An Earthy Entanglement with Spirituality

# An Earthy Entanglement with Spirituality

Critical Reflections on Literature and Art

Elizabeth Moore Willingham, Editor

LIVERPOOL UNIVERSITY PRESS

First published in 2024 by
Liverpool University Press
4 Cambridge Street
Liverpool
L69 7ZU

Copyright © 2024 Elizabeth Moore Willingham

Elizabeth Moore Willingham has asserted the right to be identified as the editor of this book in accordance with the Copyright, Designs and Patents Act 1988.

All rights reserved. No part of this book may be reproduced, stored in a retrieval system, or transmitted, in any form or by any means, electronic, mechanical, photocopying, recording, or otherwise, without the prior written permission of the publisher.

British Library Cataloguing-in-Publication data
A British Library CIP record is available

ISBN 978-1-78976-175-7 paperback

Typeset by Carnegie Book Production, Lancaster
Printed and bound by Integrated Books International, United States of America

This book is dedicated to
Anthony V. P. Grahame and Anita Grahame

# Contents

*List of Illustrations* — ix

*Abbreviations* — xi

*Acknowledgements* — xv

*Introduction: Our Earthy Entanglement* — xvii
Elizabeth M. Willingham

### ❧1❧
Out of the Depths: Recovering the Medieval Sublime — 1
Michael P. Kuczynski

### ❧2❧
Presbyterian Impulses Amid Catholicism in Kate Chopin's *The Awakening* — 25
Thomas Bonner, Jr.

### ❧3❧
Posthumanism and Inexorable Desire: Lacanian *Méconnaissance* in Walter Tevis's *Mockingbird* and Gary Shteyngart's *Super Sad True Love Story* — 50
Barbara E. Hamilton

### ❧4❧
Lynn Nottage's *Ruined*: A *Vagina Monologues* for the Twenty-first Century? — 94
Martha Greene Eads

### ❧5❧
Kinship in Translation: Colette's Animals and Divine Interconnection — 121
Lowry Martin

### ❧6❧
Sergio Ramírez's *Sara*: A Feminist Ethic in the Revision of a Bronze-Age Tale — 148
José Juan Colín

## ~7~
Patterns of Disintegration, Community, and Love in
  George Eliot's *Adam Bede* ............................................. 170
David O. Thompson

## ~8~
The Hero's Journey to Redemption: Re-envisioning the
  Dramatic Structure of *King Lear* ..................................... 205
Claudia M. Champagne

## ~9~
Overcoming the World: Strategies of the Poet and
  the Sculptor ............................................................ 227
Helen F. Maxson

## ~10~
Religious or Irreligious: The Reader's Response
  to *Pearl*, Shakespeare's *The Winter's Tale*, and
  Flannery O'Connor's "Revelation" .................................. 249
William T. Cotton

## ~11~
"Shape and Meaning and Point" in Katherine
  Anne Porter's "The Grave" ........................................... 273
Elizabeth Moore Willingham

## ~12~
New Orleans' St. Louis Cemetery No. 1 ............................ 289
Judith H. Bonner

Tomb No. 577 .................................................................. 291
Elizabeth Moore Willingham

*Appendix* ........................................................................ 294

*Notes on Contributors* .................................................... 298

*Index* ............................................................................... 303

# List of Illustrations

Chapter 4: Diagram: Cycles of Violence, ©2020 Carolyn Yoder and the STAR Team at EMU, updated 2020. Based in part on the writings of Olga Botcharova, Peter Levine, Vamik Volkan, and Walter Wink. Used by permission.

Photograph: MONUC visits a Congolese women's shelter for victims of sexual abuse, © MONUC/Marie Frechon, used by courtesy of Marie Frechon.

Chapter 5: Portrait of Colette attributed to Jean Reutlinger (d. August 1914, Battle of Ardennes, France). Used by courtesy of the Bibliothèque nationale de France. The image is made available by Wikimedia Commons.

Chapter 8: Fig. 1. Gustav Freytag's Pyramid, Ellis MacEwan. *Freytag's Technique of the Drama*. Scott Foresman, 1895. 15.

Fig. 2. Aristotle's Elements of Tragedy (*Poetics*) Plotted on Freytag's Pyramid. © 2023 Claudia M. Champagne.

Fig. 3. Champagne's Inverted Pyramid: *King Lear*'s dramatic structure supported by Aristotle's *Poetics*. © 2023 Claudia M. Champagne.

Chapter 9: Pl. 1. Michelangelo's Vatican *Pietà* (St. Peter's Basilica, Vatican City). Plates 1-6 of the *Pietà* are used here courtesy of Jebulon (Xavier Espinasse, photographer), Wikimedia Commons, CCO, Public domain.

Pl. 2. Vatican *Pietà*: Detail of the Virgin's face and upper body.

Pl. 3. Vatican *Pietà*: Detail of contrasting surfaces.

Pl. 4. Vatican *Pietà*: The Virgin's extended left arm and her fingers.

Pl. 5. Vatican *Pietà*: Details of the representation of "pliant flesh" and "subtle folds."

Pl. 6. The Virgin's strap, a color close-up showing Michelangelo's signature.

Pl. 7. The Virgin's strap, a close-up in black-and-white, showing its transcription, by the late Irving Lavin (*Artibus et Historiae* 2013, IRSA), used by permission of Professor Marilyn A. Lavin.

x | LIST OF ILLUSTRATIONS

                Pl. 8. Transcription of the Virgin's strap by Irving Lavin (*Artibus et Historiae* 2013, IRSA), used by permission of Professor Marilyn A. Lavin.

Chapter 12:  Ladies decorating tombs on All Saints' Day in a New Orleans cemetery. Unknown photographer and subjects. New Orleans, LA. Created *c.*1890–1900. Courtesies accorded by Koch and Wilson, Architects, of New Orleans and Dover Publications.

Cover photo credits—

Front cover:  Tomb No. 577, St. Louis No. 1, New Orleans, 2003. ©2023 emw.

Back cover:  A storm passes over Lake Belton, Texas, 2010. ©2023 emw.

Back cover (inset): Discovery, 2006. ©2023 emw.

# Abbreviations

| | |
|---|---|
| BL | the British Library, London |
| *Carátula* | *Carátula: Revista Cultural Centroamericana*, a Central American journal of literature and culture, accessible at Caratula.net |
| CDME | *A Concise Dictionary of Middle English (1150–1580).* Ed. A. K. Mayhew and Walter W. Skeat (Oxford, UK: Clarendon, 1888. Gutenberg.org). *See also* **MED**. |
| Dir. | Directed by; precedes one or more personal names given in natural order |
| Douay-Rheims | (Douai-Rheims, Douai) the English translation of the Vulgate (Catholic, Latin) Bible. Important critically as a document in use through historical periods of Catholic culture, it includes the Rheims New Testament (English College. Rheims [Reims or Rhemes], France, 1582) and the Douay Old Testament (English College. Douay, France, 1609–1610). The "Gibbons" edition (Baltimore: John Murphy, 1899) has the *Imprimatur* of James Cardinal Gibbons, Archbishop of Baltimore, and remains in use. In the *Catholic Encyclopedia* at Newadvent.org, see "Douai" and "Gregory Martin" |
| DRC | The Democratic Republic of (the) Congo |
| Ed. | Edited by; precedes one or more personal names in natural order |
| ed. | edition; follows an ordinal number (1st, 2nd) to indicate a book's editorial status. *See also* **ed., eds.** |
| ed., eds. | editor, editors; follows one or more personal names where the first is in inverted order, as in Fry, Carlos, ed. *See also* **ed.** |
| EETS (*EETS*) | The Early English Text Society, publisher of literary and historical texts in English (1864–), whose volumes are published on behalf of EETS by the OUP |
| *ELH* | *English Literary History*, an academic literary journal |
| EMU | Eastern Mennonite University, a private liberal arts university in Harrisonburg, Virginia |
| Englishman's | *The Englishman's Greek Concordance of the New Testament: Coded with Strong's Concordance Numbers* is the revision by Jay Patrick Green, Sr. (Peabody, MA: Hendrickson, 1996) of *The Englishman's Greek Concordance of the New Testament* (George V. Wigram. London, 1839). *See also* **Strong's**. |
| esp. | especially; directs attention to pages, sources, or details |

| | |
|---|---|
| ESV | the English Standard Version of the Bible, adapted from the Revised Standard Version (RSV), intended as a precise translation based on recent text criticism (Crossway 2001–2016, print and digital) |
| *et al* | and others; preceded by a comma, compresses a group of more than two authors or editors |
| FCE | Fondo de Cultura Económica, a publishing house based in Mexico City |
| FSG | Farrar, Straus & Giroux, a New York publisher founded in 1945 as Farrar, Straus and Company |
| IRSA | Istituto per le Ricerche di Storia dell'Arte, publisher of *Artibus et Historiae* (Poland) |
| KJV | the King James Version of the Bible (1611), also known as the English Protestant Bible, whose joint British-American nineteenth-century revision was published in 1881 |
| l., ll. | line, lines; indicates one or more lines in a drama or a poem |
| *LALT* | *Latin American Literature Today*, an online quarterly journal based at the University of Oklahoma (latinamericanliteraturetoday.org) |
| LGBTI(A) | lesbian, gay, bi-sexual, trans-gendered, inter-sexed, (asexual), indicating gendered sexual preference (L, G, B) or identity as a result of surgical intervention (T) or biological/genetic construction (I, A), and referring generally to diversity in sexual orientation |
| MEC | The University of Michigan's Libraries' online *Middle English Compendium*. *See also* **MED**. |
| MED | *A Middle-English Dictionary*, Ed. Francis Henry Stratmann (3rd ed. 1878; suppl. 1881). Its newer edition (Ed. Henry Bradley. Oxford, UK: Clarendon, 1891) was digitized in 2009 (Archive.org). The University of Michigan's Department of English began in 1925 to compile the *Middle English Dictionary*, issued by the University of Michigan Press in 115 fascicles (1952–2001). Referred to as the (print) MED, it forms "the heart" of Michigan's Libraries' **MEC**. *See also* **CDME**. |
| MLA | The Modern Language Association, a professional association and academic publisher. *See also* **PMLA**. |
| *MLR* | *The Modern Language Review*, an academic journal |
| MONUC | Organization Mission in the Democratic Republic of the Congo (UN Security Council, November 1999), renamed as the UN Organization Stabilization Mission in the Democratic Republic of Congo (MONUSCO), 1 July 2010. *See also* **UN**. |

| | |
|---|---|
| n.d. | no date of publication given in the original |
| n., nn. | note, notes; followed by a note reference number or numbers, usually in endnote cross references |
| Norton | W. W. Norton a New York publisher established in 1923 and known for its editions of literary works and criticism |
| n.p. | no known publisher and/or place of publication |
| NPR | National Public Radio, Washington, D.C. |
| *NYT* | *The New York Times*, a daily newspaper known as "the Gray Lady" |
| *OED* | *The Oxford English Dictionary*. 2nd ed. Ed. J. A. Simpson and Edmund Weiner. 20 vols. (OUP, 1989); digital format by subscription |
| OUP | Oxford University Press (Oxford UP), a UK publisher with New York offices; a department of Oxford University |
| p., pp. | page, pages; followed, respectively, by a number or numbers |
| P | Press. *See also* U, UP. |
| Perf. | Performer(s), actor(s); followed by one or more personal names |
| *PMLA* | *Publications of the Modern Language Association*, the MLA's academic journal |
| qtd. | quoted (in/by); followed by a personal name or title |
| [Rev.] | review; designates a book review in a list of works cited |
| Rpt. | reprint, reprinted; a reissue of a previously published piece |
| s., ss. | stanza, stanzas; indicating, respectively, one or more formal, numbered divisions of a poem |
| SEP | *The Stanford Encyclopedia of Philosophy*, Ed. Edward N. Zalta (Stanford University online) |
| Strong's | *The Exhaustive Concordance of the Bible* (1890) compiled under the direction of James Strong (d. 1894) |
| Stuttgart | St. Jerome's Vulgate Bible, *Biblia Sacra iuxta Vulgatam Versionem* (Ed. Bonifatius Fischer, *et al.* Stuttgart: Deutsche Bibelgesellschaft, 1983), also called "Weber-Gryson" for recent editors, Robert Weber and Roger Gryson |
| TEAMS | The Consortium for the Teaching of the Middle Ages |
| THNOC | The Historic New Orleans Collection, a museum, research center, and publisher preserving the history and culture of New Orleans and the Gulf South |
| Trans. | Translated by; followed by one or more personal names in natural order |
| U | University (in publishing data). *See* UP. |
| UN | the United Nations, New York City |

| | |
|---|---|
| **UP** | University Press (as a publisher) |
| **Vulgate (Bible)** | St. Jerome's Vulgate translation of the Bible, referring to the **Stuttgart** edition unless otherwise specified. *See also* **Douay-Rheims**. |
| **WMU** | Western Michigan University, Kalamazoo, Michigan |

# Acknowledgements

A book whose reach in materials and critical approaches exceeds the bounds of artistic movements, geographies, and categories requires significant outside support, and many institutions, scholars and experts, librarians, curators, photographers, graphic artists, and colleagues have lent their skills and resources to this project. We are grateful, variously, for guidance and advice, expert research assistance, and permissions from Marie Frechon, UN photographer in the DRC, 2007–2009; Carolyn Yoder, Hannah Kelley, and members of the STAR team at EMU; Dr. Karen Saupe of Calvin College and Dr. Marjorie L. Harrington of Medieval Institute Publications at WMU; Xavier Espinasse, known as "Jebulon," for his sumptuous color images of the *Pietà*; Professor Marilyn A. Lavin, for use of two of the late Professor Irving Lavin's *Pietà*-related images; Dr. Joanna Wolańska of IRSA; Eric Vigneron of the Reproductions Department of the Bibliothèque nacionale de France for much support with photographic holdings; Kendall Gunter of *Commonweal Magazine* (New York) for access to an archived article; Koch and Wilson, Architects, of New Orleans, and Dover Publications; Judith Bonner, Howard Margot, and Mary Lou Eichhorn of THNOC; Curator Amber M. Kohl of the University of Maryland's Katherine Anne Porter Collection; and Baylor University librarians Janet Jasek, Libby Ehlers, and Kenneth L. Carriveau. Support lent to this project has been constantly formative and literally indispensable.

With humility and deep appreciation, I gratefully acknowledge the unfailing erudition, quick responses, ready guidance, exacting standards, infinite patience, insightful queries, constant kindness, and thoughtful readings of my fellow contributors to this book and of our editors and proofreaders. We are indebted to Sussex Academic Press and the Liverpool University Press for all the best reasons involving editorial, production, and marketing genius and generosity.

Those of us associated for decades with the South Central Conference on Christianity and Literature's annual meetings in New Orleans and New Mexico are ever grateful to Claudia Champagne, Tom and Judith Bonner, and Sister Donna Marie Gould for the spirit of warm friendship and challenging critical insights—*et le bon temps*—that initiated this project and moved it to completion.

*Elizabeth Moore Willingham*
Waco, Texas, U.S.A.
December 12, 2022

What is art but an entanglement—or perhaps rather a synthesis—of the most earthy and the most spiritual?

> John MacCaig Thorburn
> *Art and the Unconscious.* 1925. 80.

# Introduction: Our Earthy Entanglement

### Elizabeth Moore Willingham

In the epigraph on the preceding page, John MacCaig Thorburn recorded the spare, intriguing aesthetic whose terms stand in our title.[1] Thorburn theorizes art's genesis by characterizing its existential nature as an intimate encounter between earth and spirit. In the critical readings and viewings offered in this volume, the merger between the earthy and the spiritual may be a transparent intention, as it is shown to be in a viewing of Michelangelo's Vatican *Pietà* and in readings of the "Lament of the Virgin" and the dramatic *consolatio* we call *Pearl*. It may produce gritty developments of character and plot leading to an existential crisis, as it does in Shakespeare's *King Lear* and *The Winter's Tale*, in George Eliot's *Adam Bede*, and in Kate Chopin's *The Awakening*. In the distinct, sometimes brutally earthy contexts of Lynn Nottage's drama *Ruined*, Sergio Ramírez's fictional biography *Sara*, Colette's sketches of the Great War's service dogs, and Gary Shteyngart's and Walter Tevis's dystopian-future novels, a dynamic ethic founded in self-awareness, forgiveness, justice, and love animates the human spirit. The ethical system of Nottage's *Ruined*, for example, grows organically from forgiveness discovered in pity and love, offering a redemption that transcends injustice, heals suffering, and creates community. In *Adam Bede*, when painful revelations break spirits and fracture relations in the village of Hayslope, love and forgiveness lead to reconciliation and heal the community. In the *Pietà*, *King Lear*, Katherine Anne Porter's "The Grave," and Flannery O'Connor's "Revelation," the grace of redemption—of one kind or another—prevails.

In our first essay, "Out of the Depths: Recovering the Medieval Sublime," Michael P. Kuczynski displaces Romanticism's theoretical claims on the sublime to reconsider the distinct nature of its interpretation during the Middle Ages. Kuczynski treats the idea's substantial tradition in poetry and prose examples from the Renaissance through the present day to show the nature and focal points of its development. Despite some convergence in Romantic and medieval thought on the sublime, the medieval passage through "the darkness of the self" (Kuczynski) differs strikingly from Romanticism's view, making an understanding of the medieval view essential to accessing its subsequent interpretations. Beginning in the late-eighteenth-century, Romanticism espoused critical perspectives derived from Greek creative theory's valorization of artistic, rhetorical, and thematic virtuosity, whereas the medieval concept of the sublime takes its principles from the Psalter. Romanticism's soaring magnificence and supreme, self-conscious artistry in painting, music, and literature, meant to evoke a heightened emotional response, contrasts both the spiritual lows and the serenity and thanksgiving expressed in the psalms. The psalmist's profound feelings of isolation, fear, helplessness, sorrow, and shame and resort to God's peace and assurance comprehend the medieval sublime. Kuczynski shows how the after-life of the medieval *via negativa* aesthetic has engaged a range of literature that includes the poetry of Tennyson, Christina Rossetti, Gerard Manley Hopkins, and R. S. Thomas and the prose of Herman Melville, in a striking passage from *Moby-Dick*.

Kuczynski's examination of the medieval preoccupation with "dark interiority" and "imperfection and contingency" suggests the kind of inward tension concealed by external appearances that Thomas Bonner, Jr. probes in "Presbyterian Impulses Amid Catholicism in Kate Chopin's *The Awakening*." Bonner frames his reading in contexts of late nineteenth-century regional differences within the South, and he shows how Chopin's familiarity with Presbyterian life and the denomination's internal debates, along with her cradle-Catholic experience of Southern Louisiana's pervasive social and religious culture, equipped her to create Edna Pontellier's divided existence. Bonner examines Chopin's organic development of Edna's highly charged interior life from her outward signs of revulsion toward her Presbyterian upbringing through her ill-prepared efforts to escape it with a Louisiana-Catholic marriage. The depth and sharp detail in Chopin's portrait of South Louisiana's religious and social traditions are juxtaposed against her spare outlines of Edna's Kentucky society and Presbyterianism. The pervasive presence of Catholic culture across Chopin's fiction and the intellectual and social distinctions attached to her characters' denominations provide further grounding for Bonner's "negative space" reading of Chopin's most enigmatic protagonist.

While Edna Pontellier's yearnings for freedom, self-realization, and transcendent love are frustrated, the similar impulses Barbara E. Hamilton explores in "Posthumanism and Inexorable Desire: Lacanian *Méconnaissance* in Walter Tevis's *Mockingbird* and Gary Shteyngart's *Super Sad True Love Story*" find slightly more promising outcomes. Taking Jacques Lacan's idea of the psychic centrality of desire as her critical framework, Hamilton shows how *Mockingbird* (1980) and *Super Sad True Love Story* (2010) address questions about human frailty and nature with implied critiques of dystopian worlds where desire and disappointment are suppressed or re-directed according to their planners' *méconnaissance*. She finds Tevis's novel speaking to existential fear and desire and demonstrates the precariousness of the printed word in a distant future shaped by Dean Robert Spofforth, an ancient cyborg who hires Paul Bentley, a sober, thoughtful, literate young man in a drugged, illiterate world, as a professor at his university before imprisoning Paul for the crime of teaching his lover to read. Shteyngart's novel, too, achieves resonance with today's readers, according to Hamilton, in its restless, aging-salesman protagonist, Lenny Abramov, whose reading habit makes him an outlier, and whose love for the hip, muddled young Eunice Park and for his upside-down country and altered city (New York) are "sad." Paul and Lenny can be no more than contingently successful in holding off dehumanizing forces when humanity's inherent desire to transcend its vulnerabilities threatens intellectual curiosity, empathy, and love.

Desire, agency, and community that transcend trauma are central to Martha Greene Eads's comparative readings of two award-winning feminist dramas—Lynn Nottage's *Ruined* (2009) and Eve Ensler's *The Vagina Monologues* (*TVM* 1996, 1997). The interrogative format of the chapter's title—"Lynn Nottage's *Ruined*: A *Vagina Monologues* for the Twenty-first Century?"—is the basis for Eads's systematic examination of essential differences between the two dramas, and she addresses persistent, telling critical questions about them in contexts of recent events and trauma-recovery theory. *TVM*, created to be highly flexible in format, content, and venue, recently celebrated its twentieth anniversary with a 2018 edition of the play that included new monologues. *Ruined*, in contrast, is theater that organically develops a cast of characters caught in the physical and emotional effects and personal disruptions of war in the Democratic Republic of (the) Congo. Their traumas are integral to armed aggressions, wherever they occur. Acknowledging *TVM*'s decades of social significance and *Ruined*'s distinct genesis and ends, Eads suggests theoretically engaged moral and ethical approaches to viewing, teaching, and staging the dramas, and she frankly interrogates their staging of treating and healing traumas associated with sexual assault in local and global communities.

Concerns with love, war, and the long-term effects of trauma often shaped the fiction and sketches of Colette, a prolific, highly honored French author who served as a nurse to the wounded and worked as a journalist near the front lines in the Great War. She is best known in the U.S. for her novel *Gigi* in its conversion to stage and screen and for her "scandalous" early novels. In "Kinship in Translation: Colette's Animals and Divine Interconnection," Lowry Martin, who has elsewhere explored Colette's writing about the Great War's service animals, traces the genesis and effects of Colette's nature writing and her development of an adult genre featuring anthropomorphized animal protagonists. These two elements of Colette's extensive literary production have been largely ignored in criticism and literary biography, and Martin presents readings of selections from her novels, sketches, and animal "dialogues." Martin points to their literary value and cultural resonance and proposes that Colette's animal-centered stories and her descriptions of nature not only lifted Colette's benighted spirits and allowed her a measure of professional autonomy but also laid the foundation for a revision of her public persona with projects that were close to her heart and held significant interest for French readers.

José Juan Colín delves into a novelist's spiritual reimagining of a traditional biblical matriarch in "Sergio Ramírez's *Sara*: A Feminist Ethic in the Revision of a Bronze-Age Tale." Colín systematically examines the means and effects of Sara's claims to voice and agency and shows how Ramírez grounds his material securely in the biblical outline, deftly supplying plausible detail to fill out textual lacunae and to enlarge on gestures toward the biblical Sarah's personality. The lynchpins of Ramírez's proto-feminist Sara are wit and self-possession, and her interactions with Abraham, the archangels, Lot and his wife, and God—whom Sara calls "The Wizard"—confirm her as quick, fearless, and resourceful. Ramírez, a former Nicaraguan revolutionary and vice-president and a prize-winning novelist currently in exile in Spain, envisions Sara's running commentary on the patriarchy and her transgressing its code when desperate circumstances warrant.

Like Ramírez's *Sara*, George Eliot's *Adam Bede,* a novel of rural English life at the end of the eighteenth century, is structured around an eponymous character living in a socially stratified, deeply religious community. David O. Thompson, in "Patterns of Disintegration, Community, and Love in George Eliot's *Adam Bede,*" focuses on Eliot's representation of the process of myth making and revelation and its effects on the small community of Hayslope. *Adam Bede*'s earliest critics, like some of its recent ones, attributed the views of science, history, and myth they found in the novel to Eliot's intimate knowledge of contemporary European philosophy and theology, particularly that of German higher criticism. Thompson tempers that view by showing how *Adam Bede* is more accurately the product of Eliot's early skeptical inclinations and her own views of fiction, history, love, and community. He finds that rather than making a wholesale adoption or reductive distillation of others' views, Eliot is particularly attentive in *Adam Bede* to narrating organic discovery of the nature of love and community in the lives of her characters and in the Hayslope community's response to challenges to its myths.

English literature's indebtedness to a nineteenth-century German theoretical perspective is the point of departure for Claudia M. Champagne's "The Hero's Journey to Redemption: Re-envisioning the Dramatic Structure of *King Lear*." Champagne asserts that *King Lear* defies the limitations of Gustav Freytag's perennially influential "pyramid" or "triangle," a graphic representation of the structure of Shakespearean tragedy, and that leading twentieth-century views of the play's structure also fall short of addressing its distinctions. Champagne's reading views *King Lear* as presenting an earthly and spiritual journey in which a pagan-era king begins his downward path into alienation as thoughts of revenge and feelings of shame and madness crowd in on him. He moves toward the nadir of his fortunes before beginning a wayward ascent toward reconciliation and redemption. Shakespeare closes the play with Lear and Cordelia's imprisonment and stages the spectacle of Lear entering the stage in grief, bearing in his arms the dead Cordelia, executed by mischance. The play's catastrophe and its staging of Lear's restoration to sanity, fatherhood, and kingship before his death achieve an uncommon effect on the audience, and Champagne remodels Freytag's diagram as an inverted pyramid and applies Aristotle's elements of tragedy in support of her revision to accommodate these unusual features. The shape of the drama, made graphic by Champagne's inverted pyramid and her Aristotelian analysis, suggests the medieval concept of life on earth as a journey that opens with the sin of pride and continues, fraught with error, suffering, and despair, to be redeemed by the grace of love at its close.

The poignant staging of Lear supporting Cordelia's body may remind some audience members of the tableau of the Virgin holding Christ's body at the foot of the cross, a frequent subject of art and literature. Helen F. Maxson explores the interpretation and reception of the idea in two materially distinct, roughly contemporaneous representations. The first, a poetic "Lament of the Virgin" in Middle English, composed as Mary's dramatic monologue, is seldom seen except by specialists and students, and the other, Michelangelo's Vatican *Pietà*, is a sculpture of global renown housed in St. Peter's Basilica and viewed annually by several million visitors. The "Lament of the Virgin" that Maxson chooses for this reading is dated about 1450 and is one of several surviving manuscript versions of the lyric. The Vatican *Pietà*, created from a block of Carrara marble that Michelangelo personally chose from the quarry in the final years of the fifteenth century, interprets Mary's lament over Christ's body. Maxson gives close attention to the properties and constraints of materials and to signs of similar creative ends and religious awareness shared by the poet and the sculptor. Both achieve a Virgin whose layered spiritual and earthy aspects figure coherently into her role in Christianity's narrative.

Like Maxson, William T. Cotton considers a question of affective reception of diverse creative materials in "Religious or Irreligious—The Reader's Response to *Pearl*, Shakespeare's *The Winter's Tale*, and Flannery O'Connor's 'Revelation.'" Cotton's readings of the pious Middle English dream-vision composed around 1375, of Shakespeare's fantastically contrived romance, dated about 1610, and of O'Connor's gritty, comic short story of 1964 theorize the nature of responses from readers divided along theological lines. Each reading probes overt and subtle representations of religious values and ethical principles and their appeals, locating them variously couched in circumstance, discourse, or character development. Cotton's primary materials converge in their shared concerns with moral and ethical failings, spiritual disquiet, death, and redemption—earth-bound and heavenly—and each conveys moral and ethical perspectives in dialectics of character development and circumstance. Cotton speculates on readers' likely reactions to those appeals, offering innovative approaches to reader-response theory in his treatment of the dramatic climax of *The Winter's Tale* and in examining the discursive pathetic appeal attached to the father's loss in *Pearl*. Cotton's theory of the complicity of the reader in O'Connor's "Revelation" is its own revelation in the story's critical history.

As Cotton's primary sources and his readings show us, certain examples of literature pose ethical questions and represent the tension of internal conflicts. Katherine Anne Porter's short story "The Grave," the subject of our eleventh chapter, with its titular gesture pointing, like Scrooge's third ghost, toward mortality, is one of those. Often considered a coming-of-age tale of disquieting sexual knowledge or interpreted by means of biblical types and narratives, "The Grave" is one of Porter's series of so-called Miranda stories. It recalls a summer day in 1903 when Miranda was nine, a self-absorbed little wanderer seeking adventure along country trails on a "burning day" in Texas. Miranda's disturbing experience of that day is soon buried away, covered over on the earth and in memory, only to rise unbidden, decades afterward, in a stark tableau before her mind's eye. The horrifying vision is quickly replaced by another that gives her childhood experience—and the story—its shape, meaning, and point.

Our final chapter, in two brief parts, dedicates its commentary to our front cover image and its famous geographical site. Turning again to the theme of "the grave" and to art as an encounter between the "most earthy" and "most spiritual," we address features of New Orleans' highly visible interest in death through its various funereal and spiritual cultures. New Orleans art history expert Judith Bonner's first section addresses the famed St. Louis Cemetery No. 1, and I provide details for the cemetery's "Tomb No. 577," shown in the cover photograph. Bonner, Senior Curator at The Historic New Orleans Collection (THNOC), considers St. Louis Cemetery No. 1's history of prominence and highlights local customs, intersections of popular and funerary culture, and physical evidence that reflect the aesthetics of mourning and remembrance in its multi-cultural milieu. Tomb No. 577, the subject of my discussion, is among the older tombs in St. Louis No. 1. Its architecture and inscriptions imply a family's private and public lives in the colonized South, its multi-generational familial and spiritual bonds, and its desire for remembrance. The tomb's physical evidence testifies to its remarkable survival and the ravages of its exposure to New Orleans' climate. Efforts to catalogue, restore, and preserve the structure both enable and complicate the present-day reception of its art and history.

Reception indeed may be slippery, changeable, and indeterminate. We see the earthy-spiritual entanglement, *prima facie*, in the tomb, and our gaze on it may also inspire notions that respond to the Humanities' essential question—What does it mean to be human? Such existential questions are the work of criticism, though they're rarely the largest furniture on the stage. These chapters, too, each in its own way, imply responses in studies of better-known and more gently preserved primary materials, offering up critical truth, resonant insights, and the best kinds of critical surprises.

**Note**
1 Thorburn's article "Art and the Unconscious" (1921) and an essay dealing with symbolic interpretation (1924) preceded the release of *Art and the Unconscious* in 1925, available through Google Books, courtesy of the University of California at Berkeley (pp. i–xiii; 1–242). Bibliographical details of primary materials cited here and treated in the chapters are found in the respective chapter's Works Cited.

**Works Cited**
Thorburn, J. M. [John MacCaig]. "Analytic Psychology and Religious Symbolism." *The Monist* 34.1 (January 1924): 96–111.
—. "Art and the Unconscious." *The Monist* 31.4 (October 1921): 585–600.
—. *Art and the Unconscious: A Psychological Approach to a Problem of Philosophy*. The International Library of Psychology 31. London: Kegan Paul, Trench, Trübner, 1925.

CHAPTER

# 1

# Out of the Depths
## Recovering the Medieval Sublime

Michael P. Kuczynski

> O the mind, mind has mountains; cliffs of fall
> Frightful, sheer, no-man-fathomed.
> Gerard Manley Hopkins, "No Worst"[1]

The sublime as an aesthetic category is normally associated by critics with the rise of Romanticism, especially its idealized vision of art and artists. In this essay, I argue for a reevaluation of the sublime that recovers its medieval dimension, the necessary connection that artists of the Middle Ages regularly trace and traverse between height and depth, magnificence and humility, grandeur and rudeness.[2] This connection weakened under the influence of Romantic ideology's identification of sublimity with the spectacular and the thrilling. It nevertheless survived beyond the Middle Ages into the early modern period and was also revived after the Renaissance as part of the Victorian fascination with medieval culture generally, in the work of poets such as Alfred, Lord Tennyson (d. 1892), Christina Rossetti (d. 1894), and Gerard Manley Hopkins (d. 1889).[3] Today, the recovery of the medieval sublime is important both to an accurate understanding of the Middle Ages themselves and to our appreciation of an aesthetic that values more than the superficial allure of works of art, no matter how compelling, and the celebrity of artists, no matter how talented.

"Sublimity," from Latin *sublimitas*, means in the physical and spatial sense "an elevation," "loftiness," a "high position or altitude" rather than a depth.[4] To write of the sublime in terms of depth as well as height, therefore, suggests an approach that may seem paradoxical. Many twenty-first-century readers, influenced by attitudes toward literary history that still regard the Middle Ages as relatively "dark" or ignorant, would not associate "greatness of artistic or intellectual conception; grandeur of language or style"—the *OED* definition of sublimity[5]—with medieval culture at all. The Middle Ages is currently experiencing yet another waning in the Academy, a struggle for relevance. Non-academics, for their part, are more likely these days to identify medieval grandeur with the elaborate computer-generated special effects—castles, armies, forests and mountains—in the HBO series, *Game of Thrones*, based on George R. R. Martin's fantasy novels, rather than with the real architectural expressiveness of the great cathedrals or the rhetorical artistry of Chaucer's verse.

Typical expressions of the Romantic sublime include those popular atmospheric paintings by the German Romantic Caspar David Friedrich (1774–1840) that capture mysterious and solitary wanderers, standing by the sea or on the peaks of great mountains, staring away into the fog with their backs turned to us. This is the sort of mysterious doppelgänger Percy Bysshe Shelley (d. 1822) imagines as the speaker of his poem, "Mont Blanc: Lines Written in the Vale of Chamouni," whose turbulent rhetoric recreates for the reader the sublime landscape of the Alps, where

> The everlasting universe of things
> Flows through the mind, and rolls its rapid waves,
> Now dark—now glittering—now reflecting gloom—
> Now lending splendour, where from secret springs
> The source of human thought its tribute brings
> Of waters—with a sound but half its own.[6]

Shelley's pun on the word "tribute"—the branch of a river but also an act of homage—idealizes the origins of human intelligence and his own poetic ego, by relocating the streams of artistic influence from Mount Helicon, the traditional seat of the Muses, to a contemporary European landscape. The poem is full of variegated patterns of darkness and light and abrupt shifts of emphasis that mimic the atmosphere and spasmodic eruptions of water in the terrain around Mont Blanc itself. "Mont Blanc" the poem anticipates in its imagery and meter the lofty measures of a musical composition such as Beethoven's Symphony No. 9. It is quintessentially sublime—in the strictly Romantic sense.

Unlike medieval poets, Shelley seeks to stimulate rather than to discipline the passions. His subject is the "awful" or awe-inducing "thou" of Nature, embodied in a specific mountain and the experience of that place as he reconstitutes it artistically for his reader. Because Shelley is not a theist, his poem does not consider God as Mont Blanc's Creator. In God's absence, the poet is supreme artificer, his persona dwarfed physically perhaps but not spiritually by the grandeur he describes. In an early draft of "Mont Blanc," instead of subtitling his poem "Lines Written in the Vale of Chamouni," Shelley prefaces his work with the theatrical direction "Scene—Pont Pellisier in the Vale of Servox." The note suggests that the poet and his speaker are stage-managing Nature's performance, commanding the elements that have provoked his imagination.[7]

Even critics sensitive to the nuances of the medieval sublime can be distracted by this kind of Romantic virtuosity. A recent collection of essays that seeks to explore the sublimity of medieval art comprehensively, in terms of its architecture, literature, and music, concentrates on the local qualities of grandeur and magnificence in specific works, their lofty aesthetic effects.[8] This approach serves as a useful riposte to certain clichés about the culture of the Middle Ages as drab. It does not, however, explore at all medieval art's almost obsessive concern with what I would call dark interiority, the artist's scrutiny of his own imperfection and contingency. This emphasis distinguishes medieval sublimity definitively from its Romantic counterpart, which glamorizes exteriority and ego. C. Stephen Jaeger, the editor of the essay collection to which I refer, does attempt in his introduction to reconcile discrete moments of sublimity in medieval art with the *sermo humilis* or humble style that Erich Auerbach once identified as one of the most distinctive features of the culture of the Middle Ages:

> The grand style lives right behind the humble in many significant instances, as the other world lives or is perceived to live, just behind the created world; its brilliance is concealed by a veil of realism. Divinity lifts the veil now and then, as an occasional epiphany or theophany breaks through the surface of lived reality—a mystery occasionally emerges in the everyday—in the imagination of the medieval Christian author.[9]

Jaeger's metaphor of layering, however—of one reality situated behind another—depends on a Classical and Romantic aesthetic that gives priority to surfaces and is ahistorical when applied to the art of the Middle Ages. The experiences of "epiphany," "theophany," and "mystery" that Jaeger mentions as possible in the presence of great medieval art are not however the primary element in our appreciation of its beauty. Magnificence in the art of the Middle Ages, I would argue, is always strictly coherent with and thus inseparable from another vital aspect of the medieval artist's vision: its acute awareness of the ordinary, including a range of subjects and emotions that threaten to undermine rather than to transport the human ego, such as fear, doubt, self-abasement, and even despair.

## The Classical Sublime

The Romantic understanding of the sublime is of Greek origin and was not known to the Latin Middle Ages. An anonymous first-century treatise once attributed to Longinus, *Peri Hypsous* ("Concerning Loftiness"), lays out a systematic theory of literary sublimity in terms of the disposition of the artist himself and his role as an agent inspired from on high to compose his works; the subject matter of his productions, which must be dignified rather than base and designed to provoke in the first instance feeling rather than thought; and the style in which the inspired artist treats his elevated subject, by using extensive rhetorical ornament such as dramatic imagery and aureate diction.[10] A sublime rhetorical passage, according to Pseudo-Longinus, captures and conveys a writer's greatness of spirit and the grandeur of his theme, communicating these immediately to a listener or reader, so that he too is caught up in the strange origins and effects of the rhetorician's words: "For by some innate power the true sublime uplifts our souls; we are filled with a proud exaltation and a sense of vaunting joy, just as though we had ourselves produced what we had heard."[11] The unknown author of *Peri Hypsous* finally emphasizes inspiration over technique as essential to poetic sublimity. The rules of rhetoric can be learned but inspiration cannot, and the deploying of rhetoric without inspiration produces only a false sublimity or "mere bombast."[12] Pseudo-Longinus, then, prefers those gems turned up by a great artistic spirit in a field of imperfect writing to more consistent hack work by second-raters, who may be good at following the rules of composition but whose conceits do not flash out and flame. As the medieval proverb, adapting Horace, puts it: "The grete Homerus slepeth somtyme."[13] The pagan bard who intones, "Father Zeus, kill us if thou wilt, but kill us in the light," or the Old Testament heroic poet who declared, "God said, 'Let there be light,' and there was light," can be forgiven certain blemishes in their works, because these allow the sublime moments to radiate in contrast.[14]

There is a pedantic quality to *Peri Hypsous* and to the Romantic ideology it engendered that anticipates, oddly enough, the nineteenth-century criticism of Matthew Arnold, who established as a standard for true sublimity "high seriousness" in writing over a commingling of noble and ignoble verbal effects.[15] Pseudo-Longinus's critique of Hesiod for his description of the allegorical figure Trouble with "Rheum [. . .] running from her nostrils" foreshadows Arnold's infamous dismissal of Chaucer for his description of the murdered choirboy in the *Prioress's Tale*, who has his throat cut "vnto [his] nekke boon": "The charm," Arnold writes, the magic that he associates with the sublime in poetry, "is departed."[16] There is of course much in *Peri Hypsous* that the Middle Ages would have found congenial, such as its emphasis on the supernatural basis for the poet's inspiration and the principle of decorum, whereby the style of a composition should be fitted as exactly as possible to its subject. Medieval poets would have found less acceptable, however, Pseudo-Longinus's concentration on the constituent parts of a work of art rather than its wholeness and, among these parts, his focus on the work of art's surface effects of grandeur or magnificence. This selective approach to art's form and content gets transferred in the Romantic sublime to the character of the artist himself, whose entire nature as a person becomes less important than the drama of his performance as a divine surrogate.

## The Medieval Sublime

The valorizing of the artist and his work throughout *Peri Hypsous* is alien to medieval ideas about art and artists. Geoffrey of Vinsauf (d. 1210), whose *Poetria Nova* directly influenced Chaucer and many other medieval writers, does not imagine the poet as an impulsive demigod but rather as a careful architect, who composes his work only after he has thoroughly planned it in his mind.[17] Passion, Geoffrey of Vinsauf cautions, is to be avoided:

> If a man has a house to build, his impetuous hand does not rush into action. The measuring line of his mind first lays out the work, and he mentally outlines the successive steps in a definite order. The mind's hand shapes the entire house before the body's hand builds it. Its mode of being is archetypal before it is actual. Poetic art may see in this analogy the law to be given to poets: let the poet's hand not be swift to take up the pen, nor his tongue be impatient to speak.[18]

In this analysis, Geoffrey gives priority in poetic composition to reason over passion, deliberation over inspiration. His cautions have precedent in the writings of the Church Fathers, who encourage distrust of the self-indulgent aims of rhetoric and poetry. St. Augustine recalls in his spiritual autobiography, the *Confessions*, how he gave up rhetoric for biblical exegesis,[19] and Jerome warns in one of his letters to Pope Damasus, "Devils feed on the songs of poets" [*Daemonum cibus est carmina poetarum* ].[20] Indeed, Jerome's sentence goes on to deride altogether worldly wisdom [*saecularis sapientia*] and ostentatious rhetorical display [*Rhetoricorum pompa verborum*], elements that are at the very heart of the Classical and Romantic concept of the sublime. The safest path for writers who seek to honor patristic warnings about poetry is deference to Sacred Scripture, where as the Venerable Bede had observed in his handbook *On Schemes and Tropes* [*De Schematibus et Tropis*], anything worth doing rhetorically had already been executed to the highest standard and along the most edifying lines.[21]

In a similar vein, St. Bernard of Clairvaux derides the plastic arts and their Cluniac proponents who insist on adorning places meant for worship with eye-catching decorations:

> The church is adorned with gemmed crowns of light—nay, with lusters like cartwheels, gird all round with lamps, but no less brilliant with the precious stones that stud them. Moreover, we see candelabra standing like trees of massive bronze, fashioned with marvelous subtlety of art, and glistening no less brightly with gems than with the lights they carry. What, think you, is the purpose of all this, the compunction of penitents or the admiration of beholders? O vanity of vanities, yet no more vain than insane![22]

From a twenty-first-century perspective, it is easy to dismiss such a passage as proto-Puritanism, to see in it a resistance to all that must have struck at least certain monastic gazes as most inspirational about medieval liturgical display. It is more difficult to understand the passage as correcting an attitude that places the artist and his achievements before the presumed purposes of his art—praise of the Creator and the edifying instruction of his creatures.

The word *sublimitas* is infrequent in the Latin Bible and, when it occurs, does not refer to human productions. It appears only six times in the Vulgate: four times in the Old Testament and twice in St. Paul's epistles. Some of the Old Testament instances describe false sublimity—not the sort that Pseudo-Longinus derides (*i.e.*, rhetoric without passion) but the equivalent in the artist of what John Milton calls in Book II of *Paradise Lost* Satan's "bad eminence"—an inflated sense of one's own power and worth. The prophet Isaiah warns, for example, that "The loftiness of men [*sublimitas hominum*] shall be bowed down, and the haughtiness of men shall be humbled, and the Lord alone shall be exalted" (Isaiah 2:17).[23] Later in his book (33:16), Isaiah further explains that true sublimity is accessible on earth only to those who walk in the ways of justice: the just man "shall dwell on high, the fortifications of rocks shall be his highness [*sublimitas*]: bread is given him, his waters are sure." The just man, it might be said, derives his sublimity—his spiritual loftiness—secondhand from God, who is the very foundation of justice. Or as St. Paul explains in his second letter to the Corinthians (4:7), our "light of the knowledge of the glory of God," our apprehension of sublimity, which Paul says is a real "treasure," we have "in earthen vessels, that the excellency [*sublimitas*] may be of the power of God and not of us." The incarnation of God in Christ, of the divine *logos* in the words of Scripture, and of edifying truth in human discourse, such as the compositions of religious poets, are all instances of the coherence of height and depth, magnificence and humility, grandeur and rudeness that typify the inescapably paradoxical nature of the medieval sublime. The Romantic wanderer, as we have seen, seeks sublimity by mountaineering and then writing about the experience; the Christian pilgrim who longs for the sublime must first journey within, confronting his own humility: *sublimitas sit virtutis Dei et non ex nobis*. Francis Petrarch's account of his ascent of Mount Ventoux in pursuit of sublimity offers an apt counterpoint to Shelley's experience of Mont Blanc. Petrarch's only motive, at least initially, is to wonder at the elevation. By his own admission, he is "led solely by a desire to view the great height of it."[24] Once he achieves the summit, however, instead of marveling at the majesty of the peak, he takes out his copy of St. Augustine's *Confessions* and reads thus: "And they go to admire the summits of mountains and the vast billows of the sea and the broadest rivers and the expanses of the ocean and the revolutions of the stars and they overlook themselves."[25] The locus of the true sublime, Petrarch implies by this exemplum of his spiritual maturation, is not outside the self, in awe-inspiring views, but within the heart and soul of each person. The sublime in biblical and medieval aesthetics is a phenomenon that arises from the artist's conflicted awareness of having been created in God's image and from his intractable fallen nature. As St. Paul observes in his letter to the Ephesians (3:17–20), that person who is "rooted and founded in charity" [*in caritate radicati et fundati*] is able amid his turbulent life "to comprehend, with all the saints, what is the breadth and length and height and depth [*sublimitas et profundum*]." This person, Paul insists, can be "filled unto all the fullness of God" by understanding, in contrast with his own imperfection, the perfect and sublime love of Christ.

Sublimity, then, in the writings such figures as St. Paul, St. Augustine, and Petrarch, is not primarily a product—an intense aesthetic experience, provoked by literary special effects. It is a process—a painful journey through sin and into God's magnificence. Students of medieval contemplation will be familiar with the metaphor of a "negative path" [*via negativa*], the way of apophatic or dark mysticism. The anonymous author of a fourteenth-century treatise on contemplation called *The Cloud of Unknowing* instructs his reader to "put a cloud of forgetting beneath you, between you and everything that was ever created," so that he can focus attention where it belongs, on God.[26] Such comprehensive forgetting, which the *Cloud*-author understands is difficult and perhaps impossible for most people is a figurative pilgrimage through the profundity of one's own nature, which is imprinted with the Divine image [*imago Dei*] but distorted by sin. The discipline itself requires a complete suspension of all spatial and temporal consciousness, any sense of one's precise coordinates in space and time. As the *Cloud*-author further explains, his injunctions that the reader should "put a cloud of forgetfulness beneath him," that he should "look within," and that he should "climb above the self" toward God must be understood only in the spiritual sense. To take these instructions otherwise is to get lost, the unnamed writer cautions, in "literalism and ingenuity."[27]

This sort of contemplative discipline and the metaphorical language used to describe it makes clear that the interior landscape of the medieval sublime can be even more vertiginous than the exterior one Shelley depicts in "Mont Blanc" and more challenging than Shelley's landscape is to traverse. The literary byproduct of a writer's meeting this challenge is an art that, arguably, is richer in scope than Shelley's, for it confronts with brutal honesty the radical alterity between God's magnificence and human wretchedness. This alterity is the central theme of the following fifteenth-century religious lyric:

> O Radiant luminar of light eterminable,
> Celestiall father, potenciall god of might,
> Of heyven & erthe, o lorde incomparable,
> Of all perfeccions essenciall most parfight!
> Of maker of mankynd thow formed day & nyt,
> Whose power imperiall comprehendithe every place;
> My hert, my mynde & all my holl delite
> Ys, after this lyf, to se thy glorious face.[28]

The confinement of the speaker's heart, mind, and will—his entire being—to a single, nearly perfunctory line of verse, following his hyper-aureate diction and heavy anaphora in describing the godhead, suggests not only the estrangement but also the intimacy between infinity and finitude, heaven and earth, height and depth, sublimity and profundity. God's grandeur and human insignificance are twin halves of a medieval diptych: in this lyric, each clarifies the other's meaning. Moreover, the anonymity of the poem prevents its author's ego from intruding on the power of his statement and on the generality of its application. The lyric speaks not only in its author's voice but also, collectively, in the voice of all believers.

The opening lines of Shelley's "Mont Blanc" also move abruptly from a magnificent summit to a "deep" and "Dizzy Ravine" below: an Alpine landscape, after all, cannot have mountains without valleys. For the Romantic poet, however, the magnificent and the profound are equally imposing and "awful," whereas for medieval religious writers, who are concerned with the geography of faith and sin, height and depth while codependent nevertheless remain in a perpetual, hierarchical contrast. Engaging the true sublime, for a medieval Christian poet, means exploring and eliminating the false sublimity of one's own pride. Whereas the Romantic sublime often results in a deliberate flight from the everyday in search of vertiginous landscapes, the medieval sublime, frequently coexists alongside the quotidian. The religious lyric quoted above, for instance, survives in a pocket-sized fourteenth-century manuscript now in London, BL Additional MS 20059, that consists mainly of legal notes connected with an aristocratic household in Cheshire. On its front and back flyleaves, recorded in a later hand, are this poem, three hymns to the Virgin, a prose vision of the Mother of God first recorded by St. Thomas Becket, and verses on the Trinity. The book insists by its contents and structure on the relationship between the mundane and transcendent.[29]

Furthermore, whereas Romantic figures tend to depict their engagements with the sublime as feverishly exotic, medieval writers, who accept that they can only grasp true magnificence by working through the darkness of the self, can often sound remarkably nonchalant about the relationship between God's sublimity and human profundity. Many critics extol Chaucer's writing for its "naturalness," the matter-of-fact way in which the poet explores all of the great human subjects—love, the cosmos, God's pity and anger, the humor at the heart of our most humiliating moments (including sexual ones), the dignity of a plowman's hard labor, the delicate beauty of a daisy. At the same time, however, Chaucer's writing also comprehends despair: Dorigen's obsession with her husband Averagus's imagined death by shipwreck in the *Franklin's Tale*, for instance, or the eerily bland, taxonomic analysis of the many species of self-inflicted misery that Chaucer adapts from a Scholastic *summa* on penance and the Seven Deadly Sins as the last of his *Canterbury Tales*, told by the Parson:

> Now comth wanhope, that is despeir of the mercy of God, that comth somtyme of to muche outrageous sorwe [*sorrow*], and sometyme of to muche drede [*fear*], ymaginynge thart he hath doon so muche synne that it wol [*will*] nat availlen [*help*] hym [i.e., to repent], though he wolde repenten hym and forsake synne, thurgh [*through*] which despeir or drede he abaundoneth al his herte to every maner [*kind of*] synne.[30]

One cannot imagine the magnificent moments of the *Canterbury Tales* without the base ones. Indeed, a key element in Chaucer's vision is the juxtaposition of the ordinary and everyday with sublime aesthetics and theology. Just as the nobility of the Knight's chivalric romance is matched as part of Chaucer's design by the ignobility of the Miller's *fabliau*, the rebellious vitality of the Wife of Bath is chastened by the sobriety of the Parson. The poet's most sublime moment in the *Tales* is in fact his most self-effacing—his prayer, immediately following the Parson's discourse, that anything virtuous in his work be attributed to Christ and that anything vicious in it be blamed on his own lack of talent [*defaute of myn unkonnynge*].[31] That the success of the entire *Canterbury* project might depend on Chaucer's penance, a canceling out rather than assertion of his artistic ego, points to a fundamental difference between Romantic and medieval notions of poetic sublimity.

## Medieval Sublimity in the Psalms

Like Chaucer's prayer, many of the tropes and figures of the medieval sublime have their *locus classicus* in the biblical Book of Psalms. Throughout the Middle Ages, the Psalter was regarded as a digest of the wisdom of all of Scripture or, in the words of the Middle English contemplative, Richard Rolle (d. 1349), "perfeccioun of dyuyne pagyne" [the magnificence of the sacred page], in that the Psalms encompass all the "lare" [spiritual wisdom] that other biblical books "draghes langly" [treat at greater length].[32] Traditionally, medieval exegetes interpreted the three-part structure of King David's sequence of 150 psalms as a map of the tripartite progress of every human soul: from sin, through penance, and on to justification by grace. Medieval monks read or chanted the entire Psalter through each week, until its language became part of the monastic literary subconscious.[33] Lay people, by contrast, engaged the Psalter's profundity less expansively, often by reciting during private prayer a small but coherent subgroup, the Seven Penitential Psalms. St. Augustine had these psalms painted on his bedroom walls during his final illness:

they were, from his point of view, the Bible's most sublime poetic statement.

One of the simplest and most powerful of the penitential psalms, Psalm 129 (*De Profundis*) in the Vulgate numbering, is also one of the most influential lyric poems ever written and an important biblical source for the medieval sublime:

> Out of the depths I have cried to thee, O Lord:
> Lord, hear my voice. Let thy ears be attentive to the voice of my supplication.
> If thou, O Lord, wilt mark iniquities: Lord, who shall stand it.
> For with thee there is merciful forgiveness:
> and by reason of thy law, I have waited for thee, O Lord.
> My soul hath relied on his word:
> My soul hath hoped in the Lord.
> From the morning watch even until night, let Israel hope in the Lord.
> Because with the Lord there is mercy: and with him plentiful redemption.
> And he shall redeem Israel from all its iniquities.

In a heavily glossed Wycliffite psalter, Oxford, Bodleian Library MS Bodley 554, marginal commentary connects Psalm 129 with David's crimes of adultery and homicide as recorded in the second Book of Samuel; with Israel's Babylonian captivity; and with the moral imprisonment of every person who cries out to the sublime majesty of God in heaven for deliverance from sin.[34] Throughout the Middle Ages, commentators understood Psalm 129 and the entire Psalter as having a dual private and public identity, an individual and communal voice. The Psalms speak of David's engagement with his own deep sins, his salvation by way of God's mercy, and how his exemplary fall and rise, out of the depths and into the heights, is worked out within the entire nation of Israel and across time in all devout people. The Psalms are perfect templates, for all Christians, of prayer and meditation, rhetorical models of the soul's extravagant and even violent emotions in flight from and in pursuit of God. It is no wonder that Petrarch, inspired by his reading of Augustine's sermons on the Psalms, describes the Psalter as a textual profundity, "a deep ocean" upon which everyone at some point in her or his life must voyage.[35]

In addition to its connection with David's biography and its usefulness as a model of penitential prayer, Psalm 129 was part of the medieval Office of the Dead, one of those psalms sung or spoken liturgically to commend the soul of the deceased and all souls still suffering in purgatory to Christ.[36] John Lydgate, a monk of Bury St. Edmund's and one of Chaucer's fifteenth-century disciples, wrote a brief verse treatise on *De Profundis* in which he notes that his abbot, William Curtis, charged him with explaining why the Church especially values this psalm for private and public prayer:

> Another charge was vpon me leyd,
> Among psalmys to fynde a cleer sentence [*meaning*],
> Why De Profundis specyally ys seyd
> For crystes sowlys, with devout reverence. ("On *De Profundis*" ll. 9–12)

Once Lydgate fulfills this charge by composing his poem, his abbot instructs that *De Profundis* be displayed on a carved panel on the abbey church's wall. This gesture formalizes the psalm's importance not only as the Psalmist's personal statement of despair but also as a communal declaration concerning the emotional depths of our human nature.[37] One could, in fact, argue that this single biblical poem lays out, by way of its imagery and sentiments, the principles of a comprehensive Christian existentialism, an ontology of the sinful, penitent, and justified soul. It traverses, in its rhetoric and cultural afterlife, the Christian depths and heights.

Medieval commentators loved Psalm 129's opening image of depth because it is at once specific and general, particular and vague. On the one hand, it signifies overwhelming affliction, either in the form of tribulation or persecution. On the other hand, it betokens a troubling indistinctness of suffering and instability of spirit, becoming thereby a powerful analogy for the soul set adrift within its own chaotic selfhood. Its image of the deep occurs as well in other psalms. For example, in Psalm 41:8–9 (*Quemadmodum desiderat*), the same image expresses a condition of what might be called metaphysical involution:

> Deep calleth on deep, at the noise of thy flood-gates.
> All thy heights and thy billows have passed over me.
> In the daytime the Lord hath commanded his mercy;
> and a canticle to him in the night.
> With me is prayer to the God of my life.

The phrase "Deep calleth on deep" describes, in an especially dense way, the maelstrom of the soul's self-involvement—in sin but also in persistent self-investigation, which is the way to grace. *Abyssus abyssum invocat* is a figurative expression at once frightening and alluring, like Shelley's "Dizzy Ravine" in "Mont Blanc":

> [. . .] when I gaze on thee
> I seem as in a trance sublime and strange
> To muse on my own separate fantasy,
> My own, my human mind [. . . ]. (ll. 34–37)

Here, in his "trance sublime and strange," Shelley intuits retrospectively something of the pre-Romantic, medieval meaning of sublimity as not only an encounter with magnificence but also an involvement with the soul's obscurities. Shelley's trance is a hypnagogic condition in which the poet's encounter with the physical merges with the metaphysical. St. Augustine, in his sermon on Psalm 41, identifies this meeting place between body and spirit with the dark interiority of every human heart:

> What then is the abyss that calls and to what other abyss does it call? If by abyss we understand a great depth, is not man's heart, do you not suppose, an abyss? If deep signifies profundity, isn't the human heart a deep abyss? For what is there more profound than that abyss? Men may speak, may be seen by the operations of their members, may be heard speaking in conversation: but whose thought is penetrated, whose heart seen into?[38]

On the one hand, such a vision would seem to condemn the individual to a life of solipsism. On the other hand, as Augustine further interprets the phrase "deep calleth on deep," this vision actually enables communication between individual souls, God, and each other during their anxious pursuit of self-knowledge:

> If man then is an abyss, in what way does abyss call on abyss? Does man call on man as God is called upon? No, but *calls on* is equivalent to *calls to him*. Deep calls on deep, then, is man calls to man. Thus it is wisdom is learned, and thus faith, when man calls to man.[39]

For Augustine, the Psalms reflect our individual and our social identities as Christians. These divine poems offer, by way of their meditations on sin and redemption, a transcendent experience of sublimity that unites the Church as a Mystical Body, Christ the Head and his members. The poems are a powerful *cri de cœur* out of, across, and beyond our mortal depths.

## Early Modern and Victorian Echoes

The medieval idea of one soul struggling "out of the depths" while enlightening another continued to inspire, beyond the close of the Middle Ages, a lengthy and inventive tradition of Psalm translation and imitation. Sir Thomas Wyatt, for instance, a sixteenth-century diplomat and courtier best known today for such erotic lyrics as "They Flee from Me" and "Blame Not My Lute," composed a moving imitation of all the Penitential Psalms. In his version of *De*

*Profundis*, Wyatt explores masterfully the Psalmist's image of human depth:

> From depth of sin and from a deep despair,
> From depth of death, from depth of heart's sorrow,
> From this deep cave of darkness' deep repair,
> Thee have I called, O Lord, to be my borrow.
> Thou in my voice, O Lord, perceive and hear
> My heart, my hope, my plaint, my overthrow,
> My will to rise, and let by grant appear
> That to my voice thine ears do well intend.
> No place so far that to thee is not near;
> No depth so deep that thou ne mayst extend
> Thine ear thereto. Hear then my woeful plaint.[40]

Wyatt exhibits his poetic genius by amplifying the opening image of *De Profundis* in two different but complementary ways: he uses the noun "depth" and the adjective "deep" to describe not only his spiritual condition—"this deep cave of darkness' deep repair"—but also the verbal space of the poem itself, to which the poet withdraws from his daily responsibilities to perform the hard work of self-scrutiny. It is only in the final line of his stanza, after his long fugue of distress, that Wyatt demands the attention and grace of God, by way of a simple, unornamented imperative: "Hear then my woeful plaint." The poignancy of the moment is more pronounced because of its distressed prelude.

Another slightly later Renaissance psalmist, the Elizabethan soldier-poet George Gascoigne, mimics Wyatt's psalm paraphrase while also taking a more agitated poetic route toward the divine. His thoughts in his own version of *De Profundis* are less orderly than Wyatt's and marked by hyperbole and even bathos:

> From depth of doole [*sorrow*] wherein my soule dooth dwell,
> From heauie heart which harbors in my brest,
> From troubled sprite whych sildome taketh rest,
> From hope of heauen, from dreade of darksome hell,
> O gracious God, to thee I crie and yell:
> My God, my Lorde, my louely Lorde alone,
> To thee I call, to thee I make my mone.
> And thou, good God, vouchsafe in gree [*in good will*] to take
> This wofull plaint
> Wherein I faint:—
> Oh, heare me then, for thy great mercies sake![41]

The accretive monotony of the opening parallel structures—anaphora reinforced by labored alliteration—erects a kind of metric wall against which the surprise of the poet's culminating, desperate shout reverberates. "Yell" did not yet have in the sixteenth century quite the vociferous meaning it carries today. Nevertheless, it signals in these lines the poet's shift from a tone of stiff formality to one that is more colloquial. The abrupt and onomatopoetic monosyllable "yell" anticipates the truncated meter of the eight-syllable couplet that epitomizes Gascoigne's distress: "This wofull plaint / Wherein I faint." Here we can sense, as the poet uses rhyme to pull the reader up short metrically, the breathless desperation of a solitary soul at the very point of swooning. The entire passage reflects the poet's simultaneously artful and artless engagement with the sublimity of Wyatt's paraphrase as well as its Old Testament original.

These early modern examples from the English tradition of metrical psalm versions suggest continuity between the medieval sublime and certain Renaissance attitudes toward religious poetry. This continuity was renewed in nineteenth-century literature in both America and England as part of a popular revival of interest in the Middle Ages. None of the examples that follow, unlike those of Wyatt and Gascoigne, is a psalm translation or paraphrase, except in the very loosest sense of those terms. Rather, they are independent literary productions inspired by Psalm 129 and its medieval popularity. They develop along freer imaginary lines the Psalmist's powerful image of a direct encounter with human profundity as our sole means of approaching the heights of divine magnificence.

One of these creative engagements with Psalm 129 has been overlooked by critics because it appears very briefly in a vast book sometimes identified as the "Great American Novel," Herman Melville's masterpiece, *Moby-Dick*. Like his contemporary, Nathaniel Hawthorne, Melville was much obsessed with the Middle Ages. In what is arguably the key chapter of his novel, "The Whiteness of the Whale" (Chapter 42), Melville invokes the Psalmist's image of one deep calling out to another to express the confounding and yet hopelessly intriguing processes of human intellection, brought on by Ishmael's meditation on Moby Dick's absence of color: "In a matter like this," Ishmael explains, "subtlety appeals to subtlety, and without imagination no man can follow another into these halls."[42] Melville implies that imagination, the human power to create art out of a terrifying metaphysical blankness, is the soul's chief means of achieving the sublime. His decision to pursue this theme by way of a psalm figure and its medieval interpretation suggests that the whaling vessel's "Knights and Squires," as the author describes the

Pequod's crew collectively earlier in *Moby-Dick* (Chapter 26) are on a mystic pilgrimage as well as a sea voyage.

The English Victorians are less cryptic than Melville in their engagements with medieval sublimity. In his *Ballads and Other Poems* (1880), Tennyson entitles one of his most personal poems simply, "De Profundis," explaining in a subtitle that this poem is one of two verse "greetings" that he composed for his newborn son, Hallam, whom he named after his friend and the subject of *In Memoriam*, Arthur Henry Hallam, who was drowned at sea.[43] Tennyson uses Psalm 129's image of depth in his poem to represent the turbulence of his mourning as well as the primal chaos over which the Holy Spirit broods in Genesis 1:2. Just as God once brought forth all manner of life from nothingness, the birth of Hallam Tennyson brings forth some measure of hope from Tennyson's despair over the death of Arthur Henry Hallam:

> Out of the deep, my child, out of the deep,
> From that great deep, before our world begins,
> Whereon the Spirit of God moves as he will—
> Out of the deep, my child, out of the deep ,
> From that true world within the world we see,
> Whereof our world is but the bounding shore—
> Out of the deep, Spirit, out of the deep,
> With this ninth moon, that sends the hidden sun
> Down yon dark sea, thou comest, darling boy.[44]

Tennyson's effect is almost that of a metaphysical conceit, a violent yoking together of the personal and the cosmic, the depths and the heights. The poet repeats an English version of Psalm 129's Latin cue, "Out of the deep," several times within a relatively few lines as a kind of incantation, capable itself of conjuring birth from death, light from darkness, hope from despair. This interpolated refrain reminds the reader that Tennyson is simultaneously using the medieval text while updating its ideas philosophically, to bring them in line with his own metaphysical musings. That Tennyson deliberately composed his poem in a simple ballad meter, recounting his descent into the self and ascent into the empyrean by way of one of the humblest lyric forms, may in fact be his most profound tribute to medieval sublimity in his idiosyncratic treatment of *De Profundis*.

Unlike Tennyson's poem, Christina Rossetti's "De Profundis" manages to evoke Psalm 129's depths without once mentioning its image of the deep. Rather, the speaker of her lyric laments in the plainest terms the chasm between heaven and earth, between the sublime beauty of the night sky—imagined brilliantly as a vault from which the stars hang and as a dark ocean on which they drift—and her own desperately extended heart and hands:

> Oh why is heaven built so far,
>     Oh why is earth set so remote?
> I cannot reach the nearest star
>     That hangs afloat.
>
> I would not care to reach the moon,
>     One round monotonous of change;
> Yet even she repeats her tune
>     Beyond my range.
>
> I never watch the scatter'd fire
>     Of stars, or sun's far-trailing train,
> But all my heart is one desire,
>     And all in vain:
>
> For I am bound with fleshly bands,
>     Joy, beauty, lie beyond my scope;
> I strain my heart, I stretch my hands,
>     And catch at hope.[45]

The impossibility of the speaker's achievement of the sublime, so long as she is "bound" to her body, is a reminder that the Psalms and poetry that imitates them can do nothing more than verbalize, out of the depths of mortal experience, the soul's aspiration for the heights of salvation and union with God. The poetic act, as Rossetti depicts it with compelling honesty, is a gesture toward the sublime but should never be identified, the Romantic view notwithstanding, with sublimity itself. Her tone in the lyric becomes progressively petulant and nearly despairing, until the last line of her final stanza, which ends with the word "hope." She does not, however, embrace this "hope" fully; she snatches at it, longing to secure what remains beyond her reach. Rossetti's faith is an impulse, a sudden lurching beyond the earthbound and thought-imprisoned self toward something or maybe even Someone on high.

It is tempting to think of Rossetti's lyric as a reply—one abyss calling out to another, as Augustine might put it—to Hopkins's use of the medieval sublime in "No worst," one of his so-called Terrible Sonnets. Indeed, Hopkins's "No worst" itself could even be read as *his* answer to the extravagances of Shelley's "Mont Blanc":[46]

> No worst, there is none. Pitched past pitch of grief,
> More pangs will, schooled at forepangs, wilder wring.

> Comforter, where, where is your comforting?
> Mary, mother of us, where is your relief?
> My cries heave, herds-long; huddle in a main, a chief
> Woe, wórld-sorrow; on an áge-old anvil wince and sing —
> Then lull, then leave off. Fury had shrieked "No ling-
> ering! Let me be fell: force I must be brief."
>
> O the mind, mind has mountains; cliffs of fall
> Frightful, sheer, no-man-fathomed. Hold them cheap
> May who ne'er hung there. Nor does long our small
> Durance deal with that steep or deep. Here! creep,
> Wretch, under a comfort serves in a whirlwind: all
> Life death does end and each day dies with sleep. (Hopkins 167 ll. 1–14)

Here, in the mental geography of the sonnet's sestet, we recall distantly the sublime landscape of Shelley's "Mont Blanc," shrouded however in a fog of grim irony. The horrifying scene Hopkins's speaker describes is a psychological mountain range, crags and ravines that appear on no map because they are concealed beneath the surface of the self. Like the towering, Alp-like mountain ranges that deep submersibles reveal to us on the ocean floor, these "cliffs of fall / Frightful" are all the more terrifying because, unlike the looming mass of Mont Blanc itself, they are hidden from human perception. The soul's "small / Durance," its ability barely to hang onto itself while traversing such a landscape, is the Holy Spirit's weak answer to the strong question posed by Hopkins's speaker earlier in the octet, when he challenges God in his absent sublimity: "Comforter, where, *where* is your comforting?" (italics added). The language of "No worst" doubles back on itself as a metonym for the despairing soul's self-involvement. At the same time, the ability of the speaker of the poem to make out of his personal turbulence a verbal icon is a gesture beyond the abyss, one that has its special grandeur, since it is enabled by grace.

Writing not only in but through his despair, Hopkins, like his medieval predecessors, achieves the only sublimity available to any honest Christian poet: an imperfect and gradual ascent toward Truth. For him, the dark depths of the self, while frightening, are also evocative—magnificent in their purpose and potential, as they are in the twentieth-century Welsh poet R. S. Thomas's psalm-inspired poem, "This to Do":

> I have this that I must do
> One day: overdraw on my balance
> Of air, and breaking the surface
> Of water go down into the green

Darkness to search for the door
To myself.⁴⁷

Thomas's demonstrative pronoun and his categorical imperative imply that a religious poet is obligated, at some point during his career, to engage the sublime by plunging uncertainly but hopefully into the deep recesses of the self. This view of the poet's role and indeed of the role of poetry draws its power from a persistent, if sometimes neglected tradition of the medieval sublime. Such a poet's journey, in his life and in his work, from height to depth, from heaven to earth, from the air up above and then down into the waters of the soul's dark interiority may put him in mortal danger. It will also, however, connect him with his readers in a more profound way than the grandeur of much Romantic verse can, despite its self-evident literary genius and cultural allure.

**Notes**

1  For the epigraph, see Catherine Phillips's edition of Hopkins's poetry (167 ll. 9–10).
2  An earlier version of this essay was delivered as the keynote address to the South Central Conference on Christianity and Literature in New Orleans, LA, 2013. I am grateful to the conference participants and especially to William V. Davis, for helpful comments.
3  For a useful introduction to the Romantic sublime, see James Kirwan's *Sublimity: The Non-Rational and the Irrational in the History of Aesthetics*.
4  *OED*, sense 3.a. *Cf.* P. G. W. Glare on *sublimitas*, sense 1: "Height (*i.e.* either altitude or upward extent), elevation; a high place, a height" (2032).
5  *OED*, sense 4.
6  Friedrich's *Wanderer above the Sea of Fog* or *Chalk Cliffs on Rügen* (both, 1818) are examples; see Christina Grummt's *catalogue raisonné* of Friedrich's work. See Shelley (120 ll. 1–6).
7  See Shelley (124). In editors Leader and O'Neill's notes, they contrast the atheism of Shelley's 1817 poem with the theism of Samuel Taylor Coleridge's 1802 "Hymn before Sun-Rise, in the Vale of Chamouni," although they stop short of suggesting that the later poem is a response to the earlier (721).
8  See Jaeger's edited collection on the sublime in medieval arts and letters.
9  In his Foreword to the English translations of Auerbach's *Literary Language*, Jan M. Ziolkowski writes that Auerbach marked the dominant strain of realism in Western literature as emerging from "Christian belief" and from a cultural sense that "special value" attached to "the humble, the earthly, and the common" (xxi). Auerbach's earlier articles

"Sacrae scripturae sermo humilis" and "Sermo humilis" are prefacing studies to his "*Sermo Humilis*" chapter in *Literary Language* (xxi n. 42). Also see Jaeger (11).
10 Citations of Pseudo-Longinus' text of *Peri Hypsous* come from Penelope Murray and T. S. Dorsch's translation. Earlier commentators often translated the title of *Peri Hypsous* as *On the Sublime*.
11 Pseudo-Longinus (120).
12 Pseudo-Longinus (120).
13 See John Simpson and Jennifer Speake's entry "Homer sometimes nods" (156).
14 The prayer to "Father Zeus" is Ajax's in Homer's *Iliad* (Bk. 17). The Hebrew narrative is found at Gen. 1:3.
15 See Matthew Arnold's *Essays in Criticism* (12–27). Arnold, to be fair, derives his concept of high seriousness from Aristotle and equates it, during his discussion of the relationship between Classical and modern verse, with the quality of a poet's sincerity.
16 Pseudo-Longinus quotes Hesiod (*Shield of Heracles*, l. 267). Arnold refers to Chaucer, l. 197 ("The Prioress's Tale"). See Arnold (17).
17 Geoffrey's influence is partly measured by the fact that his treatise survives in over 200 manuscript copies, some of them heavily glossed. For Chaucer's reference to Geoffrey of Vinsauf in the mock-heroic context of the *Nun's Priest's Tale*, see Larry D. Benson's edition (260 ll. 3347–3351).
18 See Geoffrey of Vinsauf (16–17).
19 See Augustine's *Confessions* (163), where he describes with distaste how as a teacher of rhetoric he had become nothing more than a "salesman of words."
20 Jerome, Epistola XXI.13 (*PL* 22:385).
21 See Bede (169).
22 See Caecilia Davis-Weyer on medieval art (169).
23 All biblical quotations in this essay are taken from the Douay-Rheims (Douai-Rheims) translation. The Latin is taken from the Stuttgart edition of the Vulgate.
24 See "To Dionigi da Borgo San Sepolcro" in Petrarca's *Rerum familiarum libri I–VIII* (172).
25 See Augustine, *Confessions* (X.8.15), quoted in Petrarca, *Rerum familiarum libri I–VIII* (178).
26 See A. C. Spearing's translation, *The Cloud of Unknowing and Other Works* (26).
27 See Spearing (75).
28 See Carleton F. Brown's edition (80 ll. 1–8).
29 I am grateful to the British Library, London for allowing me to examine this manuscript.
30 See Chaucer (311 ll. 693–695).
31 See Chaucer (328 ll. 1–2). For a superb analysis of this element of medieval sublimity in Chaucer's work, which associates it with some of

the theological and ethical concerns of William Langland, the author of *Piers the Plowman*, see George Kane's 2010 essay.
32 See H. R. Bramley's edition of Rolle's work (4).
33 See especially Paul Gehl's 1984 article.
34 I am grateful to the Bodleian Library, Oxford for allowing me to examine this manuscript. See Kuczynski, *A Glossed Wycliffite Psalter*.
35 See Petrarca's "To Giovanni Boccaccio" (47).
36 See editor F. L. Cross's *Oxford Dictionary of the Christian Church* for "De Profundis" (390).
37 I discuss Lydgate's poem at much greater length in terms of the private and public significance of the Psalms in my book, *Prophetic Song: The Psalms as Moral Discourse in Late Medieval England* (135–143).
38 For Augustine's remarks on this passage from Psalm 41 (in the Vulgate numbering), see *Nicene and Post-Nicene Fathers* (136a). Schaff and Coxe's 1888 translation of Augustine is available through Archive.org, Google Books, and Newadvent.org (section 12).
39 See Augustine (Schaff and Coxe 136b) and section 13 in digital formats.
40 See Wyatt's *Complete Poems* (213–214 ll. 50–61).
41 For Gascoigne, see G. W. Pigman's edition (290–291 ll. 1–11). Also see a useful discussion on Gascoigne by Gillian Austen (32–53).
42 See Melville (209).
43 The passage from Tennyson that follows is the first section of the second part of a poem entitled, in the standard edition of Tennyson's works, "The Two Greetings." See Tennyson in Christopher Ricks's edition (III 67–70). Ricks groups "The Two Greetings" with another Tennyson lyric entitled "The Human Cry" under the general heading "De Profundis" (Ricks's no. 383). Ricks's headnote explains the complicated publication history, including Tennyson's own changes of title to the material.
44 See Tennyson (68–69 ll. 24–34).
45 See Rossetti (302).
46 Rossetti briefly met the much younger Hopkins, who admired her poetry and its deliberate medievalism, in 1864. See Norman White's biography of Hopkins (82). The Terrible Sonnets, however, were not discovered and published until after Hopkins's death. Shelley, especially his *Prometheus Unbound*, was an early influence, but Hopkins moved rapidly beyond it. See White (40, 398). On Hopkins's conflicted response to Shelley's Romantic sublime, see, for example, Paul Mariani's biography of Hopkins (175–176).
47 R. S. Thomas, *Pietà* (14).

**Works Cited**

Arnold, Matthew. *Essays in Criticism: The Study of Poetry; John Keats; Wordsworth*. Ed. Susan S. Sheridan. Boston: Allyn and Bacon, 1896.
St. Augustine. *Confessions*. 10.8.15. *The Confessions of St. Augustine*. Trans. E. B. Pusey. London: Dent. New York: Dutton, 1907, 1920. 212–213.

—. *Confessions*. Trans. Henry Chadwick. Oxford: OUP, 1992.

—. *Nicene and Post-Nicene Fathers: First Series. Volume VIII St. Augustine: Exposition on the Psalms*. Ed. Philip Schaff and Arthur Cleveland Coxe. 1888. New York: Cosimo, 2007.

Auerbach, Erich. *Literary Language and its Public in Latin Antiquity and in the Middle Ages*. Trans. Ralph Manheim. Foreword, Jan M. Ziolkowski. Bollingen Series 74. Princeton, NJ: Princeton UP, 1993.

—. "Sacrae scripturae sermo humilis." *Neuphilologische Mitteilungen* 42.2 (1941): 57–67.

—. "Sermo humilis." *Romanische Forschungen* 64.3/4 (1952): 304–364.

Austen, Gillian. *George Gascoigne*. Cambridge, UK: D. S. Brewer, 2008.

St. Bede, The Venerable. *Libri II De Arte Metrica et De Schematibus et Tropis: The Art of Poetry and Rhetoric*. Trans. Calvin B. Kendall. Bibliotheca Germanica 2. Saarbrücken: AQ-Verlag, 1991.

Bodleian Library, Oxford, MS Bodley 554. A mid-15th c. Wycliffite Psalter.

Bramley, H. R., ed. *The Psalter or Psalms of David and Certain Canticles, with a Translation and Exposition in English by Richard Rolle of Hampole*. Oxford, UK: Clarendon P, 1884. Digital version, Ann Arbor: U of Michigan Library, 2006.

British Library, London, MS Additional 20059. An anonymous 15th c. religious lyric.

Brown, Carleton F., ed. *Religious Lyrics of the XVth Century*. Oxford, UK: Clarendon P, 1939.

Chaucer, Geoffrey. *The Riverside Chaucer*. Ed. Larry D. Benson. 3rd ed. Boston: Houghton Mifflin, 1987.

Cross, F. L., ed. "De Profundis." *The Oxford Dictionary of the Christian Church*. London: OUP, 1957. 390.

Davis-Weyer, Caecilia. *Early Medieval Art 300–1150: Sources and Documents*. Toronto: U of Toronto P, 1986.

*Game of Thrones*. Creators David Benioff and D. B. Weiss. HBO. 2011–2019.

Gascoigne, George. *A Hundreth Sundrie Flowres*. Ed. G. W. Pigman, III. Oxford, UK: Clarendon P, 2000.

Gehl, Paul. "Mystical Language Models in Monastic Education Psychology." *Journal of Medieval and Renaissance Studies* 14 (1984): 219–243.

Geoffrey of Vinsauf. *Poetria Nova*. Trans. Margaret F. Nims. Rev. ed. Toronto: Pontifical Institute of Mediaeval Studies, 2010.

Glare, P. G. W., ed. "sublimitas." *Oxford Latin Dictionary*, 2nd ed. Oxford: OUP, 2012. Vol. 2. 2032.

Grummt, Christina. *Caspar David Friedrich: Die Zeichnungen, das gesamte Werk*. 2 vols. München: Beck, 2011.

Homer. *The Iliad*. Trans. A. T. Murray. 2 vols. Cambridge, MA: Harvard UP, 1924.

Hopkins, Gerard Manley. *Gerard Manley Hopkins*. Ed. Catherine Phillips. Oxford: OUP, 1986.

Jaeger, C. Stephen. *Magnificence and the Sublime in Medieval Aesthetics: Art, Architecture, Literature, Music*. New York: Palgrave Macmillan, 2010.

Jerome (Sancti Eusebii Hieronymi). Epistola XXI. *Epistolae*. Ed. Jacques Paul Migne. *Patrologiae cursus completus. Series Latina* [*Patrologia*

*Latina (PL)*]. Paris: Migne, 1864. 22. 379–394. Electronic text at Patristica.net/latina (Migne. Patrologia Latina).

Kane, George. "Poets and the Poetics of Sin." *The Morton W. Bloomfield Lectures, 1989–2005*. Ed. Daniel Donoghue, James Simpson, and Nicholas Watson. Kalamazoo: Medieval Institute, 2010. 1–19.

Kirwan, James. *Sublimity: The Non-Rational and the Irrational in the History of Aesthetics*. New York: Routledge, 2005.

Kuczynski, Michael P. *A Glossed Wycliffite Psalter: Oxford, Bodleian Library MS Bodley 554*. EETS, OS 352, 353. 2 vols. Oxford: OUP, 2019.

—. *Prophetic Song: The Psalms as Moral Discourse in Late Medieval England*. Philadelphia: U of Pennsylvania P, 1995.

Langland, William. *Piers [the] Plowman: A New Translation of the B-Text*. Trans. A. V. C. Schmidt. Oxford World's Classics. Oxford: OUP, 1997.

Longinus. See Pseudo-Longinus.

Lydgate, John. "On *De Profundis*." *The Minor Poems of John Lydgate*. Pt. I. Ed. Henry Noble MacCracken. EETS Extra Series, 107. London: Kegan Paul, Trench, Trübner; Henry Frowde, OUP, 1911 (for 1910). 77–84.

Mariani, Paul. *Gerard Manley Hopkins: A Life*. New York: Viking, 2008. 175–176.

Martin, George R. R. *A Game of Thrones*. A Song of Ice and Fire 1. New York: Bantam, 1996.

Melville, Herman. *Moby-Dick or, The Whale*. New York: Penguin, 1992.

*The Oxford English Dictionary (OED)*. 2nd ed. Ed. J. A. Simpson and Edmund Weiner. 20 vols. Oxford: OUP, 1989. Electronic text by subscription.

Petrarca, Francesco. "To Dionigi da Borgo San Sepolcro of the Augustinian Order and Professor of Sacred Scripture, concerning some personal problems." *Rerum familiarum libri I–VIII*. Trans. Aldo S. Bernardo. Albany: SUNY Press, 1975. 172.

—. "To Giovanni Boccaccio, an expression of gratitude for sending Augustine's book on the Psalms of David." *Letters on Familiar Matters, Rerum familiarum libri XVII–XXIV*. Trans. Aldo S. Bernardo. Baltimore: Johns Hopkins UP, 1985. 4.

Pigman, G. W., III. See Gascoigne, George.

Pseudo-Longinus. *Peri Hypsous [Concerning Loftiness*, formerly, *On the Sublime]*. Trans. Penelope Murray and T. S. Dorsch. *Classical Literary Criticism*. London: Penguin, 2000. 113–166.

Rossetti, Christina. *Christina Rossetti: The Complete Poems*. Ed. R. W. Crump. Intro. Betty S. Flowers. London: Penguin, 2001.

Shelley, Percy Bysshe. *Percy Bysshe Shelley: The Major Works*. Ed. Zachary Leader and Michael O'Neill. Oxford: OUP, 2003.

Simpson, John, and Jennifer Speake. "Homer sometimes nods." *The Oxford Dictionary of Proverbs*. 5th ed. Oxford: OUP, 2009. 156.

Spearing, A. C., trans. *The Cloud of Unknowing and Other Works*. London: Penguin, 2001.

Tennyson, Alfred, Lord. "The Two Greetings." *The Poems of Tennyson in Three Volumes*. Ed. Christopher Ricks. London: Longman, 1987. Vol. 3. 67–70.

Thomas, R. S. *Pietà*. London: Rupert Hart-Davis, 1966.

White, Norman. *Hopkins: A Literary Biography*. Oxford, UK: Clarendon P, 1992.
Wyatt, Thomas, Sir. *The Complete Poems*. Ed. R. A. Rebholz. New Haven, CT: Yale UP, 1981.
Ziolkowski, Jan M. Foreword. Ed. Auerbach. *Literary Language*. 1993. ix–xl.

# ~2~
# Presbyterian Impulses Amid Catholicism in Kate Chopin's *The Awakening*

## Thomas Bonner, Jr.

Most discussions of Kate Chopin's *The Awakening* that address the novel's treatment of religious culture focus on the French Catholicism of Louisiana, and indeed, many concrete details in the novel encourage that approach. It is also true that nearly every scholar who has studied *The Awakening* mentions Presbyterianism as an element of Edna, its central character, and of her father, the Colonel, calling attention to the contrast between the Protestant religious culture of Edna's Kentucky and Mississippi homes and the Catholic Creole one into which she marries in South Louisiana.[1] Among twentieth-century Chopin critics who examine Chopin's treatment of local color, Catholicism, and identity, Catholic priest Daniel S. Rankin, her first biographer, is also the first commentator (1932) to cite the cultural conflict. In *Kate Chopin and Her Creole Stories*, Rankin emphasizes distinctions between the Presbyterian Edna and her Catholic husband, Léonce (171), as Chopin's biographers and some critics of the novel would later do. For example, Per Seyersted's 1969 *Critical Biography* notes Edna as a child "running away from the Presbyterian service" (154), and Emily Toth's 1990 biography (*Life*) refers to Edna's "stodgy Kentucky Presbyterian family" (330).[2] Though recent critical attention to *The Awakening*, like much twentieth-century criticism on Chopin's fiction generally, is marked by feminist commentary on her frank and realistic treatment of women characters and their sexuality, the question of Chopin's reflections on and of religion in *The Awakening* have had interest for feminist critics like Sandra M. Gilbert and Susan Gubar (1989).[3] They describe Chopin as "this daughter of a distinguished and pious Catholic family" who, early in her widowhood, "abandoned the Catholicism of her girlhood" to become "an acolyte of the 'direct and simple' stories of [Guy de] Maupassant" (II 85–86).[4] Gilbert and Gubar, commenting on Chopin's Catholicism and her inclinations toward myth, describe her as viewing the "triumph of the female through the power of the pagan" (II 114).[5]

*The Awakening*, then, possesses a critical history that is relevant to the study of Edna as a character in the full context of her and her creator's times. It was first published in 1899 and was initially rejected by many of Chopin's critics, not only for Edna's sexuality, but also for her apparent detachment as a mother, elements that foreground the disconnects Chopin presents between Kentucky Presbyterianism and French-Creole Catholicism. The novel essentially languished in obscurity for over fifty years, during which time, Chopin's critical reputation for fiction through the mid-twentieth century rested on her regional stories, often considered by critics and anthologists of the time as part of the "local color" movement. In 1956, the novel was recalled to life by Kenneth Eble in a brief essay in the *Western Humanities Review*, and about six years later, *The Awakening* was introduced to a "larger audience than Eble could have reached" when Edmund Wilson gave an "authoritative notice" of it in his 1962 study of the South's Civil War fiction, *Patriotic Gore*.[6]

The setting of *The Awakening* in Roman Catholic and French New Orleans creates a contrast with Edna's native Presbyterian milieu. Chopin has a habit of setting up contrasts in her long and short fiction, and this one especially reveals a character forged by her youthful experiences with Protestantism having difficulty being integrated into the culture and society of New Orleans and South Louisiana. Catholic churches are geographically never far away from Edna: the St. Louis Cathedral in the French Quarter of New Orleans near their Esplanade home and Our Lady of Lourdes Catholic Church, a customary boat ride across the bay from Grand Isle. Presbyterianism exists in Edna's distant past, and she will experience a visceral response to its reintroduction into her life with the visit of her father in chapter twenty-three.

The novel begins on Grand Isle on the Gulf of Mexico, south of New Orleans, where Edna and Léonce Pontellier and their two sons, Raoul (age five) and Étienne (age four) are on summer vacation with others from the city. The seaside atmosphere and the attentions of a young man, Robert Lebrun, expose Edna's emotional vulnerabilities, and she begins to rebel against the wishes of her husband. Meanwhile, her Creole friend Adéle Ratignolle warns Robert about Edna's taking his flirting seriously because, as Edna is not of their culture, she fails to understand their social customs. When Edna returns to New Orleans, she continues her independent conduct, much to the consternation of her husband. With her sensuality aroused, she falls victim to Alcée Arobin, a well-known rake, and when Robert returns to her from a trip to Mexico, she realizes the impossibility of her and Robert's romantic affection and fears her newly heightened vulnerabilities. With her husband away on business and her sons with their paternal grandmother, Edna goes alone and out of season to Grand Isle, orders fish for supper, frees herself from her bathing dress, enters the Gulf, and disappears beneath its waters.

## The Catholic Milieu

As in much of her other French-Louisiana fiction, Chopin uses the trappings of Catholicism to shape character and atmosphere in *The Awakening*.[7] For this, her second novel, she creates a deeply Catholic, South Louisiana motif when she describes recurring images of "the lady in black," whom one may assess by her clothes, manners, and the company she keeps as a devout and financially comfortable Catholic widow. "The lady in black" is first introduced "walking demurely up and down" in front of the cottages of Grand Isle "telling her beads" (882), and on a Sunday, she is observed "reading her morning devotions on the porch of a neighboring bath-house" (895). "The lady in black" appears again, carrying "her Sunday prayer-book, velvet and gold-clasped, and her Sunday silver beads" to join a group of other island visitors who will journey across the bay to attend Mass (913). Further on, when Robert announces his intention to go to Mexico, "the lady in black" thinks of a rosary brought to her from Mexico and wonders about the supposed limits of an indulgence attached to it (923–924), showing her awareness of the post-Reformation Catholic Church's legalisms. This point is perhaps Chopin's subtle criticism of those practices.

Against such crisp, suggestive, and compelling regional Louisiana images of older Catholic womanhood, however, the youthful Edna's upper mid-South Presbyterian background operates like negative space in a painting, echoing here a duality that draws Edna away from the influence of both religious institutions toward a life in which her very self is outside their bonds. Chopin describes Edna with light strokes, as Edna merely "talk[s] about her father's Mississippi plantation and her girlhood home in the old Kentucky blue-grass country" (884) and thinks of her life in Kentucky only in vague recollections and images, a narrative technique that renders Edna's earlier life merely impressionistic.[8] Other characters in the novel allude to Edna's religious formation and its differences compared with Catholicism in vague terms. In chapter twenty-two, for example, Léonce, in response to Dr. Mandelet's question about there being anything "peculiar about [Edna's] family antecedents," replies, "Oh, no, indeed! She comes of sound old Presbyterian Kentucky stock" (948). In chapters twenty-three and twenty-four, Chopin paints Edna's mixed responses toward her father and what he stands for in a catalogue of simply sketched scenes that take place during the Colonel's visit to New Orleans. Although presented briefly, the scene of Edna's drawing her father's portrait proves critical: before the sitting, he is described in considerable physical detail: "His hair and mustache were white and silky, emphasizing the rugged bronze of his face. He was tall and thin, and wore his coats padded, which gave a fictitious breadth and depth to his shoulders and chest," and he moved with a "military bearing" (950); nevertheless, the narrator omits any description of Edna's portrait—though based on the narrator's description and Edna's nuanced sense of her father, Edna's image of the Colonel would have reached far deeper than his physical appearance. As the Colonel's visit wears on, however, Edna notes that she "had not much of anything to say to her father," even though "for the first time in her life she felt as if she were thoroughly acquainted with him" (951). In their argument over Edna's not going to her sister's wedding, the space—and silence—between them simply widens, illustrating the Colonel's "rigidity" (951) and his unchanging attitudes.[9]

In spite of her focus on Edna's family, Chopin offers the reader no direct narrative detail about the marriage of Edna's Kentucky-Presbyterian culture to that of her Louisiana Catholic husband, Léonce, but, given what I have termed the negative space of Edna's formative religious life set into Léonce's nineteenth-century South Louisiana society, the union of the two traditions serves to dramatize Chopin's concerns about the inner life of the outsider and her keen awareness of cultural differences and conflicts. In chapter sixteen, for example, where Edna and Adèle are involved in a "rather heated argument" over what a mother owes her children, Adèle affirms her position by challenging what she views as Edna's faulty understanding of maternal duty with an ironic reference: "Your Bible tells you so" (929). It is unlikely that Adèle would use the phrase "*your* Bible" (emphasis added) to a fellow cradle Catholic, and Adèle's choice of words and authority—"your Bible"—implies that she perceives a meaningful difference between Edna's Protestant Bible and the Bible as it is viewed by Catholics.[10] Along with Chopin, the attentive reader may also be aware that at Edna's marriage she would have had to convert to Catholicism or take an oath that her children would have Catholic baptism, education, and rearing. Though these principles are not expressed as a part of Edna's remodeling of her religious allegiance and views, the sacrament of marriage in Roman Catholicism was precisely this "binding" on Edna.[11]

Although Chopin never explicitly addresses any ideological or emotional struggle of Edna's having to do with religious and cultural differences, that inner contest underlies some of the most important considerations suggested by the novel, and it has been understood by many readers as lying at the center of Edna's angst. An examination of scenes in the novel in contexts of history and society during Chopin's residences in St. Louis and Louisiana, along with material from Chopin's other fiction, offers further rationales upon which to base considerations of religious culture and its social effects in *The Awakening*, giving definition to that "negative space" around Edna and making it more interesting and suggestive.[12] One of the modernist aspects of *The Awakening* is its use of purposely drawn ambiguity and vagueness. Much like Ernest Hemingway's "iceberg theory" of the narrative text lying above water and the greater narrative being below it, Chopin's text often offers clues and implied narratives, using spaces for the readers of her time to fill from their experiences.

## Considerations from Chopin's Biographical Criticism

Chopin's biography offers several circumstances and events that suggest rationales for her subtle handling of the religious and cultural questions that shape her characters and situations in the novel. The earliest investigator to consider the meeting of two cultures in *The Awakening* was Rankin, who implied that the culture of the novel lay in the "mixed marriage"—a common term in pre-Vatican II Catholicism—of Catholic Léonce and Presbyterian Edna (171), a circumstance sometimes acted out in real life, and one with which Chopin was undoubtedly familiar.[13] Toth (*Life*) reveals an interesting genealogical circumstance of which Chopin was certainly aware: Chopin's maternal grandfather was a Protestant, and her maternal grandmother's family, the Charlevilles, came from La Rochelle, France, a "center of Protestantism,"[14] and Toth proposes that Chopin was the product of a "somewhat mixed" marriage because of the "branches of Huguenots" along her family tree (41). While Kate's mother's marriage to an older man, the Irish widower Thomas O'Flaherty, might seem to suggest a model of differing cultures for Chopin, I suggest otherwise because at the period, older men often married younger women; furthermore, the intense Catholicism of both parents worked to mediate whatever gaps may have existed between their experiences and backgrounds. Seyersted (*Critical Biography*) relates an incident that affirms the unswerving Catholic commitment in Chopin's childhood home: the young Katie O'Flaherty—who would become Kate Chopin at her marriage to Oscar Chopin in 1870—asks to spend the night at a friend's home and is forbidden because the friend's family is not Catholic (19).

Catholic consciousness in the O'Flaherty household, Toth also notes, is apparent in Thomas O'Flaherty's being very pleased that George, his son from his first marriage, could attend a university in America. In Ireland, by contrast, few Catholics could go to university (*Life* 30) because only a limited number could be admitted, and their attendance required the Church's approval.[15] The issue of religion was alive in the young Chopin's mind, for in her "Commonplace Book," where she recorded salient passages from her reading and made her own observations, she copied a paragraph from Thomas Babington Macaulay's *Ranke's History of the Popes* and then appended a comment, reflecting that history was "a ceaseless combat between Catholic and non–Catholic forces."[16] As these observations from Seyersted and Toth and Chopin's early writing tend to confirm, the young Kate had a conventional religious upbringing, strongly influenced by the Sacred Heart nuns, but her wider intellectual contacts during her thirties in St. Louis moved her toward what Toth describes as "religious non-conformity" (*Life* 36).

It is clear that despite her parents' evident efforts to limit her interactions with non-Catholics, Chopin had contacts beyond her Catholic community from childhood through adulthood. The St. Louis of "Katie's" time had a large Catholic population, and, as in New Orleans, the Catholic presence in St. Louis had a strong influence on the culture of the city, yet the Protestant communities had a presence as well, as elements cited from Chopin's early biography have already indicated. Besides the Catholic and Protestant presence, communities of Jews prospered in St. Louis—Chopin published in *The American Jewess* in April 1895—as did Unitarians. Toth writes that Chopin knew many Unitarians in St. Louis, and that in December 1890, Kate and Charlotte Stearns Eliot had been accepted as charter members of the Wednesday Club (*Life* 207–208).[17] In addition, Chopin's association and friendship with Dr. Friedrich Kolbenheyer, an agnostic, also provided her a wider window of thought about religion, and Rankin remarks that through this contact, Chopin "no longer remained a Catholic in any real or practical way." Chopin's physician since the early 1870s, Kolbenheyer was a force in her intellectual and creative life as well.[18] It is important to note that Rankin, writing in the 1930s, held conservative Catholic views with an emphasis on the outward signs of the practice of Catholicism in contrast to the broader effects of post-Vatican II reforms.

## Religion and Society in Chopin's Other Fiction

Chopin's pre-*Awakening* Louisiana fiction frequently uses Catholicism as an element in her portraits of Creole and Acadian (Cajun) communities. Her first novel, *At Fault*, published in 1890, addresses the issue of divorce and contrasts a liberal perspective with stricter Roman Catholic dogma, echoing the conflict in the passage that she copied years earlier from Macaulay.[19] Curiously, in *At Fault*, Chopin provides detail about the Catholicism of her protagonist Thérèse Lafirme, a young widow in love with a divorced man, but Chopin is, at first, vague about the specific religion of Hosmer, the man who is courting Thérèse, and Chopin reveals only further on in the story that he is a Unitarian (ch. 11). When Hosmer, the newly arrived manager of a lumber mill, expresses surprise at Thérèse's religion, he implies his assumption that Northern Louisiana would be like the Protestant South he knows from his time in neighboring states. Chopin gives the seventh chapter of *At Fault* to the issue of divorce, examining its role in religion as applied to Thérèse—whose surname, Lafirme, is a pun emphasizing Thérèse's position on divorce and religion. Here, as is often the case in Chopin's other fiction, her writing is poised between exegesis and narration in her use of dialogue to achieve a debate of the issue. Chopin's narrator characterizes Thérèse's internal debate on her position to illuminate the emotion behind her subsequent discussion with Hosmer: "With the prejudices of her Catholic education coloring her sentiment, she instinctively shrank when the theme [of divorce] confronted her as one having even a remote reference to her own clean existence" (764). When Hosmer says that he did not know she was Catholic, Thérèse explains, "Because you have never seen any outward signs of it [her Catholicism]. But I can't leave you under a false impression: religion doesn't influence my reason in this" (765–766). Chopin gives Thérèse so strong a voice for her views on divorce that her words overpower Hosmer's concern with his own happiness at the expense of his wife's: "A man owes to his manhood, to face the consequences of his actions" (769).

Of interest in *At Fault* in the context of *The Awakening* is Chopin's exploring religious orthodoxy and its relation to "self" because she would again broach the subject nearly a decade later in *The Awakening*. In the twelfth chapter of *At Fault* when Texan Rufe Jimson reports Grégoire's death to Thérèse, Chopin draws the linguistic distinction between Rufe's offer of "proyer meetin's and sich" with Thérèse's correction of his Protestant-influenced phrase to "Masses" (852). In this scene Chopin privileges class distinction—as she does in *The Awakening*—subordinating the imperfect Protestant knowledge and rustic dialect to the informed Catholic ones. The outward-inward tension of *The Awakening* appears in *At Fault* as well, for Chopin makes distinctions about the practice of Catholicism with Lorenzo and Belle Worthington of St. Louis, with the conversationally "loud" and "aggressive" Belle (789), who simply observes Catholicism's physical requirements, and quiet and studious Lorenzo's having an intellectual approach to his faith because it is deepened by his wide and prodigious reading (791).

In *At Fault*, as in other examples of Chopin's short fiction, she follows the pattern of many regional realist or local color writers by presenting Catholicism as part of the Louisiana settings from which her characters emerge. As noted in the *Companion* (Bonner), language associated with Catholicism permeates Chopin's stories, indicating the intense presence of Catholicism in the locales and lives of her characters; for example the word "Assumption" in "Odalie Misses Mass"(1895) refers to a Roman Catholic feast day, and in "At the 'Cadian Ball" (1892), "Assumption" refers to an actual civil parish in Louisiana (xiii). Priests, like Father Fochel, who appears in both Chopin's novels and in the story "A Sentimental Soul" (1895. 388 *ff.*), frequently have roles in Chopin's fiction, as do churches like Our Lady of Lourdes in *The Awakening*, where the church name recalls a nineteenth-century Marian miracle.[20] Chopin's naming Our Lady of Lourdes as the church in *The Awakening*—and in the story "At Chênière Caminada" several years later—resonates with Chopin's personal experience of religious obligations and their patriarchal nature during her marriage; these regional cultural elements have a strong presence in *The Awakening*.[21] Religious place and personal names, such as "the village of Saint Louis" and "Saint Phillippe" [*sic*] in "The Maid of Saint Phillippe" (1892. 116 *ff.*), abound in Chopin's fiction. The names of Chopin's characters, too, like Marianne in "The Maid of Saint Phillippe" and Jean Baptiste Plochel in "The Return of Alcibiade" (1892. 249 *ff.*), often have religious foundations; the former baptismal name honors St. Anne and the Virgin, and the latter, Saint John the Baptist. In contrast, among her stories, Chopin's references to the man teaching the Bible in "The Night Came Slowly"(1895. 366) and to the minister's wife in "Loka" (1892. 212) are her only references to non-Catholic clerics.[22]

## The Presbyterian Question

The question of why Chopin chose Presbyterianism for the religion of her protagonist's family in *The Awakening* is impossible to answer definitively, but, with a further consideration of biographical criticism, I suggest that the religious composition of Chopin's own family and her contact with friends' families in St. Louis probably contributed to the choice: if Chopin's intent were to create an undercurrent of personal and domestic tension to affect the mind and spirit of a female protagonist in nineteenth-century Southern fiction, she could hardly have chosen a more effective device. It is also worth noting that Chopin as a bride was very much "the other" in the eyes of her father-in-law when she arrived in Louisiana from St. Louis because of her mixed Irish and French family, though Nancy Walker emphasizes Chopin's sophistication and her stake in Louisiana's Creole culture. Nonetheless, if Chopin sought to make Edna "the other" in South Louisiana, Edna's Kentucky Protestant background would serve dramatically to accomplish that end. Indeed, the growth and nature of Presbyterianism in Missouri in Chopin's time may have particularly impressed her—as one might gather from its oppositional role in the novel—because of developments in the Kentucky branch of the church, and she appears to have been aware of its late nineteenth-century incarnation in Missouri.

About 1810, the Cumberland Presbyterian Church was founded from the schism between American Presbyterianism's frontier "revival" group (that became the Cumberland faction) and the established Kentucky Synod.[23] The reasons for the division lay in the interpretation of church authority and doctrine and in sociological matters. The basic beliefs of Presbyterianism come from the Westminster Confession (Westminster), along with the longer and shorter catechisms adopted from 1643 to 1649. These include the basic principles of Calvinism and the following standards: sovereignty of God, the primary authority of scripture as a guide to church doctrine, the Bible as rule of government and discipline as well as Faith, and "the "sacraments of Baptism and Lord's Supper."[24] The Presbyterians that Chopin likely encountered in St Louis more likely belonged to the Presbyterian Synod of Missouri, which developed from the missionary revivalist impulse of the Southern Presbyterian Church. In *The Awakening*, Edna's father's authoritarian and conventional thinking reflects the narrowness of this religious culture in attitude and perspective. It is significant that at the period of the novel, Presbyterian churches in Missouri—and in Edna's Kentucky home—followed the Calvinist tendencies of the missionary revivalist-oriented Southern church, and their emphasis on the authority of the Bible under that theology has resonance in Chopin's novel. Perhaps even more significant is their patriarchal and paternalistic position toward women, who were denied voting privileges in church matters. That only male heads of households could vote was a dictum that took its authority from St. Paul's Letter to the Corinthians (1:14:34): "Let your women keep silence in the churches; for it is not permitted unto them to speak" (KJV), and the principle apparently had force in Edna's Kentucky home, as we will discover. Through the nineteenth century, according to Lois A. Boyd and R. Douglas Brackenridge in *Presbyterian Women in America*, "churchmen" expected females to be "silent, subordinate, and submissive" in church affairs (vii).[25] Such expectations, no doubt, carried into the homes, as Edna's father indicates when he gives Léonce a harsh directive (treated more fully below) to manage Edna with "[a]uthority" and "coercion." Chopin's narrator then observes, "The Colonel was perhaps unaware that he had coerced his own wife into her grave" (954).

Another matter with which external criticism charged the Cumberland group was that it admitted ministers who lacked education and who were often described as uneducated and ill-suited to the ministry by appearance and temperament.[26] Chopin presents a reflection of this sentiment in her fictional sketch "The Night Came Slowly," based on notes she made in July 1894 while she was vacationing in Sulfur Springs, Missouri. Chopin closes her story as follows: "A man came to-day with his 'Bible Class.' He is detestable with his red cheeks and bold eyes and coarse manner and speech. What does he know of Christ? Shall I ask a young fool who was born yesterday and will die tomorrow to tell me things of Christ?" (366).[27] In the response of her fictional narrator, Chopin perhaps expresses a view close to her own sensibilities on the question of an educated clergy, her response being grounded in her own religious background. Chopin's Catholicism valued church tradition as much as, if not more than "Bible readings," and the attentive reader will note elements of class and denominational superiority in conversations and descriptions in *The Awakening*, elements yet to be addressed.[28] Chopin's process of inquiry and formal doubt definitely had matured, along with her skill as an author, by the time she created Edna to grapple with being an outlier in her own family and an outsider in the society of her family-by-marriage in *The Awakening*.

## *The Awakening*'s Cultural Encounter

If Chopin saw *The Awakening* as a microcosmic glimpse of a meaningful divide in American culture, namely, that between the Calvinistic Protestant norm of the nation's midlands and the variations at its borders, in the Spanish- and French-colonized coasts along the Gulf of Mexico, she saw religious culture and its effects as defining elements of character. While Chopin overtly advances this notion only in her youthful diaries and commonplace book—for example her referring to Christianity in 1867 as "that great source whence springs all good" (*Private* 31)—she handles the idea subtly in *The Awakening*, where Edna Pontellier is the novel's invading force.[29] Edna is a Presbyterian, so a cultural division figures into her entering the Catholic family of her husband. But she is outnumbered and less equipped to navigate the culture, so she outwardly adapts, but, ultimately, cannot exert herself to adapt inwardly or to change the social environment in which she finds herself. Of the considerable number of references to Edna's mother-in-law, the senior Mrs. Pontellier, and in the scenes where she appears, no word or act indicates her hostility toward Edna, yet she shows an eagerness beyond what might be expected to have her grandsons stay with her, away from Edna. On one occasion, old Mrs. Pontellier comes to New Orleans for the children when Léonce is away, but she does "not venture to say she was afraid they would be neglected" (955). Chopin's negative couching of Mrs. Pontellier's motivation reveals her unspoken suspicion and allows Chopin to reveal the grandmother's attitude by her implied reticence. Unlike Madame Adéle Ratignolle, who actively gives Edna her advice, the senior Mrs. Pontellier refrains from direct intervention, simply placing herself in position to ease strains when they occur in her son's family by doing what many grandmothers do: taking the children. The tacit manner of old Mrs. Pontellier's "taking the children," however, suggests to the reader that she is concerned about Edna's difficulties in acclimating herself to the Creole Catholic community and, perhaps, consequent effects on the Pontellier heirs.

Chopin creates Léonce's mother, then, as a vigilant force in support of the Catholic Creole culture in her family's life. When, after Edna's affair with Arobin in New Orleans, Edna visits little Raoul and Etienne at their grandmother's home upriver in Iberville, Edna engages them more intensely than at any earlier point in the novel, as if she were attempting to recompense her neglect. In this section, too, Chopin gives the boys greater dimension as characters. Old Mrs. Pontellier "was charmed with Edna's visit, and showered all manner of delicate attentions upon her" (978), but the grandmother sees an opportunity in Edna's news about Léonce's remodeling of their home: she "was delighted to know that the Esplanade Street house was in a dismantled condition" because its disrepair "gave her the promise and pretext to keep the children indefinitely" (978). Old Madame Pontellier's anxiety for Raoul and Etienne and her doubts about Edna remain unspoken, but given the example of Edna's family's disapproval of her marrying a Catholic, the cultural climate of Catholic Louisiana, and Mrs. Pontellier's evident concern for her grandchildren, one cannot doubt that Léonce, too, faced familial antipathy to his choice; nonetheless, Chopin does not allow the question to break the surface on the Catholic side. When, for example, Raoul sends his mother a letter in "delicious printed scrawl" (987), one can see the hand of the grandmother in this necessarily collaborative gesture, a prompt that presses Edna to be more aware of her children.

A close reading shows that Chopin's introduction of Edna's character and the development of narrative about Edna's struggle are wound closely into her Protestant upbringing in her "girlhood" home in the bluegrass country of Kentucky and at her father's Mississippi plantation. These geographies, like the death of Edna's mother and the primacy of her father, are linked at the outset of the novel (ch. 2). Throughout the narrative, other characters, particularly Adèle, are aware of Edna's cultural difference and conduct themselves accordingly with her. The narrator describes Edna as having "a small infusion of French which seemed to have been lost in dilution" (884), and the first two-thirds of the novel focus on Edna's differences from the Creole culture she joins with her Pontellier marriage.[30]

An incident in the fourth chapter, where Edna is impressed with the seeming freedom and paradoxes of Creole society in comparison to women's roles and functions in the society of her youth, illustrates this tension, and reminders of these contrasts come in subsequent scenes that feature Adèle Ratignolle at her needlework, making edgy—even judgmental—observations to Edna. When Adèle suggests that Edna sew winter clothing for her children, she points to a perceived lapse in Edna's motherly care for her children. Edna resents the suggestion: "[Her] mind was quite at rest concerning the needs of her children, and she could not see the use of anticipating and making winter night garments the subject of her meditations" (888–889). Later, on a breezy Sunday at Grand Isle, Adèle, engaged in needlework, asks Edna of what—or whom—she is thinking, and Edna replies, "Nothing" in an annoyed tone, and then offers to "retrace" her thoughts, to which Adèle responds with good humor, "Oh, . . . I am not quite so exacting. I will let you off this time" (896). Edna persists, however, and generates thoughts of herself walking through a Kentucky field, waving her arms as if the tall grass were an ocean and she were swimming through it. When Adèle asks, "Where were you going that day in Kentucky?" (896), Edna muses: "'I don't remember now. . . . Likely as not it was Sunday,' she laughed, 'and I was running away from prayers, from the Presbyterian service, read in a spirit of gloom by my father that chills me yet to think of'" (896). As she exposes her personal feelings about her father and Presbyterian Sundays in this speech, Edna "laugh[s]," perhaps to camouflage the tension apparent in her response. Edna also recalls having been quite religious as a child of twelve and then gradually becoming indifferent to religion, although she and a close female friend of similar temperament regularly discussed "religious . . . controversies" (897). Edna's yearning for independence, reflected in this Sunday image, bears a close relation to her role as a woman in society, a woman whose path to adulthood has been affected by her experiences as a Presbyterian.

The narrator reveals, at the opening of *The Awakening*'s seventh chapter, another telling thought of Edna's childhood: "At a very early period [Edna] had apprehended instinctively the dual life—that outward existence which conforms, the inward life which questions" (893). Edna's youthful observation of her "dual life" is precocious: she knows that she lives for herself, and that her "self" may not be observable to nor accepted by her family, friends, and the church of her youth.

Edna's youthful orthodoxy and rebellion mirror Chopin's experience to an extent, despite the difference between their religions. Chopin's early reading and writing are rooted in an orthodox Roman Catholic rearing and education for her time, and Chopin's narrative commentary on Edna's distancing herself from Presbyterianism may parallel Chopin's eventually freeing herself from the legalistic and hierarchical aspects of Roman Catholicism.[31] Edna's recollection of her past is probably comparable to those of many privileged girls growing up in rural areas in the mid-nineteenth century: she was one with nature and saw the grassy meadows of Kentucky as large and endless as the sea (896). She later has a crush on a "sad-eyed cavalry officer" (897), and she remembers the haunting photographic image of "a great tragedian." With these recollections, the narrator also describes Edna's infatuation with a young man engaged to another and observes that, like those others, "he too went the way of dreams" (898).

As Edna becomes more inclined to reveal her thoughts to her companions in this chapter (ch. 7), the narrative reveals details about the level of disapproval Edna faced when she accepted Léonce's proposal. Edna's father and her sister Margaret expressed "violent opposition" to her marriage to a Catholic, leading directly to Edna's acceptance of Léonce's proposal: "[W]e need seek no further for the motives which led her to accept Monsieur Pontellier for her husband" (898). Chopin describes the misleading nature of Edna's acceptance: "Her marriage to Léonce Pontellier was purely an accident, in this respect resembling many other marriages which masquerade as the decrees of fate" (898). Edna's seeing marriage as an escape from her unaffectionate family—dictatorial father, elder sister, Margaret, "matronly and dignified," (897), and younger sister, Janet, with whom Edna "quarreled a good deal"—is also likely to have enticed her to accept Léonce. But the narrator records that Edna, first influenced by youthful passion, dreams, and the ardor of her suitor, marries an illusion and quickly discovers that her and her new husband's supposed mutual "sympathy of thought and taste" (898) do not exist. In chapter twenty-three, for example, Edna matter-of-factly recognizes the distance between her and Léonce when Adèle suggests that the couple "would be"—look, at least—"more united" if Léonce were at home with Edna during her "*soirées musicales*," but Edna counters that it would not be so, asking rhetorically, "What should I do if he stayed home?" and providing the answer: "We wouldn't have anything to say to each other" (951).[32]

Confirming her perception of Edna and Léonce's separateness much earlier, in chapter eight, Adèle emphatically reminds the flirtatious Robert of Edna's "otherness" and her susceptibility to error: "She is not one of us; she is not like us. She might make the unfortunate blunder of taking you seriously" (900). With this unequivocal pronouncement, Adèle confirms not only what Edna's father and sister perceived about the considerable distance between their world and that of Catholic South Louisiana, but also what Adèle has observed about Edna's sentimental vulnerability. In a subsequent scene, when Edna and Robert cross the bay by boat, Edna's outsider status is again the narrative focus: Robert talks with Mariequita, a barefooted Spanish girl whom he knows, and no one aboard understands "what they said" (914). Robert and Mariequita may speak Spanish—or perhaps, a patois—but their conversation makes Edna an outsider, and the sly Mariequita queries Robert about Edna as Edna looks on with suspicion. While Léonce refuses to consider Edna's problems of adjustment as stemming from a mental defect when he consults Dr. Mandelet in chapter twenty-two (in a scene previously cited and to which I will return), Elizabeth Fox-Genovese pathologizes Edna's position, observing that in the character of Edna, "We are dealing with personal pathology—with a proclaimed 'outsider'" (262). Elmo Howell, on the other hand, revisits Chopin's sense of place, finding Edna seduced by nature and "becom[ing] a sort of pantheist" (217). Whichever of these opposed views strikes a chord with the reader, Edna clearly persists in her exercise of an "outward existence that conforms" (893), going to the shore with her children and traveling to Mass on Sunday across the wide bay from Grand Isle (ch. 13), for example.

The latter instance is particularly telling because the trip across the stretch of bay requires considerable effort, and Edna could easily make excuses to remain behind. Crossing the bay in Beaudelet's lugger (a fishing boat) was uncomfortable as the passengers were seated in close quarters, but Edna likely felt it necessary to observe the convention of Sunday Mass at the "quaint little Gothic church of Our Lady of Lourdes" in Chênière Caminada (916), but once inside, she falters. Edna soon gets sleepy and leaves the chapel during the service (916), just as she will later "gr[ow] sleepy" reading Emerson as "a course of improving studies" (56) that she never afterward resumes. The sleeping-waking motif, a frequent pattern in Romantic literature, usually suggests a shift in character, as it does here, and Emerson's emphasis on the individual's inner experience and self-reliance in his essays echoes Edna's growing sense of her interior self. Furthermore, "the crossing" by water to the chapel, with its mythic qualities, is more than a physical and communal journey:

> Edna felt as if she were being borne away from some anchorage which had held her fast, whose chains had been loosening—had snapped the night before when the mystic spirit was abroad, leaving her free to drift whithersoever she chose to set her sails. (915)

When Edna "drifts" out of the chapel, Robert follows and encounters her standing "outside in the shadow of the church" (917). Edna, having departed the regimen of the Mass and Church, nevertheless, continues to feel its influence on her "inward" *self*, as an inescapable presence. Outside the church with Robert, Edna stands in that position metaphorically as well, a reflection of her "inward life which questions" and coexists with her "outward existence that conforms" (893).

## Edna's "change of heart"

Despite Edna's cultural and religious differences with her Louisiana family, she finds their ways more open, possibly more sympathetic than otherwise, toward her longing to live for her *self*, beyond social conventions, loosening "her own habitual reserve" (894). She begins to distance herself from her Kentucky Protestant heritage—a movement perhaps accelerated, in part, by her surprising emotional responses to Robert's attentions. Edna acknowledges his waking her "from a life-long, stupid dream" (993), and Nancy Walker expresses Edna's changing perspective as simply "denying what she has been raised to believe" (254), while Sandra M. Gilbert explains that Edna is "running away [. . .] from the dictations and interdictions of patriarchal culture, especially of patriarchal theology" and is embarked on "a quest for an alternative theology [. . .] an alternative mythology" (273). It is evident, as Walker and Gilbert also imply, that the current of Catholic and Creole culture, into which we might say Edna has been "baptized" by her marriage, has carried her willingly away from the asceticism of the Colonel's Presbyterianism into a more sensual and self-expressive society.

Kenneth Eble long ago observed that Edna, "despite her Kentucky Presbyterian upbringing and a comfortable marriage, must struggle with the sensual appeal of physical ripeness itself, with passion of which she is only dimly aware" (192), and Larzer Ziff casts her, not as a woman merely "struggl[ing]" with her sexual feelings, but as a victim of "the Protestant mistrust of the senses" and its designation of "sexual desire as the root of evil" (197), essentially making repressed sexuality—and Edna's rejection of that repression—the medium by which we are able truly to recognize and read the nature of Edna's struggle. While most readings of the novel credit Edna's personal and sexual "repression," with its source in her Presbyterian upbringing under the Colonel's domination, and view her movement as connected with her attraction to Catholic "sensuality" and French-Creole society,[33] it is important to recognize that the Catholic and Creole atmosphere to which Edna feels drawn also honored patriarchy and had its social code, but these are easier for her to bear than other aspects of the culture because of their offsetting freedoms.

A further indication of Edna's intellectual movement toward a convergence of her inner and outer lives appears in chapter sixteen where she remembers "a rather heated argument" with Adèle over Edna's quest to discover herself and to make choices accordingly, including a mother's limiting her degree of self-sacrifice for her children. Edna focuses on her inner self, and Adèle perceives Edna's argument as relating only to her physical life. After stating that she would only give up "the unessential," Edna truly confuses this Creole "mother-woman," who remarks to her, "I don't know what you would call the essential, or what you mean by the unessential" (929).[34] Adèle reminds Edna of a mother's responsibilities to her children—that a mother would give her life for her children—affirming her argument against Edna's view of the limits of mother-love with the textual foundation cited above, "Your Bible tells you so" (929).

Edna's religious formation would have been dominated by American printings of the King James Bible, but Chopin's would have been influenced by the Douay-Rheims version of the Bible. Chopin's father's close friend Archbishop Peter Richard Kenrick of St. Louis had independently revised the Douay-Rheims Bible (1849–1852), and while *The Awakening* was being written, a new authorized American version would be published in 1899, the same year as the novel's publication. In Chopin's day, as I have suggested, the writings of the Church fathers, such as Augustine and Jerome, had as strong an influence as the Bible on religious practice and culture, and maternal virtues and responsibilities were persistent topics for the Church in the later nineteenth century. As the Catholic mother of six children, Chopin knew intimately the Church's views on womanhood and maternity, with its exemplar of the Virgin Mary, whose immaculate conception was declared dogma in 1854.[35] Four years later, fourteen-year-old Bernadette Soubirous saw visions of the Virgin at Lourdes in southwestern France between February and July 1858 (Bertrin), and Leo XIII granted the Office and Mass to the Virgin of Lourdes in 1892.[36] In Chopin's New Orleans, the Virgin Mary was honored yearly as Our Lady of Prompt Succor, to whom the Ursuline nuns had prayed for an American victory over the British in 1815 at nearby Chalmette. Chopin would have been cognizant of these events converging around the most sacred figure of motherhood in the Christian church, and she has Edna display her consciousness of the attraction of Marian images: She "liked to sit and gaze at her fair companion [*i.e.*, Adèle] as she might look upon a faultless Madonna" (890), a traditional image of Mary with the child Jesus. As a nineteenth-century woman reared Roman Catholic, Chopin reverentially capitalizes "Madonna," and when Adèle pleads with Edna, "Think of the children, Edna. Oh think of the children! Remember them!" (995), Adèle appeals in the context of these teachings and religious practices to Edna, whom she sees as outside their influence.

In chapter twenty-two, in a scene previously cited, Léonce consults Dr. Mandelet about Edna's changing temperament. Léonce describes the Colonel as "aton[ing] for his weekday sins with his Sunday devotions" and Edna's older sister Margaret as having "all the Presbyterianism undiluted" (948). Though Edna has often enjoyed her father's company and taken his part in minor conversational differences (952), Edna disagrees with the Colonel on some points. He adamantly disapproves of Edna's decision not to attend her sister's wedding, and Edna is "glad to be rid of [him]" when he sets off without her for the wedding. In her pleasure at his departure, Edna thinks of her father's "Bible reading" negatively, placing it between visions of "his padded shoulders" and "his 'toddies' and ponderous oaths" (954). In chapter twenty-four, the Colonel adopts the patriarchal manner of a minister of the Cumberland Church when he instructs Léonce on what he should do to straighten out his altercations with Edna: "You are too lenient, too lenient by far, Léonce [. . .]. Authority, coercion are what is needed. Put your foot down good and hard; the only way to manage a wife" (954). With this passage, Chopin exposes again the patriarchal elements shared by the two systems of belief and reinforces the primacy of the old Colonel in the home.

When Chopin describes Edna in chapter thirty-two as possessing "a feeling of having descended in the social scale, with a corresponding sense of having risen in the spiritual" (977), Chopin acknowledges that Edna's "inward life" has begun to have primacy over her "outward life." In moving away from the communal practice of Catholicism, Edna reinforces her position beyond overt religious practices and the physical structures of faith. The narrative makes clear that Edna grows away from the Presbyterianism of her upbringing, as we see in the scenes and events described, but she never gives any indication of fully accepting the Catholicism of her husband's family, despite its more liberal effects on her daily life, including the general frankness of discussions about sensuality.

Through *The Awakening*'s thirty-nine chapters, Edna attempts to navigate the traditional expectations for women of her time, her life, and choices informed, at first, by Presbyterianism and, then, by Catholicism. Her religious experience in New Orleans and Grand Isle is part of a personal journey toward greater liberty from the Anglo-Saxon Protestant world of her upbringing and through the Creole-French Catholic culture of her adult life, which she seems to accept but not embrace. She rejects the patriarchal attitudes of her father, for whom male primacy is absolute, as she does those of her husband, Léonce, who cares for her, but who looks at her on one occasion as if she were "a valuable piece of personal property which has suffered some damage" (882).[37] In her conflict, Edna finds her *self*, but she never places her discovery in an intellectual context that prepares her to negotiate a life in the social and religious contexts that surround her. George Arms, in an early essay on *The Awakening*, observes that Edna's new "individualism lacks philosophical grounding" (200) and supposes that had she possessed such "grounding," she might not have followed her impulse in swimming to her death. Edna's uncertainties about her future emotional, sexual, and marital life, as well as the strict social, religious, and cultural conventions affecting her, overwhelm any possibility of Edna's finding a livable space between the external life she must lead and the interior life that she has discovered.

## Notes

1 See, for example, David Z. Wehner's 2011 treatment of Chopin's "idiosyncratic and syncretic religious temperament," with his note on older work on the subject (167 n. 3), and my earlier consideration (1982) of Christianity and Catholicism in Chopin's fiction. Wehner, in fact, blames Chopin's "complicated" and "unique" religious views for the poor public reception of her stories, as well as of *The Awakening*. Critics more often blame her feminist treatment of women's lives and sexuality in the nineteenth century—a frequent focus of *The Awakening*'s critics—for the novel's negative reception (167). For example, Thomas F. Haddox, in his 2005 study of Catholicism in Southern literature, views Chopin's writing as "decadent" in contexts of sexuality and Catholicism, and provides a historical overview of relevant strands of Chopin criticism in his chapter on the fiction of Chopin, Carson McCullers, and Anne Rice (82–111). For a comprehensive treatment of Chopin's Catholicism, see Heather Ostman's *Kate Chopin and Catholicism*.

2 See Toth's *Life*, where she emphasizes that Edna's position—between "the puritanical sternness of her father's world" and the easy "familiarity" of the Pontellier's culture—casts Edna, with her "Presbyterian reserve," as the perennial outsider among Louisiana Creoles, whose ways she is apt to misunderstand. Among critical perspectives, see also, for example, Walker's 1988 essay on the "Historical and Cultural Setting" of the novel. Walker views the distinctions between the Creole world and Edna's "stern Kentuckian Presbyterian background" as providing the novel's tension. Janet Beer and Elizabeth Nolan's *Sourcebook* contains a good number of references to Edna's characterization as dependent on her Presbyterian background in their analyses of document extracts, critical articles, and book chapters (16, 63–64, 73–74, 78–79, for example).

3   In *Patriotic Gore* (1962), Edmund Wilson asserted that Chopin "anticipated D. H. Lawrence" in her "treatment of infidelity" (590. See also 529–593). Seyersted (*Critical Biography*) expands on Wilson's reading of *The Awakening*, writing that it may be read as "a eulogy on sex and a muted elegy on the female condition" (160). See also Seyersted's Introduction to the Feminist Press's 1974 edition of selected Chopin fiction that includes *The Awakening*.
4   Chopin's response to reading De Maupassant appears in an 1896 manuscript in which she describes him as "a man who had escaped from tradition and authority, who had entered into himself and looked out upon life through his own being and with his own eyes; and who, in a direct and simple way, told us what he saw" (Seyersted. *Critical Biography* 51). Chopin knew De Maupassant's short fiction intimately from having translated a substantial number of his stories in the 1890s. See Bonner's *Companion* for Chopin's translations of eight De Maupassant stories.
5   Gilbert and Gubar offer a challenging reading that builds on the final scene's ocean imagery and views Edna as Venus amid the waves.
6   For the assessment of Eble's potential audience, see George M. Spangler's historical view of criticism on *The Awakening* (249).
7   Citations of *The Awakening* and Chopin's other fiction come from Seyersted's 1969 edition of *The Complete Works of Kate Chopin* (*Works*). See n. 29, below, on Chopin's view of religion as a force for shaping fiction.
8   Edna remembers herself as "a little miss, just merging into her teens" on her father's Mississippi plantation "after they went to Mississippi [from Kentucky] to live" (897–898).
9   The idea of "rigidity" is used several times to describe the Colonel's bearing: the narrator reports, "Before [Edna's] pencil he sat rigid and unflinching, as he had faced the cannon's mouth in days gone by" (950) and as he sits for his portrait, "he is he loath to disturb fixed lines of his countenance, his arms, or his rigid shoulders" (951).
10  Elizabeth Willingham suggests that Adèle's words may reflect the last line of the refrain of "Jesus Loves Me" (the Protestant hymn of the last half of the nineteenth century). "The Bible tells me so" perhaps implies an ironic play on the words with a thought of the hymn as well as the otherness implied in "*your* Bible" (emphasis added). As the hymn dates from 1859, Chopin would have come to knowledge of it in her pre-teen or later years.
11  "Binding" is used here advisedly. At a party Edna hosts, "binding" is used in a paradoxical sense toward Edna: " a feeling of good fellowship passed around the circle like a mystic cord, holding and binding these people together with jest and laughter," but Edna "stands alone" and set outside the circle by her otherness (972). Religious practices, however, constrain her, and at the end of the novel, she sheds social and religious constraints of several kinds to free herself in death.

12 Walker (1988) stipulates that *The Awakening* is not "autobiographical" (67), and my theory of Chopin's presentation of Edna as a product of a Presbyterian household in the north-central reaches of the South accords with Walker's assertion.
13 The term "mixed marriage" is used neither by Chopin nor Rankin, but the phrase was in continuous use through Vatican II in the mid-1960s to refer to a marriage between a Catholic and a baptized non-Catholic, and it continues to be used in recent work on Vatican II. See references in Pawley, *et al*, (307, 386) and in Attridge, *et al*, (80–83, 110–111, 116, 550), for example.
14 The characterization comes from Toth, who writes that Alexandre Dumas located "a nest of Huguenot subversives" in La Rochelle in *The Three Musketeers* (*Life* 36). Kate's closest childhood friend and Sacred Heart classmate, Kitty Garesché, who became a Sacred Heart nun, also had a Huguenot strain in her family, according to Toth (*Chopin* 41).
15 See details of my review of Toth's first biography of Chopin (*Life*), which I characterize as "the most complete study" of the author's personal life (Bonner. 1992).
16 Toth notes Chopin's observation (77). See *Kate Chopin's Private Papers* (14–15) for the paragraph young Chopin copied from *Ranke's History*.
17 Charlotte Champe Stearns Eliot (b. 1843), a few years senior to "Katie," was the mother of T. S. Eliot (b. 1888). Charlotte's father-in-law, William Greenleaf Eliot established the Unitarian Church in St. Louis.
18 On Kolbenheyer, see Toth (*Unveiling* 105–106; *Life* 258–261). Toth quotes Rankin (260).
19 See above, n. 16.
20 Where the year of a story's publication has not previously been cited, the year is given parenthetically, preceding the page number.
   The Miracle at Lourdes has inspired thousands of believers to go on pilgrimage to its shrine.
21 Our Lady of Lourdes Church stood at Chênière Caminada until a hurricane destroyed it in 1893.
22 See Bonner, "Christianity" (118–125). Citations from the Bible in this chapter may best be consulted in the KJV, the English translation of the Bible in general use in Presbyterianism and other Protestant denominations in the U.S. in the late nineteenth century. Bonner's Companion provides a complete guide to Chopin's fictional characters.
23 Ben M. Barrus (1967) provides an example of documentation for the 1810 date (278 and n. 17) for founding the Cumberland Presbyterian Church (CPC) and presents a brief historiography of the "independent" CPC, taking the position that the "beginning" of the CPC finally occurred in 1813, when three years of efforts to reconcile factions had failed (280).
24 In the American church, the Reunion of 1869, according to David Calhoun's study of the Princeton Seminary, spurred change and debate between centralized and decentralized models of Presbyterianism. See

the *Westminster Confession*, Chapter 7 ("Of God's Covenant with Man") and Questions 52, 176, and 177, as examples.
25 Boyd and Brackenridge observe, however, that women's involvement with foreign missions expanded their roles in the U. S. Presbyterian Church.
26 Barrus (1967) notes that issues of doctrine and authority undoubtedly figured in the formation of the Cumberland church (277) and cites pejorative descriptions of uneducated Cumberland ministers among historical treatments and documents (279) that support Chopin's depictions of unlettered ministers. Barrus records that a "critical account" of the Cumberland Presbytery's frontier revival ministers described them in 1847 as "illiterate exhorters with Arminian sentiments" (275), and in 1856, three revival ministers were described as "uneducated men of advanced age" (278). See also Barrus's 1968 essay on CPC history (64–65 n. 78, 69–70) on "literary qualification." Barrus, Baughn, and Campbell's history of the CPC (esp. 2.83–104) describes public controversies with which Chopin may have been familiar. See also Gary North's work.
27 The young Chopin's reaction to this forward and uncouth young Bible study leader embodies the response that the leaders of the Princeton (Presbyterian) Seminary feared when members were presented with uneducated clergy and is indicative of its worst imaginings. Toth (*Life*) records Chopin's impression (232). "The Night Came Slowly" ends with the narrator's view of the unlettered minister.
28 Ted Cotton's treatment of Flannery O'Connor's Catholic perspective in her fiction (chapter 10) is of comparative interest.
29 By no means would Chopin be alone in this position, for Michael Shaara's 1974 novel, *The Killer Angels*, views the War between the North and the South as an extension of the English Civil War between the Roundheads and the Cavaliers. The conflicts Chopin represented as essential to Southern character and culture are an extension, from this perspective, of cultural conflicts arising from the Reformation, and Catholic and Protestant settlers in the South are viewed as having transported the historical conflict with them across the Atlantic.
30 The description resonates with Chopin's negative reception from her father-in-law because her degree of French ancestry was slighter than he found acceptable.
31 As an example of Chopin's view on religion as fertile ground for a fiction writer, consider her essay on Christian art in which she states rhetorically: "Where is there a more prolific theme for the rovings of fancy than religion, with all its beauties celestial and terrestrial" (*Private* 31). The "rovings of fancy" refer to the creative imagination.
32 Marriage for many women in the nineteenth century was part adolescent dream and part economic necessity.
33 See, for example, chapter seven, with the scenes at Grand Isle (esp. 894).

34 Edna fails as "mother-woman," but Adéle is "delicious in rôle," as the "embodiment of every womanly grace and charm" (887–888).
35 The Immaculate Conception of the Virgin Mary signifies that the mother of Jesus was conceived as "immaculate"—without the stain of Original Sin by virtue of Christ—and was declared in the *Constitution Ineffabilis Deus* (8 December 1854) by Pope Pius IX (Holweck).
36 In 1894 Chopin wrote a review of Émile Zola's *Lourdes*, in which she cites a character's telling of "clerical abuses prevailing" (698) at Lourdes—where the clerics are obviously priests—and she attributes the view to Zola. While Chopin seems to have a less critical perception of the clergy than Zola, she sees fit to include the pejorative passage in her review.
37 In the opening chapter, Edna has "bathed" in the Gulf of Mexico with Robert Lebrun at a hot time of day, and Léonce remarks, "You are burnt beyond recognition," as he surveys her in regretful appraisal (882).

**Works Cited**

Arms, George. "Contrasting Forces in the Novel." Kate Chopin. *The Awakening*. Ed. Margo Culley. 198–202.
Attridge, Michael, Gilles Routhier, and Catherine E. Clifford. *Vatican II: Expériences Canadiennes / Canadian Experience*. Religion and Beliefs Series. Bilingual ed. Ottawa: U of Ottawa P, 2011.
Barrus, Ben M. "The Cumberland Presbyterian Church." *Journal of Presbyterian History (1962–1985)* 46.1 (1968): 58–73.
—. "Factors Involved in the Origin of the Cumberland Presbyterian Church: Author's Preface." *Journal of Presbyterian History (1962–1985)* 45.4 (1967): 273–289.
—, Milton L. Baughn, and Thomas H. Campbell. *A People Called Cumberland Presbyterians: A History of the Cumberland Presbyterian Church*. Vol. 2. Eugene, OR: Wipf & Stock, 1972. Chapters 1–6.
Bertrin, Georges. "Notre-Dame de Lourdes." *The Catholic Encyclopedia*. Vol. 9. New York: Robert Appleton Company, 1910. Newadvent.org.
Bonner, Jr., Thomas. "Christianity and Catholicism in the Fiction of Kate Chopin." *Southern Quarterly* 20.2 (1982): 118–125. Rpt. *In Old New Orleans*. Ed. Kenneth Holditch. Jackson: UP of Mississippi, 1983.
—. "[Rev.] Emily Toth, Kate Chopin. New York: William Morrow, 1990. 528 pp. $27.95." *South Central Review* 9.1 (1992): 110–111.
—. *The Kate Chopin Companion: With Chopin's Translations of French Fiction (Companion)*. New York: Greenwood P, 1988.
Boyd, Lois, and R. Douglas Brackenridge. *Presbyterian Women in America: Two Centuries of a Quest for Status*. Contributions to the Study of Religion 46. Westport, CT: Greenwood, 1996.
Calhoun, David. *History of Princeton Seminary: Faith and Learning: 1812–1868*. Carlisle, PA: Banner of Truth, 1996.
Chopin, Kate. "At the 'Cadian Ball." *Works*. 219–227.
—. "At Chênière Caminada." *Works*. 309–318.
—. *At Fault*. *Works*. 741–877.
—. *The Awakening*. *Works*. 881–1000.

—. *The Awakening: An Authoritative Text: Biographical and Historical Contexts: Criticism.* Ed. Margo Culley. 2nd ed. New York: Norton, 1994.
—. *The Complete Works of Kate Chopin* (*Works*). Ed. Per Seyersted. Baton Rouge: Louisiana State UP, 1969. Paper ed. 2006.
—. "Emile Zola's *Lourdes.*" *Works.* 697–699.
—. *Kate Chopin's Private Papers.* Ed. Emily Toth and Per Seyersted. Bloomington: Indiana UP, 1998.
—. "Loka." *Works.* 212–218.
—. "The Maid of Saint Phillippe." *Works.* 116–123.
—. "The Night Came Slowly." *Works.* 366.
—. "Odalie Misses Mass." *Works.* 406–410.
—. "The Return of Alcibiade." *Works.* 249–254.
—. "A Sentimental Soul." *Works.* 388–397.
Culley, Margo. *See* Chopin, Kate. *The Awakening.*
Eble, Kenneth. "A Forgotten Novel." Kate Chopin. *The Awakening.* Ed. Margo Culley. 188–193.
—. "A Forgotten Novel: Kate Chopin's *The Awakening.*" *Western Humanities Review* 1 (1956): 261–269. Rpt. *Critical Essays on Kate Chopin.* Ed. Alice Hall Petry. New York: Hall, 1996. 75–82.
Fox-Genovese, Elizabeth. "Progression and Regression in Edna Pontellier." Kate Chopin. *The Awakening.* Ed. Margo Culley. 257–263.
Gilbert, Sandra M. "The Second Coming of Aphrodite: Kate Chopin's Fantasy of Desire." Kate Chopin. *The Awakening.* Ed. Margo Culley. 271–281. *The Kenyon Review* 5.3 (1983): 42–66.
—, and Susan Gubar. "The Second Coming of Aphrodite: Kate Chopin's Fantasy of Desire." *No Man's Land: The Place of the Woman Writer in the Twentieth Century.* Gilbert and Gubar. Vol. 2. New Haven, CT: Yale UP, 1989. 83–120.
Haddox, Thomas F. *Fears and Fascinations: Representing Catholicism in the American South.* New York: Fordham UP, 2005.
Holweck, Frederick. "Immaculate Conception." *The Catholic Encyclopedia.* Vol. 7. New York: Robert Appleton Company, 1910. Newadvent.org.
Howell, Elmo. "Kate Chopin and the Creole Country." *Louisiana History: The Journal of the Louisiana Historical Association* 20.2 (1979): 209–219.
North, Gary. *Crossed Fingers: How the Liberals Captured the Presbyterian Church.* Tyler, TX: Institute for Christian Economies, 1996.
Ostman, Heather. *Kate Chopin and Catholicism.* London: Palgrave Macmillan, 2020.
Pawley, Bernard C. *Observing Vatican II: The Confidential Reports of the Archbishop of Canterbury's Representative, Bernard Pawley, 1961–1964.* Ed. Andrew Chandler and Charlotte Hansen. Camden Fifth Series 43. Cambridge, UK: Cambridge UP for the Royal Historical Society, 2013.
Rankin, Daniel S. *Kate Chopin and Her Creole Stories.* Philadelphia: U of Pennsylvania P, 1932.
Seyersted, Per. Introduction. *"The Storm" and Other Stories with* The Awakening. Feminist Press Reprint 5. Old Westbury, NY: Feminist P, 1974. 7–18.

—. *Kate Chopin: A Critical Biography*. Baton Rouge: Louisiana State UP, 1969. *See also* Chopin, Kate.
—. *See also* Chopin, Kate. *Complete Works*.
Shaara, Michael. *The Killer Angels: A Novel of the Civil War*. New York: David McKay [Random House], 1974.
Spangler, George M. "Kate Chopin's *The Awakening*: A Partial Dissent." *NOVEL: A Forum on Fiction* 3.3 (1970): 249–255.
Toth, Emily. *Kate Chopin: A Life of the Author of* The Awakening. New York: Morrow, 1990. London: Random Century, 1990.
—. "Kate Chopin's *The Awakening* as Feminist Criticism." *Louisiana Studies* 15 (1976): 241–251.
—. *Unveiling Kate Chopin*. Jackson: UP of Mississippi, 1999.
Walker, Nancy. "Feminist or Naturalist?" Kate Chopin. *The Awakening*. Ed. Margo Culley. 252–256.
—. "The Historical and Cultural Setting." *Approaches to Teaching Chopin's* The Awakening. Ed. Bernard Koloski. New York: MLA, 1988. 67–52.
Wehner, David Z. "'A Lot Up for Grabs': The Idiosyncratic, Syncretic Religious Temperament of Kate Chopin." *American Literary Realism* 43.2 (2011): 154–168.
Wilson, Edmund. Foreword. *Works*. Ed. Per Seyersted. 13–15.
—. *Patriotic Gore: Studies in the Literature of the American Civil War*. Oxford: OUP, 1962. New York: FSG, 1962. New York: Norton, 1994.
Ziff, Larzer. "From *The American 1890s*." Kate Chopin. *The Awakening*. Ed. Margo Culley. 196–198.

# 3

# Posthumanism and Inexorable Desire

## Lacanian *Méconnaissance* in Walter Tevis's *Mockingbird* and Gary Shteyngart's *Super Sad True Love Story*

BARBARA E. HAMILTON

A steady stream of literature recounting human attempts to transcend biological limitations runs from the writers of the book of Genesis and the *Epic of Gilgamesh* through authors such as the Pseudo-Apollodorus, Ovid, the medieval mystics of Europe, John Milton, the English Romantics, Friedrich Nietzsche, J. M. Barrie, and beyond. Since Marvin Minsky's project to reverse engineer the human brain began in the 1950s, writers of futuristic novels and screenplays have also tapped this rich, imaginative vein by creating stories around posthuman attempts to transcend human fallibility and mortality.[1] These narratives are typically framed as conflicts between the collective strength of seemingly undefeatable cyborgs and the determined ingenuity of the few remaining humans capable of critical thought. In raising and then alleviating anxieties about the growth of technology and humanity's future, most writers of this form of dystopian fiction adhere to the archetypal quest-and-conquer model of heroic literature. Both Walter Tevis's 1980 Nebula-nominated *Mockingbird* and Gary Shteyngart's award-winning 2010 *Super Sad True Love Story* (*Super Sad*) present a more nuanced analysis of the interactions of human and cyborg in the posthuman world.

Tevis and Shteyngart situate posthumanism's origins in the attempt to give anxious, fearful people what they think they want: the end of desire and unhappiness through merging the best of humanity with technology. Because this vision of utopian perfection is based on its designers' hubristic misreading of reality—or *méconnaissance* in Jacques Lacan's terminology—the utopian project in neither novel is sustainable. The engineered society of Tevis's *Mockingbird* collapses due to its flawed psychic model; the book can be read as a postmodern fable culminating in a seeming return to human agency following the demise of misguided, dysfunctional techno-sociolinguistic control. Read today, forty-odd years after its first release, *Mockingbird*'s ambiguously happy ending seems intentionally naïve. Shteyngart, writing in 2010 of a not-too-distant, eerily recognizable world, gives scant hope for any resuscitation of individual human agency due to the networked triumph of multinational corporations, totalitarian governments, and omnipresent media saturation. His protagonist's inability to keep up with a competitive, pressurized lifestyle, his retreat into aspirational dreams of romance, and his nostalgia for an illusory, more "natural" past are the painful center of the novel.

Neither Shteyngart nor Tevis presents his principal posthuman character as an enemy to be defeated by non-engineered humans; instead, both implicate the human social engineers as developing inherently neurotic, misguided theories leading to the creation and inevitable demise of their purportedly helpful posthuman projects. Tevis portrays the main character Robert Spofforth—a cyborg who is tortured by half-memories of the depressive engineer whose consciousness has been downloaded into his metal brain—as a prisoner of his programming who must follow the coding of his designers. Spofforth, despite his outstanding abilities, remains enslaved to long-dead humans who made him and, in the novel's present time, to the much-diminished humans he currently serves. The posthuman, highly engineered Joshie Goldmann of *Super Sad* is driven by his own fears of aging and death; Shteyngart presents him as an increasingly pathetic figure representing humanity's inability to cope with inevitable mortality, a latter-day Gilgamesh without the epic trappings. Nor is Joshie Shteyngart's only misguided character; the would-be immortal maintains his rock-star influence as Director of the Post-Human Services Division of a major corporation by capitalizing on other humans' vulnerability and fear of death. In both novels, people are responsible for their own desires to transcend human limitations and for the subsequent surrender of their autonomy to who- or whatever promises to alleviate their pain through technology and medication. As MIT researcher Sherry Turkle writes in *Alone Together*, "Technology is seductive when what it offers meets our human vulnerabilities. And as it turns out, we are very vulnerable indeed."[2] To be human is to be vulnerable to an endless cycle of

Lacanian *méconnaissance*, and for both Tevis and Shteyngart, an overdependence on technology is the inevitable result of the desire to escape vulnerability and limitation.

## The Misperceptions of Recursive Desire: *Mockingbird*

Tevis, a popular English professor and Milton scholar at Ohio University before becoming a full-time writer, was closely attuned to the critical problem of hubristic drives in literature through his teaching and study of Milton's poetry. His fiction consistently examines aspiration along with the neurotic social and individual forces that undercut and doom it. While his 1963 *The Man Who Fell to Earth* documents the emotional dangers of pushing our limits and desiring too much—dangers that for Tevis resulted in his alcoholism—*Mockingbird* reflects the writer's post-recovery abilities to embrace desire without being neurotically consumed by it.[3] Combining his interests in Milton's 1667 *Paradise Lost* and contemporary psychological theory, Tevis critiques the transgressive desires of late-twentieth-century American culture along with media-driven substitutions for passion and engagement. In a 1984 interview with CBS's Don Swaim, Tevis called his "comic psychological fiction" an "exaggerated fairytale story-telling to say something profound about our own times," comparing *Mockingbird*'s elements to those of mythology and medieval romance, and affirming that his Everyman characters are meant to tap the substrate of human experience. Shortly after *Mockingbird*'s publication, Tevis told reporter Andrew Weiner, "Science fiction [...] is something of a religious medium [...] I'm writing about the seductiveness of the ways of avoiding living your life that our society offers right now, the drugs and the television and all the other inducements to trivialize your life." Ostensibly predicated by Tevis's despair over students becoming less literate each year, *Mockingbird* is, at least in part, his homage to the works students should have appreciated had they been better prepared, and it is an investigation into an individual's power to forge a radically better human condition.

*Mockingbird* is set in a crumbling Eden, Tevis's prescient vision of twenty-fourth century New York City, where robots enable a distraction- and stress-free existence. Based on the premise that the achievement of happiness is humankind's strongest desire, a long-ago group of well-intentioned social scientists called "the Designers" engineered robots to serve that end.[4] Most of the novel's robots are unthinking functionaries programmed to fulfill tasks in order to free humans for personal creativity and innovation, but the highest-level androids—"Make Nines," like the cyborg Robert "Bob" Spofforth—have been given a downloaded, somewhat-edited human consciousness and are therefore capable of decision-making and the semblance of emotion. In the centuries between the death of the Designers and the opening of the novel, the cyborg caretakers follow their programming to equate happiness with the absence of unhappiness, seeking to eliminate anything that causes humankind pain or effort. Because humans have become emotionally and cognitively suppressed with heavy marijuana intake, media streams, and mandatory, contraceptive-laced sedatives called "sopors," they cannot use their free time as the Designers intended: to self-actualize as creative, engaged agents. Lacking any meaningful occupation and unable to communicate successfully with each other, they pass their days attending to basic physical needs and being entertained with violent pornography that offers virtual sensation without the potential discomfort or risk of actual human connection.

Because relationships were considered a primary source of inner turmoil by the Designers, the individual's Privacy is now prioritized over "dangerous" social bonding. By the same rationale, the Designers found child-rearing psychically disturbing and gradually weakened family life. The last generation of children following the onset of mass sterilization and contraception had been born just over thirty years before the novel begins, taken from their parents and reared in dormitories to be indoctrinated in the alienating Rules of Mandatory Politeness by their robot caretakers. Students in Tevis's world take classes that encourage self-focus—Interior Development, Serenity Training, and Mental Hygiene. The course sequence on Interpersonal Relations emphasizes individual development over the Mistake of Proximity (26) and teaches students to resist "the whims of another person" (74). The Designers' robotic representatives warn against socialization with facile slogans like "Don't ask—relax" (24), "Alone is best" (26), and "Quick sex protects" (75). In situations where avoidance of others is impossible, frightened humans quell anxiety with sopors, marijuana, and immersion in porn.

Toward the end of *Mockingbird*, one of the two human protagonists, film studies professor Paul Bentley, muses on the motives of the Designers as he recognizes that misunderstanding, not lust for power, has perpetuated this inflexible system:

> They would have thought of themselves as grave, serious, concerned men—the words "caring" and "compassionate" would have been frequently on their lips [. . .] planning the perfect world for Homo

sapiens, a world from which poverty, disease, dissension, neurosis, and pain would be absent, a world as far from . . . the world of melodrama and passions and risks and excitement—as all their powers of technology and "compassion" could devise. (242–243)

In Paul's ability to see beyond the need to blame others for the unfortunate results of their bad decisions, Tevis allows Paul—and readers—to realize that he has progressed from being the frightened victim of the Designers' misrecognition of human nature to a magnanimous critic of their attempts to eliminate human suffering. The enlightened professor recognizes that the best of intentions can have disastrous consequences, and that *méconnaissance* is part of the universal human tendency to reach for a life of more pleasure and less pain.

In "Beyond the Pleasure Principle," Sigmund Freud posits that this tendency to avoid pain culminates in the death drive (*Todestreib*), an "urge in organic life to restore an earlier state of things,"[5] a desire to regress to a preverbal state of origin. Romantic poets such as William Wordsworth would interpret this drive as a desire to recapture a lost Eden, a childhood memory of "clouds of glory,"[6] a completeness and unity that is gradually worn away by the exigencies of civilization. In Lacanian terms, the preverbal state outside of human law and culture is the register of the Real. *Mockingbird's* Designers tried to eliminate the death drive by minimizing the inarticulately needy psyche and thereby invigorate its opposite: the creative drive toward love and life-affirming actions. However, in attempting to reduce the death drive that leads humans toward both anxiety-producing danger and *jouissance*[7]—"the passions and risks and excitement" in Paul's words—they reduced humans to an infantile, dependent, almost preverbal state.

Because the Designers reasoned that stressful higher-level thinking leads to unhappiness, they suppressed once basic skills such as reading and mathematics from the curriculum as too difficult and relational; Paul is cautioned by Spofforth, "Reading is too intimate. It will put you too close to the feelings and the ideas of others. It will disturb and confuse you" (78). He and his fellow humans, along with the robots and cyborgs in *Mockingbird*, rely strictly on images, voice recordings, and videos for the information they need. Time, characterized by philosopher Milič Čapek as that "chronic hallucination of the human mind,"[8] leads to unnecessary stress in a postindustrial, postcapitalist world where humans no longer need schedules or deadlines; it is divided into segments—"blues" and "yellows"— that lack points of reference, rendering chronology impossible. To convey a world in which most humans are fairly inarticulate, speech averse, and incapable of measuring time, Tevis uses a layered, almost epistolary approach to trace the progress of his characters through chapters entitled "Spofforth," "Bentley," and "Mary Lou," starting with Spofforth, whose thoughts and actions are narrated omnisciently. Initially, the two human characters, Paul and Mary Lou Borne, present first-person narratives as voice recordings of their experiences and recaptured memories; further on, as they reclaim the ability to read, write, measure time, describe their world, speculate, feel, and articulate, they speak through elegant and evocative journaling.

For the Designers, doing away with upsetting emotional and genetic tendencies of the past was meant to usher in a new era of potential fulfillment, a typical posthumanistic goal.[9] Tevis interrogates this endeavor through two interwoven and complementary plots: one involving the posthuman Spofforth's death drive toward annihilation, and the other involving the humans' drive toward integration and love, a *thanatos-eros* conflict in which both sides ultimately win. Yet under this simple concept is a more complex rendering of Lacan's interlocking registers. Spofforth, due to his downloaded memories, also desires love and tries to recreate it, while Paul and the intellectual renegade Mary Lou do all they can to recapture "the passions and risks and excitement" (243) of being human by challenging their world. The Designers' misrecognition of reality culminates in suppressing Lacan's registers of the Real (too frightening and chaotic for anxious people) and the Imaginary (requiring what the Designers regard as disruptive human imagination), leaving only the tyranny of the Symbolic, the linguistically structured register of civilization and law. Tevis emphasizes the Designers' stamp on language by his Orwellian capitalization of their codified rules, for instance, Mandatory Privacy. If there is an Imaginary in the drugged opening of *Mockingbird*, it is vestigially present only in the *méconnaissance* coded into stunted clichés and codes that are meant to align human desire with the Designers' law.

Tevis's triangle of protagonists may be read as representative of Lacan's three interlocking registers of the Imaginary, Real, and Symbolic; Spofforth, Paul, and Mary Lou also interlock in important ways, as none of them can approximate psychic integration without the others to provide elements of the registers each lacks. In Lacan's Seminar XI, he defines the Real—that disturbing, indescribable, unattainable source of our desires—as "the essential object which is not an object any longer, but this something faced with which all words cease and all categories fail, the object of anxiety *par excellence*"

(*Seminar* 164). The Real, only fully experienced between birth and language acquisition, is impossible to approximate in time, binary code, or linguistic constructs. As the locus of unattainable desire, its pressure on the Imaginary and the Symbolic is psychically necessary, according to Lacan. Without the intrusion of the Real pushing them toward action, humans have no need to question their own imaginings or sociolinguistic structures and no reason to recognize or overcome the limitations of their lives. To eliminate fragmentation and subdue the disturbing desire of the Real, *Mockingbird*'s social Designers had to suppress the Imaginary—the socially constructed world that humans imagine is reality—by stunting the population's ability to perceive anything other than the Symbolic (the rules as given by socially powerful father figures, the Designers themselves). They could then reduce the Symbolic to its least effective state through their hollowing out of language.

Paul, having discovered an ancient cache of silent films, has taught himself to read using their captions and moves from Ohio to New York seeking permission to teach his new skill. There he meets the younger, beautiful social misfit Mary Lou. Spofforth, who, along with his many other tasks, is Dean of New York University, is fascinated by Paul's inexplicable initiative because the cyborg has seen nothing but subdued humans for centuries. Although he denies Paul permission to teach, Spofforth offers him the job of recording captions of other silent films. Under the influence of his film viewing and the forgotten books that he later discovers in basements and buildings slated for demolition, Paul begins to build an alternate vision of humanity, transforming himself from a frightened, sedated manchild into a socially confident, intellectually curious adult, equipped to rediscover past systems of meaning.

As Tevis's representative of the Imaginary, Paul is sure that his new realizations are more accurate than his childhood teachings, while readers are shown that some of Paul's conclusions persist as misreadings of reality. From a passive recipient of numbness and gratification, Paul becomes an active shaper of his world, a "fixer" like Spofforth and a questioner like Mary Lou, and he transforms and saves himself using literacy as his primary tool. Serving a prison sentence for cohabiting with Mary Lou and teaching her to read, Paul is able to bond with other prisoners and to escape from prison. As he makes his way, wounded and ill, along the Atlantic seacoast, he avoids the fate of human sacrifice at the hands of a remnant cult of pseudo–Christian fundamentalists, owing his escape primarily to his ability to read.

At the end of his journal, Paul celebrates his delayed coming into manhood as a result of rediscovered literacy: "All of those books—even the dull and nearly incomprehensible ones—have made me understand more clearly what it means to be a human being. And I have learned from the sense of awe I at times develop when I feel in touch with the mind of another, long-dead person and know that I am not alone on this earth" (254). His connection with minds outside his own through reading unlocks core human emotions—cleansing anger, wonder, imagination, loneliness, love, and the indefinable restlessness of metaphor—that the Designers of Privacy sought to eliminate. For Paul, literacy provides a vocabulary that allows him to escape from his society's dysfunctional norm of ingrained solitude and disengagement; the more he reads, the less frequently Paul resorts to the mandated addictions of sopors and porn. Paul's Day Fifty-Seven journal entry records his sexual and intellectual awakening as he and Mary Lou teach each other a sensual alphabet, reflecting the combined potency of literacy and physical intercourse (69–72). "Knowing" by all definitions is the forbidden fruit that brings Paul to life, releasing him from his innocence and alienation. Paul is the Everyman of the Imaginary, the character who joyfully celebrates his growing competency and imagines he knows how his world works.

Mary Lou, a Candidate for Extinction at birth due to her extreme intelligence, escaped from her dormitory "around puberty time" (49) and was raised in the wilderness by Simon, a gruff, elderly widower from whom she absorbed some of the underground radicalism he had learned from his father (50). Described as emotionally stronger and more intelligent than Paul from the beginning of the novel, Mary Lou is Eve to his Adam. She is an instigator who introduces Paul to freethinking, but when she becomes pregnant with his child, his influence over her grows as he matures emotionally and intellectually. Later, she is briefly dominated by Spofforth, who kidnaps her to explore human love. While Mary Lou is a directional signal and catalyst of radical social change for the other two characters, her lack of personal development in the narrative renders her static in comparison to Paul. In this way, Mary Lou is important as the outlier and representative of Lacan's register of the Real; like the residual wildness of the zoo she inhabits, she is the "not-all" (*pas-toute*), the motivating exception that exists as more than a negation.

As Ellie Ragland interprets Lacan's message from *Le sinthome* (Book XXIII, 1975–1976), "This [concept] places man within the logic of the finite, the *faute*, as opposed to women who dwell within the logic of the particular and the infinite, not all (*pas-toute*) under the sway of phallic law." As women are closer to the Real than men, Mary Lou is the clarifying m/Other by which both Paul and Spofforth define themselves.[10] Mary Lou disturbs the Symbolic peace and the constructed Imaginary, motivating the risk–reward behavior that allows Paul to question his perceived reality and enables Spofforth to resist his role as Detector and Enforcer of the Symbolic. Like them, though, Mary Lou lacks an integral component; having been raised outside the system, she does not completely understand the power or significance of the law. Mary Lou misses important sociolinguistic codes Spofforth and Paul recognize; for instance, she assumes the Symbolic has no control when she mistakenly proclaims, "The Detectors don't detect anymore" and then insists, "The Detectors don't detect *anything*" (41). As she gives birth as a captive in Spofforth's apartment, Mary Lou experiences a double confinement that makes her appear to have passively accepted the Symbolic as represented by both Paul and Spofforth. Even at her most constrained, though, she makes the arrangement with her cyborg captor that will destroy the dystopic world of the Designers and allow humans to thrive; with this action she remains a female outlier "not all under the sway of phallic law."

Spofforth, as an ancient cyborg, is one of "the strongest and most intelligent creatures ever made by man" (4) and is responsible for fostering the exponential infantilization of humans in his world's decaying infrastructure. Spofforth's intelligence is an edited copy of the brain of a depressive engineer named Paisley, and his exterior is cloned from the living tissue of a beautiful African American. Due to the suicides of his fellow Make Nine cyborgs, Spofforth is the last in his line and has been programmed to remain in service to humans despite his longing for death. The only way the weary Spofforth can fulfill his death wish is to let humanity succumb by attrition, so as Director of Population Control, he prevents all further conception and waits to be released from his burden. He represents the Symbolic as a social construct, having no preverbal experience of the Real and only partial snatches of Paisley's edited memories to serve as his Imaginary. As Turkle writes, "Thinking about robots [. . .] is a way of thinking about the essence of personhood" (xvii),[11] and Spofforth is a character who makes readers question the nature of mortality, friendship, love, duty, and "human" rights. Tevis depicts Spofforth as Detector of wrongdoing, fixer of the broken, and Enforcer of Rules, so that the cyborg embodies the inhumanity of the engineered world. At the same time, the author eloquently portrays the terrible impact of Spofforth's contradictory programming and his designers' lack of concern for his well-being despite his overwhelming yet thankless responsibility. The cyborg's anger, vulnerability, and untenable loneliness are Tevis's greatest indictment of the posthuman project. As a shadow image of Milton's Satan, Spofforth gives Paul and Mary Lou, along with the reader, an Other by which to define desire and humanity.

Readers never hear Spofforth's voice directly, adding to his Otherness. His actions and emotional life are narrated in the third-person in "Spofforth" chapters and reported in the others' journaling, yet his story begins and ends the novel. Tevis presents Spofforth's ambiguity in the book's opening paragraph through a series of literary and media allusions that resist the reader's attempt to sort them into a coherent image:

> Walking up Fifth Avenue at midnight, Spofforth begins to whistle. He does not know the name of the tune nor does he care to know; it is a complicated tune, one he whistles often when alone. He is naked to the waist and barefoot, dressed only in khaki trousers; he can feel the worn old paving beneath his feet. Although he walks up the middle of the broad avenue he can see patches of grass and tall weeds on either side of him where the sidewalk has long before been cracked and broken away, awaiting repairs that will never be made. From these patches Spofforth hears a chorus of diverse clickings and wing rubbings of insects. The sounds make him uneasy, as they always do this time of year, in spring. He puts his big hands into his trouser pockets. Then, uncomfortable, he takes them out again and begins to jog, huge and light-footed, athletic, up toward the massive form of the Empire State Building. (1)

This passage may spur the attentive reader to various questions: Why is Spofforth dressed like a field hand, walking barefoot up the middle of Manhattan's busiest street? Why is Fifth Avenue deserted and crumbling? Why won't it be repaired? Why is the phallic metonomy of the Empire State Building, with its libidinal echoes of rebirth, the goal of his spring pilgrimage?[12]

As the journey continues, Tevis piles on more literary echoes: the wise but troubled Spofforth may echo Tithonus' eternal longing for death, Simeon awaiting his people's Messiah, Milton's Lucifer fighting against his creator, Merian Cooper's King Kong defending himself against society and technology, Hegel's self-aware bondsman (*Knechtschaft*) seeking an emancipation, Lacan's "dark god" (*dieu obscure*), or Mary Shelley's monster.[13] Spofforth is all of these and more: an impotent, angrily incredulous collection of figures, characters, and symbols from Western civilization's cultural past. No longer willing to serve the humans who created him, Spofforth as described by Tevis is a projected image, necessarily reliant on humans to understand himself and fulfill his drive toward annihilation; he is an indictment of his designers' sterile perception of achieved desire as mere efficiency, not as Lacan's *jouissance*. In Lacan's view, a sane person must accede to the demands of the Symbolic—even a dysfunctional Symbolic—to become part of the shared world of mutually agreed-upon ideas, and the individual submits to a figurative castration to become a speaking subject who can engage and be understood by others. Spofforth's lack of genitalia demonstrates how imprisoned he is by his Designers' programmed *méconnaissance*, and despite his castration and centrality in the novel, how unable he is to be completely understood.

When Mary Lou meets Paul and introduces him to the concepts of "memorizing her life" and "learning by heart" (30)—subversive invitations to the Imaginary, as well as challenges to the Symbolic law—his first reaction is that she must be mentally ill: "*My God! I thought. She can't be sane!* But here she was, and the Detectors had left her alone. And then I thought, *It's the not taking drugs.* What could have happened to her *mind* . . . ?" (30). Here, at the beginning of the story, Paul's responses show he is also under the control of the Symbolic. When the only reality is the law engineered by the Designers, the sedated humans are incapable of imagining anything else, yet the reader's awareness that this Symbolic is based on a *méconnaissance* cries out for the resistance Mary Lou instigates as representative of the Real. As the characters' inability to interact socially and the incoherence of their speech in the first half of the novel reflects, the world of *Mockingbird* is not a Symbolic register that fulfills Lacan's definition of its purpose, which is to integrate the child into the world of adults. It is a system designed to keep adults in a childlike, unquestioning, supposedly happy state of mind forever.

Tevis suggests that reading provides Paul and Mary Lou the necessary skills to develop an alternative, less deceptive and limiting Symbolic; they certainly think so. However, he continually undercuts that suggestion with scattered hints that their pieced-together history and realizations are also deceptive. As Paul and Mary Lou begin to mirror the culturally driven desires they uncover in a previous Symbolic discovered through books and films, they think they are recovering a lost and more natural reality. Just so, Lacan characterizes the situation of the preverbal infant; in his Mirror Stage, the child seizes upon the specular image of an integrated self (the m/Other) as a promise of future unity and individual competence, but the image is deceptive. On the other hand, while most readers applaud each of Paul's and Mary Lou's newly attained insights, a critical reader will also recognize the deception and recursion inherent in Tevis's manifestation of specularity in *Mockingbird*.

While Paul's emerging maturity seems like a great victory over forces that would keep him an infant, close reading of the character shows that he often replaces the deceptive, engineered Symbolic of his own world with the previously deceptive, engineered Symbolic made available to him in ancient film and literature. For instance, he navigates the scenes most freighted with potential risk or danger by mirroring actors in silent films, and he develops a personal chronology based on his realization that he is "older than Douglas Fairbanks in *Captain Blood*" (31). Films are Paul's constant points of reference in even his most whimsical choices, as two examples attest. Making his way back to New York and Mary Lou after escaping from prison, Paul is threatened with being thrown into the "lake of fire" (a small-scale fusion reactor) by the cult leader Edgar Baleen; he saves himself by repeating lines from the Bible and asking to be baptized as the actor H. B. Warner does in *King of Kings*. Further along on his journey, Paul decides to have a "roadside picnic," consciously mimicking ZaSu Pitts' picnic in *The Lost Chord* (254). It should be understood that Hollywood films are an egregious example of media misrepresentation of real life, but Paul's misreading goes beyond that. Even though H. B. Warner did play Jesus in a 1927 version of *King of Kings*, the swashbuckling Douglas Fairbanks was not in *Captain Blood*, and ZaSu Pitts did not appear in any version of *The Lost Chord*. Without a human parent to mirror, Paul's attempt to mirror film stars in order to recreate historic cultural norms is still deeply flawed, as is his memory of the films.

The excavated film norms create psychic tension and provide Paul with a new set of sociolinguistic expectations and demands, including love. By the end of the novel, his ability to expansively love humans and the world is one sign of his maturity, yet Tevis provides even more incongruity in the way Paul uses the past. As pseudo-Adam and Signifier, he becomes steward of a female pet in prison, the cat he names Biff, erringly choosing the name of a male dog from a child's reader. Each instance of Paul's random and slightly off-kilter use of the past echoes Lacan's claim that the Imaginary (our perceived reality) is a deception. Referring to Stéphane Mallarmé's image of language as a worn coin in the *Écrits*, Lacan writes that this "metaphor is enough to remind us that speech, even when almost completely worn out, retains its value as a *tessera*," (43), a broken piece of pottery that fits with another to function as the "password" of early mystery religions.[14] In *Mockingbird*, Paul perceives each clue from the past as a password to a more fulfilling reality, but the linguistic *tesserae* do not align perfectly for him or for readers. Even Paul's insights about the motivations of his society's Designers may be off base, as they differ from Spofforth's rendition.[15] His surname signifies that he is, after all, functioning "bent-ly" from beginning to end.

Each character contributes to a lack of textual coherence that mirrors his or her anxieties and encourages the reader to reject possible resolutions of that incoherence as unoriginal or inconclusive. Like the mockingbird of the title that repeats the songs of other birds rather than singing its own, the characters pursue their desires for integration by repeating images borrowed from others. Mary Lou quotes her foster parent Simon repeatedly, measuring Paul and Spofforth against the dead "father" she yearns for. In the absence of Paul, she strategically accepts Spofforth in the father-lover role and fretfully compares the two. Members of the Baleen family cult desire to know the word of God, but when Paul reads from the Bible, they cannot comprehend or apply it. Edgar Baleen spouts mangled quotations from scripture to subjugate his cult and justify his power over them, and his followers lack the interpretive capital to understand how he twists the verses or to protest his abuse.

In a similar way, Paul and Mary Lou, in an early scene in the Bronx Zoo, re-enact Adam and Eve's fall from innocence using a robot snake and plastic fruit, yet have little idea they are performing a formerly archetypal scene. In his journal, Paul records his longing to assign their performance some significance: "When I got back I put the fruit on top of *Dictionary* that sat on my bed-and-desk [*sic*]. Then I took three sopors. And slept until noon today. [¶] The fruit is still sitting there. I want it to mean something; but it doesn't" (42). At this stage in his coming to consciousness, Paul's immediate recourse when faced with confusing alterity, despite his drive to make sense of his life, is fear and a desire for oblivion through medication and sleep. Later, he becomes more able to accept a central absence of meaning, even as he still yearns for connection to something outside of himself.

After his strategic request to be baptized by Edgar Baleen, he wonders, "Does baptism really work? Could there be a Holy Spirit? I do not believe so" (196). Paul finds a copy of the Bible and reads it, finding Jesus to be "a sad and terribly knowing prophet—a man who had grasped something about life of the greatest importance and had attempted, and largely failed, to tell what it was" (252). Despite this intellectual rejection of belief in something extra-human, Paul emotionally returns to the idea that there was some reality that Jesus could not put into words—something beyond human ability to articulate—and this instinct comes even after months of living in a family compound with the abusive, Bible-misquoting Edgar Baleen.[16]

Spofforth is also plagued by recursive incoherence in the form of irritatingly redundant snippets of memory from Paisley's life, including a partial line from Robert Frost's "Stopping by Woods on a Snowy Evening"—"Whose 'something' these are, I think I know" (105)—and recurring dream images he can't identify. The only way for Spofforth to pursue the psychic unity he desperately wants to find before dying is to recreate and then mirror what it means to be a *bona fide*, functional human of old. As the embodiment of Lacan's *nom du père* (Name of the Father—the Symbolic representative of the law), Spofforth can function for Tevis as both Satan and God. Spofforth as Satan reenacts the transgression of Adam and Eve by providing Paul access to books and films and by allowing him to cohabit temporarily with Mary Lou. As God, he banishes Paul from the Garden by sending him to prison. However, in a twist on the Genesis story, Spofforth's quest to "resurrect his lost self" (104) impels him to cast out Adam (Paul) and move in with Eve (Mary Lou). As the Lacanian *Urvater*, the chaotic "dark god" who is both lawgiver and transgressor, Spofforth "castrates" Paul by removing him from the scene in order to enjoy the now-pregnant Mary Lou and moves her into his apartment in order to enact a fantasy of human love.[17]

Mary Lou reports in her journal that Spofforth, like all fragmented children, is trying to recapture or mirror the imagined coherence of his father-creator: "I suppose that dream has much to do with my living here in this three-room apartment with him. It was almost certainly the beginning of his desire to live and act like an ordinary human being of a long time ago, to try to live a life like the life of the dream's original dreamer" (99). Spofforth, however, unlike Paisley, the "original dreamer," lacks genitalia, so he can only attempt to restage scenes from Paisley's past or recast Mary Lou into the image of a woman he desired as a young cyborg, buying Mary Lou a red coat similar to one worn by the long-dead object of his infatuation. Incapable of love himself, Spofforth also acts as a specular mockingbird by approximating what he intuits of love from Paisley's half-memories and what he gathers from the interactions of Paul and Mary Lou. Locked by his programming into the Symbolic, Spofforth highlights the futility of an endless, unfulfilled quest for integration of the Lacanian registers into a synthesized psyche.

Although the cyborg subdues Mary Lou during her pregnancy by providing an endless supply of beer, he interrogates his own creation and existence through the course of their conversations, mirroring her process of "memorizing my life." Beginning with his creation, Spofforth has held the role of supervisor over human behavior; throughout his long existence, then, he has been the almost-worshiped, certainly feared, never-understood God figure of the law. Spofforth's contact with the Real through the catalyst Mary Lou gradually allows him to react, expressing centuries of repressed anger. Mary Lou records: "Once when I was bored I taunted him with the name 'Robot' and he became furious—frightening—and shouted at me, 'I did not choose my incarnation'" (101). When she later unthinkingly reaches out to him in a sexual overture, he shows her the blank area between his thighs and bites out, "I was made in a factory in Cleveland, Ohio, woman. I was not born. I am not a human being" (103). Like Milton's Satan who did not choose to be incarnated, Spofforth becomes ferociously aware that despite his godlike status, he is not a Christ figure choosing to ransom humankind through self-sacrifice.[18] Gradually, he realizes that despite the way humans perceive him, he is not a heroic engineer/creator like Daedalus, but an Icarus, the doomed son who is not sufficiently prepared for or guided to execute the impossible task he was given.

Indeed, the story of Icarus, one of the prime myths of human striving toward transcendence of limitation, haunts all of Tevis's work. A character's despairing or dismissive response to the Breughel painting *Landscape with the Fall of Icarus* appears first in *The Man Who Fell to Earth* and motivates the title.[19] The novel's chemistry professor Nathan Bryce, who is out to prove that Thomas Jerome Newton—the title's eponymous "man who falls"—is an alien, ruminates on the Breughel print above his stove:

> It was a picture that he had once loved but was now merely used to. The pleasure it gave him now was only intellectual—he liked the color, the forms, the things a dilettante likes—and he knew perfectly well that was supposed to be a bad sign. [. . .] Finishing the coffee he quoted, in a soft, ritualistic voice, without any particular expression or feeling, the lines from W. H. Auden's poem about the painting:
>
> ". . . the expensive delicate ship that must have seen
> Something amazing, a boy falling out of the sky,
> Had somewhere to get to and sailed calmly on." (*The Man* 25)[20]

Bryce, aware of the Symbolic codes that he should feel awe, pity, and fear at the sight of hubris and its punishment, is nevertheless more disturbed by his own apathy than by Icarus's fate. Bryce's lack of affect toward the boy's death and the indifference of others in the painting are echoed in *Mockingbird* by Mary Lou, who, unlike Bryce, has no cultural grounding in the painting and lacks knowledge of Auden's responsive model:

> The other day Bob brought me a hand-painted ancient picture from the archives to hang over a big ugly spot on the living-room wall. [...] There is a body of water in the picture—an ocean or a large lake—and sticking up out of the water is a leg. I don't understand it; but I like the stillness of the rest of the scene. Except for that leg, which is splashing in the water. I might try to get some blue paint someday and paint over it. (109)

While Bryce knows the story well enough to feel guilty about his lack of response, like Mary Lou, he wants the painting to mean something, to speak to him, but it doesn't.

Mary Lou's narrative attributes the painting's presence in the apartment to Spofforth, who, she writes, brought the painting home to cover an ugly spot; readers, however, are led to awareness that Spofforth hangs the painting to commemorate his new self-knowledge and anticipation of his end as one who will fall to his death unnoted by the passing world. Mary Lou, of course, has no knowledge of Ovid's "Daedalus and Icarus" in the *Metamorphoses*, and she is disturbed merely by the incongruity of a leg protruding from the sea. Breughel's design for the painting decenters the landscape by situating the inverted leg in the lower right, squeezed between the ship and the land, so the viewer's eye is drawn to almost everything else first; only those who know the story recalled by the painting's title know to look for Icarus's body being swallowed into the sea. As in similar passages, the educated reader will have the cultural capital, the missing half of the *tessera* that literacy and knowledge bring in order to make the pieces fit, while the character sees only discord. Just as Paul initially retreats into oblivion when faced with things that don't fit, so Mary Lou seeks to eliminate incongruity in this instance by painting over Icarus' leg. With Mary Lou's intention, Tevis again demonstrates her *méconnaissance* to be a product of her ignorance of the Symbolic. Nevertheless, she unwittingly gives Spofforth his password to the Real when she says the word "woods" (178), ending his quest to complete Frost's line of poetry after over a hundred years. Having worked in cities his entire life, Spofforth gains with this word the *tessera* he needs: a metonymic reference to wildness, a chink in the rule of law that has chained him to eternal servitude. It's a small victory, and while he can't escape his programming, with Mary Lou's help, he is able to recover one tiny piece of what the programmers deleted from Paisley's memory.

The pleasure of reading Tevis comes not just from recognizing his echoes of Western literary and film classics, but from grappling with potential meaning instigated by his juxtaposition of these hints and the lacunae the reader must fill. Paul and Mary Lou gradually replace their world's simple *dicta* with phrases that remain evocative but inexplicable for them, such as "Only the mockingbird sings at the edge of the woods" (20) and "My life is light, waiting for the death wind" (4).[21] Gradually, the reader moves from seeing the novel as a simple fable or a psychological allegory to recognizing it as a fundamental inquiry into integral human desire to transcend limitations. Tevis entices his readers to become actors in the human plot of resurrecting and creating meaning, as shared desires for integration and mythmaking compel readers to amplify resonant images from the narrative and from the past. Readers may substitute a variety of possibilities in Tevis's more elusive allusions, replicating the questions and discoveries of the characters. The reader also becomes a "mockingbird at the edge of the woods," repeating lines from the Bible, Geoffrey Chaucer, Milton, Mary Shelley, Percy Bysshe Shelley, Mark Twain, T. S. Eliot, and Auden, searching for the *tessera*, the password, and Tevis—the supreme mockingbird—strategically pulls his readers into the narrative by dangling the possibility of resolution in front of them.

The novel's conclusion presents readers with an obvious plot closure, which is yet replete with signs that lead in opposing directions. Spofforth, longing for death, pressures Mary Lou to abort her child, but Mary Lou bargains to keep the baby and stop the flow of contraceptives and sopors for humanity by agreeing to push Spofforth off the Empire State Building at his next spring pilgrimage. Paul, the unaware father of Mary Lou's baby, arrives back in New York on an empathetic Thought Bus along with his cat Biff, a growing collection of books and record albums, new clothes and chocolates, and love for Mary Lou. When Mary Lou introduces him to his daughter and explains the dawning era of human recovery from addiction, she and Paul decide to travel in the Thought Bus to California, leaving the decay and imminent chaos of New York City behind. Before they can leave, however, Spofforth must have his resolution.

Spofforth and the archetypal family of father, mother, and child make the long trek up the crumbling stairs of the Empire State Building for the last time, and he begins an evening of meditation upon the history of human hubris and misunderstanding. In the opening of the novel, Tevis had introduced the solitary Spofforth as an Other with no true connection to humanity or nature, as the insects' mating rituals of clicking and wing rubbings merely made him inexplicably anxious. In the closing pages, Tevis again recalls Chaucer's evocation of the rising fecundity and restlessness of April, but with a difference. Spofforth's new understanding of love is shared by his human companions and by nature in the "small dark presence" of the sparrow who keeps vigil with him atop the building. "Perched on his arm, a sparrow, a city sparrow—tough and anxious and far too high. And it stays with him, waiting for dawn" (274). As the human couple is now joined in their definition of the Imaginary, the sparrow serves as harbinger of the Real, recalling Chaucer's "smale fowles . . . / That slepen al the night with open yë / So priketh hem nature in hir corages—[. . .]."[22] Faced with imminent death, the cyborg has his moment of integration and is filled with the *jouissance* that eluded him throughout his life: "He is joyful as he had been joyful one hundred seventy years before, in Cleveland, when he had first experienced consciousness, gagging to life in a dying factory, when he had not yet known that he was alone in the world and would always be alone" (274). After years of being alone, Spofforth feels Mary Lou's and Paul's hands push on his back, feels her goodbye kiss, and descends headlong into love:

> And oh, [he] continues to fall. Finally then, with his face serene, blown coldly by the furious upward wind, his chest naked and exposed, his powerful legs straight out, toes down, khaki trousers flapping above the backs of his legs, his metallic brain joyful in its rush toward what it has so long ached for, Robert Spofforth, mankind's most beautiful toy, bellows into the Manhattan dawn and with mighty arms outspread takes Fifth Avenue into his shuddering embrace. (275)

While Spofforth's ending provides surface closure in the death of the oppressive Symbolic and the integration of mutual love, the reader again must choose which symbol is most telling, as the cyborg is once more, alternatively, Icarus, a freed slave, and Lucifer falling head first. He is also Lacan's "dark god" of human imagining, falling cruciform to save humanity not from sin, but from himself, realizing that the greatest service he can give them is to take himself out of their way in a final act of *plus du jouir*, "an excess and cessation of *jouissance* at the same time."²³ In his ending, Spofforth combines the drives of *thanatos* and *eros* as he resolves the ambiguity that his unchosen incarnation bequeathed upon him.

Tevis here relies on his readers to recall more lines from Eliot's "A Song for Simeon" (1928) to attend the departure of his weary, dark god:

> I have walked many years in this city,
> Kept faith and fast, provided for the poor [. . .]. (ll. 9–10)
> [. . .].
> I am tired with my own life and the lives of those after me,
> I am dying in my own death and the deaths of those after me.
> Let thy servant depart,
> Having seen thy salvation. (ll. 35–38)

If Spofforth, as faithful slave to his creators, is a parallel for the faithful Simeon who can finally die upon seeing the long-promised Messiah, then how should readers parse the ending for Paul, Mary Lou, and little Jane? Are they a Holy Trinity for a new epoch of humanity? Is Jane to be the rabbi for a law-changing flock of followers? Will Paul and Mary Lou become the next spiritual and intellectual leaders for a new society? For the humans, like Spofforth, the novel begins in complete individuality and ends in the integration of love, family, and the planned restoration of community: a "happy ending" that Tevis was willing to risk at the price of his reputation as a serious writer.²⁴

If, as Tevis told Swaim in his 1984 interview, *The Man who Fell to Earth* was about falling into addiction and *Mockingbird* is about falling into sobriety, then we are meant to take the obvious formal unification of comedy—reconciliation and the forming of a family—at face value, despite the pervasive sense of irresolution throughout the narrative. With Tevis's many references to Milton's *Paradise Lost*, the reader could well interpret the exit of Paul and Mary Lou as an echo of Adam and Eve's banishment from the garden in Book 12 when the Archangel Michael responds to Adam:

> "This having learned, thou hast attained the sum
> Of wisdom; hope no higher [. . .]." (ll. 575–576)

And the twelfth book closes by relating their future prospects:

> The world was all before them, where to choose
> Their place of rest, and Providence their guide,
> They, hand in hand, with wandering steps and slow,
> Through Eden took their solitary way. (ll. 646–649)

If *Mockingbird* is a reworking of *Paradise Lost*, then the new family, having previously reenacted the Fall, leaves the pseudo-Eden of the Designers' utopia with all the wisdom they need to create their way through a world that is there to be discovered, with Providence their guide.

An unresolved question that echoes throughout *Mockingbird* is whether there is a Providence that undercuts its Lacanian message of an empty center, a God who is not there. Tevis offers the reader optional interpretations. Paul is fairly sure there is no God despite his strong admiration for Jesus. In Mary Lou's frequent interjections—"Jesus, Paul!" and "My God, Paul!"— she links Bentley with both divine beings. It is reasonable to project Paul as a future prophet of literacy and consciousness for the newly sober population of North America, but a strictly human one because the Bentley-Bornes—or Borne-Bentleys—are a fallible family in a fallible world. While Spofforth's assisted suicide is surely Tevis's rejection of a Kurzweilian *theosis*,[25] he gives the reader a vestigial hope of something beyond, and so does Lacan, who claims God is "not there" yet frequently refers to God as an influence on the human psyche.

As the critic Michel de Certeau explains in his book *The Mystic Fable*, in order to be a poet in Lacan's world, one must be essentially lost and frustrated. Certeau writes that the poet meanders "unmoored" from origins like a ship lacking ballast, unable to communicate glimpses of a nonexistent truth to an uncomprehending world. He writes, "Henceforth this desire can no longer speak to someone. It seems to have become *infans*, voiceless, more solitary and lost than before or less protected and more radical, ever seeking a body or poetic locus. It goes on walking, then, tracing itself out in silence, in writing" (299). The paradox of being able to glimpse something nonexistent perfectly captures the atmosphere of *Mockingbird*, in which longstanding cultural archetypes should mean something but do not, spiritual leaders seem to have grasped something but cannot express it, interpretations are often misinterpretations, poetry creates inchoate sensations that cannot be articulated, and the desire for faith remains as powerful as faith itself once was.

Regardless of whether he is quoting an old film or the Bible, Paul admits that he desperately wants to believe that "the way, the truth, and the life" (254) exist, but toward the end of his journey in the Thought Bus he takes from the Baleens' compound back to New York City, he is also aware that he can erroneously assume emotions are truths. For instance, even though Paul feels Biff is intelligent, the bus shares that "It's just that she's very *real*—is very much a cat—and that makes her seem intelligent to you. I can read her whole mind at a glance, and there's very little there" (249). In the same conversation, the Thought Bus explains that it cannot detect a God figure in the universe: "As far as I know there is no God. [. . .] It doesn't bother you. You may think it does, but it doesn't. You're really on your own. You've been learning that" (249). To appease Paul's desire for something beyond himself, the Thought Bus reminds him that he wants to be happy and is searching for someone he loves, and that temporarily suffices. Tevis leaves the question unresolved as to whether readers should grant spiritual authority to a Thought Bus programmed by the Designers.

The poetics of endless, unfulfilled, inarticulate desire that Lacan and Certeau describe may be recognized by Tevis's readers but would be unappealing to *Mockingbird's* characters after their difficult struggle to mature into consciousness, connection, and autonomy. Such an "unmoored" fate for Paul and Mary Lou would also undermine Tevis's characterization of the book as a celebration of recovery. The author's clearest hint that there may indeed be a hidden Providence comes via the caches of forbidden books Paul finds in his journey; for example, these books carry uncannily helpful titles: *Woodworking for Fun and Profit, Holy Bible, Audel's Robot Maintenance and Repair Guide, A Backpacker's Guide to the Carolina Coast*, and *Cooking Shore Dinners: Let's Have a Party!* (138). Everything Paul stumbles over in his travels providentially provides him with exactly what he needs to survive on his quest to become a more functional human and return to Mary Lou. Whether this is Providence or just the growth of Paul's capacity to think critically, seeking purpose and synthesis in all things, is left up to the reader, an ambiguity perfectly in keeping with a Lacanian perspective.

An equally plausible interpretation of the book's conclusion is suggested by its unmistakable reference to the final lines of Twain's 1885 *Huckleberry Finn*, in which the outlier Huck justifies his escape from civilization: "But I reckon I got to light out for the territory ahead of the rest, because Aunt Sally she's going to adopt and civilize me, and I can't stand it. I been there before" (274). Like Huck and other Romantics before him, Paul and Mary Lou recognize the detrimental effects of "civilization" and join the historical parade of European and American urbanites fleeing the corruption of the city for a distant, unspoiled wilderness, the kind of place where they will want to raise Jane.[26] In celebrating the individual restlessness and mythic American resistance to limits and strictures, Tevis's plot resolution of heading west validates the centrality of desire and hope within the elusive call of the inarticulable, wild Real.

Given the recursive and unsuccessful nature of the novel's references to other attempts at utopia, the overt "happiness" of Tevis's ending remains covertly tenuous. No matter what new Symbolic the family expects to create as they move west, pessimistic—or realistic—readers will assume that their project is as destined for failure as all previous efforts have been. Of course Paul and Mary Lou are now in a much better state to cope with life than they once were, as most humans will be once they detoxify from their mandatory drugs and develop their thinking skills. However, now that Spofforth is dead, Paul's treasured busload of books and record albums form the new Symbolic; the travelers carry with them the legacy of thousands of years of human civilization that they idealistically hope to improve upon as they create a new world. Given the unavoidable nature of desire and the inevitable *méconnaissance* produced by that desire, the Bentley-Borne's new world is one from which their grandchildren will likely one day also flee as they, too, restlessly move on.

### Reiterative Desire as Parody: *Super Sad True Love Story*

A first reading of Gary Shteyngart's *Super Sad* elicits immediate comparison to *Mockingbird*. The novels share formal characteristics such as using New York City as a setting and calling attention to its iconic, metonymic buildings; the narratives are produced by the journaling—and in the case of *Super Sad*, also the texting—of older-male–younger-female couples. The divided format enables similar explorations of generational differences and highlights the unreliability of the narrators as they communicate their layered, often conflicting perspectives. Both Tevis's and Shteyngart's male characters exhibit a nostalgic attraction to past systems of meaning, but each ultimately rejects them: like Paul, Shteyngart's protagonist Lenny Abramov is moved by elements of Christianity and has sympathy for Jesus, and he also resists the emotional pull of organized religion as represented by a ranting, power-mad evangelist. Given their existential disavowal of achievable Truth, Paul and Lenny pursue similar compensatory quests, including artifact collection and transfer of meaning to a romantic partner.

Regardless of their shared disavowal, the rejected past is ever present for both protagonists. Where Paul uses films as models for his relationship with Mary Lou, Lenny refers to characters from Chekhov and Tolstoy to encourage optimism for his chances with Eunice Park, and both novels contain a metanarrative raising anxiety about the fate of literature in a world of images and slogans.[27] Central to each is an examination of desire, the role of nostalgia, and resistance to what Evgeny Morozov calls "the folly of technological solutionism," in other words, seeking utopia and the cessation of pain through technology.[28] Like Mary Lou, *Super Sad's* Eunice is psychologically locked into measuring all partners against a dominant father figure; for Eunice, the narcissistic, abusive podiatrist Dr. Sam Park is at the center of her perceptions of men. She is also "captured" by a post-human *Urvater*[29]—Lenny's boss and father figure, Joshie Goldmann. The male protagonists mirror their respective creators (*i.e.*, Paul as a professor from Ohio and Lenny as a son of Russian immigrants in New York), and both narratives can be read as *Bildungsromane* with adult heroes.

Despite these similarities, the novels are radically different in tone and atmosphere. While Tevis sympathetically portrays the alienated, dreary life of a posthuman cyborg in Spofforth and the even drearier, purposeless lives of humans who merely, mindlessly survive, Shteyngart focuses almost completely on the fear-driven and quixotic quest for posthuman immortality, starting with the first sentence: Lenny's proclamation that "Today I've made a major decision: *I am never going to die*" (3).

*Mockingbird's* events take place centuries after human-directed social evolution created an emotional wasteland, a mythological desert in which all systems are irretrievably broken and the past is almost forgotten; *Super Sad's* characters live in a recognizably dysfunctional, ultra-competitive world perhaps ten years in America's future, a culture so inhumane that it could explain why the Designers in *Mockingbird* had first sought to eliminate anxiety and desire. While Tevis's characters are so brainwashed and drugged that they must rediscover emotional needs, Shteyngart's New Yorkers are consumed by unappeasable desires and fears stoked by the relentless judgment via media streams of their indispensable wearable technology, the *äppäräti*. *Super Sad's* world is one of active cruelty in which people, according to Lenny's friend Vishnu, "form a community" (88) by opening themselves to public humiliation and ruthlessly broadcasting their harsh rankings of others; in comparison, the world of *Mockingbird* is passively cruel when juxtaposed to its Designers' utopian intentions.

Readers first meet Lenny Abramov, a BA, MBA "Life Lovers Outreach Coordinator (Grade G) of Post-Human Services" (5), through an anxious, self-deprecating yet sporadically hopeful diary entry written on his flight to New York from Rome, where he has supposedly spent a year recruiting High Net Worth Individuals as clients for Indefinite Life Extension. Instead, he has spent the year in wine-drinking, pasta-eating, woman-chasing self-indulgence, frequenting favorite historical sites and enjoying what he considers a natural "good life" unavailable to him in the United States, where every aspect of existence is quantified and found inadequate. As an average, rather unsuccessful man pushing forty, Lenny knows he is too unimportant and too poor to gain life extension treatments, but by working for Post-Human Services, he hopes to qualify for them through an employee rewards package for top recruiters. However, his instinctive drive toward pleasure coupled with his knowledge that he can never succeed on his own in such a high-risk environment distract him from trying hard enough; instead, he looks to others to guarantee his immortality.

The United States portrayed in the description of Lenny's fraught attempt to re-enter the country teeters on the brink of complete disintegration produced by the merger of media outlets, technology companies, government entities, security organizations, and multinational corporations like Staatling-Wapachung, the owners of Post-Human Services. There is only one political party, the Bipartisans, and televised news is delivered through a choice of "FoxLiberty-Prime and FoxLiberty-Ultra" (11). Due to the U. S. government's weakened state and failing technology, a wide swath of citizens' personal data from credit rating, age, cholesterol level, body-mass index, registered ethnicity, social media contacts, and recorded conversations is the determiner of all decisions, yet the data are often wrong, lost, or corrupted, leading to potentially disastrous consequences for the individual. Benjamin Barber's envisioned fall of the nation-state in the overwhelming wake of efficiently capitalist economic, media, and military control—sold to the public by stoking fears of terrorism—provides the backdrop for *Super Sad*'s characters' desperate attempts to rise above unfortunate others.[30] To survive in the present and perhaps even into the future through life extension, they must assure their place in the new power structure created by Staatling-Wapachung's alliance with the invading Chinese People's Capitalist Party and incongruously merged corporations like ColgatePalmoliveYum!BrandsViacomCredit.

Given his inability to cope with this reality, Lenny turns to both his boss and his love interest to escape his anticipated status as an unsuccessful Low Net Worth Individual who is deemed Impossible to Preserve. Lenny's almost-seventy-year-old employer Joshie Goldmann is head of Post-Human Services and is its greatest advertisement. Joshie's nanobot-aided eternal youth and Steve Jobs-like status as prophet of technology hide his own deep-seated fear of death. Lenny's significant other is Eunice Park, the anorexic daughter of Korean immigrants from Fort Lee, New Jersey, whom Lenny meets at a party on his last night in Italy. The unemployed Eunice, a major in Images with a minor in Assertiveness at the elite Massachusetts Elderbird College, spends her time and her abusive father's money with constant online shopping, intensive texting on her GlobalTeens account, and avoiding her parents' pressure to retake the LSAT. Lenny's desperate attempts to get Joshie and Eunice to love and help him are evident in a document he entitles "STRATEGY FOR SHORT-TERM SURVIVAL AND THEN IMMORTALITY FOLLOWING RETURN TO NEW YORK AFTER EUROPEAN FIASCO":

> 1) Work Hard for Joshie— [. . .] make excuses for poor performance in Europe; get raise; lower spending; save money for initial dechronification treatments; double own lifespan in twenty years and then just keep going at it exponentially [. . .].
> 2) Make Joshie Protect You—Evoke father-like bond in response to political situation [. . .]; evoke Jewish feelings of terror and injustice.
> 3) Love Eunice—Even if she's far away, try to think of her as a potential partner; [. . .] make yourself feel loved by her to lower stress levels and feel less alone. [. . .] and let her become, in short order, reluctant lover, cautious companion, pretty young wife. (50–51)

Lenny, like the others, is a deliberate user, and his own needs determine how he will relate to his acquaintances. Joshie is never respected, admired, or fawned over for himself, but for what he can give Lenny. Despite Lenny's protestations of love and devotion, he is always calculating how having Eunice on his arm will raise his ratings, attract Joshie's attention, and lead to dechronification treatments. This strategic assessment culminates in Lenny's calculated introduction of Eunice to his equally Machiavellian boss (214 *ff.*), which leads to Joshie's assumption of sexual control over Eunice. Eunice, in turn, uses her youth and sexuality to control Lenny and Joshie, ultimately leaving them both for an artistic hunk in Scotland as the former United States disintegrates completely. Despite their moments of charm and readers' occasional sympathy for their plight, these characters are basically unsavory due to their Darwinian survivalist mentality and ruthless disregard of anything not of immediate service to themselves. Shteyngart is clear, however, that they are socially constructed products of their world rather than inherently evil.

Michael E. Zimmerman describes posthuman evolutionary development as "indifferent to the fate of what came before" and concerned only with future progress (355). In *Super Sad*, the future promises of technology are dangled before Americans in a way that minimizes the importance of anything else, especially of things related to the past. Throughout the novel, Shteyngart portrays the diminished value of history in the lack of respect toward elders, veterans, and parents—anyone not steeped in youth culture. This devaluing of the past is exacerbated by the impact of the data avalanche constantly rolling over the populace, obliterating their ability to develop an historical framework. The perpetual media stream presents a certain kind of literacy, but not the type that encourages deep thought; the main purpose of online outlets such as CrisisNet is to keep people in a perpetual state of cortisol-spilling anxiety, flipping the context to a new crisis before reasoning can occur. Even the novel's text-dependent social media promotes a transition to visuals rather than words in an effort to decrease the human capacity for reflection and thought. Eunice's GlobalTeens texting account, for example, is prefaced by a daily Super Hint like "Switch to images today! Less words = more fun!!" (27), with an erring adjective to modify "words," or "Harvard Fashion School studies show excessive typing makes wrists large and unattractive. Be a GlobalTeen forever—switch to images today!" (44). Consistent with the denigration of words, Eunice's Elderbird College has closed its library based on disuse and irrelevance. Like the shuttered library, Lenny is hopelessly *outré* due to his "smelly" Wall of Books—books that Lenny reads and remembers instead of "text-scanning for data" (158).

Minimizing the value of literacy and thoughtful conversation also works in the breakdown of government communication, which is replete with acronyms and clichés that echo both Orwell and Tevis. The American Restoration Authority (ARA) engages in peppy but oft-misspelled slogans like "Together We'll Surprise the World!" (43) and "America Celebrates It's [*sic*] Spenders" (208), while its disintegrating voice-to-text technology misinterprets user input, transcribing "some Italians" as "Somalians," for instance, in a *méconnaissance* with irreparable and even lethal personal consequences (9, 12–13). The ARA's security directives end with the paradoxical phrase, "By reading this sign you have denied existence of the object and implied consent" (43). In the last days of the United States, despite complete and lethal governmental and corporate control over the people, all official outlets of the Symbolic law fall into disarray as power structures shift unpredictably and language becomes dysfunctional.

In keeping with Zimmerman's characterization of the evolutionary march of posthumanism as "indifferent," a Lacanian analysis of the characters and their situations puts them in an infantile, comfort-lacking, needs-driven state that overpowers any of the socially coded moralities or ethical systems that perhaps gave their parents' lives meaning. They lack a sense of social coherence that might help them transcend self-focus to claim a more other-directed and connected life. Lenny is somewhat familiar with Lacan, as a volume of his writings is a part of the Wall of Books, but he confesses that Lacan is prominently displayed there only to help him pick up women. Lenny, Eunice, and certainly Joshie lack the psychic means to integrate Lacan's registers in a way that would allow them to love authentically. In fact, the New York City environment is so beyond human functioning that it resists clear demarcation of the registers, and the characters are not as discretely representative of them as they were in *Mockingbird*. In contrast, *Super Sad* is parody rather than allegory, yet Shteyngart repeatedly alludes to the Lacanian concepts of compelling, unfulfilled desire, nostalgia for perceived historical meaning, the need for love and approval from a father figure, the broken Symbolic, and *méconnaissance*. His characters are more likely than those in *Mockingbird* to consciously misperceive reality as a defense mechanism because to perceive it would be too painful for Shteyngart's humans to handle. Whereas Tevis's characters were left with a relatively blank slate from which to rebuild a humane society after the death of Spofforth, Shteyngart's are still faced with a crushingly powerful and inhumane world in which survival is the prime directive, as one form of the Symbolic is replaced by an even more powerful one.

In the chaotic shifting, merging, and renaming of the Symbolic structures like government agencies, political alliances and powerful corporations, the elusive, inarticulate Real is not a post-Romantic place of resistant wildness functioning as a necessary corrective to the Symbolic as it did in *Mockingbird*, but an impassive, amoral landscape that rewards only survival. Eunice, as a female connected to the Real, is strictly a survivalist, able to rationalize any behavior in order to keep herself in control and to keep her family prosperous, at least until she abandons them for a less complicated life in Scotland. The protagonists' frantically optimistic Imaginary is symptomatic of posthumanism, but only in the sense that posthumanism is an offshoot of the American Dream and immigrant aspiration. In fact, as Lenny travels through "natural" Italy, he finds a marked hostility to

Americans and the equation of American ideals with the posthuman project; Italians, instead, embrace mortality as a means of loving life.

It is hard to underestimate the impact of the American immigrant strategy of claiming status and cultural legitimacy through wealth in adding to the novel's cruel demarcation of successful High Net Worth Individuals, those worthy of life extension, from the unsuccessful Low Net Worth Individuals. Shteyngart's protagonists and their colleagues are all second-generation citizens whose parents came from Eastern Europe, Korea, China, the Philippines, or India. Lenny relates that once his family had achieved lower-middle-class status with their tiny Westbury, Long Island, Cape Cod home, "[M]y parents used to drive me around in their rusted Chevrolet Malibu Classic to neighborhoods poorer than my own, so that we could laugh at the funny ragtag brown people scurrying about in their sandals and pick up important lessons about what failure could mean in America" (12). The immigrants' drive to "dream big," to scramble over others to the top, and to keep buying and believing while maintaining a persistent nostalgia for the places they have left makes them complicit in the pragmatic brand of efficient and unethical capitalism that leads to Goldmann's delusory Post-Human Services Division. Yet as they cling to their codes of success and competitively outrank each other, they are also efficient capitalism's most likely victims; their personal anxieties keep them in a deep state of perpetual desire just right for a market-driven economy that thrives on its consumers' feelings of inadequacy, and their fears also prevent them from being able to love.

Lenny's college friend Vishnu and Vishnu's wife, Grace, are the only characters whose treatment of others seems genuinely solicitous and motivated beyond a personal agenda. Grace, who is also Korean American, warns Lenny about Eunice's compulsive neuroses, stemming from "the worst kind of combination of abuse and privilege, and growing up in this, like, greenhorn southern-California Asian upper-middle-class ghetto, where everyone is *so* shallow and money-craven" (162). As children of immigrants, Lenny and Eunice's understanding of each other's needs is what draws them self-destructively together: "the craving for money and respect, the mixture of entitlement and self-loathing, the hunger to be attractive, noticed, and admired" (165), but shared desire and insecurity isn't enough to sustain their relationship. They will never be able to appease their own needs through each other or supply what the other craves. Despite moments in which they seem to bypass self-preoccupation and care for each other unselfishly, their partnership disintegrates within four months once Joshie entices Eunice, using his greater wealth and access to a world of specialized goods, even as he targets her family for extra leverage to force her to comply with his sexual plans (269, 280, 295).

Lenny, whose hopeful lists and plans show him to be the Imaginarian in this novel, eventually realizes what is happening to his world, to his relationship, and to himself. Despite his pervasive nostalgia for the past, the books that once served as his reference point are no comfort. Reading through Eunice's eyes, he becomes impatient with Milan Kundera's philosophizing and recognizes that the constant flow of information from the media outlet CrisisNet is more helpful than Kundera's ironic commentary on the recursiveness of experience. Lenny begins to measure his "progress" by the amount of time spent without reading or talking about books. Unlike Paul's paean to literacy in *Mockingbird* that allows him to "feel in touch with the mind of another, long-dead person and know that I am not alone on this earth" (Tevis 254), Lenny's musings lead him to conclude, "I'm learning to worship my new äppärät's screen, the colorful pulsing mosaic of it, the fact that it knows every last stinking detail about the world, whereas my books only know the minds of their authors" (Shteyngart 78).

While rightly reading the survival strategies for his dysfunctional world, Lenny necessarily misreads human nature through the lens of his own needs. Instead of valuing literature as he once did—as a means of intellectual and empathetic sharing across cultures and generations—he casually writes it off as one more diseased perspective, a rationalization that allows him to keep pace with the youth culture around him. Readers of the 331-page novel could interpret Lenny's assessment of literature as one more worthless *méconnaissance* as a Lacanian insight from Shteyngart, but it also comports with Lenny's self-deprecating yet self-serving way of embracing whatever trend he thinks will lend him relevance. In spite of his integral Imaginary tendencies, Lenny, in self-defense, tries to interlock with the Symbolic to enter the supposed "adult" world—which, unfortunately for Lenny and other humans, is a world of psychic infancy in *Super Sad*. This again echoes the misdirected role of the Symbolic in *Mockingbird*.

The failure of *Super Sad's* world to nurture its inhabitants' emotional lives shows in the oral-stage neediness of most characters and is reflected in their simultaneous desire for and paranoia about consumption. They rank and shame themselves and each other over who consumes and shares the most via social media, obsessively posting their personal trait scores, largely based on their weight, age, economic worth, and media usage. Information about consumption of the proper food and their ability to "become full" by spending are recurring means of public confession via äppäräti and other technology (57–58, 88–92). For instance, "credit poles" display individuals' credit ratings as they walk along the street, a public function that keeps Lenny's parents hidden in their home (135), while those with high ratings promenade like peacocks. In a perfect, market-driven storm of public shaming, the demand to meet the advertised standards of successful, conspicuously consuming citizens keeps the characters in a state of constant insecurity about their social legitimacy, enhancing the psychic neediness of those brave enough to wade into such competitive waters. The demand for perfection in order to succeed in a world in which transitory success is improbable forces the characters to remain in a state of childlike neediness. Lacan, in "The Subversion of the Subject and the Dialectic of Desire," writes that all demand is a demand for love.[31] The inescapability of measurement and comparison in *Super Sad*'s America points to an eternal Mirror Stage in which its inhabitants can never measure up, producing for them a fragmenting anxiety rather than the promise of eventual maturation. Stalled in the self-focused, infantile stage of development, Lenny and Eunice—and even the socially powerful posthuman Joshie—struggle to be worthy of love and approval from the *nom du père*, the Name of the Father, a desire for love that renders their actions as potential *méconnaissance*.[32]

To gain his desired dechronification treatments, Lenny needs his "*ersatz* papa" (50, 328) Joshie's approval to keep a high salary despite his lack of productivity. Lenny labors under the burden of less-than-perfect SAT scores and the encroaching decay signaled by his 40th birthday. He compulsively lists impossible goals to meet the standards of his American pseudo-father, who inhabits the Symbolic codes of self-assessment and social judgment of the United States. He is also trying to offset the "old world" Symbolic of his real parents, the janitor Boris Abramov and his wife Galya, who still speak Russian to him. Eunice is Lenny's big roll of the dice for getting on Joshie's A-list. Knowing a beautiful young girl will pique his boss's interest, Lenny sets the stage for his pseudo-father's betrayal by showing him her photograph in order to gain recognition of his ability to attract such a prize (127). Lenny makes his conflicted motivations clear in his journal:

> If you don't pull this off, if you hurt this poor girl in any way, you will not be worthy of immortality. But if you harness her warm little body to yours [. . .] then both of you will be shown the kingdom. Joshie may

slam the door on you, may watch your heartbeat stutter to a stop in some public hospital bed, but how could anyone deny Eunice Park? How could any god wish her less than eternal youth? (100)

To "pull this off," Lenny must first keep the difficult-to-please Eunice, the angry, damaged child who starts to treat him as if she were his "*ersatz* mama" by choosing his clothes and teaching him how to brush his teeth.[33] Eunice, the critical pseudo-parent, becomes not only Lenny's talisman but also one more person from whom he must seek approval.

Eunice, of course, has conflicts of her own to resolve. She is constantly harangued by her parents about her low test scores and is locked into an angry cycle of avoidance and approval-seeking behavior toward her abusive father; moreover, her sense of responsibility for her mother and younger sister, layered into her anorexia-inducing lack of self-confidence, sabotages all of her relationships.[34] Whenever Eunice feels the need for her father's approval, she mentions her volunteer work at a refugee shelter in Rome where she was more notable for her absence than for her aid to refugees. When she helps the senior citizens of Lenny's apartment building and the homeless veterans in Tompkins Square Park, Eunice makes certain that her father knows about it. In her unreliable role as a purveyor of immortality for Lenny and Joshie, Eunice's psychological fragmentation causes her to lash out narcissistically in critical anger or to retreat into mute, compulsive online shopping in order to secure their validating, slavish dependence on her. Highly self-conscious, Eunice the social performer rationalizes every self-destructive move in confessional texts to her sister Sally and to her California friends that show readers what she is (perhaps) truly thinking.[35]

Joshie, despite his theotic attempts to become an incredibly wealthy, rock-star purveyor of immortality, is also locked into the past; his Upper West Side apartment is, for Lenny, no more than a nostalgic nod to the former Jewish intelligentsia who once inhabited the neighborhood. Joshie has filled its walls with beautifully framed posters of old science fiction films from his youth. In contrast to "noble" Prometheans like Victor Frankenstein and Ray Kurzweil, who were catalyzed by the death of a parent, Joshie's bathetic quest for immortality stems from his youthful, heartbroken response to the death of his Pomeranian, his "stalwart and only best friend, felled by doggie cancer on a Chevy Chase lawn" (217).[36] Joshie's purchase of a former synagogue and office graced with a stained glass representation of the first commandment—"You Shall Have No Other Gods Before Me" (64)—betrays his Jewish roots and hubristic self-identification. Considering himself a latter day Messiah, Joshie charismatically engenders the worship of his disciple-employees as long as he can sustain their hopes in the efficacy of his life-extension treatments. As Joshie demonstrates the injected, system-cleansing nanobots' revitalizing power, his increasingly muscular, youthful appearance is marred only by his thick, "tribal" nose and an odd, schleppy gait that makes him walk "as if a Philip Glass piece were playing commandingly behind him" (64).[37] He is ultimately unable to escape his biological parentage or the fact that he is 50 years older than Eunice. In a nod to Freud's and Lacan's Oedipal theories, Shteyngart has the would-be artist Joshie display to Eunice one of his twenty drawings of his naked mother, each one exactly, recursively alike. Even before his own dechronification treatments fail, Joshie's breathless reactions to Eunice are perverted rather than godlike, and beneath his assumed glamour, Joshie is merely a creepy stereotype, trying to dress and talk like a teenager, grasping for youth by making love to the younger woman he has won in an Oedipal conflict with his "son" Lenny. Joshie, like Dr. Frankenstein and the Designers in *Mockingbird*, is not a good parent to his "creation" Lenny—or an adequate lover for Eunice.

The denizens of *Super Sad* recognize the brokenness of their world and its imprisoning patterns, and each one, in his or her *méconnaissance*, has the illusion of breaking free of them. Like Joshie, Lenny and Eunice are quite good at diagnosing each other, and sometimes even themselves, yet they cannot escape their family origins. Like Lenny's parents, who migrated from Soviet Russia but now decorate their Westbury home with framed postcards of Red Square and the Kremlin, *Super Sad*'s immigrant children nostalgically incorporate and commemorate the corruption from which they flee. In this way, they are similar to Paul and Mary Lou in their attempt to found a new, better society based on the books, music, and film of an older one. Lenny, for instance, is horrified by the white elite's crass disregard for people of color and by mass stereotyping based on race or class; he takes pride in living in the only remaining diverse neighborhood of the city. Even so, he frequently slides unconsciously into casual white privilege; by the third short paragraph of the book, Lenny destabilizes reader sympathy with a parody of Whitney Houston's dialect. He and his friends bond by calling one another "Nee-gro!" and Lenny jokingly relates that the white sales team at Post-Human Services are "Cowboys," while scientists at the research division are "Indians"—albeit of South Asian origin (180–181).[38]

Eunice is also unable to break free from her immigrant past, hating her father yet desperate for his approval, and angry with her mother for her old ways and Korean-laced English. She responds ironically to her sister's suggestion that she date a Korean because "it's easier," showing that she recognizes the cycle of abuse and her potential participation in it: "Yeah, maybe I'll date a Korean guy like dad. That's called 'a pattern'" (32). Actively seeking an alternative to her father, she ends up with the 40-year-old dependent child, Lenny, and with the 70-year-old, narcissistic, equally abusive Joshie, who gets her to move in with him by reminding her that only he can ensure her parents' safety during the change in government. Like *Mockingbird*'s survivalist Mary Lou held captive by Spofforth, Eunice makes a bargain with the current Symbolic, consciously and expediently choosing a faulty dynamic.

*Super Sad*'s characters' hunger to be better than others—to be good enough, to be approved, to be special—is centered in the anxiety produced by the absent Father in the broken Symbolic, the *nom du père*, and the m/Other who first presents that Symbolic in anticipation of the father's arrival. Manipulative and abusive representatives of the *nom du père* like Joshie keep their minions in fearful thrall to the past. Won Choi, in his interpretation of Lacan's Seminar V, explains,

> Fanaticisms of various kinds emerge when the subject's passion for the real fails to find a way to integrate itself into the symbolic order proper, regresses to the level of the desire of the Other (wherein the symbolic is hopelessly tangled with the imaginary), and thus turns into a blind aspiration for recognition of the maternal charismatic figure who promises to satisfy all the needs the subject has. (260)

Shteyngart's New York City is a landscape in which the registers are not interlocking, but tangled, as Won Choi explains. Lenny and Joshie see a charismatic maternal figure in Eunice, who, once she moves in with Joshie, starts to choose his clothes and to scrub him with a loofah, just as she did with Lenny (298, 317). As female, she represents both the unpredictability of the Real and the Symbolic of American youth culture, and both men fanatically pursue youth through her. Desperate to escape the emotional pull of her own father, she locks herself into abusive relationships with men who want her for what she can give them.

In seeking to defeat death, the sterile, needy, elite members of *Super Sad*'s "creative class" remain uncreative, self-directed, narcissistic children who seek "parents" to fulfill their needs in the one-sided, non-reciprocal way they need to be loved. They value their own preservation over relational ties to others, chafing against kinship responsibilities while secretly envying the overt familial affection shown by the "brown" Low Net Worth Individuals. Lenny's first "young American mama" is Nettie Fine, the social worker who had helped his parents settle in the U. S. (10–13). Nettie once calmed his childhood fears of death by explaining that having children of his own will stop that anxiety because they "will become your life" (326). Yet, just as he dismisses the connective power of literature in favor of isolating data-feeds, Lenny never has children, proclaiming that the idea of a biological legacy is "utter nonsense. The children are our future only in the most narrow, transitive sense. [. . .] The phrase, 'I will live for my kids,' for example, is tantamount to admitting that one will be dead shortly and that one's life, for all practical purposes, is already over" (3–4). Rather than risk adult responsibility to transcend the self and care for others, *Super Sad*'s protagonists are firmly stuck in the Mirror Stage of deception and comparison as their world falls apart. In his last diary entry, Lenny writes, "Today I've made a major decision: *I am going to die*" (304)—as if the choice of death were his to make.

In contrast to Tevis's ambiguously open window of opportunity for Paul and Mary Lou to create a better world, Shteyngart's characters have no such option. The adamantly silent Eunice retreats to Aberdeen with a young Scottish artist; Joshie grotesquely falls apart and must confess, "We were wrong. [. . .] There was no way to innovate new technology in time to prevent complications arising from the application of the old. [. . .] In the end, nature simply would not yield" (329). After years of bouncing from country to country, the still solitary Lenny returns to Italy, where the novel began among the ruins of another fallen empire. There, Lenny is faced with a reminder of his humiliating attempt to thwart reality when his and Eunice's GlobalTeens texts are distributed globally by a Chinese publisher (327). Even in the relative safety of his friends' ancient villa, he must watch a performance of the texts, in which his part is played by a theatrically sobbing woman (330–331). Admitting the defeat of his idealistic plans, Lenny retreats into the elegiac, regretful silence described by Certeau: "*infans*, voiceless, more solitary and lost than before" (299). Shteyngart offers his protagonist no ambiguity; for Lenny, everything is lost—the American dreams of success and eternal life, the battles for superiority, reassurance, love, and approval from his broken god.

## The Inevitability of Transcendental Desire

Both Tevis and Shteyngart frame their novels with references to iconic buildings—the Empire State Building in *Mockingbird* and the Pantheon in *Super Sad*—representing the transcendental impulse as integral to the human psyche. Both buildings are monuments to the persistence of desire and the mortality of the human race; in their representation of the repeating cycles of ill-fated hope and *méconnaissance* for generations of humankind, both are also referred to as grave markers. Tevis's narrator juxtaposes "the height and bravado" of 1932 New York City with its brokenness in 2387 in the novel's conclusion: ". . . it truly towers above Manhattan in singleness of form and intent in the way that it must have first sprung to the hopeful minds of its architects. New York is nearly a grave. The Empire State Building is its gravestone" (273). Just so, Shteyngart's Lenny had journaled in euphoric assurance of posthuman immortality at the novel's beginning:

> Ended up where I always end up. By the single most beautiful building in Europe. The Pantheon. [. . .] this is the most glorious grave marker to a race of men ever built. When I outlive the earth and depart from its familiar womb, I will take the memory of this building with me. I will encode it with the zeros and ones and broadcast it across the universe. See what primitive man has wrought! Witness his first hankerings for immortality, his discipline, his selflessness. (6)

Lenny describes the Pantheon, ancient Roman temple to all the gods—now recycled as a church—as a comforting, sheltering, darkened womb lit by an open oculus providing a heavenward view, drawing a visitor's eyes upward. Inside this darkness, pure light shines from the central opening, undefined and unmediated by human-created images of the Divine in stained glass.

As central metaphors, the buildings memorialize the human desire to reach beyond the limitations of their present state and search for an aspirational goal, whether that is celebrating a projected economic empire in the middle of the Great Depression or circling an empty center to commune with whatever or whoever may be beyond sentient reach. The same impulse that led human engineers to erect these buildings has also led to the development of the posthuman technology Tevis and Shteyngart critique. "Inside every utopia is a dystopia striving to get out," asserts John Crowley in his review of the Depression-era futurist designer Norman Bel Geddes.[39] The inevitability that desire and aspiration will speed the transition of utopia into its dystopic result never seems to dissuade humans from trying again.

Although Shteyngart does not mention it, the Pantheon contains the sarcophagus of the artist Raphael (1483–1520), who grandiosely commissioned his tomb within the temple, perhaps half-believing the deification accorded him by his peers. Inscribed on the tomb is the epitaph by Pietro Bembo: "This is that Raphael, by whom in life / our great parent Nature feared defeat / and in whose death did fear herself to die."[40] Bembo eulogizes the human artist's desire for immortality and the discipline and selflessness required for his almost-successful attempt to overcome nature; at the same time, he recognizes Raphael's inevitable failure. Lenny, too, eventually realizes, as the eighth-century antiphon proclaims, *media vita, in morte sumus*—"in the midst of life we are in death." In their novels, Tevis and Shteyngart show us a key psychological reason for that. In resisting the finality of death, humans live more fully; as many artists and engineers will attest, without a deadline and an impetus, production is difficult. It is hard to imagine a model of human life without an expiration date, just as it is hard to imagine writing off humanity's glorious and ill-fated attempts to transcend mortality through the arts and sciences as the mere detritus of one more superseded species, or to conceive of reducing the evocative Pantheon to the efficiency of binary code.

As Tevis and Shteyngart imply, the human drive to accurately perceive and overcome material limits is heroic, inevitable, iterative—and a ceaseless round of *méconnaissance*. No matter how much the dreamers seek transcendence into something better, according to Lacan they perpetually look back in nostalgia, seeking approval and validation from the imperfect past they drag forward into their new reality. The oculus and the vision remain the open and indefinable center around which they circle.

### Notes

1 I use the terms "posthuman" or "posthumanism" to refer to both post- and transhumanism, which seek to reduce or eliminate what plagues us by a sped-up process of biotechnical evolution that involves fighting disease, gene editing, increasing longevity, or even eliminating death. Researchers in these fields also work toward enhancing our capabilities through the development of artificial intelligence and convergence of machine and human intelligence in Ray Kurzweil's term, "The Singularity."
2 See Sherry Turkle (1).
3 James Sallis, in his review of the 1999 Del Rey Impact editions of *The Man Who Fell to Earth* and *Mockingbird* for *Science Fiction and Fantasy*

magazine, commented on Tevis's pattern of returning to a despairing story with an open-ended revision years later. Just as *The Queen's Gambit*, published in 1983, is a more hopeful re-telling of Tevis's 1959 *The Hustler*, *Mockingbird* is in many ways a revision of *The Man Who Fell to Earth*. Citations here from *The Man Who Fell to Earth* come from the Avon-Hearst issue of 1976.

4  Phrases capitalized in the novels to designate various kinds of entities, principles, and groups of people will hereinafter be given in capitals without quotation marks. Citations here from *Mockingbird* come from the 1999 Ballantine edition.

5  See Freud (308).

6  In Stanza 5 of Wordsworth's "Ode: Intimations of Immortality from Reflections on Early Childhood" (1807), he captures the sense that an infant's life before exposure to the corrupting influence of human civilization has meaning and glory that fades "into the light of common day" (l. 76) as the child reaches adulthood: "Our birth is but a sleep and a forgetting; / The Soul that rises with us, our life's Star, / Hath had elsewhere its setting, / And cometh from afar: / Not in entire forgetfulness, / And not in utter nakedness, / but trailing clouds of glory do we come / From God, who is our home:..." (ll. 58–65). In Lacan's formulation, God is removed, but the longing for God remains or is replaced by the Real, which lives on the subconscious nostalgia for a unity that preceded the acquisition of language and, hence, culture.

7  In Seminar IV, "*La relation d'objet* 1956–57," Lacan defines *jouissance* as an inarticulable, transgressive escape from the sociolinguistic structures of meaning that govern the human world. Connected to the death-drive of the Real, *jouissance* transcends the "pleasure principle": "For it is pleasure that sets limits on *jouissance*, pleasure as that which binds incoherent life together" (*Écrits* 319).

8  As with language, the sectioning of life into measurable units of time is a human phenomenon that enables civilization and communication. Čapek reminds us that time is a construct, so we can include it with language as part of Lacan's register of the Imaginary.

9  The extreme of this desire for transcendental human achievement through merging with technology is promoted by one of posthumanism's most influential proponents, Ray Kurzweil, founder of Singularity University. In a 2015 campus session on the subject of God (archived online), Kurzweil explained,

> Evolution creates structures and patterns that over time are more complicated, more knowledgeable, more creative, more capable of expressing higher sentiments, like being loving. It's moving in the direction of qualities that God is described as having without limit. [...] Evolution is a spiritual process that makes us more godlike. There is beauty and love and creativity and intelligence in the world—it all

comes from the neocortex. And so we are going to expand the brain's neocortex so we're going to become more godlike.

In his 2006 book *The Singularity is Near: When Humans Transcend Biology*, Kurzweil described the final stage of human-directed evolution to go beyond Singularity, the merger of human and machine intelligence, into an infusion of this convergence into the universe: "In any event, the 'dumb' matter and mechanisms of the universe will be transformed into sublime forms of intelligence, which will constitute the sixth epoch in the evolution of patterns of information. This is the ultimate destiny of the Singularity and of the universe" (21). As the universe is infused with human and machine intelligence, it transforms from inert matter to a spiritualized realm of infinite knowledge and connectivity. Michael E. Zimmerman's 2008 article "The Singularity: A Crucial Phase in Divine Self-Actualization?" links Kurzweil's vision with a long history of *theosis*, the attempt to become god. Kurzweil would restore Lacan's missing "God who is not there" with one created by the merging of human with technology. The *Mockingbird* Designers' goals were not quite so divine, but comparing Spofforth's despair and death wish to Kurzweil's anticipated sublimity shows that the most hoped-for outcome of posthumanism is not inevitable.

10  Lacan writes in his Seminar XX that "woman dwells on the dark side of God who is weighty and fecund. To believe in the impossible, in the real, is weighty. [. . .] The profundity of being *as* a woman, albeit fictional, concerns accepting a position in the social gaze of displacing the Other who does not exist" (qtd. in Ragland). Lacan echoes this idea—that women exist somewhat outside the tyranny of the phallic Symbolic—in "God and the Jouissance of The Woman," where he asserts that women are "capable of a *jouissance* beyond the phallus" (145). This means they are at once the fecund creators of new life and closer to the annihilation of death-drive.

11  Donna Haraway in "A Cyborg Manifesto" called the posthuman the ultimate Other against which we measure ourselves. She writes, "In a sense, the cyborg has no origin story in the Western sense—a 'final' irony since the cyborg is also the awful apocalyptic *telos* of the 'West's' escalating dominations of abstract individuation, an ultimate self untied at last from all dependency, a man in space" (151–152).

12  Tevis's allusion here is to Chaucer's "General Prologue" of *The Canterbury Tales*, in which spring is portrayed as a time when all of nature is restless, motivating humans toward pilgrimage. Spofforth's uneasiness at the clicking of insects shows that despite his lack of distracting genitalia and emotion, the disturbance of the Real remains effective upon Spofforth in Paisley's residual half-memories.

13  Tithonus, a mortal beloved by the goddess Eos, is given immortality but not eternal youth; his story appears in the Homeric hymn 5, "To Aphrodite" (158–181). The narrative of Simeon seeing the Messiah

after his long wait appears in Luke 2:25–35. See the aftermath of Satan's unsuccessful rebellion in Book 1 of John Milton's *Paradise Lost*, as Satan exhorts his allies, and various debates and confrontations ensue before Satan leaves Hell for Earth at the close of Book 2. Cooper directed the science fiction film *King Kong*, released in 1932, in which Kong's captors exhibit the captured ape to New York society and harry him to the top of the Empire State Building where marksmen in biplanes cause him to fall to his death. On Hegel's "lordship and bondage" chapter of *Phenomenology*, see Ludwig Siep's 2014 study (93–95). Mary Shelley's novel of Dr. Frankenstein's creation was first published anonymously in 1818. Of Lacan's "hidden" or "dark god," Herman Westerink explains how "Moses' Thing" (the God of Exodus 3:14) is shown by Lacan to be a "dark god" because the dark god's "desires and demands are not restricted by a rational law," and while the dark god may fulfill desire, he "also demands an obedience" that may produce "suffering and death" (35).

14 Mallarmé's comparison comes from "To Extract the 'Pure Notion' that Lies Within" in his essay "The Crisis of Poetry" (1896).

15 While Paul attributes the Population Control and Dormitory System to human social engineers, Spofforth tells Mary Lou that another Make Nine cyborg, Solange, invented that non-familial social structure to enable human happiness. Later, readers find that Spofforth himself was Director of Population Control and may have set the system in motion.

16 Following his escape, Paul's sojourn with the Baleen family immerses him in what passes for evangelical Christianity in an illiterate world, and Paul again functions as an autobiographical representation of Tevis. In his interview with Andrew Weiner, Tevis shares that he considers the Jesus story from his troubled, fundamentalist youth to be "a very powerful story" that he "once believed to be historical fact."

17 I use here Freud's term *Urvater*, translated as "forefather" or "primal father," but for Lacan, the term also alludes to the "hidden God" or "dark god" he called the Real Other. The *Urvater* represents the controlling authority figure who, as representative of the Symbolic, hands out laws to others, but who, as representative of the Real, breaks them with impunity for his own satisfaction. On the "dark god," see also nn. 13 and 23.

18 Spofforth's bitter remark about his incarnation refers to Milton's prefatory argument to Book 3 of *Paradise Lost*.

19 Though the painting is traditionally attributed to Pieter Breughel the Elder, the attribution has been debated since the late 1990s based on tests on its materials and dating. Tevis, who died in 1984, attributed the painting to Breughel in his novels.

20 Tevis quotes lines 19–21 of Auden's 1938 poem "Musée des Beaux Arts."

21 The line is the fourth in the first stanza of Eliot's "A Song for Simeon" (1928), while the mockingbird at the edge of the woods is Tevis's creation.
22 These are ll. 9–11 from Chaucer's Prologue to the *Canterbury Tales*. Chaucer's famous image of tiny birds that can't stop singing and can't wait for dawn because their hearts are instinctively full of *eros* in the spring—"So priketh hem nature in hir corages" (l. 11)—captures the general restlessness of desire that is the human condition. Tevis's second nod to Chaucer's image shows that for Spofforth, at least, resolution is possible through the knowledge and death he has longed for. Also see n. 12, above.
23 See Lacan ("God" 144–145). Westerink explains the "dark god" as "a destiny, as the constitutive cause of and that around which the symbolic coalesces, and although the symbolic law is capable of binding a large part of desire, the Thing always exerts its presence and calls into question the law" (33).
24 Tevis explains, "It was an honest ending for me. I felt that way about life. It's very easy to write an unhappy ending and then announce yourself as a serious writer, less easy to write a happy one" (Weiner interview).
25 For Kurzweil's vision of apotheosis, see n. 9, above.
26 Interestingly, California was the location of Tevis's childhood happiness before his family's move from San Francisco to Kentucky, a transition Tevis described to Don Swaim as traumatic.
27 In a 2011 interview with Shteyngart, NPR's Terry Gross asks, "Do you feel like Lenny, like somebody who is an artifact of the past because you read books and, even more artifact-ful, you write books?" He answers, "Yeah, no, it's so depressing. I feel like I'm insane to write novels. I'm like one of those, you know, those last Japanese soldiers on one of those islands who's like hiding in a cave and still shooting at the Americans, who are advancing; he still hasn't heard that the emperor has surrendered. That's what I feel like all the time. I'm one of those guys."
28 Morozov questions the appropriateness of Silicon Valley's "amelioration orgy" to fix all human problems by data collection, research, and the development of new technologies in his book *To Save Everything, Click Here*. His premise is that the quest to "fit us all into a digital straitjacket by promoting efficiency, transparency, certitude, and perfection—and by extension, eliminating their evil twins of friction, opacity, ambiguity, and imperfection" (xiii–xiv) will ultimately curtail human freedom and the desire to innovate. The societal endeavor to monetize and gain "silicon Eden"(xiv) through constant data-mining is more obvious in *Super Sad* than it is in *Mockingbird* due to the deterioration and unreliability of vast global tracking systems that resist even Spofforth's ability to repair them—which is just what allows someone like Mary Lou to live untracked for most of her life. Shteyngart's characters are trapped in a world of omnipresent, competitive quantification and surveillance.

29 Both Spofforth in *Mockingbird* and Joshie Goldmann in *Super Sad* fulfill the role of the *Urvater* (see nn. 13 and 17). Perhaps because he is less programmed than Spofforth and therefore more responsible for his own decisions, the less sympathetic Joshie reflects a greater tendency to create laws but break them himself for his own psychic or sexual satisfaction.
30 Benjamin Barber predicted the weakening and demise of the nation-state torn between anti-democratic forces of terrorism and multinational corporations in his 1995 *Jihad vs. McWorld*.
31 The full passage reads as follows:

> It will seem odd, no doubt, that in opening up the immeasurable space that all demand implies, namely, that of being a request for love, I should not leave more play to the question; but should concentrate it on that which is closed this side of it, by the very effect of demand, in order to give desire its proper place. [. . .] Desire begins to take shape in the margin in which demand becomes separated from need." (*Écrits* 311)

32 In keeping with the oral-stage neediness of the characters, most descriptions of physical intimacy in the book are of oral sex (25, 143, 261).
33 For the nature of Eunice and Lenny's relationship, see, for example, 25, 28, 75, and 113.
34 For Eunice's background and issues, see, for example, 30–32, 72–74, 114, and 169–171.
35 See, for example, Eunice and Sally's texting (170–172), along with the exchange between Eunice (Precious Panda) and her friend Jenny (Precious Pony) (172–177).
36 In Mary Shelley's *Frankenstein*, the young Victor Frankenstein is first motivated to reanimate dead tissue by the untimely death of his vivacious, loving mother in childbirth, a loss that propels the narrative. His hubristic attempt to defeat death for all of humankind ends in failure when he rejects and refuses to parent his "child," the Monster. The young Kurzweil's interest in pursuing life extension and The Singularity (see n. 9, above) was also motivated by the premature death of a parent— his beloved father, Frederic. In Barry Ptolemy's 2009 film *Transcendent Man*, the childless Kurzweil shares that he stores everything he can find of his father in a warehouse and has downloaded all memories of him into a database. He hopes to live long enough for technology to revive his father, restoring his rebuilt personality and consciousness from the warehoused memories and memorabilia.
37 Philip Glass (b. 1937) is an American minimalist composer of symphonies, operas, and film scores.
38 For Lenny's grating uses of "nee-gro," see 83, 89, 91, for example.
39 Crowley describes Bel Geddes, designer of the Futurama pavilion at the 1939 New York World's Fair, as someone whose work captures the hopeful *méconnaissance* in futurist imaginings that inevitably conflict with present reality.

40 For the translated text, see Francis Ames-Lewis (107). Bembo's Latin inscription reads, *Ille hic est Raphael, timuit quo sospite vinci / Rerum magna parens, et moriente mori.*

**Works Cited**

Ames-Lewis, Francis. *The Intellectual Life of the Early Renaissance Artist.* New Haven, CT: Yale UP, 2002.
Auden, W. H. "Musée des Beaux Arts." *Collected Poems.* Ed. Edward Mendelson. New York: Vintage, 1991. 179.
Barber, Benjamin R. *Jihad vs. McWorld.* New York: Crown, 1995.
Breughel, Pieter, l'Ancien. *La chute d'Icare. c.* 1588, Huile sur panneau, transposée sur toile. Musées Royaux des Beaux-Arts de Belgique, Bruxelles.
Čapek, Milič. *The Philosophical Impact of Contemporary Physics.* Princeton, NJ: Van Nostrand, 1961.
*Captain Blood.* Dir. Michael Curtiz. Perf. Errol Flynn. 1935.
Certeau, Michel de. *The Mystic Fable.* Vol I. Trans. Michael B. Smith. Chicago: U of Chicago P, 1992.
Chaucer, Geoffrey. "General Prologue." *The Canterbury Tales: Fifteen Tales and the General Prologue.* Eds. V.A. Kolve and Glending Olson. 2nd ed. New York: Norton, 2005. 3–23.
Choi, Won. "Lacan's Double Battlefront in the 1957–58 Seminar: Constructing the Graph of Desire." *Psychoanalysis, Culture, and Society* 17.3 (2012): 244–261.
Crowley, John. "Inside Every Utopia is a Dystopia." *Boston Review.* 19 April 2017. Boston: bostonreview.net, 2022.
Eliot, Thomas Stearns. "A Song for Simeon." *The Complete Poems and Plays 1909–1950.* New York: Harcourt Brace, 1971. 69–70.
Freud, Sigmund. "Beyond the Pleasure Principle." *On Metapsychology.* Middlesex, UK: Penguin, 1987.
Gross, Terry. "Gary Shteyngart: A 'Love Story' in a Sad Future." *Fresh Air.* NPR. 13 May 2011.
Haraway, Donna J. "A Cyborg Manifesto: Science, Technology, and Socialist-Feminism in the Late Twentieth Century." *Simians, Cyborgs, and Women: The Reinvention of Nature.* New York: Routledge, 1991. 149–181.
*King of Kings.* Dir. Cecil B. DeMille. Perf. H. B. Warner. 1927.
*King Kong.* Dir. Merian C. Cooper. 1933.
Kurzweil, Ray. *The Singularity is Near: When Humans Transcend Biology.* New York: Viking, 2006.
—. "Ray Kurzweil Responds to the Subject of God." Alexander Esenov Techno Channel. *YouTube.* 29 August 2015.
Lacan, Jacques. *Écrits: A Selection.* Trans. Alan Sheridan. New York: Norton, 1977.
—. "God and the Jouissance of T̶h̶e̶ Woman. A Love Letter." Ed. Juliet Mitchell and Jacqueline Rose. *Feminine Sexuality.* London: Macmillan, 1985. 137–161.
—. *The Seminar of Jacques Lacan: Book II: The Ego in Freud's Theory and in the Technique of Psychoanalysis 1954–55.* New York: Norton, 1991.

*The Lost Chord.* Dir. Wilfred Noy. Perf. David Powell, Alice Lake, and Dagmar Godowsky. 1924.

Mallarmé, Stéphane. "The Crisis of Poetry." Ed. Martin Travers. *European Literature from Romanticism to Postmodernism: A Reader in Aesthetic Practice.* London: Bloomsbury, 2006. 149–152.

"Media vita, in morte sumus." *The Canterbury Dictionary of Hymnody.* Norwich, UK: Canterbury, 2013. The online revision of John Julian's *Dictionary of Hymnology* (1892).

Milton, John. *Paradise Lost. Paradise Lost and Selected Poetry and Prose.* Ed. Northrup Frye. New York: Holt, Rinehart & Winston, 1965. 5–304.

Morozov, Evgeny. *To Save Everything, Click Here: The Folly of Technological Solutionism.* New York: Public Affairs, 2013.

Ovid. "Daedalus and Icarus." *Metamorphoses. A Complete English Translation and Mythological Index.* Trans. Anthony S. Kline. Bk. VIII: 183–235. The Ovid Collection. Charlottesville, VA: University of Virginia Library, Electronic Text Center, 1999.

Ragland, Ellie. "What Lacan Thought Women Knew: The Real and the Symptom." *The Symptom* 14. Lacan.com. Ipswich, MA: EBSCO, 2013.

Sallis, James. "Books: *The Man Who Fell to Earth* and *Mockingbird.*" *Fantasy and Science Fiction.* July 2000.

Shelley, Mary Wollstonecraft. *Frankenstein; or The Modern Prometheus.* 3 vols. London: Lackington, *et al*, 1818.

—. *Frankenstein.* Ed. J. Paul Hunter. Norton Critical. New York: Norton, 2012.

Shteyngart, Gary. *Super Sad True Love Story: A Novel.* New York: Random House, 2010.

Siep, Ludwig. *Hegel's Phenomenology of Spirit.* Cambridge, UK: Cambridge UP, 2014.

Swaim, Don. "Walter Tevis Interviewed by Don Swaim January 6, 1984." *Book Beat.* Don Swaim Collection. Athens, OH: Ohio University Libraries Digital Archival Collections, 2021.

Tevis, Walter. *The Hustler.* New York: Harper & Row, 1959.

—. *The Man Who Fell to Earth.* Greenwich, CT: Gold Medal Books, Fawcett Publications, 1963. Oxford, UK: Alpha Science Fiction, 1963.

—. *The Man Who Fell to Earth.* New York: Avon-Hearst, 1976.

—. *Mockingbird.* New York: Doubleday, 1980.

—. *Mockingbird.* Intro. Jonathan Lethem. New York: Del Rey-Ballantine, 1999.

—. *The Queen's Gambit.* New York: Random House, 1983.

"To Aphrodite." *Homeric Hymns, Homeric Apocrypha, Lives of Homer.* Ed. Martin Litchfield West. Loeb Classical Library. Cambridge, MA: Harvard UP, 2003. 158–181.

*Transcendent Man.* Dir. Barry Ptolemy. Perf. Ray Kurzweil, 2009.

Turkle, Sherry. *Alone Together: Why We Expect More from Technology and Less from Each Other.* New York: Basic, 2011.

Twain, Mark. *The Adventures of Huckleberry Finn.* Intro. Lionel Trilling. New York: Holt, Rinehart & Wilson, 1948.

Weiner, Andrew. "Tevis, Now on the Wagon, Rides on to New Success." *The Globe and Mail.* Toronto, Ontario, Canada. 11 April 1981. E-10.

Westerink, Herman. *The Heart of Man's Destiny: Lacanian Psychoanalysis and Early Reformation Thought.* Psychoanalytic Explorations. London: Routledge, 2012.
Wordsworth, William. "Ode: Intimations of Immortality from Reflections on Early Childhood." *The English Romantics: Major Poetry and Critical Theory.* Ed. John L. Mahoney. Lexington, MA: D.C. Heath, 1978. 170–173.
Zimmerman, Michael E. "The Singularity: A Crucial Phase in Divine Self-Actualization?" *Cosmos and History: The Journal of Natural and Social Philosophy* 4.1–2 (2008): 347–370.

# ❦ 4 ❧
# Lynn Nottage's *Ruined*
## A *Vagina Monologues* for the Twenty-first Century?

### Martha Greene Eads

Since well before the emergence of the #MeToo movement, communities have struggled to address instances and patterns of sexual violence. Particularly on college campuses, where faculty and administrators aspire to help all students thrive, complex questions emerge. Which courses of action empower survivors? As social media messages fly, is shaming perpetrators helpful? What penalties are tough enough to deter and punish appropriately? When, if ever, can forgiveness be a goal?

Theatre and drama educators seeking to foster conversation around these questions might expect Eve Ensler's *Vagina Monologues* (1996) to serve as the teaching text they need. While some of the show's monologues celebrate women's embodiment and sexual agency, others address the devastation sexual violence causes. Ensler's project has thus done vital work in the areas of truth-telling and justice-seeking around abuse, but Lynn Nottage's far more artistically accomplished, pedagogically responsible, and politically nuanced *Ruined* (2008) advances further in depicting a path toward healing. In stretching students' perceptions to regard bystanders as potential allies and even perpetrators as complex, wounded human beings, *Ruined* can help university communities envision mercy and peace as well as truth and justice in response to abusive acts.

While any educator has ample reason to denounce sexual violence, encourage healing, and cultivate resilience that will empower resistance to further wrongdoing, faculty and administrators at church-related institutions should aspire to lead the way. Jesus healed emotional and social as well as physical ills. Leaders at some Christian colleges, however, have stifled open conversations, even those about healthy sexual behaviors, fearing that such discussion might signal acceptance of practices their traditions prohibit. That administrators have refused to permit productions of *The Vagina Monologues* on some religious campuses and that students of faith have protested such productions elsewhere surprises no one. Many of the show's early proponents anticipated such opposition, expecting that the institutional Church would little appreciate a theatrical event that simultaneously celebrates women's sexual fulfillment and exposes abuses that are all too common in patriarchal systems.

Even so, a striking number of students, faculty, and staff at church-related colleges do care about these issues and long for honest dialogue that will promote sexual responsibility and discourage abuse. Several church-related colleges have staged *The Vagina Monologues*, and Notre Dame law professor Cathleen Kaveny has argued vigorously for doing so on Roman Catholic campuses. Those who hold out against staging *The Vagina Monologues*, however, have a basis for doing so other than disapproval of its sexual content. Whatever the show's merits, *The Vagina Monologues* fails to take into account men's potential to serve as allies in advocating and enacting sexual wholeness. Delia D. Aguilar notes that the kind of violence *The Vagina Monologues* aims to eliminate is "of the impersonal sort, never institutional or systemic. It's men who are the problem" (22). In fact, the only exceptions to this "rule" are Bob in "Because He Liked To Look At It," whose adoring, hour-long examination of a narrator's vagina frees her from self-loathing; Randy in "The Vulva Club," who joins his wife in naming her genitals in front of a body chapel; and another unnamed husband in "I Was There in the Room," who is "sternly counting, [. . .] telling [his wife] to focus harder" as she struggles to give birth, attended by three women who are obviously wiser and more sympathetic than the husband. On the whole, then, *The Vagina Monologues* suggests that men are superfluous, at best. At worst, they are villains.

*Ruined*, in contrast, features fully realized male characters who illustrate men's capacities to serve as women's companions on a path to healing and peace. Set in the Democratic Republic of Congo (DRC), which United Nations (UN) officials have declared the "the rape capital of the world," the play dramatizes the impact of sexual violence at least as powerfully as *The Vagina Monologues* does (Deroze 172). In so doing, however, *Ruined* suggests that even the worst perpetrators are fully human and demonstrates that when women suffer in a society, men sustain damage, too. Reading, staging, and discussing *Ruined* can therefore help students resist the impulse of the wider U.S. contemporary culture to vilify men, marginalizing perpetrators of sexual violence as "the other," an isolation that exacerbates destructive attitudes and behaviors.[1] Acknowledging a perpetrator's humanity does not minimize his wrongdoing nor necessarily entail forgiveness, but it is an act of mercy that can lead to peace. Moreover, having female and male students reflect together on systemic as well as personal injustice in another part of the world creates opportunities for collaboration that can build resilience and resistance to further injustice at home. Although some male viewers of *The Vagina Monologues* have expressed appreciation for the play and have enlisted in Ensler's fundraising and consciousness-raising campaigns, *Ruined* does a far better job of demonstrating that sexual violence is a problem men and women share and can best tackle together.

## The Two Plays' Origins and Receptions

Despite their deep dissimilarities, *The Vagina Monologues* and *Ruined* have superficially similar origins. Moreover, both plays have strong records of popular and critical support: besides its central role in the lucrative fundraising campaign connected with V-Day events, *The Vagina Monologues* won an Obie in 1997, whereas *Ruined*, which has enjoyed more critical acclaim if less popular buzz than *The Vagina Monologues*, took the Pulitzer Prize in 2009. The two dramas also share a vital element of their respective beginnings, but Ensler and Nottage narrate creative processes and methods that are distinct in important ways. Those approaches, as well as the playwrights' dissimilar attitudes toward the material, have shaped each play's reception and dramatic effectiveness. Ensler and Nottage had already established themselves as playwrights when they each interviewed a series of women about personal experiences of embodiment and abuse, subsequently shaping those interviews into stage presentations. From that point, however, the playwrights' accounts of their compositions differ dramatically.

Ensler's narrative about her creation of *The Vagina Monologues* has both mysterious elements and surprising omissions. In the 2001 V-Day edition of *The Vagina Monologues*, for example, Ensler mentions an unsettling conversation with an older woman that prompted her to interview over 200 more women, yet she declares, "I don't really remember how [writing the *Monologues*] began" (xxiv). Ensler elaborates on her theme of writing in a fugue state elsewhere in her recollection, musing, "I am not sure why I was chosen [to write the play . . .]. I don't think I had much to do with *The Vagina Monologues*. It possessed me. [. . . .] I definitely do not remember writing the piece. Simply put, I was taken—used by the Vagina Queens" (xxiii, xxv).

In contrast, Nottage's account of her writing process is straightforward, and *Ruined* is simultaneously more dramatically conventional and more thoughtfully crafted in plot and characterization than *The Vagina Monologues*. Aiming to adapt Bertolt Brecht's *Mother Courage and Her Children* for black actors, Nottage traveled in 2004 to a Ugandan refugee camp, where she met with more than thirty survivors of brutal sexual assaults by both government soldiers and rebel fighters in the DRC. Longstanding political rivalries and fierce competition for access to mineral resources have exploded into conflict that includes an unprecedented level of sexual violence. While the number of men who have been targets of sexual violence in the DRC is growing and drawing increasing attention, Nottage focused on interviewing female survivors and subsequently developed four especially dynamic women's roles for *Ruined*.[2]

## Changing Critical Responses to *The Vagina Monologues*

Although several of the women with whom Ensler spoke had also survived sexual violence, some of her individual monologues address topics with which nearly all women will be familiar, such as attitudes toward pubic hair and experiences of menarche. Ensler's claimed receptivity to all of this material, as well as her craft in shaping and delivering the resulting monologues, quickly won her an enthusiastic following. Two and a half decades after she launched her one-woman show in 1996 and then re-introduced it a year later as a full-cast production, some university students in the U.S. still clamor to produce it as a part of the annual V-Day campaign that began in February 1998. Over time, Ensler added sections that address injustices associated with cultures outside the U.S., including rape as a war tactic in the former Yugoslavia and female genital mutilation. In 2012, the V-Day campaign went worldwide by directing fundraising efforts toward addressing violence against women in such high-risk regions as the DRC, Afghanistan, Haiti, and Juárez, Mexico.[3] To celebrate *The Vagina Monologues*' fifteenth anniversary the following year, Ensler and like-minded activists staged "One Billion Rising," or "The Biggest Mass Global Action to End Violence Against Women and Girls in the History of Mankind."[4] In addition to offering tens of thousands of performers and audience members an array of opportunities to consider diverse experiences of female embodiment, *The Vagina Monologues* has helped raise over $100 million through ticket and souvenir sales for anti-violence and women's empowerment organizations around the world (Swan and Ensler 3).

As a stage play, however, *The Vagina Monologues* has serious flaws. Granted, the individual monologues are dramatically and theatrically powerful: "If Your Vagina Got Dressed" and "The Vulva Club," for example, elicit guffaws and sometimes even uncontrollable laughter, while accounts of abuse in "My Vagina Was My Village" and "The Little Coochi Snorcher That Could" evoke gasps of horror and exclamations of outrage. Furthermore, actors and viewers alike offer moving accounts of having identified with the show's various characters and feeling more empowered through their encounters with the project.[5] Nonetheless, drama scholars with widely ranging perspectives have questioned the play's artistic quality. In a November 2015 South Atlantic Modern Language Association meeting, for example, where participants discussed *The Vagina Monologues*' merits and shortcomings as a script for university performance, one commentator acknowledged her students' appreciation for the play but went on to observe, "It's not really a play. It's a theatrical event " (Modern Drama I). Although the loosely linked monologues drive home a profound concern for women's sexual safety and empowerment, Ensler has failed to provide a logical dramatic structure or unifying framework for the monologues that the "Vagina Queens" transmitted to her.

Ensler's failure to achieve coherence and integration is perhaps a minor point for critics who cite shortcomings in the play's ethical framework, and many feminists, queer theorists, and global studies specialists have raised objections to Ensler's script as well as to her proscriptions against revising the text to reflect specific communities' commitments and concerns (Reiser 3). While many religiously conservative critics and educators denounced *The Vagina Monologues* from its earliest days, some feminist critics, including Alyssa Reiser, Michele L. Hammers, and Christine Cooper, have more recently complained that the play's focus on female genitalia is offensively essentialist. For related reasons, many on the LGBTQI spectrum and their allies have objected to the play's failure to accommodate the diversity of sexual experience, and a number of campuses have suspended their annual productions. An email describing a Mount Holyoke College student group's 2015 movement to discontinue production stated, "Gender is a wide and varied experience, one that cannot simply be reduced to biological or anatomical distinctions, and many of us who have participated in the show have grown increasingly uncomfortable presenting material that is inherently reductionist and exclusive" (Laughland).[6] Ensler has also developed a script about violence against women based on essays by a more diverse group of people entitled *A Memory, a Monologue, a Rant, and a Prayer* (2006), to which some theatre groups have shifted, but 438 college groups and 329 community groups still staged *The Vagina Monologues* in February 2015, many of them extending an annual tradition (Swan and Ensler 56).

Despite the show's continuing appeal for many, Shelly Scott asserted as early as 2003 in "Been There, Done That: Paving the Way for *The Vagina Monologues*" that several of Ensler's monologues are potentially harmful, especially to young performers. Even as she acknowledges *The Vagina Monologues*' cultural significance, Scott warns about the "possibility for exploitation in a global movement using young, impressionable women to raise funds by publicly performing monologues of explicit sexual and violent content" (417). Scott contends that the show's content and its visceral impact are intentional: "The issues presented in the monologues are included in the script to provoke strong emotional responses, and I wonder how prepared the performers and directors are for handling their own reactions to the stories" (418). Even as she hints about *The Vagina Monologues*' appeal to viewers with prurient interest in women's sexual suffering, Scott points more directly to its capacity to trigger the kinds of traumatic responses that Ensler hoped her play would help heal.

Ensler's instructions about staging the show increase this risk. Certainly, the conscientious theater director or professor of theater, literature, or gender studies can do much to facilitate students' processing of ideas, but the *V-Day Organizer's Handbook*, according to Erin Striff, urges campus casts "to have as *few* rehearsals as possible" because performing *The Vagina Monologues* should be "fun, educational and empowering, not a burden."[7] Striff asserts that directing the production as the 2004 *Handbook* instructs "deprives the cast of discovering what is empowering about their own and each other's work" and "has a detrimental effect on those interested in creating feminist theatre" (83). Denying student actors sufficient time to discuss, reflect on, and perhaps take issue with the script minimizes their opportunities for intellectual as well as emotional and social growth. Ensler's efforts to control performers' interactions with her text thus constrain them as artistic co-creators and intellectual agents.

While Reiser, Scott, and Striff have objected to *The Vagina Monologues*' treatment of gender identity and handling of emotionally and intellectually demanding material, Carolina Sánchez-Palencia and Eva Gil also contend that the script's very form impedes serious intellectual engagement with important issues, asserting that "the play fails to open a real dialogue and manifests itself as flagrantly mono-logic" (147). Striff advances a similar argument. Noting that Brecht condemned realistic theatre not only for its dissimulation of conventions but also for its hegemonic quality, Striff explores the way in which Ensler's play appears to present "actual women's stories" in order to evoke a highly emotional rather than an intellectually critical experience and suggests that *The Vagina Monologues* provides a hegemonic discourse of its own (73).

Comparing Ensler as a playwright with writers of theatrical agitation propaganda, Striff notes that the latter typically provide more historical and social context than Ensler does, even as they steer viewers toward the perspectives they deem "correct." Rejecting Ensler's kinship with agitation propaganda theater on that basis, Striff concludes that *The Vagina Monologues* is more closely related to docudramas favored by the Lifetime cable channel, which she notes regularly sponsors V-Day events and aired the premiere of Ensler's V-Day documentary (73, 74). *The Vagina Monologues* resembles docudrama, Striff points out, by "obscur[ing] facts and distort[ing] events," "blend[ing] facts and speculation," and "simplify[ing] complex issues." She observes that a highly motivated audience member might learn more about those issues by joining one of the organizations V-Day promotes, but cautions that if spectators feel they have contributed to women's causes "simply by donating money instead of time, further education about these complex issues may never occur" (75). In other words, while the play has opened important conversation and raised money for worthy causes, its script oversimplifies its subject matter and context in order to sell tickets and souvenirs.

## *Ruined*: Dramatic Foundations and Distinctions

*Ruined*'s carefully constructed plot, in contrast, presents memorably complex characters entangled in complicated personal and systemic relational webs. The play's protagonist, Mama Nadi, is a madam in a conflict-zone brothel who resembles *Mother Courage*'s title character in being a morally ambiguous survivor of an armed conflict. Her staff includes Josephine, Sophie, and Salima. Josephine prides herself in being a chief's firstborn daughter, but she bears physical scars from the abuse she suffered at the hands of soldiers who raided her village. While Josephine and Salima work as prostitutes, Sophie has been "ruined" for the sex trade by a rape-induced fistula and therefore sings for the clientele in the brothel bar.[8] Salima's past has been even more harrowing than Josephine's or Sophie's: after being held in sexual slavery by the soldiers who killed her baby, she returns home to face rejection by Fortune, her husband. Describing Fortune's spurning of her, Salima says, "He called me a filthy dog, and said I tempted them. Why else would it happen? Five months in the bush, passed between the soldiers like a washrag. Used. I was made poison by their fingers, that is what he said. He had no choice but to turn away from me, because I dishonored him" (45). Salima is, then, "ruined" for marriage and family life in her community. Fortune eventually has a change of heart and comes to take her home, but Salima fears he will reject her again when he discovers that she is pregnant by one of her captors.

Each of the younger female characters' backstories helps to create a picture of life for women in the DRC sex trade, but Sophie's work as a singer also serves an important artistic purpose, one well worth noting to theatre and literature students. Barbara Ozieblo notes in "'Pornography of Violence': Strategies of Representation in Plays by Naomi Wallace, Stefanie Zadravec, and Lynn Nottage" that *Ruined*'s use of music, along with its rapid succession of short scenes, helps viewers reach a level of Brechtian detachment, even though the play is in many ways realistic (76).[9] Similarly, Sánchez-Palencia and Gil call Nottage's decision to cast the same male actors as soldiers on both sides of the conflict a "Brechtian strategy" (151). These fairly subtle expressionist staging strategies remind audiences gently but repeatedly that *Ruined* is a play, not a slice of life.

While teaching *Ruined* affords instructors an opportunity to discuss German expressionism, it also facilitates the introduction or review of other concepts from global theatre. Christopher Olsen asserts that *Ruined*'s staging demonstrates not only Nottage's skill in drawing from Brecht but also her sensitive appropriation of traditional African performance practices: "[D]espite the naturalistic setting, characters sing and dance as well as tell stories. Sophie's lyrics often have the feel of cynical cabaret songs from the 1920s but are sung with freshness and exuberance like a griot foretelling the future [. . . . ¶] Dances and songs are familiar to the audience and allow them to participate as they would in a religious festival [. . .]" (85). Olsen draws from Sandra L. Richards's 1989 essay "Wasn't Brecht an African Writer?" to assert that some of the expressionistic elements Nottage employs are centuries old in Africa (85). Educators seeking to cultivate appreciation for non-Western dramatic forms may thus find here another reason to teach *Ruined*.

## *Ruined*'s Qualified Brechtianism

While her globally inflected dramatic strategies provide rich teaching material, Nottage qualifies her reading of *Mother Courage* as an inspiration for *Ruined*, recalling that she realized early on that Brecht's epic dramatic form offered what she calls a "false frame" for the volatile content yielded by her interviews with Congolese women.[10] Whereas Brecht strove to establish and maintain a significant emotional distance between his characters and audiences, Nottage relies on some realistic strategies to foster viewers' connections to her characters. In an *LA Times* interview, she explained, "I didn't want to be sensationalistic. The audience had to be ready to hear the horrors; otherwise it would be too easy to dismiss them. I knew I had to seduce them first" (Pacheco).[11] Nottage's use of the term "seduce" to describe her artistic goal for *Ruined* is provocative, given the play's focus on sexual violence. The prostitutes whose lives she depicts sometimes behave provocatively on stage toward their customers, too, so Nottage walks a tightrope as she acknowledges the nature of their work while avoiding their sexual objectification, partly through her employment of the distancing elements described above. In contrast, while *The Vagina Monologues*' form also calls attention to itself as a theatrical event, Ensler includes some monologues that seem intended to stir audience members' sexual desire. She repeatedly interweaves potentially arousing accounts of erotic fulfillment with troubling stories of violence, with perhaps the most notable juxtaposition occurring within one monologue, "The Little Coochi Snorcher That Could," which celebrates a twenty-four-year-old woman's sexual grooming of a thirteen-year-old survivor of abuse by both an older child and her father's best friend.

Nottage's goals differ from Ensler's, of course, but far fewer viewers are likely to find anything sexually stimulating in *Ruined*. Nottage's careful balance of cultivating sympathy for her characters while reminding viewers that they are watching a performance also enables her to resist what Abraham Kaplan has called "the pornography of violence." Ozieblo, in fact, describes Nottage as having been "'determined to avoid the 'pornography' she thinks has pervaded much Western reporting on Africa."[12] Drawing from Charlotte Canning's discussion of the ways in which "re-enactment or even discussion of brutality and rape can become 'pornographically erotic,'" Ozieblo affirms *Ruined*'s success in "play[ing] with the possibilities of absences . . . or surreal juxtapositions in order to evoke unpalatable realities and so to achieve a Brechtian distancing that, while shielding the spectator from the immediate horror of the action, makes an empathetic connection possible" (67, 79). Nottage has thus worked creatively through her understanding of her mission to "seduce the audience" through compelling, realistic characterizations and situations while employing certain Brechtian elements to support the audience's entry into distressing content.

## Identification as a Call to Action?

In praising *Ruined*, Ozieblo concludes that Nottage's skill not only "enables us to contemplate what is happening" but also "forc[es] us to think, and perhaps even act, for ourselves" (79). Nottage herself has given mixed signals about whether she intends the play to prompt readers to take any particular kind of action, saying she believes "it is important that [*Ruined*] not become a documentary, or agitprop [*i.e.*, agitation propaganda]."[13] When asked by Dayo Olopade whether she considered *Ruined* "to be a domestic play, a political play, [or] a fantasy," Nottage replied, "Our relationship to art shifts, and something that was not political can suddenly become political and something that seems political can suddenly become apolitical. So I am hesitant to label the play, and just [want to] allow the audience to have whatever relationship they want with the play." Later in the same interview, however, Nottage responded more pointedly when asked what she hopes audiences will take from *Ruined*:

> Act. . . . Put down your newspaper and actively get engaged. It's very easy for all of us to be armchair activists. And very easy for all of us to be outraged in the moment—but very difficult to choose to do something tangible to implement change. So hopefully there will be one or two people compelled to do something.

In spite of her expressed hope for an active audience response from a small number of people, she does not—as her response about theater's political role might suggest—directly tell her audiences what to do, a significant distinction from Ensler's expectations of audiences who watch *The Vagina Monologues*.

While Nottage has appeared on several occasions with Dr. Denis Mukwege, a Nobel Laureate renowned for his work on fistula repair in the DRC, *Ruined*'s producers have never engaged in fundraising campaigns, not even on behalf of Dr. Mukwege's hospital. Nottage's modest desire for "one or two people" who see *Ruined* to feel "compelled to do something" is both more nebulous and less ambitious than Ensler's plan to "first [end] violence against women and girls and then [eliminate] violence against all persons" worldwide through sales of theatre tickets and, during V-Day events, of vagina-shaped lollipops, gourmet chocolates, and designer purses (qtd. in Hammers 221).

The merchandising associated with V-Day prompted Srimati Basu to report being "struck by the ways in which the 'global' is invoked as innately distant but consumable." The global aspect of V-Day, Basu notes, is "marked simultaneously [. . .] as both primitive and ultra-chic," and its "exotic products" then work "as parallels to emergent discoveries of 'global' forms of sexual violence in remote settings, forms of cultural capital to be displayed and elaborated on" (36–37). The jarring juxtapositions to which Basu calls attention also get a damning critique from Delia D. Aguilar, who cites these items of V-Day material culture as evidence of the disconnects set up between the enthusiasms of the play and the harsh, daily realities of many other women's lives:

> [T]he presentation I saw the other night was very clearly class-bound and, worse for us colonials, reeking of imperial hubris. "What would your vagina wear?" The recommended apparel—Louis Vuitton boots and a matching bag, cashmere and Lolita Lempicka perfume, Birkin bag, etc.—is hardly within the reach of U.S. white, working-class women, who, by these standards, would be reduced to sporting vaginas au natural. So where does this put those of us, members of the non-elite, living in the "Third World"? The references to "saving" Afghan women and those poor benighted African "sisters" whose clitorises are cut up, labias infibulated, and who in all other ways are subordinated and repressed by their men, well, we've got to rescue them, too! Who's the "we" here? *The Vagina Monologues* is curiously devoid of social context, except where Bosnia and other such places are cited [. . .]. I must say that, as it stands, *Vagina Monologues* is just one more conduit of cultural imperialism. (22–23)

Unfortunately, as Aguilar contends, Ensler's appropriation of St. Valentine's Day both to celebrate the varied pleasures of female embodiment and to denounce sexual violence and suffering promotes materialism that may exacerbate the injustices she claims to address.

While Ensler's project has therefore come to strike many scholars as insensitive to and even exploitive of its subject matter and audiences, most have praised Nottage for the way in which *Ruined* brings questions of global injustice to its audiences' attention. Sharon

Friedman asserts that Nottage is unusual in "[striving] for [. . .] 'ethical encounters' with distant 'others' in ways that avoid a kind of cultural imperialism in appropriating their stories" (127). Wendy Arons and Theresa J. May laud Nottage for reminding audiences that "we . . . wear African diamonds on our fingers or carry conflict minerals from the Congo—coltan, gold, tungsten, tin, tantalum—in the digital devices in our pockets," and *Ruined*, they declare, emphasizes "the ways in which we are all knotted into those systems, tied together by the things we consume" (186). Although Arons and May's ecodramaturgical discussion gives particular attention to *Ruined*'s messages regarding resource use and the physical environment, they contend that such a reading in no way minimizes the power of Nottage's depiction of the Congo's scarred survivors of sexual violence. Rather, the ecological subtexts of Nottage's play illuminate the complexity of her project and the people she aims to honor by also acknowledging the violation of their ties to their landscape through the extraction of resources, the destruction of landscapes, and the repeated displacement of individuals and entire communities.

## *Ruined* and Its Detractors

While *Ruined* has thus enjoyed noteworthy critical favor for its layered presentation of the causes and effects of Congolese violence, a few scholars complain that it falls short of its Brechtian model, betraying its own uncompromised and subjective view of suffering by providing a romantic conclusion.[14] Jill Dolan contends that *Ruined*'s "conservative happy ending" undercuts its feminist message as well as its "Brechtian vision of the consequences of war for women" (Online). In the play's final scene, Mama Nadi responds at last to romantic overtures by Christian, her suitor-salesman who delivers not only supplies but also women to staff the brothel behind the bar. Régine Michelle Jean-Charles finds that the play's conclusion "undermines [Mama Nadi as a] model of empowerment and independence because eventually [she] joins . . . Christian, creating a love story that ends happily ever after" (225). Arguing that Nottage betrays the characters and situations of her play, Jean-Charles explains that "Mama's initial resistance to [Christian's] advances were based on her desire for independence, recognition for how much she had sacrificed to [. . .] construct a world where men were disposable" (225 ). For Jean-Charles, the relative authority Mama Nadi wields over male customers in the brothel as well as the relative protection she is able to offer her prostitutes demonstrates Nottage's noteworthy capacity to illuminate the creative agency of women survivors of sexual violence. Jean-Charles finds, however, that Nottage's decision to "marry off" Mama Nadi undercuts the play's initial promise.

Jean-Charles's discussion of *Ruined* is complex and demands serious consideration, particularly by Christian scholars. Jean-Charles's own confession of religious faith ("Acknowledgements"), unusual in contemporary academic studies, affirms that her work is "first and foremost a product of God's grace" and that it is an essential element of her "prolonged meditation" on the biblical injunction to "remember those who are suffering, as though you yourselves were suffering" (ix).[15] From this perspective of attention to the suffering of victims, she asserts that much well-intended writing ultimately fails to "remember" the victims by turning away from "the bodily and subjective significance of violence" to perpetuate the patriarchal license of sexual violence (19). With these failures, literary works intended to validate the personal suffering and agency of victims do quite the opposite. Pointing to a number of authors who address life in Africa and the Caribbean, Jean-Charles shows the frequency with which literary works, including some that foreground stories of women in trauma-inducing circumstances, view women's experience and suffering through objectifying, patriarchal eyes.

Jean-Charles concedes that despite its conventional ending, *Ruined* does succeed in presenting a subjective representation of women characters' lives in the play's violent, patriarchal world, where mayhem is economically driven. Referring to Susan Sontag's critique of works about suffering in distant places that fail to acknowledge colonialism and globalization as contributing factors, Jean-Charles praises Nottage's depiction of the DRC conflict's complex context in the following excerpt, cited by act and scene:

> A casual conversation [between Mama Nadi and the mineral merchant Mr. Harari] about coltan [1.2] seems to indict the global community's complicity in the war. The presence of a diamond [1.5] that Mama obtains from a miner occasions a plot twist as well as a reminder that the conflict also revolves around natural resources. A quick reference to Mbotu [2.4] vaguely reflects a fraught history of the DRC. These moments of dialogue offer a larger context for the conflict, though ultimately this conflict—its origins and details—is not as important as what happens to the women as a result. (221)

Nonetheless, Jean-Charles ultimately contends that in spite of Nottage's achievement in consistently privileging the victim's subjective experience, the conclusion of the play makes an appeal to audience expectations that "undercuts the production of subjectivities that were previously at [the play's] core" (218). Jean-Charles emphasizes that the protagonists and their subjective experience must maintain distance from conventional ideas of love and romance and thus reproaches Nottage as unworthy of the trust that she may have earlier won from discerning members of the audience, based on the play's feminist view of the world.[16] According to Jean-Charles's perspective, in order to honor Mama Nadi's subjectivity fully, *Ruined*'s concluding scene should have featured her final rejection of Christian—or, at the very least, have left the two characters stalled in a perpetual impasse.

## Hopefully Ever After

However valid Jean-Charles's criticism may be from a feminist point of view, Nottage's having Mama Nadi accept Christian's invitation to a shared life reflects not only Nottage's sensitivity to the story's cultural context but also something akin to poetic justice. In "Staging Gender Violence in the Congo: Reading Lynn Nottage's *Ruined* as a Documentary Drama," Phyllisa Smith Deroze suggests that the conclusion honors productive cultural norms. She points out that people in the DRC generally privilege "family, motherhood, and heterosexual marriage over material possessions, autonomy, and homosexuality" (186). Moreover, Mama Nadi's receptivity to love from a man becomes dramatically significant when she reveals in the play's final moments that, she, like Sophie, has suffered a rape-induced fistula. The injury will likely prevent her from ever engaging in vaginal intercourse, much less enjoying it, and the shame associated with her condition has surely contributed to her keeping Christian at arm's length throughout the play. To move into his embrace in a dance as the play concludes, to move forward in life with him after the curtain falls, requires tremendous hope.

Such hope is, in its essence, spiritual. Furthermore, whether or not Nottage intended such a message, her play affirms a worldview, common to all three Abrahamic faiths, in which it "is not good that the man"—or the woman—"should be alone" (Gen. 2:18). Instead, each person is to find companionship through complementarity in a partner of the opposite sex. In contrast to the significant number of characters in *The Vagina Monologues* who seek ecstasy in sometimes-fleeting sexual encounters with women or in masturbating alone, Nottage's protagonist risks the profound vulnerability of embarking on a potentially long-term and assuredly complex relationship with a man.[17]

While a real woman in Mama Nadi's circumstances might understandably find companionship (sexual or non-sexual) with other women or choose to remain alone, the character simultaneously finds a kind of closure as well as a new avenue for growth in heterosexual partnership. When Mama Nadi finally reveals to Christian (and to the audience) that she herself is "ruined," his devotion to her does not waver. Instead, he tells her, "God, I don't know what those men did to you, but I'm sorry for it. I may be an idiot for saying so, but I think we, and I speak as a man, can do better" (67). Christian, as a proxy for the man or men who brutalized Mama Nadi, hears her truth, accepts responsibility, and offers to join her in moving forward. Mama Nadi's acceptance of Christian thus provides not a *happily*-ever-after but instead a *hopefully*-ever-after conclusion.

The complexity with which Nottage endows both Christian and Mama Nadi makes their hopeful union plausible as well as satisfying. Christian is clearly flawed, having pandered Sophie, his own niece. Obviously wounded and fragile emotionally and physically, he is an alcoholic who resumes his drinking under pressure. Still, despite his failings, he has tried to protect Sophie from further violence by bringing her to the relative safety of the brothel. He has demonstrated selfless love for Mama Nadi throughout the play, even compromising his recovery from alcoholism by submitting to a military commander's bullying insistence that he drink in order to prevent an episode of violence in the bar.[18] Similarly, Nottage nuances Mama Nadi's character with emotional and physical complexity. She profits from other women's sexual labor, yet she eventually offers her most precious possession, a valuable diamond, to pay for Sophie's fistula-repair surgery rather use it for her own medical care or to make a fresh financial start elsewhere. Even in the nightmare setting of a DRC war zone, in which they have both witnessed and experienced profound trauma, Christian and Mama Nadi have grown in vulnerability and generosity, validating the audience's sympathy for them and making them fitting companions for one another. Each is "a rare bird," the title of the guitar tune to which they dance as the lights fade on the stage.

## *Ruined*'s Remaining Realities

Despite its romantic conclusion, *Ruined* nevertheless hammers home the reality that truly happy endings are rare, especially in conflict settings. Salima's husband Fortune, regretting his earlier rejection of her, comes looking for her at the brothel. When a cousin accompanying him tries to dissuade him from pursuing reconciliation, Fortune justifies his choice absolutely: "I've prayed on this" (49). Although Nottage's depiction of Fortune could have continued the pattern that Jean-Charles laments in so many other texts—that of focusing on violence against women as violations of men's property and assaults on men's pride—Nottage instead secures Salima's subjectivity by having her declare to the brothel patrons, "[Y]ou will not fight your battles on my body anymore" (63) and later perform what Phyllisa Smith Deroze calls a "doubly-fatal" self-induced abortion (184). Salima is beyond overcoming her traumatic experiences when Fortune re-enters her life, and whether Fortune's commitment to their marriage would have held, no one can predict, but their moment of reunion ends with her death.

Nottage's depiction of Fortune thus shows realistically how violence extends beyond its immediate victims, creating cycles that typically encompass family members, neighbors, and even entire communities. Facing his painful personal failure to protect his family in addition to living in an area of intense fighting have surely contributed to Fortune's initial rejection of Salima. While Salima responds to violence by adopting what trauma scholar Elaine Zook Barge calls "acting-in" behaviors, including withdrawal, hopelessness, feelings of numbness, anxiety, self-blame, and shame, Fortune's responses fit the "acting-out" pattern: aggression, irritability, blaming, an inability to be flexible or tolerant, and lack of empathy (Barge 17). Often, couples struggling with such emotional and behavioral patterns experience domestic violence.

While Fortune's most obvious suffering is as a bystander to his wife's kidnapping and their daughter's murder, other men in the play are, of course, obvious perpetrators of sexual violence—and possibly victims, as well. Kate Whoriskey, Manhattan Theatre Club's production director and Nottage's companion on her interview trip to Uganda, notes the irony of the cycle of sexual violence in the DRC: "[T]he men and boys who raped were themselves victims of unspeakable violence," she observes, and "they spend the rest of their lives terrorizing and destroying others."[19] In recognition of this brutal irony, Nottage gives even a brothel customer who never appears on stage a complex history. Salima compares him and his fellow-soldiers unfavorably to the miners who also frequent the brothel, complaining, "Them soldiers don't respect nothing. Them miners, they easy, they want drink, company, and it's over, but the soldiers, they want more of you, and—" (22). Salima breaks off, and when Sophie, perceiving Salima's distress, urges her to continue, Salima recounts the soldier's gloating over having brutally murdered one of her tribesmen, "bragging like I should be congratulating him. And then he fucked me, and when he was finished[,] he sat on the floor and wept. He wanted me to hold him. Comfort him." Without shifting her focus from the abused Congolese women who need healing, Nottage demonstrates that societies in which women suffer are hostile places for men, too.

While Ensler's variety of feminism minimizes this reality in *The Vagina Monologues*, Deroze marvels at Nottage's achievement in dramatizing it: "Even within a play about women, Nottage highlights that the war also has devastating impacts on men who are encouraged to put their humanity aside and engage in savage behavior. From a womanist perspective, communal healing includes men and children" (183). Deroze reminds admirers of this play set in the DRC that even in the U.S., "black feminism and womanism are not gender-separatist movements like traditional white feminism," emphasizing that racism is a "shared experience" that unites men and women in the black community in a common cause, "prevent[ing] their total abandonment of one another even if some black men are perpetrators of violence" (183, 186). In other words, the devastating effects of entrenched racism in the U.S. deserve to be acknowledged, not as excuses for but as possible contributors to the development of abusive patterns among some African-American men.

That Nottage's Congolese characters are also caught up in longstanding regional and even global conflicts that complicate and intensify their suffering. The "Cycles of Violence" diagram (p. 112) illustrates the ways in which personal and larger-scale traumas are likely to exacerbate each other. Interpersonally and among groups, those who perceive themselves to be victims often cultivate an us-versus-them mentality that justifies increasing levels of violence in the interest of self-defense, honor, or justice. That Nottage uses the same male actors to portray both government soldiers and rebel fighters in successive scenes shows that she understands, if only intuitively, the universal temptation among those in conflict to demonize opponents who resemble them more than they can bear to admit.

*A delegation of MONUC's female staff visited a Congolese women's shelter in Goma to donate supplies, such as blankets, sheets, cookware, and toiletries. Local women run the shelter for other Congolese women. The survivors we met showed remarkable strength and courage in their interactions with us and with one another, but the violence they suffered would leave anyone broken. One woman, for example, had not uttered a word since being raped three years earlier, and many bore children conceived in sexual violence. One survivor gave birth to triplets following two gang rapes, and very young girls now have the responsibility of caring for a child. Despite their trauma, an ambiance of celebration was in the air because of MONUC's visit, which was humbling. Any helping gesture, big or small, is much appreciated, as these women's needs are great. In this photo: A young adolescent who is now parenting her own child is seen at left. On the right, a survivor of two gang rapes carries one of her triplet children. Identities and chronology are concealed. — Marie Frechon—*

© MONUC/Marie Frechon. *The image is used by permission of the photographer.*

112 | MARTHA GREENE EADS

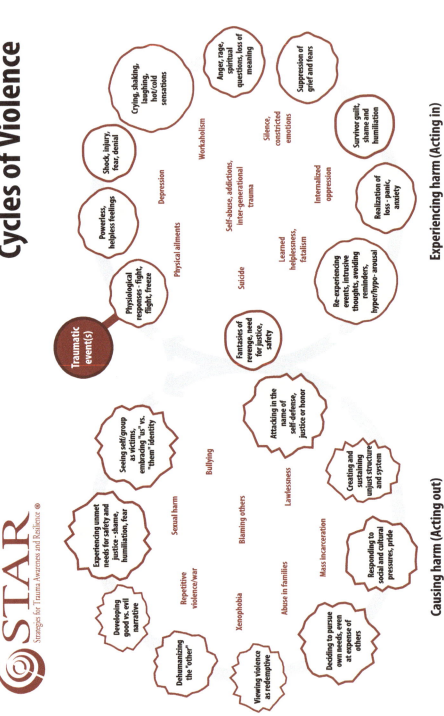

*The STAR diagram is © Carolyn Yoder and the STAR Team at Eastern Mennonite University, creators of the material. It is used here by the gracious permission of Ms. Yoder, the STAR Team, and Hannah Kelley on behalf of STAR at EMU.*

## "Don't Forgive and Forget, But Remember and Change"

Understandably, survivors, bystanders, and perpetrators of trauma often wish they could forget their pain and the past that caused it. Sophie's signature cabaret song addresses this desire, suggesting that song and dance are insufficient to erase regret, guilt, and fear, and that to find peace, at least for the night, the bar patrons must "have another beer":

> Have another beer, my friend,
> Douse the fires of your fears, my friend,
> Get drunk and foolish on the moment,
> Brush aside the day's heavy judgment.
>
> Yes, have another beer, my friend,
> Wipe away the angry tears, my friend.... (14–15; 17)

The song serves as an appropriate accompaniment to the activities through which Mama Nadi profits: her customers attempt to forget the pain they've experienced by abusing alcohol, engaging in risky sexual behaviors, and gambling, and in so doing, they inflict pain on others (Barge 17). Subsequent action in the play demonstrates, of course, that such "acting-in" behaviors lead to more violence: harassment of the prostitutes, brawling, and repeated returns to conflict zones.

Not forgetting but instead remembering in the right way is a requirement for any individual or society seeking to break out of the acting-in and acting-out cycles of violence, and *Ruined* both illustrates and enables right remembering. Barge observes that truth-telling includes acknowledging suffering, often through ritual; facing a new reality, including fears associated with it, frequently through storytelling; and memorializing what happened, often through works of art. Song and dance within *Ruined* serve some of these purposes for the characters, as does the women's sharing their stories with each other and Mama's vital exchange with Christian at the play's conclusion. The play itself, however, functions significantly as ritual, a storytelling event, and a memorial around the harrowing violations of individual bodies, communities, and landscapes in the DRC.

Eve Ensler deserves credit for similar achievements in *The Vagina Monologues*; however, her storytelling succumbs to the temptation Elaine Barge describes in her work on trauma as the "pressure to only tell one version or one part of the story—the one that makes our side look good and the other side look bad. Usually there are multiple sides of a story, all claiming to tell the truth" (23). Undoubtedly, sexual violence not only looks bad but *is* bad, and characterizing it otherwise would hardly be telling the truth. Marrying mercy to truth, however, as Nottage does in *Ruined* through highlighting male characters' own wounds, begins to trace trauma's origins. "Reflecting on the history of the 'other' helps us understand and address root causes of the trauma [. . .]. Understanding why THEY harmed us may lead us to realize that we ourselves can feel safe only if everyone feels safe," Barge observes (25). Sometimes, parties on both sides of a conflict meet to share and reflect on their differing accounts of events, as documented by the film *Fambul Tok*, in which survivors and perpetrators of unspeakable violence in Sierra Leone conducted a series of meetings in pursuit of healing, or in the Coming to the Table project here in the U.S., in which descendants of enslaved Africans meet with descendants of those who owned their ancestors, functioning as proxies to address harms done. In such contexts, forgiveness sometimes takes place. Such forgiveness has not emerged from forgetting; instead, individuals remember together and move toward change.

## Justice and Peace Through *Ruined*

Mama Nadi and Christian model this kind of remembering, and the plan Christian ultimately proposes—to "stay, help you run things. Make a legitimate business. A shop" (66)—aligns with Barge's observation that those from opposite sides of a conflict can sometimes move beyond trauma to genuine peace through "working on a project together, learning together" (25). While their new partnership thus reflects truth, mercy, and even a measure of justice in the form of Christian's proxy apology, wide-scale sexual violence, regional conflict, and economic and environmental devastation rage on beyond Mama Nadi's place while she and Christian dance inside.

Deroze has observed that Nottage's decision to name her most admirable male character "Christian" symbolizes the playwright's challenge not only to Congolese Christian men to stand by their wives but also to followers of Jesus elsewhere to respond compassionately to the DRC crisis (186). To those ends, performing and studying *Ruined* opens interdisciplinary fields of inquiry church-related institutions might be eager to explore: what minerals go into our electronic devices, and from where do they come?[20] How common is sexual slavery—there and here? How have African tribal conflicts, historic European territorial colonialism, and twenty-first-century

U.S. economic expansion intersected? Asking such questions in community and responding to them productively can help campus communities build collective resilience, as Barge suggests. "When societies are resilient," Barge observes, "they are able to respond to adversity and change, can respond to crises in ways that strengthen communal bonds, exhibit creative thinking and flexibility, have the ability to improvise in new and challenging situations, [and] use misfortune to strengthen communal solidarity and renovate the social fiber" (33). Such resilience is often in short supply when colleges must confront their own crises. Engagement with *Ruined*, then, is an opportunity educators—particularly those in Christian colleges and universities—can embrace for many reasons.

## Notes

1  In *So You've Been Publicly Shamed* (2015), journalist Jon Ronson offers a relevant observation from an 1867 commentary on public whippings: "If [there] had previously existed in [the convicted person's] bosom a spark of self-respect[,] this exposure to public shame utterly extinguishes it. Without the hope that springs eternal in the human breast, without some desire to reform and become a good citizen, and the feeling that such a thing is possible, no criminal can ever return to honorable courses" (qtd. in Ronson 55). "Hope springs eternal in the human breast" is found in Alexander Pope's *Essay on Man*.
2  Marie Frechon's photograph of survivors is of interest to this discussion of women's experiences and resilience in the DRC. On the matter of raping men in order to "feminize" and degrade them in armed conflict, see articles on the general subject, including its practice in the DRC, by Sandesh Sivakumaran; on practices in the DRC specifically, by Mervyn Christian, *et al* (2012); and Will Storr's article in *The Guardian*. Christian, *et al*, found this type of violence "multi-dimensional" and heavy with consequences of all kinds for the surviving victim and his family.
3  See Penny Farfan and Leslie Ferris's introduction to an anthology of women playwrights' work (2). See also Elaine Aston's disciplinary standard, *Feminist Theatre Practice*.
4  In 2022, Vday.org continues to promote "One Billion Rising," describing the movement as having "launched on Valentine's Day 2012."
5  See "Letters and Stories" (145–171).
6  In response to Mount Holyoke's decision, Ensler told Oliver Laughland, "I think it's important to know that I never intended to write a play about what it means to be a woman, that was not what the *Vagina Monologues* ever intended to be [. . .]. It was a play about what it means to have a vagina. It never said, for example, the definition of a woman is someone who has a vagina [. . .]. I think that's a really important distinction." She also pointed out that she adds an additional monologue

each year, noting that a 2005 addition, "They Beat the Girl Out of My Boy," which focuses on a transgendered character's experience, remains optional for performance.
7 Striff quotes from the "V-Day Organizers Handbook" [sic], available online in February 2004 (81 and Striff's n. 22) just prior to V-Day. The document is apparently no longer available.
8 Theorizing the sexually victimized woman's altered identity, Rajeswari Sunder Rajan observes that her "newly recognized identity—[. . .] her function in an economy of sexual propriety and property—becomes an emotional war-cry and prelude to the virtual disappearance of the concerns of the woman herself" (68). A rape-induced fistula is a tear or hole in the tissue between the vagina and the anus that results in permanent urinary and/or fecal incontinence. See the Fistula Foundation website for a discussion of obstetric fistula, the more common type of fistula; the results of either type are similar.
9 In cinematic terms, Sophie's songs are diegetic because they are perceived by the characters (as well as the audience) and contribute internally to the development of character and plot, as well as to audience involvement, an element of the play that deserves attention.
10 Ozieblo cites the report of Nottage's being interviewed by the *Los Angeles Times* (76); subsequent references in this section to Nottage's interview come from Ozieblo's account.
11 See Ozieblo (67). The "immersive power" of cinema is critically translatable to the effects of the theater on its audience. For example, see Mary Galbraith's 1995 essay "Deictic Shift Theory and the Poetics of Involvement in Narrative." Deroze (173) calls *Ruined* a successful "documentary," drawing from the genre studies of Gary Fisher Dawson and Alan Filewood, and suggests that the "journalism" of documentary style deploys elements of drama to "manipulate the real world."
12 The phrase "pornography of violence" has been in use in the fields of aesthetics, law, and censorship since the 1950s when Abraham Kaplan ("Obscenity as an Esthetic Category") wrote: "A new category of the obscene emerges: the *pornography of violence*" (558, italics *sic*).
13 The passage is quoted in Sanchez-Palencia and Gil (152).
14 Addressing Nottage's acknowledged debt to Brecht, Marike Janzen argues that the former fails to achieve the latter's capacity to invite reflection on the deep structural roots of injustice (174). Arons and May, however, argue convincingly otherwise.
15 The scriptural reference is from Hebrews 13:3. Its key words are given various translations. KJV: "Remember them that are in bonds, as bound with them; and them which suffer adversity, as being yourselves also in the body. ESV: "Remember those who are in prison, as though in prison with them, and those who are mistreated, since you also are in the body."
16 Jean-Charles writes: "Though the drama initially offers a female-dominated and female-inspired universe as an alternative to the war,

or, perhaps, in spite of the war, it ultimately reproduces the notion that such a world is unsustainable and that women need men for protection, partnership, and romance. This romantic ending destabilizes the previously articulated messages of female survival devoid of male protection. The use of the romance as a method of narrative closure for the play appeals to the viewer's sensibilities and emotional need for a felicitous ending to a bleak story" (231).

17 The narrator in "The Little Coochi Snorcher" says that the twenty-four-year-old woman who seduced her when she was thirteen urged her "to always know how to give myself pleasure so I'll never need to rely on a man [. . .]. I realized later she was my surprising, unexpected, politically incorrect salvation" (82). In a monologue celebrating digital penetration in a lesbian encounter, the narrator says, "I did not desire women, for example, because I disliked men. *Men weren't even part of the equation* [. . .]. For example [. . .] I'm having sex with a woman. She's inside me. I'm inside me. *Fucking myself* together with her" (115, italics added). The protagonist in "The Vagina Workshop" recounts "[lying] there, thrashing about on [her] little blue mat" in an autoerotic orgasm (50). In thus urging women to eschew partnership with men, these monologues ultimately preach a sexuality of self-absorption.

18 Christopher Olsen misses the sacrificial nature of this act, writing, "By the end of Act I [. . .], Christian, who has sworn off liquor for many years, returns to drinking and finds a drunken stupor to be the easiest place to hide his pain" (85).

19 Arons and May (185) quote Whoriskey.

20 For example, a student-led campaign in 2013 succeeded in making EMU's campus a conflict-mineral-free zone (Zucconi and Yoder). See Mary Beth Marklein's reporting on the reception of Ensler's play on college campuses. The "blood coltan" trade involves child labor, rebel militias, violence, and death. See, for example, stories by Morgan Winsor, Jake Flanagin, and Jeffrey Gettleman and Marcus Bleasdale. Smartphone capacitors use tantalum derived from coltan, or columbite-tantalite (Los Alamos).

**Works Cited**

Aguilar, Delia D. "On Vagina Monologues." *Kritika Kultura* 2 (2002): 22–23.

Arons, Wendy, and Theresa J. May. "Ecodramaturgy in/and Contemporary Women's Playwriting." *Contemporary Women's Playwrights*. Ed. Penny Farfan and Leslie Ferris. New York: Palgrave Macmillan, 2013. 181–196.

Aston, Elaine. *Feminist Theatre Practice: A Handbook*. Abingdon, UK: Routledge, 1999, 2005.

Barge, Elaine Zook. *Village STAR—Breaking Cycles of Violence: Building Healthy Individuals and Communities*. Harrisonburg, VA: EMU, 2016.

Basu, Srimati. "V is for Veil, V is for Ventriloquism: Global Feminisms in *The Vagina Monologues*." *Frontiers* 31.1 (2010): 31–62.

Brecht, Bertolt. *Mother Courage and Her Children (Mutter Courage und ihre Kinder: Eine Chronik aus dem Dreissigjahrigen Krieg)*. Trans. John Willett and Ralph Manheim. New York: Penguin, 2007.
Christian, Mervyn, Octave Safari, Paul Ramazani, Gilbert Burnham, and Nancy Glass. "Sexual and Gender Based Violence against Men in the Democratic Republic of Congo: Effects on Survivors, Their Families and the Community." *Medicine, Conflict and Survival* 27.4 (2011): 227–246.
Cooper, Christine M. "Worrying about Vaginas: Feminism and Eve Ensler's *The Vagina Monologues*." *Signs* 32.3 (Spring 2007): 727–758.
Dawson, Gary Fisher. *Documentary Theater in the United States: An Historical Survey and Analysis of Its Content, Form, and Stagecraft*. London: Greenwood, 1999.
Deroze, Phyllisa Smith. "Staging Gender Violence in the Congo: Reading Lynn Nottage's *Ruined* as a Documentary Drama." *Documenting Gendered Violence: Representations, Collaborations, and Movements*. Ed. Lisa M. Cuklanz and Heather McIntosh. New York: Bloomsbury, 2015. 171–192.
Dolan, Jill. "*Ruined* by Lynn Nottage." *Feminist Spectator*. Princeton.edu, 16 March 2009.
Ensler, Eve. *The Vagina Monologues: The V-Day Edition*. New York: Villard, 2011.
—. *V-Day Until the Violence Stops*. Dir. Abby Epstein. Prod. Vincent Farrell. Lifetime Television. 2003.
—. See also "Letters and Stories." Swan, Susan Celia.
Ensler, Eve, and Molly Doyle. *A Memory, a Monologue, a Rant, and a Prayer*. New York: Villard, 2007.
*Fambul Tok*. Dir. Sara Terry. 2011.
Farfan, Penny, and Leslie Ferris, eds. *Contemporary Women Playwrights: Into the Twenty-first Century*. New York: Palgrave Macmillan, 2013.
— "Introduction." *Contemporary Women Playwrights: Into the Twenty-first Century*. 1–14.
Filewood, Alan. *Collective Encounters: Documentary Theatre in English*. Toronto: U of Toronto P, 1987.
Fistula Foundation. "What is Fistula?" fistulafoundation.org. San Jose, CA: 2005–2023.
Flanagin, Jake. "Ethically Sourced iPhones Are Ruining the Congo: Go See the Gorillas and Help." *Quartz*. Manhattan, New York: 6 December 2014, updated 20 January 2016.
Friedman, Sharon. "The Gendered Terrain in Contemporary Theatre of War by Women." Ed. Penny Farfan and Leslie Ferris. 115–130.
Galbraith, Mary. "Deictic Shift Theory and the Poetics of Involvement in Narrative." Ed. Judith F. Duchan, Gail A. Bruder, and Lynne E. Hewitt. *Deixis in Narrative: A Cognitive Science Perspective*. Hillsdale, NJ: Lawrence Erlbaum, 1995. 19–60.
Gettleman, Jeffrey, and Marcus Bleasdale. "The Price of Precious Metals: Conflict Minerals." *National Geographic* 224.4. 125th Anniversary Collector's Edition (October 2013): 38–42, 46–47, 50, 52, 54–58, 60–61.

Hammers, Michele L. "Talking about 'Down There': The Politics of Publicizing the Female Body through *The Vagina Monologues*." *Women's Studies in Communication* 29.2 (2006): 221–243.

Janzen, Marike. "Solidarity, Human Rights, and the Poetics of Connection: Articulating Community in Bertolt Brecht's *Mother Courage and Her Children* and Lynn Nottage's *Ruined*." Ed. Edith W. Clowes and Shelly Jarrett Bromberg. *Area Studies in the Global Age: Community, Place, Identity*. DeKalb, IL: Northern Illinois UP, 2016. 159–177.

Jean-Charles, Régine Michelle. *Conflict Bodies: The Politics of Rape Representation in the Francophone Imaginary*. Columbus: Ohio State UP, 2014.

Kaplan, Abraham. "Obscenity as an Esthetic Category." *Law and Contemporary Problems* 20.4 Obscenity and the Arts (1955): 544–559.

Kaveny, Cathleen. "Be Not Afraid: *The Vagina Monologues* on Catholic Campuses." *Commonweal* 136.5 (2009): 13–18.

Laughland, Oliver. "*Vagina Monologues* Playwright: 'It Never Said a Woman Is Someone with a Vagina.'" London: theguardian.com. 16 January 2015.

"Letters and Stories." *The Vagina Monologues: The V-Day Edition*. New York: Villard, 1998, Rev. ed. 2001 (for December 2000). 144–171.

Los Alamos National Laboratory (LANL.gov). *Periodic table of elements: LANL*. "Tantalum [73]." Washington, DC: U. S. Department of Energy (energy.gov), 2021.

Marklein, Mary Beth. "*Vagina Monologues* Becoming College Phenomenon." *USA Today*. 2 March 2004.

"Modern Drama I" (Regular Session). The South Atlantic Modern Language Association Conference. Research Triangle Park, NC. 11 November 2015.

Nottage, Lynn. *Ruined*. New York: Dramatists Play Service, 2010.

Olopade, Dayo. "The Root Interview: Lynn Nottage on 'Ruined' Beauty." *The Root* (theroot.com). 1 March 2010.

Olsen, Christopher. "Performative Body Language in Suzan-Lori Parks's *Venus* and Lynn Nottage's *Ruined*: African Female Bodies Through African American Eyes." Ed. Benita Brown, Dannabang Kuwabong, and Christopher Olsen. *Myth Performance in the African Diasporas: Ritual, Theatre, and Dance*. Lanham, MD: Scarecrow P, 2014. 71–88.

Ozieblo, Barbara. "'Pornography of Violence': Strategies of Representation in Plays by Naomi Wallace, Stefanie Zadravec, and Lynn Nottage." *Journal of American Drama and Theatre* 23.1 (2011): 67–79.

Pacheco, Patrick. "Lynn Nottage Always Points a Provocative Pen." *Los Angeles Times*. 19 April 2009.

Rajan, Rajeswari Sunder. *Real and Imagined Women: Gender, Culture and Postcolonialism*. London: Routledge, 1993.

Reiser, Alyssa. "Our Vaginas, Not Ourselves: A Critical Analysis of *The Vagina Monologues*." *MP: An Online Feminist Journal* 1.4 Popular Culture (2006): academinist.org.

Richards, Sandra L. "Wasn't Brecht an African Writer?" *Brecht in Asia and Africa: The Brecht Yearbook* 14 (1989): 168–183.

Ronson, Jon. *So You've Been Publicly Shamed*. New York: Riverhead Books, 2015.

Sanchez-Palencia, Carolina, and Eva Gil. "'She'd Make a Splendid Freak': Female Bodies on the American Stage." *Revista de Estudios Norteamericanos* 16 (2012): 141–156.

Scott, Shelly. "Been There, Done That: Paving the Way for *The Vagina Monologues*." *Modern Drama* 46.3 (Fall 2003): 404–423.

Sivakumaran, Sandesh. "Lost in Translation: UN Responses to Sexual Violence against Men and Boys in Situations of Armed Conflict." *International Review of the Red Cross* 92.877 Women (2010): 259–277.

—. "Sexual Violence against Men in Armed Conflict." *European Journal of International Law* 18.2 (2007): 253–276.

Storr, Will. "The Rape of Men: The Darkest Secret of War." London: theguardian.com, 16 July 2011.

Striff, Erin. "Realism and Realpolitik in Eve Ensler's *The Vagina Monologues*." *Journal of Dance and Theatre* 17.2 (2005): 71–85.

Swan, Susan Celia, and Eve Ensler. *#Rise4Revolution: ({V-Day}) [sic]: 2016 Annual Report*. San Francisco: vday.org, 2017. A 68-page pamphlet printing; also in digital viewer format at Joomag.com.

Winsor, Morgan. "Congo's Conflict Minerals: US Companies Struggle to Trace Tantalum, Tungsten, Tin, Gold in Their Products." *International Business Times*. New York: IBT Media, 18 September 2015.

Yoder, Carolyn. "Cycles of Violence [pdf]." *Strategies for Trauma Awareness and Resilience [STAR] Program*. Center for Justice and Peacebuilding. Harrisonburg, VA: EMU, 2021.

Zucconi, Mike, and Chris Yoder. "EMU Joins 14 Other Higher-Ed Institutions as a Conflict-Free Campus." Harrisonburg, VA: EMU. 23 April 2013.

# ❦ 5 ❧
# Kinship in Translation
## Colette's Animals and Divine Interconnection

### Lowry Martin

The French writer known as "Colette" to the global reading public, was an influential, controversial, and contradictory figure, as well as one of France's most prolific, innovative, and accomplished authors. This chapter turns to the substance and significance of a body of Colette's work that has attracted relatively little critical attention, namely, her fiction and sketches that treat animals as thinking, feeling participants in the world and her descriptions of the natural world.[1] Colette's skill with these themes is evident in her first four novels, all ghostwritten under her husband's authorship between 1900 and 1903, and in 1904, as she was ghostwriting *Minne*, her fifth novel, Colette was busy creating dialogues between two emotionally nuanced, anthropomorphized animal protagonists of her own invention. Her sympathetic representations of animals' personalities and perspectives and her nature writing also validate Colette's lifelong insistence that she was happiest in the countryside and in the company of animals. The body of her work most closely aligned with that sentiment has significant value, not only for Colettian criticism but also as an element of her literary biography. Though the material has not been systematically examined to those ends, biographers have noted Colette's interactions with nature and her love of animals, along with her writing "landscapes" in her early career to help support herself. This chapter argues that for Colette, natural surroundings and animals were a source of spiritual delight, kinship, and strength. They provided her with peace, interest, community, and inspiration in times of crisis and became essential to developing her career and giving her creative, personal, and financial autonomy.[2]

## A Provincial Child of Nature and the Claudines

Sidonie-Gabrielle Colette, called Gabri by her family, was born in France in 1873 in the village of Saint-Sauveur-en-Puisaye in Bourgogne (Burgundy) as the youngest child of Adèle Eugénie Sidonie Landoy, known as Sido, and Jules Joseph Colette.[3] Under the guidance of Sido and a local herbalist called La Varenne, and in the company of her older brothers, Achille and Léo, Gabri became intimate with the plant and animal life of her mother's garden and the nearby waterways, woods, and hills. Achille was Gabri's rival for their mother's attention and approval and also Gabri's model and teacher. His love of nature and animals mirrored—perhaps surpassed—their mother's, and Colette described Achille as "'lov[ing] plants more than human beings and animals more than plants.'" Achille, like their mother, emphasized to Gabri the principle of close, sustained observation of nature and animals, and he and Sido indelibly and irreversibly shaped Gabri's habits and view of the world.[4] She grew to adulthood in a highly literate household with her freethinking, anti-establishment mother, her disabled war-hero father, her older siblings, a beloved cook, a few servants, and a series of pets. The family valued books, individuality, writing, music, poetry, and scientific methods. Gabri developed verbal ease and musical accomplishment, attended the secular village school, and asked to receive her First Communion. She won her classmates' respect for her ability to write quickly and well, and she was asked to perform public readings. On several occasions, her father's publishing aspirations took Gabri to Paris where they made connections with Henry "Willy" Gauthier de Villars, the wayward elder son of a Paris publisher, and Gabri was soon smitten with him.

On May 15, 1893, Willy and Gabri married at her parents' home, and as Colette, she soon settled into Belle Époque Paris with her village dresses, provincial dialect, and floor-length braids. Willy's womanizing continued following their marriage, and though Colette made her opposition evident, she decided to adapt herself to the situation with grace. Nonetheless, about a year into the marriage, she fell ill with abdominal swelling, pain, and high fever, symptoms of an infection that those around her evidently traced to Willy's philandering; moreover, when the doctor, a specialist in venereal diseases, saw that events might go in either direction, he called Sido to Paris.[5] Sido arrived and nursed her daughter in what Thurman calls a state of "silent fury" directed toward Willy (76). Colette rallied, but symptoms persisted into the following spring, and the doctor urged "a change of air" in June 1895, sending Colette to the eastern coast of Belle-Île, off the coast of Brittany, for two months. At Belle-Île, Colette saw the sea for the first time, immersed herself in it, and explored the beaches for sea creatures. Soon after Colette and Willy returned to Paris, he urged—or demanded—that Colette compose what would become the first of the Claudines, a series of "love" novels published with Willy as author.[6]

Colette obediently filled lined copybooks with narrative embroidered with the spicy elements Willy required, but her work lay unpublished for its supposed lack of marketability. About five years later, however, Willy, claiming authorship, published it as *Claudine à l'école*, and when sales were slow, he resorted to promoting it with reviewers. Willy coiffed and costumed Colette as the schoolgirl character Claudine and paraded her around Paris, sometimes in company with Colette's *Doppelgänger*, the actress Polaire, attired as Claudine for her stage role. Willy franchised products and promoted events using Colette's schoolgirl image, always gesturing toward her as the "real" Claudine of his rapidly evolving project.

## Creating Claudine as a Nature Lover

Under Willy's demands, Colette had used the blank pages of her writing notebooks to find a voice, and she developed her protagonist Claudine as an enemy to the artifice, etiquette, and snobbery of elite Belle Époque society, first associated in Colette's experience with the Villars, who strongly disdained their connection with Sido and Jules Colette's family. Colette suggests an awareness of her license as ghost-author in the opening of *Claudine à l'école*, where Claudine breaks off reading from her *Manual of Departmental Geography* to critique its entry for "Montigny-en-Fresnois"—the novel's alter-toponym for Saint-Sauveur-en-Puisaye. She pens "a loving and meticulous description of the landscape and natural beauty"[7] of Saint-Sauveur:

> Le charme, le délice de ce pays fait de collines et de vallées si étroites que quelques-unes sont des ravins, c'est les bois, les bois profonds et envahisseurs, qui moutonnent et ondulent jusque là-bas, aussi loin qu'on peut voir .... Des prés verts les trouent par places, de petites cultures aussi, pas grand'chose, les bois superbes dévorant tout. [....¶] Chers bois! Je le connais tous; je les ai battus si souvent. Il y a les bois-taillis [...] ceux-là sont pleins de soleil, de fraises, de muguet, et aussi de serpents. (2)

[The charm, the delight of this countryside, composed of hills and valleys so narrow that some are ravines, lies in its woods—the deep, encroaching woods that ripple and wave away into the distance as far as you can see.... Green meadows make rifts in them here and there, so do little plots of cultivation. But these do not amount to much, for the magnificent woods devour everything....) Dear woods! I know them all; I've scoured them so often. There are the copses... full of sun and strawberries and lilies-of-the-valley; they are also full of snakes.][8]

Claudine imparts the natural world's sensuous diversity and spiritual magnetism in the faces of delicate flowers, the promise of sweet berries, and her familiar woods, celebrating equally the branches "qui vous agrippent méchamment la figure au passage" [that cruelly grasp at the passer-by's face], "ces atroces petits corps lisses et froids" [the dreadful, smooth, cold little (snake) bodies] that cross one's path, "chenilles veloutées" [velvety caterpillars], and "araignées des bruyères, si jolies, rondes et roses comme des perles" [heather spiders, so pretty, round and pink as pearls] among the foliage.[9] Like Colette, Claudine, curious and fearless, stands in awe of nature in all its guises, despising pretension and socialized femininity. In the description are notes of pride and yearning, and in Claudine's burst of impatience with those who are fearful of nature or bored by it, the passage speaks to Colette's deep love of her native place.

In 1901's *Claudine à Paris*, Claudine confesses "une passion imprévue" [an unexpected passion] (124) for Francis Jammes, a popular provincial poet and storyteller of village life, nature, and religious feeling. Claudine is smitten upon realizing "ce poète saugrenu comprend la campagne, les bêtes, les jardins démodés et la gravité des petites choses stupides de la vie" [this absurd poet understands the country, animals, old fashioned gardens, and the seriousness of all life's small stupidities]. These are the things Colette understands and reverences most deeply, but Claudine's mockery has an extra hint of irony because the "absurd" Jammes is just the kind of fellow with whom Claudine—and Colette—imagined a spiritual kinship.

In 1904, Colette continued to be engaged in writing Willy's love novels, but she was composing her first "animal book"—*Dialogues de bêtes*—and she began corresponding with Jammes. The Bibliothèque Nationale's *Bulletin mensuel* of "recent publications" for September–October 1904 announced *Dialogues des bêtes* by Colette Willy, the name Colette chose for herself, and the November issue included an entry for *Minne* with Willy as its author. Colette was again disappointed when Willy refused her authorship—*de mon nom*—for *Les*

*Égarements de Minne* in 1905, but she continued writing for him. In 1906, she finished the final Claudine, *La Retraite sentimentale*, setting it at her much-loved Les Monts-Bouccons.[10] She executed the printer's fair copy before making a "retirement" of her own, moving from the apartment she and Willy shared on the rue de Courcelles to a ground-floor flat at the rue de Villejuste in November.[11] She writes in *Mes apprentissages*, "C'est là que j'ai affronté les premières heures d'une vie nouvelle, entre la chatte et le chien" [It's there that I faced the first hours of a new life, between the cat and the dog].[12] When *La Retraite sentimentale* was released in February 1907, its authorship was given as "Colette et Willy."[13]

The novel's nature passages drew on Colette's memories of her recuperation at Belle-Île, catching biographer Thurman's attention. Thurman writes that at Belle-Île, Colette had "been restored to her element—nature," and had found "an ally and a backdrop" in the landscape and sea that allowed her to "reclai[m] her power" and the "physical eloquence" that had been "stifled in the salons of Paris" (80). In *Mes apprentissages*, in a frequently quoted passage that refers to 1904, Colette describes finding an ally in her native values and instincts: "Je m'éveillais vaguement à un devoir envers moi-même, celui d'écrire autre chose que les Claudine. Et goutte à goutte, j'exsudais les *Dialogues de bêtes*, où je me donnais le plaisir, non point vif, mais honorable [. . .], de ne pas parler de l'amour" [I was vaguely awakening to a duty to myself, that of writing something other than the Claudines. And drop by drop, I eked out the *Dialogues de bêtes*, where I gave myself the pleasure, not lively, but more honorable . . . of not speaking of love].[14]

## Composing the *Dialogues de bêtes*

To say that Colette "did not speak of love" in *Dialogues de bêtes* is inexact because it is clearly a work of love about love, and Colette dedicates her first little sextodecimo book of four dialogues to Willy.[15] Engaging in some gender bending and blending, she presents two male household pets as protagonists: Toby-chien, an affectionate, sensitive little French bulldog, and Kiki-la-doucette, a self-centered, less-than-kind Chartreuse cat are Colette's and Willy's respective alter-egos.[16] Toby-Chien is faithful, self-deprecating, inclined to romanticize, and attached to his mistress, Elle [She], while Kiki-la-doucette is narcissistic, aloof, "cruel," and faithless. Kiki tolerates Elle but prefers Lui [Him]. Toby and Kiki's conversations express Colette's yearning for the kind of companionable married life that she had not known, and her appeal is sufficiently transparent that Thurman affirms Colette "opened her heart" to Willy in the *Dialogues* (144). Moreover, editor Françoise Burgaud finds that Colette's animal protagonists serve an existential function: "faire passer des vérités qu'à ce moment de sa vie Colette ne pouvait exprimer ouvertement, et de rêver une vie qui n'était pas la sienne" [to convey truths at this point in her life that Colette could not openly express, and to dream of a life that was not her own] (1.805). Colette's protagonists incarnate her shifting affective landscape, and for readers familiar with Colette's biography, Toby and Kiki hold a mirror to the Villar's eroding marriage, locating an undercurrent of emotional sado-masochism in Colette and Willy's lopsided relationship.

Following the publication of the four *Dialogues* in 1904, Colette published two further animal-protagonist pieces in Paris journals that year and completed a third new dialogue. These three dialogues were combined with the original four and published as *Sept Dialogues de bêtes*. Jammes' Préface to *Sept Dialogues* appeared in the *Mercure de France* (literary magazine) in March 1905, two months before *Sept Dialogues de bêtes*, with Jammes' Préface heralded on its cover, was published by the Mercure de France press in May. Jammes declared Colette a great poetess and defended her from the injustice of a personal slander, professing a grasp of what the French public had missed: Colette is not only a woman of the country, a knowledgeable housewife, engaged in ordinary pursuits, but is also "un vrai poète" [a true poet], with a profound affinity with nature and all its creatures (11).[17] "Mme Colette Willy est une femme vivante," Jammes wrote, "une femme pour tout de bon, qui a osé être naturelle et qui ressemble beaucoup plus à une petite mariée villageoise qu'à une littératrice perverse [(She) is a living woman . . . an earnest woman who's dared to be herself, and who looks much more like a little village bride than a perverse woman writer] (15). Colette considered Jammes' luminous superlatives and passionate defense to have set her on the path to redemption.

## Reading *Dialogues de bêtes*

Beyond the voices of Toby and Kiki—and the occasional comments of Elle and Lui, in "Le Voyage," for example—a distinct quality in Toby's voice ventriloquizes Colette's intense yearning to find ordinary domesticity.[18] In this evocative passage from "Le premier feu," Toby philosophizes on returning home after an afternoon outdoors:

Mais quelle ivresse quand ses capricieux pieds de bois retourneront vers la Maison, pressés de retrouver Lui qui gratte le papier, trop lents à mon gré. Je l'environnerai de bonds et de cris, vibrant de voir diminuer le coteau et raccourcir la pente, de sentir l'admirable odeur d'écurie et de bois brûlé qui rapproche de nous le gîte. (128–129)

[But what intoxication, when her capricious wooden feet turn toward the House, hurrying to find He who is scratching on the paper, (hurrying) too slowly for my liking. I will surround her with cheers and cries, quaking to see the hill diminish and the slope lessen, to smell the admirable smell of stables and burnt wood that brings the cottage closer to us].

Toby is joyfully bound for the homely pleasures and comforts of provincial life, with its familiar house and country odors. These elements are more than a break from Parisian urbanity; they are a delight and a refuge.

Where Toby anticipates ordinary comforts and revels in them, Kiki expresses his disdain for such simplicity. In the opening dialogue ("Sentimentalités"), Toby accepts Kiki's insult—"Et tu lèches la main qui te frappe" [You lick the hand that strikes you] (34), with a conciliatory response, "Oui, c'est tout à fait comme tu dis. C'est une jolie expression" [Yes, it's just as you say. That's a pretty expression]. But Kiki is dissatisfied with the soft landing his insult has had and persists, professing shame on Toby's behalf to see Toby's lack of self-respect: "Tu aimes tout le monde, tu accueilles d'un derrière plat toutes les rebuffades, ton cœur est avenant et banal comme un jardin public" [You love everyone, you greet all rebuffs without resistance; your heart is as welcoming and common as a public park] (35). In "Elle est malade," Kiki dismissively cuts off Toby's poetic description of running with Elle and her horse, telling Toby, "Tu es le dernier des romantiques" [You're the last of the romantics.] (106). Further on in the conversation, Toby charges Kiki with being amused by frightening others—"[C]ette vanité qui consiste à exagérer une cruauté très réelle" [this self-indulgence of exaggerating (is) extremely cruel]—and recalling Kiki's earlier insult, poses a rhetorical question: Is Kiki not "le premier des sadiques?" [the leading sadist] (111–112). Ironically, Toby is freer and more worldly than Kiki in spite of Toby's inclination to romanticize and Kiki's to be cynical.

When Elle and Toby return from an outing that has included stopping in at a shop in "Une Visite," Kiki asks, "C'est gai, un magasin?" [Is a shop fun?], and Toby describes the experience:

> Il y a beaucoup de gens pressés les uns contre les autres. [...] Des pieds inconnus me poussent, me froissent, écrasent mes pattes. Je crie, d'une voix qu'étouffent les jupes ... Quand nous sortons de là, nous avons l'air, Elle et moi, de deux naufragés ... [.]" (163–164)
>
> [The are many people jammed against one another. . . . Unknown feet press against me, squeeze me, crush my paws. I cry out in a voice suffocated by skirts. . . . When we get away from there, we look, She and I, like a pair of castaways . . . .]

Toby's suffering is not over, for he later recalls a portion of their walk home when he corrects their visitor's notion that the country is all lovely sand, green lawns, and milk: "Non. C'est la route en farine blanche qui cuit les paupières et brûle les pattes" [No. There's the white flour road that bakes the eyelids and burns the paws] (175). Toby has encountered discomfort that Elle "in wooden shoes" could not be expected to think of—yet Colette gives close attention to Toby's perception of the hot, sandy road.

Kiki and Toby's dialogues become lyrical as they observe the surreal light and troubling silence brought on by an impending storm in "L'Orage" and settle in to enjoy the peace and custom of a friendly autumn fire on the hearth in "Le premier feu." There is poetry in the sense of liberty one feels in the country in "Elle est malade" and in the fragrant smoke that slips under the door (la fumée *odorante qui glisse sous la porte!*) in "Diner est retard" and in the anticipation of an unknown caller in "Une Visite." Colette's ability to capture the mundane beauty, grace, and ironies of everyday life arguably finds its most authentic expression in the *Dialogues*. They inscribe Colette's life-long affection for animals and the French countryside in her works, a sentiment that resonated with the contemporary public, too, in tropes of bucolic tranquility and the private sphere held dear by the bourgeoisie of the Belle Époque. The beauty and grace of rural France with its changing seasons, traditional customs, familiar domestic pets and farm animals, and comforts that signify homely pleasures could hardly have failed to appeal in the early years of the new century. Despite the popularity of vastly different competing literary styles such as modernism and surrealism, interest in and readership of Colette's animal dialogues and later animal narratives increased and broadened through the years of wars and post-wars. Her stories, dialogues, sketches, and book projects treating nature and animals, both for themselves and in relation to humans, continue, even now, to appeal to readers and bibliophiles. Colette's locating nature and its creatures at the center of her cosmology and affective economy and her frequent emphasis on human capacity to understand and partake in animals' phenomenological experiences set Colette apart among France's writers and thinkers.[19]

## Between the *Dialogues*

Although the content of *Dialogues de bêtes* and Jammes' preface may have worked to displace earlier impressions of Colette, she would remain a controversial figure for years to come as she worked in music halls to earn a living. One particular "dialogue" with reference to a watershed moment in Colette's life and career forged a direct connection with Toby-Chien as Colette's canine alter-ego.

During the final years of her marriage, Colette learned pantomime as a way of supporting herself, and in January 1907 at Le Moulin Rouge, Colette (as a beautiful, revived mummy) and Mathilde "Missy" de Morny (as a male archeologist) engaged in a romantic kiss that signaled a pre-arranged riot in the theater. The disturbance, organized by Missy's relations, directed its mayhem chiefly at her and the Moulin Rouge, and Colette soon commented on the uproar in the press.[20] Her character "Toby-Chien" mounted Colette's public defense in a new dialogue, *Toby-Chien parle* [Toby-dog speaks], printed in *La Vie parisienne* of April 27, 1907, where Toby argues that his mistress only wants to be free to live as she pleases.[21]

Colette lived, generally, as she liked until the Great War intervened. Following her divorce from Willy in 1910 and her separation from Missy in 1912, Colette married Henri "Sidi" de Jouvenel that December, and delivered their daughter, named for Colette, in July 1913. In 1914, Sidi left for Verdun, and Colette chose to nurse the wounded in Paris and at the front and served as a war correspondent for several Paris journals. American expatriate, Stuart Merrill, living in Versailles, noted Colette's war work and public reputation in a July 1915 letter to his mother in New York:

> [Y]our last letter contained an excellent suggestion, which was to read to the blind soldiers. But they are all gathered in one hospital in Paris. I didn't send you a beautiful article written on them by a very bad woman, Colette Willy. It was too heartrending. Isn't it quite characteristic of Paris that, hissed off the stage some years ago for her outrageously immoral conduct, she should have become a wonderful writer and one of the best nurses in the Paris hospital?[22]

Merrill's sympathetic musing and superlatives imply that Colette's negative public reception may have been ameliorated early in the war by her war work, and he suggests other elements of her public reputation: the reading public's long memory of her missteps, the general (mis)conceptions about the Moulin Rouge incident, knowledge of Colette's nursing and journalism beyond Paris, and a perceived irony between Colette's peacetime and wartime conduct, giving greater weight to the latter. Her wartime stories and sketches, as Merrill writes, may be "beautiful"—even "heartrending"—as those discussed below affirm.

## Colette's War and Its Dogs

In her dispatches from the front, some collected among the forty-two sketches and stories in *Les Heures longues (1914–1917)*, Colette's tone is generally optimistic and her descriptions are often beautifully poetic despite the grim events she witnessed.[23] In "Jour de l'An en Argonne" [New Year's Day in Argonne], she records an aphoristic observation shared with her in 1914: "Il n'y a pas, me disait un Grec au mois d'août dernier, d'état auquel on s'habitue aussi vite que l'état de guerre. [There's is no state, (as) a Greek was saying to me last August, that one gets used to so quickly as a state of war] (54).[24] Colette attests to the surface adaptability of those around her in Argonne, where exigent circumstances and war's proximity quickly put the quietus on peacetime custom and comfort.[25]

Marguerite Moreno, Colette's long-time friend, remarked Colette's dispassionate demeanor as she watched Sidi leave for Verdun and probable death. Colette, ever a stoic in response to adversity, wrote in *Les Heures longues* an observation derived from her nursing the wounded: "La plupart de ces jeunes Français, échappés à la mort au prix d'un membre, guérissent, verdoient comme un arbre ébranché" [The majority of these young Frenchmen, escaping death at the price of an arm or leg, heal, bloom(ing) like a tree where a limb was lopped off].[26] But when Sidi, "in the thick of the fighting" at Verdun, complained of not getting her letters, Colette understood. "Mon amour, [. . . .]," she wrote, "Nous sommes de pauvres animaux" [My love, . . . . We're nothing but poor beasts].[27] Human and creature suffered the war together, and the "four-legged" *poilus* [French soldiers] represented in Colette's journalism and fiction express that shared experience of war.

In "Chiens sanitaires" [Rescue dogs/Ambulance dogs], Colette recalls her observations of Turco, a new member of the canine corps who, during his training exercises, carries what he regards as a real message to headquarters. Turco and his fellow canine apprentices are earnest and avid to serve, and Colette calls him "notre agent de liaison" [our liaison agent] (*HL* 92).[28] Colette observes that Turco and his "Lieutenant" seem fashioned from the same cloth: "Drap bleu-gris, et poil gris-bleu, silencieux, agiles, ils sont déjà couleur d'horizon, couleur de l'ombre azurée des haies, couleur de l'argile bleuâtre des tranchées" [Blue-gray cloth saddle, and gray-blue coat, quiet, agile, they are already the color of the horizon, the color of the azure shadow of the hedges, the color of the bluish clay of the trenches] (96). Colette conflates man and dog as a single, lovely, silent, unit—"un beau couple de chasseurs" [a beautiful pair of hunters]— attired in nature's blues and grays, moving together into the distance.

In Colette's sketch of Pick, also in "Chiens Sanitaires," she again emphasizes the bond of community between the *poilus* and service dogs. Pick is among the rescue dogs risking everything at the front to save the *poilus*:

> Chiens, nos compagnons dans la guerre et dans la paix[;] chiens, de qui la confiance humaine exige et reçoit tout[;] chiens, c'est pour notre édification que je veux dire le beau destin de Pick, chien sanitaire fameux. Il servit son pays et ses frères soldats, et mourut glorieusement, le flanc percé d'une balle allemande. (96–97).
>
> [Dogs, our companions in war and in peace; dogs, from whom human trust demands and receives everything; dogs, it is for our edification that I want to tell the beautiful destiny of Pick, the famous rescue dog. He served his country and his brothers in arms, and died gloriously, his side pierced by a German bullet.]

In this encomium, Colette anthropomorphizes Pick and his fellows as *poilus*, capable of courage, loyalty, and self-sacrifice. In the close of "Chiens sanitaires," Colette describes a fox terrier in Pick's unit (97). The terrier saved one-hundred-and-fifty wounded soldiers at the Battle of the Marne, but eventually got lost behind enemy lines. He returned to camp wounded and was rehabilitated. Colette recounts the little terrier's joy at returning to his brothers in arms at the front at Les Vosges, emphasizing not only his bravery, but also his unwavering loyalty to the French cause.

Colette reminds her readers that France's war-service dogs came from herding breeds like the Bouvier des Flandres, the Briard or Berger de Brie, the Beauceron, also known as Bas Rouge or Berger de Beauce, with his "red stockings," and, of course, the "impatient" (*intolérant*) and fiercely determined little fox terrier (95–96). To a beleaguered French public, weary of war and dismayed at reports of despairing soldiers deserting the historic carnage and horrors of trench warfare, Colette's stalwart canines are inspiring and touching exemplars of bravery and resilience—little soldiers fiercely devoted to duty and to the humans they serve. Colette grounds her war reporting—like the fiction I will shortly address—in the language and values of contemporary French popular culture, lending her narratives to France's collective memory of the war.

### "La Chienne" ("The Bitch")

Vorace, the story's titular protagonist, is a female *chienne briarde*, a sheep-country herder and guard dog with thick, gray-blue fur. She has not been to war, but was left behind by it to suffer the absence of the "Sergeant," the story's human protagonist.[29] The Sergeant returns to Paris on leave, goes home to make himself presentable, and proceeds to the home of Jeannine to whom he has entrusted Vorace (*HL* 218). Though the sergeant finds Jeannine away and only the housekeeper, Lucie, at home, Vorace provides a jubilant, affectionate reception that makes Jeannine's absence increasingly suggestive: "Mais il fut quand même accueilli par des cris, chevrotants de surprise et de joie, étreint, mouillé de baisers: Vorace, sa chienne de berger, la chienne qu'il avait confiée à sa jeune amie, l'enveloppa comme une flamme, et le lécha d'une langue pâlie par l'émotion" [But all the same, he was greeted with trembling cries of surprise and joy, embraced, and wet(ted) with kisses: Vorace, his female shepherd, the dog he had entrusted to his young friend, enveloped him like a flame, and licked him with a tongue pale with emotion] (*HL* 218).

Colette ratchets up the narrative tension with Lucie's excited, voluble explanation of Jeannine's absence. Lucie gives rapid, facile, and then stumbling pretexts, claiming that Jeannine has had to go away for two days to inventory furniture in her country house, but, Lucie observes, "Heureusement que ce n'est pas au bout du monde" [Fortunately, it's not at the end of the world], and should the Sergeant write out a telegram, Jeannine could arrive home the following morning (218–219). Lucie insists that the Sergeant stay for the night and asks whether she should turn on the water heater for his bath although he has—clearly enough—already bathed. The Sergeant notices Vorace responding to his call with a loving look (*un regard d'amour*) and thinks of Jeannine, who is "un peu trop jeune, souvent trop gaie" [a little too young, often too cheerful] (219)—adding a further doubt concerning Jeannine. With quickly sketched contrasts between presence and absence, openness and subterfuge, and loyalty and indifference, Colette develops character and events around the negative space of the missing mistress.

At dinner, the Sergeant and Vorace resume an old routine with her patiently waiting for tidbits from his plate and responding to his words in the language of barks. Afterward, they settle in for a quiet evening, with Vorace lying at the Sergeant's feet as he smokes and reads the paper (219–220). Vorace keeps vigil as the Sergeant contemplates a snapshot of Jeannine wearing a summer outfit in the countryside and notices its date, June 5, 1916—in an unfamiliar hand—a day he recalls having been at the front at Arras. The incongruities the Sergeant encounters and the carelessness implied in the photo's being in plain sight fail to impress the war-weary man, and he falls asleep before the hearth as Vorace, obediently remaining in place, continues to observe him.

As the clock strikes ten, the dog insists on going outside, and the Sergeant accedes (221). At first, Vorace behaves as if she is merely happy to be out with the Sergeant, who plays with her, his head filled with thoughts of seeing Jeannine and the seven days of his leave they will spend together. Soon though, the Sergeant lags behind as Vorace takes them toward the less populated outskirts, and, well ahead, she waits for him to catch up before turning down a lane at a brisk trot, obviously intent on a particular destination (222). Vorace's determined behavior heightens the Sergeant's anxiety, and he quickens his pace as Vorace, "joyeuse . . . le précéda, en bon guide" [joyful . . . goes ahead of him like a good guide], and he orders her forward from time to time (222). The distinction between Vorace's knowledge and the Sergeant's more worldly perspectives become increasingly differentiated as the Sergeant takes command.

Vorace stops before a house created for a lover's betrayal: "une maisonnette basse, chargée de vigne et de bignonier, une petite maison peureuse et voilée" [a little, low house laden with vines and scarlet jasmine, a small, fearful, veiled house], and she announces, "Voilà, on est arrivé." [Here we are, we've arrived] (223).[30] As the Sergeant hesitates before gate, Vorace urges him, "Eh bien, ouvre donc" ["Well, open it then"]. The Sergeant moves to open the latch but lets his hand fall when he notices "[. . .] un fil de lumière au long de volets clos" [a thread of light along the rim of shuttered windows] (223). Fragments of doubt gathered through the evening assume a vague shape of betrayal, and instead of passing through the gate, the Sergeant asks his guide for confirmation, "Qui est là? . . . Jeannine?" [Who's there? . . . Jeannine?]. Vorace's answering bark assures the Sergeant that she has guided him to his heart's desire.

Following this climactic exchange, the Sergeant takes hold of Vorace's collar, and they withdraw to the opposite side of the lane to stare at the house with its "fil de lumière rosée" [thread of rose-colored light] along the shuttered margins. Suddenly feeling quite alone and weak (*singulièrement seul, et falible*), the Sergeant whispers to Vorace, "Tu m'aimes?" [Do you love me?] (224). Vorace licks his cheek in affirmation, and the Sergeant commands, "Viens, on s'en va" [Come, let's go]. The Sergeant withdraws definitively from whatever skirmish might have ensued between the lovers, and—to paraphrase Colette's description of abandoning the field of the "domestic hearth" in 1906—he takes the first steps of a new life with only his dog for company.

They return to the house, where the Sergeant begins repacking his rucksack, by which Vorace understands that he is again leaving without her. She is obedient, vigilant, and anxious: "[r]espectueuse et désespérée, elle sui[t] tous ses mouvements, et des larmes trembl[ent], couleur d'or, sur ses yeux jaunes" [respectful and desperate, she follows his every move, and tears the color of gold quiver in her yellow eyes] (224). Seeing her distress, the Sergeant takes her by the neck and whispers to her, "Tu pars aussi. Tu ne me quitteras plus. [. . . .] tu ne dois pas rester ici" [You're leaving also. . . . You will not be without me again . . . . You mustn't stay here]. Musing aloud, he considers what entrusting Vorace to Jeannine has meant: "[T]on âme n'est pas faite pour d'autres secrets que les miens . . . " [Your soul was not made for secrets other than mine], and the Sergeant whispers, "[T]on âme . . . ton âme de chienne . . . ta belle âme" [Your soul . . . your dog's soul . . . your beautiful soul]. Colette repeats "soul" four times in her final two sentences, emphasizing the Sergeant's realization—and Colette's conviction—that dogs share human attributes, but in purer form than humans are generally capable of. "La Chienne" juxtaposes the hazards of love in wartime and the enamored soldier's vulnerability with Vorace's unadulterated adoration and her determined effort to act as "a good guide."[31]

## "Celle qui en revient" ("The One who Came Back")

Canine constancy toward beloved humans is a trope Colette validates repeatedly in her war-dog stories, and it is foundational to "Celle qui en revient," a dialogue featuring three animal characters living together in a peaceful town (*Œuvres* 2.59).[32] Its protagonist is a nameless "chienne de berger, briarde osseuse" [a female herding dog, a bony Briard] that the story refers to only as "La Bergère" [the Shepherd]. She is a traumatized veteran of trench warfare and a former prisoner of war thrust into peacetime culture. Shepherd, as her soldier calls her, is literally *poilu*, her long, heavy coat making her emblematic of the Every-soldier and Every-animal of the war whose vivid memories are reenacted by ordinary events in civilian life.

Shepherd has "eyes the color of fire" and a new collar, a sign of her newly acquired civilian status, replacing "un bout de corde qu' Il avait trouvée là-bas" [a bit of rope He'd found out there] (2.59). He—her "Soldier"—has returned, too, and Shepherd remains alert to his goings and comings, while the Mistress's "La Chienne Bull" and "la Vieille Chatte" [the Bulldog and the Old Cat] pass comfortable, idle, tranquil days dedicated to inconsequential, familiar events and exchanges. When Bulldog inquires where "là-bas" may be, Shepherd responds tersely (*laconique*), "Là-bas,—d'où je reviens avec Lui . . ." [Out there,—where I came from with Him]. In contrast, Bulldog and Old Cat share a "peaceful" parlor and the fire on the hearth with Shepherd, who becomes anxious when Soldier is absent, and her sense of a door opening makes her tremble, her thoughts confused in the desperate hope that He has returned. Old Cat and Bulldog are bewildered by Shepherd who—to their observation—reacts violently and inexplicably to ordinary sounds and events.

Attempting to resolve Shepherd's anxiety with logic and their experience of the neighborhood, Old Cat and Bulldog explain that what lies beyond the door is nothing more than a staircase with an idle concierge at the landing, raucous children playing below, and water puddles in the street. Her visceral dread and terror of "out there" rising, Shepherd responds, "Mais le reste . . . " [but the rest . . .] (2.62). Unconvinced by Old Cat and Bulldog's anodyne descriptions, Shepherd insists that other things—those she most fears—must lie beyond the door: "l'ennemi . . . l'embûche . . . la balle et l'éclat de fer, et ce bruit terrible qui remue l'air et les entrailles de la terre . . ." [the enemy . . . the ambush . . . the bullet(s) and the gunfire, and that terrible noise that stirs the air and entrails of the earth]. For Old Cat and Bulldog, these are inconceivable hazards, but Shepherd's vivid memories create her psychic and neural present. Even as she names and describes the dangers she recalls—and expects to recur— Shepherd cannot explain their effects to her companions. Old Cat scolds Bulldog to leave Shepherd alone and attributes Shepherd's reactions to a state of nervousness (2.62). Old Cat and Bulldog mirror attitudes of French citizens who dismiss the war's lasting emotional and psychological effects on the *poilus*. They suggest the microcosm, as well, in domestic failures to establish a community of empathy between uninitiated civilians and returning veterans in the postwar.

The animals' discussion of Shepherd's fears precedes—and perhaps triggers—the recurring nightmare that reenacts her trauma: Shepherd dreams of a terrifying trench battle in which waves of Germans attack her soldier. When his gun fails, she kills oncoming German soldiers, slashing their necks with her fangs, but as each falls, others arrive to take up the attack. Despite the odds, Shepherd desperately lunges to kill the next attacker, crying out to Soldier, "[L]a main de celui-ci ne te frappera pas" [This one's hand will not strike you], but Shepherd and Soldier are captured, separated, and brutalized. Shepherd becomes desperate to rejoin Soldier, to die protecting him, and she awakens, howling in rage and consternation, terrifying Old Cat and Bulldog. With the moving details of Shepherd's dream, Colette paints the battlefield experience that forms the source of psychological and emotional disconnects between those who fought and those who know nothing of war at the front (2.64).

When Solider returns to the house, Old Cat and Bulldog are atremble with fright, and Shepherd is in a state of panic. Only Soldier, having lived the events alongside her, understands Shepherd's nightmare, and he reassures her, "C'est fini" [It's over] (2.64), but soothing human words and logic, even from a fellow *poilu* cannot reason with her terror, and she replies, "Ô mon Maître, pas encore. Je t'ai trop souvent perdu. Nous avons trop longtemps habité un pays où l'âme n'a pas de repos, et où le corps désespéré veille malgré lui quand défaut l'âme" [Oh master, not yet. I have lost you too often. For too long we have lived in a country where the soul finds no rest, and the desperate body keeps vigil in spite of itself when the soul is gone] (2.64). The haunting nightmares of an incomprehensible reality are not over for Shepherd, and she is filled with an illogical sense of alarm, a rapidly beating heart, and a desire to release the frightened howls she smothered in captivity. She begs Soldier's pardon:

> Aussi, pardonne-moi si pendant bien des jours je te donne à chacun de tes retours, au lieu des cris et des saluts d'allégresse qui te sont dus, ce qui m'emplit toute et déborde au moindre choc; la folle alarme, les bonds d'un cœur qui m'étouffe et tonne dans ma poitrine, la plainte contenue pendant tant d'heures écrasantes . . . [.] Pardonne-moi, l'amour que je t'ai voué, ô mon maître, n'a pas fini d'être triste . . . [.] (2.64)

> [Also, forgive me if every time you return, instead of the shouts and joyous greetings due you, I offer you the mad alarm that engulfs me and overflows at the slightest shock, the pounding of a heart that suffocates me and thunders in my chest, a wail held inside for so many

crushing hours.... Forgive me, that the love I dedicated to you, oh, my master, has not stopped being painful.]

With these details of Shepherd's inner life, Colette renders the horror, terrors, and desperation of war, with its indelible sensory effects. Shepherd and Sergeant enact the unceasing afterlife of apprehension and alarm carried from a space "where the soul found no rest" to the Peace, where normalcy, rationality, and reassurance have little effect on their shared emotional realities. Colette's war stories often illustrate the effects of what came to be known as "shell shock" and "battle fatigue" and today as post-traumatic stress disorder (PTSD), the late twentieth century's broad rubric for lingering psychological, social, and biological effects of trauma. Colette's explorations of interspecies relations, trauma, post-traumatic stress disorder, and separation anxiety are relevant to studies of trauma and anxiety among service dogs and their handlers in twenty-first-century wars.[33]

## Colette and Her Creatures

These stories and sketches assert that dogs perceive and sympathize with human peril and suffering and are themselves susceptible, not only to having their mental faculties and emotional resources scrambled by trauma but also to reliving traumatic events long after the reality. Colette's animal-focused publishing made her a theorist of animal experience in various contexts and a public advocate of humane, sympathetic treatment of and thoughtful co-existence with animals. In 1916's *La Paix chez les bêtes*, for example, she creates "un enclos où je veux qu'il n'y ait pas la guerre" [an enclosure where 'there shall be no war'] for the animals and assembles an array of creatures in the volume's sketches.[34] In one of them, Colette reports a skirmish in St. Petersburg where students in Ivan Pavlov's labs prompt their animal subjects to react to non-organic stimuli: "il s'agit simplement de faire saliver des chiens" [it's only about making dogs salivate]. She exacts an imaginative moment of *Schadenfreude* on behalf of the dogs, suggesting a "beau cauchemar" [a lovely nightmare] in which they capture Dr. Pavlov and turn the tables on him (207).

In *En Pays connu* [In a familiar country], almost thirty-five years later, Colette takes veterinarians to task in a sardonic tone when they report that dogs exhibit what appears to be an unreasoning fear unrelated to food or rabies: "Nous voilà bien aises de savoir ce que les chiens, atteints de peur, n'ont pas. Quant à ce qu'ils ont, c'est une autre affaire" [We're glad to know what dogs afflicted with fear *don't* have. What they *do* have is another matter] (189).[35] In a second *En Pays connu* sketch, Colette engages both the question of dogs' experience of fear and their perceptions beyond human ken as she muses on the behavior of her dog Belou, a Brabantine crossed with a Brussels griffon, "assez sotte, très gaie, gourmande" [quite silly, very cheerful, greedy] (190). Taken on a walk, Belou would suddenly flatten herself against the pavement (*s'aplatir brusquement*): "Toutes les pattes écartées, tremblante, elle semblait subir un passage effrayant, le contact directe de l'invisible. Au bout d'une minute, elle se relevait, se secouait dans sa peau, et repartait non sans regarder avec inquiétude, derrière elle" [All four legs askew, trembling, she seemed to undergo a frightening event, the direct contact of the invisible. After a minute, she got up, shook herself all over, and set out anew—not without looking worriedly behind her] (190). Colette also recalls "une grande bas-rouge" [a large Beauceron] likewise attuned to the invisible world:

> [Elle] recevait les appels d'un monde où j'eusse voulu, sous sa garde, pénétrer. Sourires sans objet, faibles battements de la queue, félicité contenue, elle dédiait le plus subtil d'elle-même, à des visiteurs—plutôt à un visiteur, que je n'ai jamais vu. La première inquiétude passée, je m'y habituai, ou mieux je reconnus les droits de l'hôte. S'il eût été maléfique, la chienne me l'aurait dit. (190)

> [She received calls from a world into which I wanted, under her care, to enter. Smiles that had no object, faint tail flapping, contained bliss, she dedicated the subtlest (aspects) of herself to visitors—rather to *a* visitor—whom I have never seen. With the first disturbance behind us, I became used to it, or better yet I recognized the rights of the host. If the visitor had been evil, the dog would have told me.]

In these sketches, Colette conveys her sense of transcendence in human and animal relations. It is a sense inextricably entwined with her respect and love for the natural world, where she found power, inspiration, joy, and peace.

A good number of Colette's publishing projects reflect the sense of shared community she found in nature. Among them are her commentaries in beautifully illustrated books of the 1930s such as *Paradis terrestre* in 1932 and *Splendeur des papillons* in 1936 and an illustrated compilation, *De la patte à l'aile*, in 1943. Her collections of sketches, fiction, and memoirs honoring nature and exploring animals' inner lives include *Prrou, Poucette et quelques autres* (1913), *Sido, ou les points cardinaux* (1930), *Histoires pour Bel-Gazou* (1930), and *La Chatte* (1933). Others—like *Les Heures longues, La Paix chez les bêtes,* and selections from *La Chambre éclairée* of 1920 and *Celle qui en revient suivi de quelques autres dialogues de bêtes*—evoke war's hardships and losses, along with hope for a kinder world for "hommes et les bêtes, ennemis et frères" [mankind and beasts, enemies and brothers] in the Peace (225).[36] Some of these are odes to peace and freedom, and others, like Colette's sketch based on Pavlov's experiments, suggest ethical issues, and still others suggest a tension that connects the two elements. In the *La Paix* sketch titled "Les Couleuvres" [grass, ribbon, or garter snakes], for example, Colette concludes of the snakes she's just placed on her lap, "[I]l me semble déjà qu'elles s'humanisent, et elles croient que je m'apprivose" [It seems to me they are becoming human, and they believe I am tamed].[37] Colette emblematizes the uneasy dance between humans and creatures as we negotiate cohabitation, a theoretical and ethical concern that took shape in academe decades after her death.[38] She might well have assented in these contexts to Georges Bataille's observation, made decades later, "The animal opens before me a depth that attracts me and is familiar to me" (22). She explored that attractive depth throughout her life.

Far exceeding Colette's confessed sense in 1904 of a "vague duty" to redeem herself, she became a French institution. She was awarded the Chevalier of the Légion d'honneur alongside Marcel Proust in 1920, and by 1927, Paul Claudel named Colette France's "greatest living writer." She was elected to *les Dix* (the Ten) of l'Academie Goncourt in 1944, nominated for the Nobel Prize by Claude Farrère (Frédéric-Charles Bargone) in 1948, chosen president of l'Academie Goncourt in 1949, and made a Grand Officier of the Légion d'honneur in 1953. At her death in August, 1954, the Church refused her its rites, but she was buried with state honors, the first woman in French history to be so recognized.[39]

Colette's expressing her perspectives and philosophy through other species and celebrating the natural world in her writing turns out to have been much more than wily camouflage or emotional reticence because these subjects formed her principal source of strength and offered her a kind of religious experience. Disclaiming any conventional religious system, Colette found in her interactions with animals and nature an authentic spirituality characterized by feelings of kinship, sympathy, and respect. When Jammes asked Colette to comment on a book of his poetry, *L'Église habillée de feuilles* [The Church clothed in leaves] published in 1906 following his return to Catholicism, her self-effacing refusal revealed a disinclination to take up theological matters directly.[40] She wrote, "Vous savez, je ne peux pas beaucoup vous parler de l'Église habillée de feuilles [sic], parce que je ne connais rien à Dieu, et je ne sais pas si j'y comprendrai jamais grandchose" [You know, I can't say very much to you about *l'Église habillée de feuilles* because I understand nothing of God and don't know that I'll ever understand much].[41] Even without this protest, it is clear that Colette found faith, hope, and love outside religious rites and dogma. Her lifetime of work and her choices of where and how to live attest to the spiritual peace and strength she derived from her communion with nature and its creatures. Among all things, Colette perceived an interconnectedness, a kinship of soul or spirit gesturing toward the divine, and in representing animals' emotional lives, in giving them voices, history, and rationales, Colette has no peer in French literature.

*Colette with bulldogs. Portrait attributed to Jean Reutlinger (d. August 1914, Battle of Ardennes, France).*

## Notes

1 See *Mes apprentissages* (79–81); *My Apprenticeships* (95–97). Because *Mes apprentissages* has no chapter titles or numbers and pagination is distinct between the French and English editions, page numbers for the English translation are shown at each instance.

2 Colette's work in these areas long precedes academic movements related to animals and ecology that would arise in the late twentieth century. For essays treating Colette's animal narratives, see, for example, Cathy Comfort, Juliana Schiesari, Sharon Spencer, and Martin.
3 *Sido*, *Vrilles de la vigne*, and *La maison de Claudine* are sources of Colette's autobiography in regard to her family and her life in Saint-Sauveur-en-Puisaye. Among the many biographical efforts centered on Colette, Michèle Sarde's *Colette*, Claude Francis and Fernande Gontier's *Creating Colette* (2 vols.), and Judith Thurman's *Secrets of the Flesh* present distinct, compelling perspectives on Colette's biography with extensive documentation.
4 For biographers' views of Gabri's childhood and family life, see, for example, Francis and Gontier (1.33 *ff.*), citing Colette's description of Achille in *Pour un herbier* (esp. 58–63). See also Thurman (21–29). On Gabri's personality and literary performances during her schooldays, see Francis and Gontier (1.40–43; 79–82) and Thurman (39–42). On the Gauthier-Villars connection, see Thurman (38–39). On Willy, see Francis and Gontier (1.74–78) and Thurman (44–46).
5 See Thurman (75–76; 80–81; 96–97). Colette's ailment was likely to have been gonorrhea or genital herpes, contracted from Willy. Francis and Gontier categorically declare her illness to have been syphilis (I.128–129).
6 Colette's early "love" novels include the ghostwritten novels I refer to in the opening paragraph and eventually include two series with protagonists called Claudine and Minne. The Claudines are *Claudine à l'école*, *Claudine à Paris*, *Claudine en ménage*, *Claudine s'en va*, and *La Retraite sentimentale* of 1907. The Minne novels are *Minne* and *Les Égarements de Minne*, combined and condensed in 1909 as *L'Ingénue libertine*. See Francis and Gontier (1.150–151) and Thurman (96–97).

See Google Books or Archive.org for texts of the early novels. If the date of the first English translation is sufficiently early, both texts may be fully accessible online. Where we know of no published English translation, we translate the title within brackets immediately following the French title in Works Cited. Data for published English translations is selectively embedded in the citation of the French original. See Nicole Ward Jouve on problems in Colettian bibliography and translations (219 *ff.*).
7 See Patricia A. Tilburg (178).
8 Online, see *Claudine à l'école* (1902. 1–4). Text translations given here are usually modified from published translations or are mine or the editor's, and punctuation not in the original French may be imposed for clarity. Colette frequently used em-dashes and three-point ellipses. Only bracketed ellipses in French quotations are to be read as editorially imposed gaps. Having been noted in the original, they remain open in the English translation.
9 The *Thomisus onustus* (the crab or heather spider) female may be pink.

10 The country estate Les Monts-Bouccons (Boucons) in Besançon was to be a gift from Willy to Colette, but he did not transfer the deed to her, and on December 31, 1907, her presence was required in Besançon under court order to sign its sale papers. See Francis and Gontier (1.168–169; 264, 268) and Thurman (117–118; 183).
11 See *Mes apprentissages* (125–126. *My Apprenticeships* 105–106). See also Thurman (178–182).
12 See *Mes apprentissages* (156. *My Apprenticeships* 132–133). Schiesari (40–41) misunderstands Monts-Bouccons as the "there" of this sentence.
13 The marriage ended officially in 1910, but the process of severing the Villars' emotional and professional ties lasted for decades.
14 *Mes apprentissages* (101. *My apprenticeships* 85). See Thurman on this passage (141) and Cummins on Colette's development as a writer (second and third chapters, esp. 121–123).
15 The dedication may have been a consolatory gesture to Willy, then grieving the death of Kiki-la-Doucette, Willy's real-life domestic alter ego.
16 Citations here from the early *Dialogues de bêtes* come from *Sept Dialogues'* 1909 edition translated as 1913's *Barks and Purrs* (Google Books). See n. 18 for English titles of dialogues mentioned in the text. Citations of Colette's animal-centered writing may refer to the second volume of Colette's *Œuvres* (Pichois's Pléïade edition); to *La Paix* (*La Paix chez les bêtes*); to *Creatures* (*Creatures Great and Small*); and to *Collected* (Colette's *Collected Stories* in English). Citations for *Creatures* refer to the FSG softcover edition of 1971 (second printing); hardcover editions of 1951 by Secker & Warburg (London) and FSG are less frequently available.
17 See Jammes' Préface in *Sept Dialogues* (9–17). It is also found in *Douze Dialogues* of 1930 (v–xiii), in *Œuvres* (2.3-6), and in English translations of the *Dialogues*. See Thurman's perspectives on Jammes' Préface (143–146).
18 Dialogue titles mentioned here from *Sept Dialogues* are given as follows in *Barks and Purrs*: "Sentimentalités" (Sentimentalities), "Le Voyage" (On the Train), "Diner est retard" (Dinner Is Late), "Elle est malade" (She Is Ill), "Le premier feu" (The First Fire), "L'Orage" (The Storm), and "Une Visite" (A Caller). "Toby-Chien parle" appears in 1930's *Douze Dialogues* (217–230) and in *Œuvres* (2.3–264). Its English translation appears in 1951's *Creatures* as "Toby-Dog Speaks" (105–113). Inclusive pagination for these dialogues is not carried into Works Cited.
19 See, for example, Nicole Ward Jouve (esp. 135–145).
20 See Thurman's narrative (169–173), Sarde (197–202), and Francis and Gontier (I.250–256). On Missy, see Thurman (151–153).
21 Thurman writes that "Toby-Chien parle" describes his mistress's "passionate tirade" (esp. 144). Diana Holmes describes *La Vie parisienne* as a "fashionable weekly" that was "somewhat risqué" but "prided itself on coverage of the arts" (58, 69). Holmes notes that it serialized

Colette's *La Vagabonde* and an early version of *Mitsou* in 1910 and 1917, respectively (58, 73).
22 Some punctuation is imposed. See Mylène Catel and Rosemary Lloyd's work on Merrill's letters for the original transcription. See Thurman (esp. 262–274) on Colette's wartime experiences.
23 See Catel and Lloyd (403) noting Colette's wartime articles in *Le Matin*, *Le Flambeau*, *Excelsior*, and *La Vie parisienne*.
24 Citations from *Les Heures longues* are signaled parenthetically as *HL*.
25 The nine-month Battle of Verdun in 1916 was the War's longest battle.
26 See "Renouveau" [Revival] (*LH* 18).
27 See Thurman (272–276, esp. 274).
28 I am unaware of an English translation of this story. Another of Colette's sketches, also called "Chiens sanitaires," is translated as "The Ambulance Dogs" and set at Meudon over the winter 1913–1914, with dogs called Nelly and Polo (*Creatures* 289–290).
29 See *Creatures* (115–119) and *Collected* (417–420) for "The Bitch."
30 For *bignonia* (scarlet jasmine or trumpet vine), see "*Bignonia*" in Gerth Van Wijk's 1911 edition (175b §80); note similarities among names under a., ga., ge. and n. (English-, French-, German-, and Dutch-speaking regions, respectively).
31 This short story offers an alternative reading, one in which an animal's jealous nature is underscored. While the title has a double meaning, so might this short story. Colette firmly believed that animals had and exhibited emotions similar to human emotions, and her other works offer such examples. One might interpret Vorace's motivation as jealousy. She was able to "protect" her master by revealing Jeannine's probable infidelity while simultaneously ridding herself of a rival.
32 In a little book called *Celle qui en revient suivi de quelques autres dialogues de bêtes* [She who returned along with various other animal conversations], published in 1921, the story elsewhere titled "Celle qui en revient" is called "La Chienne qui en revient" [The bitch/dog that returned]. It appears in 1930's *Douze Dialogues* as "Celle qui en revient" (3-19) and is translated as "The One who Came Back" for *Creatures* (121–130). Citations here come from *Œuvres* (2.59–64) as the most accessible of the three.
33 As Cathy Caruth points out, PTSD's definition is contested, but she affirms general agreement that this type of trauma produces delayed responses such as repetitive intrusive thoughts, dreams, or behaviors stemming from the event, along with increased sensitivity to specific stimuli (4), effects that Colette observed, experienced, and wrote about. See my article in *Lengua franca* treating this subject in the context of Colette's service dogs.
34 *La Paix*'s English translation, *Cats, Dogs, and I* (1924), is found in full at Google Books. See also *Creatures* for selections from *La Paix*. Literally translated, "où je veux qu'il n'y ait pas la guerre" reads "where I want there to be no war."

35 Rabies (*la rage*) was historically called *hydrophobia* (fear of water).
36 See *La Paix* "Conte pour les petits enfants des poilus" [A (Christmas) Tale for the Soldiers' Little Children] (221–231). See also *Creatures* (283–288).
37 See *La Paix* (159–163) or *Œuvres* (2.127–128) and the English translation in *Creatures* ("Creature Comfort" 253–255).
38 Jacques Derrida's 1997 lectures at the Cérisy Conference, published in 2008 as *The Animal That Therefore I Am*, addressed "animality" and man's position in the world of nature and non-human animal. Colette substantially and intentionally anticipated these questions, and one might re-read Colette's work in that context. Derrida also offers a catalogue of "autobiographical animals" and "animals for autobiography" that suggests an approach to reading and viewing Colette's animals (49).
39 See biographer Sarde's epilogue (425), *The New Yorker* magazine's praise of Colette in its June 1, 1935 issue (10), and the *NYT*'s August 4, 1954 obituary, "Colette Is Dead in Paris at 81." See Nobelprize.org for nomination data and Academiegoncourt.com for "Les Membres" and "Historique." On the Church's rejection, see Norell's insights and references (esp. 300–301) and Francis and Gontier (250). Editors of *Commonweal* defended Cardinal Feltin's decision, noting its "bitter" opposition; Feltin argued that religious rites are owed only to those who have "not shown by [their] attitudes that [they] have renounced the Church," leaving it "willingly and freely" (573).
40 Jammes marks his composition of *l'Église* as "après mon retour au catholicisme qui date de 1905" [after my return to Catholicism, which dates to 1905] (Jammes' *Œuvres* 2.152). See Google Books.
41 See Colette's Lettres à ses pairs (114).

**Works Cited**
Because the English titles may not be literal translations from the French, data for English translations of Colette's books are set within the French title entries and follow its data. *Barks and Purrs*, *Creatures*, and *Collected*, three translated collections of Colette's dialogues, stories and/or sketches, have separate entries corresponding to cross-references of their contents.

Burgaud, Françoise, ed. Préface. *Colette: Romans, Récits, Souvenirs (1900-1919)*. Vol. 1. Paris: Robert Laffont, 1989. i-xxxii.
Caruth, Cathy. *Trauma: Explorations in Memory*. Baltimore, MD: Johns Hopkins UP, 1995.
Catel, Mylène, and Rosemary Lloyd. "Letters of Stuart Merrill." *Nineteenth-Century French Studies* 25.3/4 (1997): 386–414.
Colette [Sidonie-Gabrielle Colette]. *La Chatte*. Paris: Grasset, 1933. *Saha the Cat*. Trans. Morris Bentinck. London: T. Werner Laurie, 1936. *The Cat*. Trans. Antonia White. New York: Popular P, 1955.
—. "La Chienne qui en revient." *Celle qui en revient: suivi de quelques autres dialogues de bêtes*. Une heure d'oubli... 60 [sic, a series]. Paris: Flammarion, 1921. 2–9. Translated as "The One who Came Back" in *Collected* and *Creatures*.

—. "La Chienne." *Les Heures longues 1914–1917*. Paris: Arthème Fayard & Cie, 1917. 218–224. Translated as "The Bitch" in *Collected* and *Creatures*.
—. "Chiens sanitaires." *Les Heures longues 1914–1917*. Paris: Arthème Fayard, 1917. 92–97.
—. *Claudine à l'école*. Paris: Ollendorff, 1900. *Claudine at School*. Trans. Antonia White. New York: FSG, 1957.
—. *Claudine en ménage*. Paris: Mercure de France, 1902. *Claudine Married*. Trans. Antonia White. New York: FSG, 1960.
—. *Claudine à Paris*. Paris: Ollendorf, 1901. *Claudine in Paris*. Trans. Antonia White. New York: FSG, 1958.
—. *Claudine s'en va*. Paris: Ollendorff, 1903. *Claudine and Annie*. Trans. Antonia White. London: Secker & Warburg, 1962.
—. *The Collected Stories of Colette (Collected)*. Trans. Robert Phelps. New York: FSG, 1983.
—. "Les Couleuvres." *La Paix chez les bêtes*. 1916. (159–163). Collated in *Œuvres* (2.127–128); translation in *Creatures* ("Creature Comfort" 253–255). See also *La Paix*.
—. *Creatures Great and Small (Creatures)*. Trans. Enid McLeod. London: Secker & Warburg. New York: FSG, 1951. Softcover, FSG, 2nd printing, 1978.
—. *De la patte à l'aile* [From paws to wings]. Illus. André Chastel. Paris: Corréa, 1943.
—. *Dialogues de bêtes*. Paris: Société du Mercure de France, 1904. See also *Douze Dialogues*.
—. *Douze Dialogues de bêtes*. Paris: Mercure de France, 1930. "Creature Conversations." Trans. Enid McLeod. *Creatures*. 1–160.
—. *Les Égarements de Minne* [Minne's waywardness]. Paris: Ollendorf, 1905. See also Colette. *L'Ingenue libertine*.
—. *En Pays connu* [In a familiar country]. Paris: Ferenczi, 1950.
—. *L'entrave*. Paris: Librairie des Lettres, 1913. *The Shackle*. Trans. Antonia White. London: Secker and Warburg, 1963.
—. *Les Heures longues 1914–1917* [The long hours]. Paris: Arthème Fayard & Cie, 1917.
—. *L'Ingénue libertine* (Colette's edition combining *Minne* and *Les Égarements de Minne*). Paris: Société d'éditions littéraires et artistiques, Librairie Paul Ollendorff, 1909. *The Innocent Libertine*. Trans. Antonia White. New York: FSG, 1968.
—. *Les Lettres à ses pairs* [Letters to her friends]. Ed. Claude Pichois and Robert Forbin. Paris: Flammarion, 1973.
—. *La Maison de Claudine*. Paris: Ferenczi, 1922.
—. *Mes apprentissages: Ce que Claudine n'a pas dit* [What Claudine didn't tell]. Paris: Ferenczi, 1936. Paris: Hachette Livre de Poche, 1972. *My Apprenticeships*. Trans. Helen Beauclerk. New York: FSG, 1978.
—. *Minne*. Paris: Ollendorff, 1904. See also Colette. *L'Ingenue libertine*.
—. *Œuvres de Colette*. Ed. Claude Pichois. 4 vols. Collection Bibliothèque de la Pléiade 314, 327, 381, 481. Paris: Gallimard. 1984–1986.
—. *La Paix chez les bêtes (La Paix)*. Paris: Arthème Fayard, 1916. *Cats, Dogs, and I: Stories from* La Paix chez les bêtes. Trans. Alexandre

Gagarine. New York: Henry Holt, 1924. "Creature Comforts." *Creatures*. 185–292.
—. *Paradis terrestre* [Earthly paradise]. Illus. Paul Jouve. Lausanne: Gonin, 1932.
—. *Pour un herbier: Aquarelles de Manet*. Le Bouquet 43. Lausanne, Switzerland: Mermod, 1948. *for a flower album* [sic]: *watercolours by Manet*. Trans. Roger Senhouse. London: Weidenfeld & Nicolson, 1959.
—. *Prrou, Poucette et quelques autres*. Paris: Librairie des Lettres and Philippe Renouard, 1913. Selections are translated in *Creatures* ("Creature Comfort").
—. "Renouveau." *Les Heures Longues*. 18–20.
—. *La Retraite sentimentale*. Paris: Mercure de France, 1907. *Retreat from Love*. Trans. Margaret Crossland. London: Peter Owen, 1974. New York: Bobbs-Merrill, n.d.
—. "La salivation psychique." *La Paix*. 207–210. Translated as "Salivation by Suggestion" in *Creatures* (277–278).
—. *Sept Dialogues de bêtes*. Paris: Mercure de France, May 1905. *Barks and Purrs*. Trans. Maire Kelly. New York: Desmond FitzGerald, 1913. See also *Douze Dialogues*.
—. *Sido ou les points cardinaux* [Sido, or the cardinal points]. Paris: Kra, 1929. Also as *Sido*. Paris: Ferenczi, 1930. *Sido*. Trans. Enid McLeod. New York: FSG, 1975. *My Mother's House and Sido*. New York: FSG, 2002.
—. *Splendeur des papillons* [The splendor of butterflies]. Paris: Librairie Plon, 1936.
—. *La Vagabonde*. Paris: Ollendorff, 1910. *The Vagabond*. Trans. Enid McLeod. New York: FSG, 1955.
—. *Les Vrilles de la vigne* [the title story in a collection]. Paris: La Vie parisienne. n.d. [1908]. Paris: Ferenczi, 1923. *The Tender Shoot and Other Stories*. Trans. Antonia White. New York: FSG, 1975.
Comfort, Cathy. "The real *Poilus*: Colette's war dogs." *Modern and Contemporary France* 28.1 (2020): 87–98.
*Commonweal* [Editors]. "Colette's Burial." *Commonweal* 60.24 (17 September 1954): 573.
Derrida, Jacques. *The Animal That Therefore I Am*. Foreword, Marie-Louise Mallet. New York: Fordham UP, 2008.
Francis, Claude, and Fernande Gontier. *Colette* [French trans. from the English by Francis and Gontier, per Steerforth Press]. Paris: Perrin, 1997.
—. *Creating Colette. Volume I: From Ingenue to Libertine, 1873-1913*. South Royalton, VT: Steerforth P, 1998.
—. *Creating Colette. Volume II: From Baroness to Woman of Letters, 1912-1954*. South Royalton, VT: Steerforth P, 1999.
Holmes, Diana. *Middlebrow Matters: Women's Reading and the Literary Canon in France since the Belle Époque*. Contemporary French and Francophone Cultures. Liverpool, UK: Liverpool UP, 2018.
Jammes, Francis. *L'Église habillée de feuilles* [The Church clothed in leaves]. Vol. 2. *Œuvres de Francis Jammes*. 5 vols. Paris: Mercure de France, 1921. 275–343.
—. "Une Préface aux *Dialogues de bêtes*." *Mercure de France* (journal) 40 (March 15, 1905): 200–203. See *Barks and Purrs* (v–xiv).

—. Préface. *Douze Dialogues de bêtes*. Paris: Mercure de France, 1930. v–xiii.
—. Préface. *Sept Dialogues de bêtes*. Paris: Mercure de France, May 1905. 9–17.
Jouve, Nicole Ward. *Colette*. Bloomington: Indiana UP, 1987.
Martin, Lowry. "From Mascot to Metaphor: Canine Combatants and the Performance of French Patriotism in the Great War." *Lengua Romana* (2017): 69–84.
Norell, Donna M. "Ultimate Reality in Colette's World: The Quest for Unity of Sidonie-Gabrielle Colette (1873-1954)." *Ultimate Reality and Meaning* 28.4 (2005): 291–314.
Sarde, Michèle. *Colette: An Autobiography*. Trans. Richard Miller. New York: William Morrow, 1980.
Schiesari, Julianna. "Colette at Home." *Polymorphous Domesticities: Pets, Bodies, and Desire in Four Modern Writers*. FlashPoints. Oakland, CA: U of California P, 2012. 38–75.
Spencer, Sharon. "The Lady of the Beasts: Eros and Transformation in Colette." *Women's Studies: Charting Colette* 8.3 (1981): 298–312.
Thurman, Judith. *Secrets of the Flesh: A Life of Colette*. New York: Random House, 1999.
Tilburg, Patricia A. *Colette's Republic: Work, Gender, and Popular Culture in France, 1870–1914*. New York: Berghan Books, 2009.
Van Wijk, H. L. Gerth. *A Dictionary of Plant Names*. The Hague: Martin Nijhoff, Dutch Society of Sciences at Haarlem, 1911.

# 6

# Sergio Ramírez's *Sara*
## A Feminist Ethic in the Revision of a Bronze-Age Tale

### José Juan Colín

Sergio Ramírez's reductive, eponymous title for his 2015 novel *Sara* takes for its protagonist the biblical "Sarah," Abraham's wife and Isaac's mother, a woman whose supporting role in the Hebrew origins narrative reaches into Jewish, Islamic, and Christian traditions.[1] In spite of Sarah's apparently fixed, ancient anchorage in texts where she is little more than a cipher, Ramírez productively reimagines her in his novel by privileging the scant indications of her personal qualities and values and probing coherent possibilities in the narrative's lacunae.[2]

Addressing innovations in Ramírez's view of the biblical Sarah, Nicaraguan bishop and critic Silvio José Báez asserts, "The most original part of the novel [. . .] is 'point of view,' given that [the novel] is narrated from Sara's perspective, from her restlessness to her rebelliousness, from the silence of her marginality, and from her practical intelligence" (3).[3] The traits Báez assigns to Sara are broadly accurate, and indeed, Ramírez sets Sara's perspective at the center of events as his opening innovation, the first unexpected move away from the traditional story with which the reader will grapple. Sara, nevertheless, does not narrate the novel. Ramírez's third-person narrator most often presents Sara's perspective, but a good number of incidents that affect Sara's development and the novel's events are outside her witness, and the narrator heightens the reader's consciousness of Sara's perspective with further detail, sometimes offering a correction to Sara's statements. Her running commentary, informed by her personal qualities, immediate experiences, long-running frustrations, and cultural circumstances, creates a dynamic relationship between Sara and the narrative voice. Ramírez begins to develop Sara's character by drawing on glimpses of the ancient Sarah from standard narratives, and within a few pages of reading *Sara* from a feminist approach, we begin to recognize her as alert, shrewd, adept, and nimble.

## The Sarah of Genesis

Genesis focuses more often on Abraham (Abram) than on Sarah (Sarai). Its narrative tracks his decisions, conflicts, and movements, recording his interactions with God and establishing Abraham's reputation for bowing down to God. When God directs Abraham to "count the stars" as an indication of the number of his descendants (Gen 15:5) and promises Abraham that Sarah will bear a son (17:15), God demands circumcision of every male in Abraham's household as the seal on their covenant, and Abraham rigorously carries out the order (17:23–27).[4] *Sara* opens shortly afterward, finding Abraham in great pain as a result of the procedure.

The biblical Sarah, unlike Abraham, garners little fame for obedience to God or faith in his pronouncements, and God seldom acknowledges her. Sarah's laughter and her skeptical—even derisive—thoughts about God's promise of a son are usually counted against her. At several critical turns of the Genesis narrative, however, Sarah speaks on worldly matters and takes a meaningful role in each instance. In Gen. 16:1–2, for example, Sarah declares her resolve to give her Egyptian slave Hagar to Abraham in the hope that she—Sarah—will have a family by means of Hagar: "Abram's wife Sarai had borne him no child, but she had an Egyptian slave girl called Hagar. So Sarai said to Abram, 'Listen now! Since Yahweh has kept me from having children, go to my slave-girl. Perhaps I shall get children through her.'" In Gen. 16:3, Sarah acts immediately to fulfill her word to Abraham: "Sarai took Hagar [. . .] and gave her to Abram as his wife." When the pregnant Hagar disrespects her, Sarah blames God for the "outrage" and mistreats Hagar for her impertinence, and Hagar runs away (16:4–6).[5] In the eighteenth chapter of Genesis, Sarah overhears the prophecy that she will become pregnant in her old age, and she laughs in skeptical derision because of her and Abraham's ages and their history of barrenness (18:12). When God hears her, he tasks Abraham, asking why his wife had laughed and doubted God (18:13). Sarah falsely disclaims the charge, protesting, "I did not laugh" (18:15).[6] After Isaac is born (Gen. 21), Sarah again feels insulted by Hagar and Ishmael, and she demands that Abraham banish both of them for mocking Isaac.[7]

Other actions ascribed to Sarah in Genesis imply an attitude of submission toward Abraham. Sarah obeys Abraham when she prepares bread for the angelic emissaries with "the best flour" (Gen. 18:6), and she remains in the tent out of sight of the visitors according to custom (18:19). In other adventures, she protects Abraham's subterfuges with silence: he tells her he will present her to Pharaoh as his sister because of her great beauty and the danger it poses to him (Gen. 12:10–20), and she silently acquiesces further on when Abraham adopts the same strategy in Gerah to preserve his life from King Abimelech (20:1–13).[8]

Ramírez coherently invests his Sara, not only with beauty, skepticism, and discernment, but also with a thin skin for slights, avidity for righteous satisfaction, a habit of eavesdropping, and a gift for mendacity. Sara resists the patriarchy with a lively, ironic commentary that challenges authority and justifies her disdain for what she considers foolish or dangerous in Abraham or God, whom she names *el Mago*—the Wizard. She conforms to social expectations when her losses are manageable and, without breaking the peace irretrievably, claims her view of truth. When potential losses loom large, on the other hand, Sara acts swiftly, with calculation and determination, to achieve her ends. Ramírez paints Sara's emotional life by extrapolating from his source to invest her with values of justice and duty and a sense of righteous indignation. These qualities emerge from an indomitable sense of her own value and a fierce maternal identity.

## Ramírez's Politics and Women Characters

Despite Ramírez's celebrated status in the Spanish-speaking world as an author, critic, revolutionary leader, and government official, he is little known in the English-speaking world outside academe.[9] To better support points of departure for my approach to *Sara*, then, the following paragraphs briefly describe representative feminist and political elements in Ramírez's writing, contextualize the use of biblical material in Nicaraguan literature, and suggest how liberation theology in that tradition offers a critical perspective on *Sara*.[10]

Ramírez's compelling female characters include those on the story's periphery who are victimized in ways that develop characterizations and motivate events, others who intervene to alter the narrative trajectory, and others who figure as primary protagonists. The ostensible hero of Ramírez's detective trilogy, opening with *El cielo llora por mí* in 2009, is ex-Sandinista and police-inspector Dolores Morales, who leads an investigation for a missing woman and soon is working to identify her murderers.[11] Nevertheless, it is the police department's cleaning lady, Morales's neighbor in *el barrio El Edén* [the Eden neighborhood], the intrepid ex-revolutionary doña Sofía Smith whose apt deductions and perilous undercover masquerade provide essential leads in the case. Doña Sofía, with her paradoxically honorific title and Anglo surname, lives as one of the invisible poor of the city. She and Sara share essential aspects of character.

Ramirez's 2011 novel *La fugitiva*, creates a fictionalized biography of the life of Costa Rican writer Yolanda Oreamuno, who resisted standard representations of women in the 1940s and sought a Spanish American literature that went beyond folklore and regionalism.[12] Ramírez reimagines Oreamuno in his protagonist, Amanda Solano, and narrates her story in three female voices, opening the novel at the end of her life with the clandestine return of her exhumed remains to Costa Rica. In journalist Patricia Villarruel's 2011 interview with Ramírez, she describes the novel's real-life subject, Oreamuno, in words that also pertain to Ramírez's Sara: "Una mujer distinta de incontestable belleza y desafiante sentido de la libertad" [A woman apart, of unquestionable beauty and a defiant sense of freedom], and Ramírez tellingly directs attention to the trajectory of *La fugitiva*'s narrative (*la linea narrativa*) as representing the fullness of Oreamuno's life: "su tragedia, su exilio, la incomprensión de la sociedad" [her tragedy, her exile, society's failure to understand her]. It is a representation that closely parallels Ramírez's achievement in *Sara*.

Like the Nicaragua of *El cielo llora por mí* and the Costa Rica of *La fugitiva*, Sara's Bronze Age desert world is patriarchal. Speaking to Villarruel, Ramírez describes the milieu he sought to create around his character Solano in *La fugitiva*: "Yo quería hacer énfasis [. . .] en que se trata de una sociedad patriarcal muy conservadora, que pretende reducir a la mujer a un lugar, que cuando intenta sobresalir le serruchan el piso o le cortan las piernas" [I wanted to focus . . . on a very conservative patriarchal society that tries to limit women to their places and when women endeavor to excel, (men) saw out the floor from under them or cut them off at the knees].[13] Doña Sofía, Solano, and Sara are characterized as women equipped to challenge repressive norms. When Villarruel asked Ramírez why he did not merely write a biography of Oreamuno, he highlighted the distinction between genres from the writer's perspective: "Porque una biografía tiene un límite y una novela, no" [Because biography has its limits, and the novel, none]. The novel's "unlimited" possibilities offer the author a theoretical opportunity Ramírez exploits to advantage in several of his novels, including *Sara*.

## Ramírez's Nicaragua

Ramírez's continuous involvement in Nicaragua's struggles toward justice and human rights and his voluminous non-fiction production as an intimate observer, interpreter, and critic of its politics, history, culture, and literature further informs my reading of *Sara*.[14] Ramírez's fiction addresses these preoccupations in vivid, sometimes stark, sometimes darkly comic narratives. His 1963 short-story collection, *Cuentos*, followed in the late 1970s by several further collections of short stories, hold a mirror to those aspects of Central American life, and his first novel, *Tiempo de fulgor*, composed between 1966 and 1970, chronicles the private and public lives of two prominent León families through a dozen or so generations of environmental and political upheavals, from their disparate, late-colonial beginnings to their shared disintegration.[15] Ramírez's *Castigo divino*, published in 1998, fictionalizes a notorious multiple-murder case that unfolded in León shortly before Somoza came to power.[16] The first Somoza dictatorship likewise frames *Margarita, está linda la mar*, published in 1998. The novel's diachronic re-envisioning of Nicaraguan history takes its title from Rubén Darío's poem, "Margarita, está linda la mar," dedicated to Margarita Debayle, whose sister, Salvadora, married Anastasio Somoza García and was the mother of his Somoza successors. Ramírez's novel connects the poet Darío's 1907 return to Nicaragua from Europe to poet Rigoberto López Pérez's violent death in his successful effort to assassinate Somoza in September 1956. In 2017, Ramírez returned to the crime genre with *Ya nadie llora por mí* and his ex-revolutionary, now-ex-policeman protagonist, Morales, and again, doña Sofía Smith and Morales's lover Fanny figure into his search for a missing young woman.

Ramírez confirmed his view of literature in service to truth, justice, and liberty in April 2018 by asking in his acceptance speech for the Cervantes Prize that he be permitted to dedicate the award to the memory of those lost in that cause and to those young people who continue the struggle.[17] Ramírez's most recent novel, entitled *Tongolele no sabía bailar*, is the third installment of his Detective Morales trilogy. Set amid the 2018 anti-Ortega movement, *Tongolele* dramatizes Nicaragua's continuing resistance to dictatorship with Morales as its marked-for-death protagonist. In September 2021, only weeks before the book was released in Spain, Ortega's regime issued an arrest warrant for Ramírez, who had relocated to Costa Rica from Nicaragua. Shipments of *Tongolele* to Nicaragua were impounded by customs officials, and by mid-December, Ramírez announced he would be making his home in Spain.[18]

Ramírez's lifetime focus on Nicaragua and Central America, his continuing resistance to repressive regimes, and recent news about his *persona non grata* status in his homeland strongly suggest that a reading of *Sara* might well engage political and social literary theory to read the novel as a counter-hegemonic narrative or as a global fiction using biblical contexts to represent present-day circumstances. This frequent resort of Luso-Hispanic writers is often grounded in principles of liberation theology, a philosophy born from the revolutionary conscience of the 1950s and '60s.[19] Liberation theology has offered writers, philosophers, film makers, and people of religion a compelling response to brutal military dictatorships, and in Nicaragua under the Somozas, where the political and economic environment was determined by self-interest and oppression, liberation theology's counterbalancing, utopian spirit found expression in the national literature. There, as elsewhere, it is marked by a discursive embrace of anti-dictatorship messages and by its engagement with higher principles—love, justice, truth, and liberty.

## Biblical Echoes

With *Sara*, Ramírez continues a Nicaraguan tradition of creating literature whose biblical echoes engage these critical elements. Nicaraguan poets like Carlos Martínez Rivas, in *Besos para la mujer de Lot*; Pablo Antonio Cuadra, in *Libro de horas*, and †Ernesto Cardenal, in *Salmos*, avail themselves of Hebrew Bible narratives and genres to create volumes of poetry that reflect the nation's violent history and uncertainty. Cuadra's and Cardenal's verses both contest and reflect on the legacy of the Somoza dictatorship, and their poetry assumes renewed significance under Ortega's rule. *Sara*'s challenges to patriarchal authority pose a similarly skeptical resistance.

Cardenal's "Psalm 5" presents a substance made of biblical forms and characters that speak to Nicaragua's suffering and injustice in modern terms:

Escucha mis palabras oh Señor
                    Oye mis gemidos
Escucha mi protesta
Porque no eres tú un Dios amigo de los dictadores
ni partidario de su política
ni te influencia la propaganda
ni estás en sociedad con el gángster. . . . (ll. 1–7)

> [Hear my words, oh Lord / listen to my groanings / hear my protest / For you are not a God who is a friend of the oppressors / nor a partisan of their politics / nor are you influenced by their propaganda / nor are you in league with the gangster. . . .]

The narrator's plea to God in these lines is intimate and direct, where Sara's dialogues with the Wizard's manifestations are coy and indirect or ambiguously framed until their final conversation. Rather than cast Sara's commentary and inquiry into the dialogic and rhetorical pattern that Cardenal adopts or into contemporary images and phrases, Ramírez maintains Sara's aloofness and skepticism and sets her into Bronze Age desert life where she is meant to be submissive. From her largely static vantage point, Sara continuously regards the Wizard and Abraham as separate from her and oppositional, as objects of study and critical assessment. Cardenal's narrator takes a different tack, moving from an appeal that affirms God's power on the side of the people to cast himself as a believer worthy of God's blessing:

> Al que no cree en la mentira de sus anuncios comerciales
> ni en sus campañas publicitarias, ni en sus campañas políticas
> tú lo bendices
> lo rodeas con tu amor
> como con tanques blindados. (ll. 28–32)

> [To him who believes not in the lies of their commercial messages / nor in their publicity campaigns, nor in their political campaigns / you will give him your blessing / surround him with your love / as with armored tanks.]

Cardenal's final lines call for the reader's present-day awareness and skepticism when the narrator compares God's protective love to a weapon of destruction, a divinity capable of destroying the enemy and protecting ordinary people who believe in God's goodness. Sara's resistance is rooted, however, in the politics of Hebrew patriarchal tradition in the far reaches of time, and Ramírez shuns anachronistic references like those Cardenal employs. But the resistance Cardenal asserts has God's blessing for its love of truth resonates with Sara's resistance, which ultimately speaks to truth and love and provides protection from destruction. Literary reworkings of biblical and religious materials to refer to modern-day, armed oppression affirm liberation theology's continuing power and suggest the theoretical foundations of *Sara*.

## Liberation Theology and Feminist Resistance

Ramírez's imaginatively liberating the intellect and voice of the Hebrew Bible's seldom-heard matriarch to give her a place of representation correlates with the philosophy of liberation theology, deepening *Sara*'s resonance with Latin America's political and social history.[20] These elements are further sharpened by Sara's most notable biblical descriptor—her being female—and her life's overarching, gendered misfortune: in a society that prizes fecundity, Sara reaches great old age never having conceived a child. Sara's apparently irremediable disappointment—her barrenness—is a cosmic betrayal that shapes her psychological and theological outlines.

But where the biblical Sarah remains largely a peripheral figure orbiting around Abraham, in Ramírez's version, Sara is constantly present, and her flowing observations and responses tell her story as a marginalized woman in a privileged household. Though Sarah habitually keeps her thoughts to herself, the Wizard is privy to them, as the reader is. Sara's continuous, internal commentary reveals her intellectual independence and discernment, and when she speaks to Abraham, her discourse is familiar and straightforward, often resistant, and sometimes defiant. Ramírez's achievement with fictionalizing Sarah's "biography" recalls a description of his *Margarita, está linda la mar* as a history-based narrative that "desmitifica" [demythologizes] larger-than-life figures.[21] In *Sara*, Ramírez reveals the instability of the patriarchy's control in the face of Sara's keen critical observations and her willingness to leap over patriarchal boundaries when loved ones are in danger. *Sara*, in a sense, "demythologizes" the ancient figure of Sarah to create a complex female character, whose agile mind, sense of irony, and potential for action the sacred texts merely gesture toward.

## A Reading of *Sara*

Sara's self-described otherness awakens the reader's involvement as the novel opens *in medias res* on Sara's expression of disgust when she observes three figures approaching Abraham's tents from a distance. She recognizes the three young men dragging themselves along through burning sand in midday heat and knows they are the Wizard's angel-emissaries in new forms and that she will have to prepare and serve them a meal at Abraham's insistence (11). Abraham's pretense of not recognizing the "strangers" (*forasteros*) sharpens Sara's annoyance because she knows—as Abraham must—that they arrive and speak at the Wizard's command. Their failures to acknowledge her confirm her marginalization and fuel Sara's resentment of the Wizard, who has made her barren and whose "prisoner" she considers herself.[22]

Sara's responses to familiar biblical events create a micro-historical view of those incidents, characterizing her as observant, critically minded, and active. Sara's gendered, decentered position, emphasized in the opening scenes by the disregard with which the Wizard and his emissaries treat her, identify Sara with the literary trope of "the other." Moreover, the "impossibility of speech" between Sara and the Wizard—and often between Sara and Abraham—associates her with theories of the colonized subaltern.[23] Despite Sara's mandate over servants in Abraham's household, her place there and her performances from the margins of her culture are dictated by her being female, and her identity lies solely in her being Abraham's wife and Isaac's mother. Sara's enforced silence and invisibility, her birth as the daughter of household slaves (in Ramírez's telling), and her erasure from interactions and conversations rooted in power suggest Gayatri Chakravorty Spivak's title question from her influential critique of post-colonial culture, "Can the Subaltern Speak?" According to Spivak's theory, the subaltern's voice is irrecoverable because the subaltern has no space or standing from which to speak. Karina Bidaseca deduces that when the subtaltern breaks her silence—gains her place and voice and is heard—she ceases to be the subaltern.[24]

The testy Wizard, hearing Sara's inward stream of challenges and defiance, might well respond to Spivak's question, as Valeria Luiselli suggests (in a distinct context): "For Heaven's sake, tell the subaltern to shut up" (53). Indeed, Sara's flowing internal commentary and occasional speech performances inform the reader's response to the events, presence, words, and acts of every other character in the novel—the Wizard, Abraham, Lot, Hagar, Ishmael, and the Wizard's various emissaries. Sara's edgy reception of her surroundings and her ethical interrogation of her world opens with her correcting Abraham's benign description of the men coming toward their tent as "strangers": they are the very men who came three days earlier to deliver the Wizard's order that all males be circumcised forthwith, a procedure that has caused Abraham great suffering (11–12).[25] Sara silently serves the Wizard-guests, muting her verbal ire and expressing it in her manner of preparing the food, whose taste they fail to notice. When the visitors confirm that she will bear a son, Ramírez follows the biblical account of Gen.

18 and has the eavesdropping Sara laugh to herself and deride the prophecy as improbable.

Whether the Wizard's demands are expressed—as in the command for universal circumcision—or implicit—as in Sara's being required to serve the Wizard's emissaries—Sara's responses are rapid and relevant. When the story opens, she is impatient with Abraham's pretexts and weakness of character and with the Wizard's interruptions and his cruel test of loyalty. Through choices that fall to her as Abraham's wife, Ramírez's Sara reveals other aspects of her character: she acts for the greater good when she allows Hagar to have sexual relations with Abraham, and she is, at times, kind toward Ishmael and Hagar, despite her envy of Hagar and the humiliation she feels in having her handmaiden bear Abraham's son.[26]

As I noted above, Sara's perspectives on her world are filtered by the commentary of the novel's critical and wily narrator, whose omniscient voice—in accord with Sara's inward one—tends to be skeptical of history and traditional conclusions, and who may counter the Wizard's dour self-importance with irony. Furthermore, the narrator gives occasional insights into Sara's motives by countering her rationales and revealing what she leaves unsaid. Nicaraguan reviewer Ulises Huete explains that one may regard the narrator as another character in the book because the narrator poses questions about incongruities in the biblical account:

> [...] no sólo nos cuenta la relación conflictiva entre Sara, Abraham y el Mago, sino que cuestiona el proceder de los protagonistas, anota las inconsistencias de la versión canónica, propone una versión de los hechos más verosímil y completa imaginativamente las omisiones del relato bíblico. La idiosincrasia del narrador compite con la del Mago en la elaboración de la historia, porque el Mago conduce los hechos con un sentido que sólo él conoce, pero el narrador los cuenta a su manera, y este estilo de contar adquiere una voz propia, es decir, se vuelve una personalidad. (Huete 6)

> [. . . not only does he (the narrator) tell us of the troubled relations among Sara, Abraham, and the Wizard, but he also interrogates the behavior of the protagonists, takes note of inconsistencies in the canonical version, proposes a more plausible version of the facts, and imaginatively completes the biblical account's omissions. The idiosyncratic nature of the narrator competes with that of the Wizard in developing the story because the Wizard controls events in a way that only he knows, while the narrator tells them in his own way, and this style of narration acquires its own voice; that is to say, it becomes a character.]

As Huete affirms, one of Ramírez's strategies is to provide the narrative voice with omniscience and a variable, intimate tone.

The narrator and Sara, then, provide wry perspectives, and their regular resort to those kinds of observations might be construed as a recommended approach to trials and suffering. When the narrative voice provides details to support Sara's logic and observations and occasionally mediates her ire, the effect is to heighten Sara's credibility. When Sara vents her annoyance about the suffering Abraham endures by being circumcised (11–12), for example, the narrator affirms her view with the further detail that Abraham's wound has become infected, and he describes the Bronze Age home remedy for swelling and inflammation (12). The narrator's engagement as an interlocutor with the reader assumes—perhaps demands, as the Wizard does from Abraham—the reader's attention, and the narrator's "we" takes the reader's partisanship for granted.

The following representative passage from the novel, for example, nuances Sara's protest against the Wizard's incongruous plan to have her bear a child in her old age by using the narrator's better-informed perspective:

> Esto de viejos, aunque venga de labios de Sara, es un dicho de poco sustento. Si acabamos de oírselo, entendamos que es sólo una manera de pedir al Mago que la deje en paz. También se ha quejado de que se siente cansada, y ésa es una expresión que tampoco vamos a tomar al pie de la letra viniendo de una mujer enérgica que no se arredra ante nungún esfuerzo o tarea, y, perspicaz y aguda en sus juicios, tiene bien puesta la cabeza sobre los hombros. (20)
>
> [This thing about old people (having a child), even though it may come from Sara's lips, is a statement with little to back it up. Even though we've just heard her say this, let's understand it's only her way of telling the Wizard to leave her alone. She's also complained of being tired, and this, too, is something we won't take at face value because it comes from an energetic woman who's undaunted by any difficulty or task, and because she's penetrating and quick in her judgments, it's clear she has a good head on her shoulders.]

In this passage, the narrator cautions and instructs readers, implying that they must sift Sara's discourse through her character as it has so far been developed to get at its truth. Partly through the narrator's insights, the reader plumbs Sara's character more fully and precisely.

Sidelined by her gender and burdened by barrenness and resentment, Sara regards herself as "prisoner" to the Wizard's whim: "Era su prisionera" [She was his prisoner], as the narrator asserts (15). For Sara, Abraham's exclusive intimacy with the Wizard is a patriarchal conspiracy working against her potential and her desires. The Wizard's angel-emissaries—Abraham's guests—also treat Sara as a servant, unworthy of notice, and her reception of them is based on their being an embodiment of the Wizard and copying his habits, even to his treatment of her: Sara "guardaba en su corazón un sentimiento tan hostil para con aquellos hombres que los visitaban sin previo aviso" [(she) harbored such a feeling of hostility in her heart toward those men who visited them unannounced], principally because they, too, ignored her (15). "Those men" are Raphael, Gabriel, and Michael, the Wizard's archangels, according to the narrator, and they visit Abraham in the forms of lithe, effeminate young men—if we can believe Sara's assessment—to announce the Wizard's will.[27]

Spotting them out in the desert, again headed toward Abraham's tents, Sara thinks of Abraham, bed-ridden with an infected penis, and she is peeved at them. The desert code requires that Abraham, ill or well, host the visitors, offering them rest and food, and when they ask where Sara is, their question implies that she remains out of sight. Sara, understanding herself as the Wizard's "prisoner," emphasizes her disappointment and marginalization in the context of the Wizard and his emissaries when she justifies her "hostility" toward them: "[A]demás de engañada, y postergada, [Sara] se sentía excluída. Jamás le dirigían la palabra, ni cuando les servía de beber y de comer, ni siquiera para decir gracias, y nunca se despedían. *Delante de sus ojos, ella no existía* [Besides being deceived and shunted aside, she felt neglected. Never did they speak to her, not even when she served them drinks and food, not even to say "thanks," and they never took leave of her. *In their eyes, she did not exist*] (15, emphasis added). The visitors' refusal to recognize Sara—when she is right under their noses (*delante de sus ojos*), so to speak—erases her from the essential experience of desert hospitality. Her erasure in this context is especially offensive because most of the effort required to welcome them falls to Sara.[28]

Neither, Sara muses, does the Wizard see her—any more than she is permitted to see or hear him—and she only knows the Wizard is present when she sees Abraham fall abruptly to his knees: "El propio Mago, frente a quien Abraham doblaba las rodillas al no más escuchar su voz, como si un puño le golpeara la cerviz, tampoco la determinaba" [The Wizard himself, in front of whom Abraham would kneel the instant he heard (the Wizard's) voice, as if a fist were striking him in the back of the neck, also failed to see her] (15). Sara becomes increasingly intent on expressing the bitterness of her marginalization, and in the following passage, Ramírez uses rhetorical repetition to deepen Sara's sense of exclusion: "Jamás [el Mago] le hablaba, jamás le pedía conversación, ni entraba en sus sueños" [(The Wizard) never said anything to her, never sought her conversation, nor would he even appear in her dreams] (15).

In an instance that counters Sara's complaint of the Wizard's effacing her existence, the visitors assure Abraham that Sara will bear him a son within the year, and later, one of them answers Sara's telepathic urging to Abraham to ask the guests why they are in such a rush to get to Sodom, telling Abraham that they go there to destroy it (52). That Sara's thoughts and movements are known to the Wizard is central to Ramírez's use of cause-and-effect in the Sodom-and-Gomorrah episode. Sodom's pronounced fate sparks Sara's urgent interest because Abraham's nephew Lot—who once fell in love with Sara, according to Ramírez's telling—lives in Sodom with his family (72).[29] The narrator explains that Sara and Lot grew up together in the house of Abraham's father, Terah (Taré), who banished Sara's servant parents when they contracted leprosy. Sara, beautiful and industrious, remained in the household (26) and was married to Abraham. When she and the teenaged Lot find themselves unexpectedly smitten with one another, their impossible "love pact" (25) ends at the same moment it begins because Sara is married. By the time Raphael tells Abraham that the angels are en route to destroy Sodom and Gomorrah, Lot and his wife, Edith, have settled in Sodom and have two marriageable daughters.

Raphael, his voice conveying how "offended" he feels, recites the final "intolerable" transgression among the many sins of the two cities: the "most abominable of their sins" is the worship of Baal in images, temples, and celebrations. Sara immediately deduces that the Wizard's jealousy is at the bottom of the foretold destruction (57). The narrator affirms her conclusion, and Sara then wonders how the Wizard can expect people to worship him when only Abraham and she know of his "invisible, nameless, faceless" existence (58). She is further outraged that the Wizard would destroy innocents—"babes at the breast"—along with the two cities' sinners (59), and she acts without delay to intervene in what she views as the jealous Wizard's excess. Mirroring the determined action of the Wizard's angels, Sara, too, "está dispuesta a pasar de las palabras a los hechos" [is ready to move from words to deeds] (53), and she resolves, unbeknownst to Abraham, to warn Lot. Hearing the angel-messengers depart, Sara disregards the patriarchal stricture that she must remain in her husband's tents unless she secures his permission to venture out and orders a servant to saddle her donkey, the beast she usually rides to Sodom to make purchases or to visit Edith (73).

Because Sara knows various paths to Sodom, she chooses a shorter route across the desert than that the angel-messengers pursue on foot and hurries her donkey along, arriving there ahead of them to instruct Lot in what he must do to escape destruction. As she travels toward Sodom, the monotonous rhythm of the animal moving across the sand allows Sara's mind to wander, and she recalls her experience of "captivity" and release in Egypt and thinks of her later friendship with Edith, who has been Sara's confidante and advisor (85 *ff.*). In Sodom, Lot is skeptical of her demands and trivializes Sara's insistent instructions, but she insists that he immediately prepare his family to abandon the city and quickly get himself to the city gates to intercept the messengers and persuade them to come to his house for the night (141–144). Sara departs Sodom to arrive home before Abraham notices her absence. By imagining Sara's movements, Ramírez provides rationales for the biblical account of Lot's presence at the gates of the city and his invitation to the disguised angels.[30] Sara's clandestine effort to save Lot, her friend Edith, and their daughters from the Wizard's destruction foreshadows Sara's decisive movement in the climactic moment of her story.

## Sara's Triumph

For the second time, Sara's will to intervene between Abraham and the Wizard takes the form of disobedience in her leaving the tents without Abraham's permission to make another clandestine journey. This time, Sara stalks Abraham and Isaac through the cover of desert vegetation to the place where Abraham does sacrifice (228–229). From her place of concealment, she hears Isaac laughingly question his father's intentions and Abraham silencing him (230). She observes as Abraham binds Isaac's hands and feet and lifts him onto the wood of the altar (229–230). Sara, "agazapada en cuatro patas, como una pantera dispuesta a dar el salto" [concealed, crouched on all-fours, like a panther about to pounce], continues to wait as Abraham tests the sharpness of his blade and feels Isaac's neck for the appropriate place to drive it in. As Abraham's fist closes on the hilt, Sara leaps forward to deflect Abraham's blow, forcefully sending the knife and Abraham to the ground. Without a care for Abraham, Sara rushes to unbind Isaac and helps him from the altar (230).

The Wizard, ignoring Abraham's vulnerable position—sprawled on the ground, dazed, and flustered—validates Abraham's act in words inaudible to Sara and Isaac and drops the curtain on the charade, saying to Abraham, "Está bien, Abraham, ya basta" [Ok, Abraham, that's enough], and assuring him, "[E]n adelante seremos uña y carne" [From here on, we are inseparable] (231).[31] Though Abraham essays to regain his sovereignty by scolding Sara on the pretext that she followed him from the tents without his permission, she counters that he had not forbidden her, and even had he done so, she'd have paid him no mind (233). He perseverates, citing patriarchal tradition, and Sara answers him silently: "Ya he salido otras veces sin que te dieras cuenta, pensó Sara, siempre detrás de tus pasos para salvar a quien debe ser salvado" [I've left many times before without your knowing, Sara thought, always dogging your steps to save whoever ought to be saved] (233). Aloud, she affirms the compelling outcome of her disobedience, that Isaac is alive: "[S]i no llego hasta aquí por mis propios pasos, nadie habría detenido tu mano" [If I weren't here on my own, no one would have stopped your hand] (233).

The damage done, Abraham admonishes her not to speak of such things in front of Isaac, and, true to character, "Ella se [ríe] con risa llena de desprecio" [She laughs disdainfully], and she mocks Abraham inwardly—"Mira quien habla [. . .] él que iba a meterle el cuchillo en la garganta" [Look who's talking . . . the guy who was about to put his knife into (Isaac's) throat] (233). Her spoken reply to Abraham undercuts his practice of obedience and the Wizard's intentions: "[A]hora me vas a salir con que el Mago lo que quería era ponerte a prueba, a ver si eras capaz de cumplir sus órdenes, por disparatadas que sean" [Now you're going to tell me that what the Wizard was trying to do was to test you, to see whether you were prepared to follow his orders, however absurd they might be] (233). Abraham immediately adopts her cynical speculation as a pretext, asserting that the Wizard stayed his hand, using Sara as his "instrument." Sara dismisses it: the Wizard had no need of further proof of Abraham's often-tested subservience; after all, Abraham is merely the Wizard's *siervo* [slave] (233).

Confirmation of Sara's power in the scene comes in the aftermath of the interrupted sacrifice: Abraham directs Isaac to sacrifice a ram opportunely caught within their reach by its horns, but Isaac looks to Sara for approval before obeying his father (234), and the substitution goes forward. Sara's desperate leap effectively sets love between the instruments of the Wizard—Abraham and his knife—and Isaac's life, sparing him to become the foretold progenitor of a "people as innumerable as the stars." In disrupting a cruel and pointless excess of patriarchal religious fervor, Sara acts in the void created by the Wizard's demands and Abraham's blind obedience to respond to the fullness of what is sacred to her.

As with Ramírez's other female protagonists, Sara's performance of agency in this scene (228–235) undermines the traditional literary and cultural tropes attached to women—the damsel in distress awaiting rescue, the submissive servant to the husband, and the suffering wife and mother, the submissive female fulfilling her role in a patriarchal society. Sara's responses—inward and external—are authentic expressions of intellect, will, and love. As she speaks and acts, she liberates herself from gendered cultural limitations, much as she liberates Isaac from the altar. That she does so without disrupting the status quo of her marriage or losing her love for Abraham is a feature of Sara's character that diverges from the paths of many other feminist protagonists, but I leave that intriguing feature of her characterization for another time.

## Settling Accounts

Many years later, despite Sara's complaint about the Wizard's refusal to acknowledge her, Sara and the Wizard (disguised as el Niño) engage in a Socratic dialogue that closes with Sara's asking him "one more question":

> Tengo sólo una pregunta más, dijo Sara. Te escucho, dijo el Niño. ¿De verdad eres real, o siempre has sido una mentira? No te entiendo, respondió el Niño. Una ilusión, un espejismo del desierto. Mira lo que se te ocurre, dijo el Niño, además de terca eres fantasiosa. Un espejismo que se pone solamente delante de dos personas, Abraham y yo, y somos nosotros dos los que te reflejamos delante de los demás. ¿Qué quieres decir con eso?, ¿que si no estuviera en la mente de ustedes dos no existiría? Más o menos, respondió Sara. Yo soy el que soy, dijo el Niño, en tono molesto. No tiene por qué molestarte, dijo Sara. La duda siempre ofende, dijo el Niño. (249)[32]

> ["I have only one more question," said Sara.
> "I'm listening to you," the Boy said.
> "Are you truly real, or have you always been a lie?"
> "I don't understand you," responded the Boy.
> "An illusion, a mirage created by the desert."
> "Look what's happened to you," said the Boy. "Besides being stubborn, you're given to fantasizing."
> "A mirage who stands before only two people, Abraham and me, and it's we two who show you to others."

"What do you mean by that—that if I weren't in your minds, I wouldn't exist at all?"

"More or less," responded Sara.

"I am who I am," said the Boy in an annoyed tone.

"There's no reason to get peeved," said Sara.

"Doubt is always offensive," said the Boy.]

Affirming her unwavering view of the Wizard, Sara fulfills the promise of her skeptical inner dialogues and verbal challenges and moves toward her final moments on earth. The silence that ensues—"En adelante lo que habría es silencio" [Beyond, there would be only silence]—closes the novel.[33]

On several occasions before this dialogue, Sara claims persuasive physical space and responds to events in ways that have shaped outcomes. For example, before Sara diverts Abraham's knife to spare Isaac's life, she engages the Wizard's interest sufficiently that he implicitly acknowledges the value of her intellectual processes: the Wizard hears Sara laugh and hears her false denial of doing so, and the archangels directly answer her unspoken questions (52). Further on, the Wizard advises Abraham to "pay heed to Sara" (207) on the subject of what to do about Hagar and Ishmael; the Wizard speaks to Sara conversationally on several occasions in the guise of el Tuerto and enters Pharaoh's dreams to free her from captivity. In Ramírez's account, Sara's defiance of patriarchal custom to save Lot and his family and, later, to follow Abraham and Isaac and to render Abraham powerless with a body blow make Sara the author of those biblically attested outcomes. Following these events, she presumably lives on as before, denied a space of representation and voice. Her development challenges assertions that once the subaltern gains space and voice, she is the subaltern no more. In a rebellion that has no unwonted casualties, Sara enacts a theology of liberation, seizing space and voice with the truth-telling "whip" of her speech and physical resistance that extends life, peace, and new beginnings to those she loves.

## Notes

1 I use the Spanish spelling "Sara" (without English's final –h) in this chapter to differentiate Ramírez's character from the Sarai/Sarah of Genesis. Direct quotations given here from the Hebrew Bible (Torah) come from Doubleday's *New Jerusalem Bible*, annotated translation (1985). In addition to the Genesis account of Sarai/Sarah (chiefly in chapters 16–18, 20–21, and 23), the Hebrew Bible refers to her in Numbers and Isaiah. In the Christian Bible (New Testament), passages in

Romans, Hebrews, and 1 Peter allude to Sarah, generally casting her as a traditional exemplar of faith or obedience. The Qu'ran gives narratives of the news of Isaac's birth, Sarah's laughter, the angels' visits, and the destruction of Sodom and Gomorrah in 11:69–83 and the command to sacrifice Isaac in 37:99–113. In an address at Fordham University in 2011, available as an electronic pdf, Amir Hussain emphasized the frequent presence of Abraham in the Qu'ran, where Abraham is the second most-cited prophet (1) and affirmed Abraham as "crucial to the prayer life of Muslims" (3).

2  My 2017 review of *Sara* spurred my interest in the novel and led to a public presentation that developed into this chapter. †Dick Gerdes translated my presentation into English from Spanish for this volume. I refer to most characters with English spellings of their names.

3  Báez writes: "Lo más original de la novela es [. . .] el 'punto de vista' adoptado, pues es narrada desde la perspectiva de Sara, desde sus inquietudes y rebeldías, desde su silencio de marginación y desde su inteligencia práctica." Baéz's review is carried (October 2022) in *Carátula* and dated July 18, 2015. Translations into English from *Sara*, other literature, and criticism are by the editor or are a collaborative effort with Dick Gerdes's translation. *Sara* has not, to date, been translated into English. A Spanish word or phrase italicized parenthetically documents a foregoing English translation.

4  See Gen. 17:1–2 for the covenant and Gen. 15:5–6 for God's illustration of the number of Abraham's descendants. God demands circumcision at Gen. 17:9–14 and renames Sarai and Abram, respectively, as Sarah (Gen. 17:15) and Abraham (Gen. 17:5).

5  In Gen. 16:9, an angel tells Hagar to return to Abraham's tents, and she does so.

6  The Hebrew Bible presents Abraham as an exemplar of faith, yet he precedes Sarah in laughing and in expressing skepticism at the thought of an aged couple producing a son. Sarah's laughter and skepticism are, nonetheless, indelibly attached to her character.

7  Gen. 21:17–19 concerns Hagar and Ishmael.

8  Though Abraham insists that Sarah is both his sister and his wife when his lie is discovered, Ramírez's narrator makes her the daughter of household slaves and disclaims the rumor of Sara's being Terah's daughter.

9  Missael Duarte Somoza's article in *Carátula* reviews a documentary on Ramírez (*Sergio Ramírez, la herencia de Cervantes en Centroamérica.* 2020) that treats his political and literary careers.

10 Beyond the national literature of Nicaragua, Luso-Hispanic authors have frequently availed themselves of the narratives, language, forms, and figures of religious culture to make political and social commentary in fiction and poetry. Consider José Saramago, Clarice Lispector, Machado de Assis, Gabriel García Márquez, Pablo Neruda, and Jorge Luis Borges, among the many.

11 Publishing data for English translations of literary works in Spanish are cited within the Works Cited entry for the original title. Where we know of no published English translation, we translate the title in brackets immediately following the Spanish title (using roman type and sentence case) in the Works Cited entry.
12 Oreamuno is known for *La ruta de su evasión*, published in 1948, and for her journalistic pieces. Her novel *Por tierra firme* [On solid ground] was apparently lost in manuscript. Seymour Menton notes James Joyce's influence on Oreamuno's fiction (256).
13 Mozelle Foreman (584) quotes the Spanish text from Manuel Bermúdez's interview with Ramírez.
14 See Nicasio Urbina's "Essays of Sergio Ramírez" for an overview of this large body of work. Also see Gabriela Polit-Dueñas's summary of Ramírez's career in Nicaraguan politics (164–165) and her emphasis on the language and perspectives of fatherhood in his 1999 memoir of the revolution, *Adiós muchachos*.
15 Ramírez provides the chronology for writing *Tiempo de fulgor*, first published in 1970 and newly released in 1986 (Reedición). The novel remains untranslated into English at this writing. León is home to Nicaragua's national university.
16 Anastasio Somoza García's dictatorship began with a coup d'état in 1937 and continued through four decades. The dictator's elder son, Luis Somoza Debayle, succeeded to power in 1956 and controlled two successors. At Luis' death in 1967, the younger son, Anastasio Somoza Debayle, was declared president and remained so until 1979 in spite of constitutional provisions prohibiting consecutive terms. Anastasio Somoza Debayle fled Nicaragua in 1979 and was assassinated in Paraguay in 1980.
17 On April 23, 2018, King Felipe VI of Spain presented Ramírez with 2017's Cervantes Prize, the Hispanic world's highest literary award. *El País*, Spain's national newspaper announced the award and published portions of Ramírez's acceptance speech. See also *LALT* (November 2018) for the full text of Ramírez's speech in Spanish with its English translation and a summary of his literary awards in the U.S., Canada, France, Chile, and Mexico. This issue of *LALT* also includes Urbina's treatment of Ramírez's non-fiction and Colín's essay on Ramírez's literary career.
18 See reporting by Sam Jones and Porter Anderson, online.
19 For background on liberation theology, see Katie Benjamin's online list of readings (Duke Divinity School Library).
20 If one were to dedicate a reading of *Sara* to exploring its resonance with Nicaragua's contemporary political milieu, the possibilities for critical readings would multiply.
21 This characterization of *Margarita, está linda la mar* is Brian T. Chandler's.

22 For Sara's self-description as the Wizard's prisoner, see the novel (15). The biblical Sarah's (Sarai's) barrenness is cited, for example, in Gen. 11:30.
23 The "impossibility of speech" is a frequent phrase in subaltern studies. It connects to Spivak's question, "Can the subaltern be heard?" One answer is that the subaltern cannot be heard because of the "impossibility of speech" before an audience that refuses to hear her; therefore, she has no voice.
24 See, for example, Spivak (27–28) and Bidaseca (68–69).
25 See Gen. 17–18 for these events.
26 For example, see *Sara* (15–16). Sara elsewhere mistreats Hagar and conspires to put Hagar at a disadvantage (125–135).
27 The visitors appear at other times as shepherds, beggars, merchants, or Bedouins (13), and the Wizard is further embodied in the appearances of "el Niño" [the Boy], who appears to Hagar in the desert (132–134; 208–210) and to Sara (245–246), and of "el Tuerto" [the one-eyed man], whose Spanish epithet I maintain here. El Tuerto appears to Sara (for example, 244–245), and he provides the sacrificial ram.
28 Though I acknowledge the narrator's statements and other indicators that cast doubt onto Sara's complaints, I regard her experiences and feelings of being silenced, bounded, and marginalized as her reality.
29 Lot is the son of Abraham's brother, Haran, who dies in Ur of the Chaldeans or Chaldees (Gen. 11:28–31).
30 In Gen. 19, Lot, for no specified motive, is waiting at the city gates when the angels arrive, and, just as inexplicably, he urges them to lodge in his house. The next morning, the angels order Lot's family from Sodom. Edith—nameless in the Genesis account—is transformed into a pillar of salt when she disobeys God's command that they must not look back.
31 The Wizard's metaphor is literally translated as "flesh and fingernail."
32 The text formats conversations between characters as shown, mirroring the style of the KJV and Douay-Rheims. (The RSV uses quotation marks.) To support reading this dialogue in English, the editor's translation uses quotation marks, along with paragraph breaks to indicate a change of speakers.
33 Sarah's death is narrated in Gen. 23.

**Works Cited**

Anderson, Porter. "Nicaragua's Sergio Ramírez on Leaving Latin America: 'A Personal Choice.'" *Publishing Perspectives: Feature Articles*. Brooklyn, NY: Publishingperspectives.com, 13 December 2021.

Báez, Silvio José. "La novela *Sara* (July 18, 2015)." *Carátula* 110. October 2022.

Benjamin, Katie. "Reading List: Latin American Liberation Theology." Durham, NC: Duke Divinity School Library, 27 February 2020. Online.

Bermúdez, Manuel. "Sergio Ramírez: Confesiones sobre Amanda." *Semanario Universidad*. San Pedro Montes de Oca: Universidad de Costa Rica, semanariouniversidad.com. 15 June 2011.

Bidaseca, Karina. "'Mujeres blancas buscando salvar a mujeres color café': desigualdad, colonialismo jurídico y feminismo postcolonial." *Andamios* 17 (2011): 61–89.

Cardenal, Ernesto. "Escucha mis protestas: Salmo 5." *Salmos*. Barcelona: Pomaire, 1976. Madrid: Trotta, 2001. 13–14. *The Psalms of Struggle and Liberation*. Trans. Emile G. McAnany. Foreword, Thomas Merton. Freiburg im Breisgau, Germany: Herder, 1971. 29–30.

Chandler, Brian T. "La repolitización del autor en *Margarita, está linda la mar*." *The Coastal Review* 4.1 (2013): Digitalcommons@georgiasouthern.edu.

Colín, José Juan. "Sergio Ramírez, el Cervantes más que merecido / The More-than-deserved Cervantes." Trans. Arthur Malcolm Dixon. *LALT* 8 (2018).

—. "[Rev.] *Sara* de Sergio Ramírez." *LALT* 2 (2017). Norman, OK: U of Oklahoma, 2022.

Cuadra, Pablo Antonio. "Libro de horas: 1946–1954." *Obra completa*. San José: Asociación Libro Libre, 1984. 61–122. *Book of Hours*. Trans. Sarah Hornsby and Matthew C. Hornsby. Managua: Academia Nicaragüense de la Lengua, 2012.

Duarte Somoza, Missael. "*Sergio Ramírez, la herencia de Cervantes en Centroamérica*, un documental de Iván Argüello" (December 6, 2021). *Carátula* 110 (October 2022).

Foreman, Mozelle. "Scenes of Language Violence in Yolanda Oreamuno's *La ruta de su evasión*." *Revista Canadiense de Estudios Hispánicos* 39.3 (2015): 565–587.

Huete, Ulises. "[Rev.] *Sara*, una revisión irónica." *Carátula* 70 (February 2016): 5–7.

Hussain, Amir. "Abraham, Sarah, Hagar, Ishmael, and Isaac: The Bonds of Family." Response to the Spring McGinley Lecture Delivered by Rev. Patrick Ryan, SJ. April 13 and 14, 2011. New York: Fordham University: Spring, 2011. 1–11.

Jones, Sam. "'A feeling of déjà vu': Author Sergio Ramírez on Ex-Comrade Ortega and Nicaraguan History Repeating." *The Guardian*. London: guardian.com, 18 September 2021.

Luiselli, Valeria. "Contra las tentaciones de la nueva crítica." *Nexos* 34.410 (2-2012): 50–53.

Martínez Rivas, Carlos. *Besos para la mujer de Lot y otros poemas* [Kisses for Lot's wife and other poems]. Prólogo, Sergio Ramírez. Muestrario de Poesía 23. Santo Domingo: Muestrario de Poesía, 2009. Electronic pdf.

Menton, Seymour. *The Spanish American Short Story: A Critical* Anthology. Lawrence: U of Kansas P, 1964. *El cuento hispanoamericano: Antología Crítico-Histórica*. 2 vols. Mexico: FCE, 1964.

Oreamuno, Yolanda. *La ruta de su evasión* [Her escape route]. San José, Costa Rica: Editorial Universitaria Centroamericana, 1970.

*El País*. "Discurso íntegro de Sergio Ramírez, Premio Cervantes 2017." Madrid: elpais.com. 23 April 2018.

Polit-Dueñas, Gabriela. "When Politicians Construct Father-Wor(l)ds: Sergio Ramírez's *Adiós Muchachos*." *Romance Notes* 44.2 (2003): 163–172.

[Qu'ran]. *The Holy Qu'ran with English Translation*. Trans. Ali Ösek, Nureddin Uzunoğlu, Tevfik Rüştü Topuzoğlu, and Mahmet Maksutoğlu. 3rd ed. Istanbul: İlmî Neşriyat, 1996.
Ramírez. Sergio. *Adiós muchachos. Una memoria de la revolución sandinista*. Mexico: Penguin Random House, 2015. *Adiós Muchachos: A Memoir of the Sandinista Revolution*. Durham, NC: Duke UP, 2011.
—. *Castigo divino*. Mexico: Alfaguara, 1988. 30th Anniversary ed., 2015. *Divine Punishment*. Trans. Nick Castor with Hebe Powell. 2015. Kingston, NY: McPherson, 2015.
—. "Cervantes Prize Acceptance Speech / Aceptación del Premio Cervantes." Trans. Rosario Drucker Davis. *LALT* 8 (November 2018). Norman, OK: U of Oklahoma, 2022.
—. *El cielo llora por mi*. Madrid: Alfaguara, 2009. *The Sky Weeps for Me: A Nicaraguan Mystery*. Trans. Leland H. Chambers. Kingston, NY: McPherson, 2018, 2020.
—. *Cuentos* [Short stories]. Managua: Editorial Nicaragüense, 1963.
—. *Cuentos completos* [Complete stories]. Mexico: Alfaguara, 1996. Madrid: Alfaguara, 1997. Mexico: FCE, 2013, 2014.
—. *La fugitiva* [The fugitive]. Madrid: Alfaguara, 2011.
—. *Margarita, está linda la mar*. Madrid: Santanilla, 1998. *Margarita, How Beautiful the Sea*. Trans. Michael B. Miller. Willimantic, CT: Curbstone, 2008.
—. "Reedición nicaragüense de *Tiempo de fulgor*." sergioramirez.com. 27 August 2018.
—. *Sara*. Mexico: Alfaguara, 2015.
—. *Tiempo de fulgor* [Season of brightness]. Guatemala: Editorial Universitaria, 1970. *Tiempo de fulgor*. Biblioteca popular de cultura universal. Managua: Editorial Nueva Nicaragua, 1986. *Tiempo de fulgor*. Havana: Editorial Arte y Literatura, 1986.
—. *Tongolele no sabía bailar* [Tongolele couldn't dance]. Madrid: Alfaguara, 2021.
—. *Ya nadie llora por mí* [Nobody cries for me anymore]. Barcelona: Alfaguara, 2017.
Spivak, Gayatri C. "Can the Subaltern Speak?" Ed. Carry Nelson and Laurence Grossberg. *Marxism and the Interpretation of Culture*. London: Macmillan, 1988. 271–313.
Urbina, Nicasio. "Essays of Sergio Ramírez / La obra ensayística de Sergio Ramírez." Trans George Henson. *LALT* 8 (2018).
Villarruel, Patricia. "Sergio Ramírez: '*La fugitiva* es la historia de muchos en una sola.'" *El Universo*, Guayaquil, Ecuador (24 April 2011). eluniverso.com.

# 7
# Patterns of Disintegration, Community, and Love in George Eliot's *Adam Bede*

## David O. Thompson

George Eliot is known for examining her characters within the context of community, exploring how conventions of love, friendship, marriage, and religion shape development.[1] As Eliot devises these patterns in her fiction, she probes how the community, too, is transformed by the resulting dialectic, an exchange—sometimes a clash—between the individual and the community that is central to much Victorian fiction. In *Adam Bede*, Eliot's first novel, she takes this approach in a self-consciously "realistic" fiction. Published in 1859, *Adam Bede* is set in the recent past, when British industrialization was beginning to threaten village traditions. Eliot describes, probably some years afterward, her view that individual struggles are largely governed by "hereditary conditions" or "inherited nature" that come into conflict with "the general," producing a "grand collision in the human lot."[2] The "general" is the collective force of a shared culture, and Eliot theorizes that the "irreparable collision between the individual and general" wins our recognition of the "irresistible power" of the general creating "real" tragedy and our sympathy for the individual.[3] The "general" force with which Eliot's more unhappy characters—Silas Marner, Godfrey Cass, Hetty Sorrel, Arthur Donnithorne, Gwendolen Harleth—collide is a community standard set by a religious group, a village, or English society more generally, in which shared history, custom, and moral prescriptions govern values and shape perceptions, including one's view of oneself. Eliot describes this social standard as tantamount to the "will of God" in that the individual must either avoid what others "have deemed to be harmful" or face some "peril" (*Letters* 3.34).

While critics have read Eliot's novels and short fiction for signs of influence from contemporary philosophy, her adherence to realism and "scientific" approach to character development and social context are often attributed specifically to the influence of Ludwig Andreas Feuerbach and David Friedrich Strauss.[4] Eliot's intellectual labors in translating Strauss's *Das Leben Jesu, kritisch bearbeitet* as *The Life of Jesus, Critically Examined* (hereinafter, *Life*) and Feuerbach's *Das Wesen des Christentums* as *The Essence of Christianity* (hereinafter, *Essence*) prior to writing *Adam Bede* have led a good number of critics to read it as a fictional expression of principles contained in one or both of those works.[5] To clarify these matters as a preface to my reading of *Adam Bede*, I will briefly characterize Strauss's and Feuerbach's philosophies as they relate to Eliot's fiction and summarize criticism concerned with philosophical "influences" on Eliot's fiction and her approach to realism.

Strauss and Feuerbach interpret Christianity through ideas of myth and purport to "demystify" Christianity with metaphors like awakening from a dream, cracking open a nut, lifting a veil, telling a secret, translating from a foreign language, and cracking a code. Todd Gooch writes that Strauss's *Life* "precipitated the gradual dissolution of the Hegelian synthesis of faith and knowledge" by applying contemporary historical methods to his reading of the Bible ("Feuerbach"). Using the metaphor of "unveiling," Strauss describes "the miraculous in the sacred history as a drapery which needs only to be drawn aside" to "disclose the pure historic form" (*Life* 50). Strauss argues that ancient religious people, answering a basic impulse, creatively transmitted their traditions and worldview through narratives to explain abstractions like revenge, justice, and divinity. In Strauss's view, "fictitious imagery" and "supernatural effulgence" obscure the "kernel of historical fact" in New Testament narratives of Jesus' life (91). As we will see, Strauss's metaphors of "cracking a nut" or "lifting a veil" in his analysis of myth become key metaphors in Eliot's fiction. For Strauss, Christianity's meaning—its biblical truth—lies within these "myths."

Strauss, then, anticipates in important ways Feuerbach's rejection of Hegel's speculative theology of Christianity in favor of realism, and Feuerbach, like Strauss before him, aims to reveal the true nature of religious belief. Both philosophers argue that the mystification of religion originates not in fraud but in mythologizing. While Strauss values myths like the New Testament life of Jesus because the myth represents a primitive stage of development of the Hegelian "Idea of the Christ," Feuerbach espouses "only" realism and views Christianity's "actual" significance as its message "about humankind," rather than about a transcendent Hegelian idea.[6] Feuerbach rejects Hegel's philosophy because he finds it too readily looking beyond "the real" for answers and truth. The result is Feuerbach's "religion of humanity," the most frequent critical context for those who examine Feuerbach's influence in Eliot's fiction.[7] Feuerbach's assertion that one discovers the "deepest secrets [. . .] in the simplest natural things" while "pining away for the Beyond," thereby "trampling" those secrets underfoot, is but one metaphor that leads Ulrich C. Knoepflmacher to characterize Feuerbach's view as "anti-theological theology" (*Religious* 44). Similar assessments of *Adam Bede*'s philosophical and theological underpinnings have been made before and since Knoepflmacher, and, beginning with nineteenth-century critic Richard Simpson, I will outline briefly the substance of that critical tradition.

In 1863, Simpson began a line of Eliot criticism that would endure into the twenty-first century, claiming that knowledge of Strauss and Feuerbach would be necessary for a truly informed reading of *Adam Bede*. Simpson asserted that Feuerbach's "key to the cipher of the Christian religion" (*Essence* viii) was itself a key to unlock *Adam Bede* (249). Of Strauss's and Feuerbach's influence on the novel, Simpson, "go[ing] directly and with easy authority to the foundations of [Eliot's] ethical belief," declared, "It is no small victory to show that the godless humanitarianism of Strauss and Feuerbach can be made to appear the living centre of all the popular religions" (225).[8] Simpson found *Adam Bede* hiding the "atheism and pantheism" of Strauss and Feuerbach under the "garb of self-sacrifice, renunciation, and universal charity" (249). In the 1960s, Bernard J. Paris notes Eliot's "break with Christianity," her "well[-]known" lack of belief in God, and her "derivation" of "an undogmatic pantheism" based on the thought of Bray, Carlyle, Hennell, Spinoza, and Wordsworth, with which she eventually "broke."[9] In 1965, Paris argues in favor of reading *Adam Bede* as a Feuerbachian analysis of the community's spiritual life (*Experiments*), and Knoepflmacher observes that critics had already thoroughly explored "[Eliot's] typical refuge in the pantheism of Spinoza and Wordsworth" (*Religious* 44).[10] Knoepflmacher insists on a "grasp of [higher criticism's] intellectual crosscurrents" as "indispensable" for reading Eliot's fiction and laments readers "uninterested" in connecting her earlier and later novels to an "ideological background" (*Ibid*. 25–26).[11]

Some thirty years after Knoepflmacher and Paris, Kimberly VanEsveld Adams argues that Eliot idealizes Adam Bede as a "feminized Godhead" representing a "Feuerbachian Christ-figure,"[12] and shortly afterward, Jonathan Loesberg notes Eliot's frequently cited agree[ment]" with Feuerbach, charging that Feuerbach's "implicit atheism" suggests "the corrosive possibilities in Eliot's use of him" (133).[13] In 2005, John Mazaheri finds Feuerbach's view of "the consciousness [. . .] man has of his own nature" portrayed in *Adam Bede* as "not finite and limited [nature], but infinite nature."[14] J. Russell Perkin's 2009 study explores the question of biblical echoes and religious sensibility in *Adam Bede*, including considerations of Strauss's and Feuerbach's philosophies. In 2013, Terry Eagleton directs attention to *Adam Bede*'s philosophical reflections, and Jonathan Rée, in his 2019 study, emphasizes philosophical influences on Eliot's view of religion, finding her view especially indebted to Feuerbach.

As Simpson does in naming Auguste Comte and Johann Wolfgang von Goethe as *Adam Bede*'s philosophical fathers, some critics suggest influences beyond Strauss and Feuerbach on *Adam Bede* and on her later fiction. Knoepflmacher cites critical examinations of Eliot's "early essays and reviews" tracing ideas in her novels "in the light of Darwin, Huxley, Comte, Mill, Lewes, Spencer, Hennell, Strauss, or Feuerbach" (*Religious* 24). Sean Gaston notes that Eliot was an attentive reader of Comte, Spinoza, and Immanuel Kant, and they, too, according, variously, to Paris, Suzy Anger, Thomas Deegan, Tim Dolin, and Jon Singleton, left impressions on Eliot's thought and her practice as a novelist. Avrom Fleishman acknowledges Strauss's philosophy as edging Eliot away from her early beliefs, but speculates that she may "have found in Spinoza a philosophy of religion that could serve to replace her inherited and discarded one" (*Intellectual* 35).[15]

A few critics carry the question of philosophical influence further afield: Adams segues from Eliot's sympathy with Feuerbach's ideas to Marx and Engels's view of Feuerbach and observes, "Eliot is not a Marxist" and "is much more deeply engaged with the ideas of Comte, Spencer, and Lewes than with those of Marx and Engels" (47–48). Anger (*Victorian*) finds Eliot's view on the "interpretation of signs" concurs with that expressed by Nietzsche in "On Truth and Lying in an Extra-Moral Sense" and notes Daniel Cottom also linking Eliot with Nietzsche's thought (112); Anger avers, however, that Eliot's views on interpretation are "more akin" to those of the German Romantic Friedrich Schleiermacher (97–98). John Rignall suggests commonality between the thought of Friedrich Nietzsche and Eliot's fiction, particularly in *Daniel Deronda*. J. Hillis Miller, in 2012, though, demurs on the matter of Eliot's having read Marx: "[N]o evidence I know of exists that Eliot ever read Marx" and any supposed "echo" of Marx's view in Eliot must be regarded as "coincidental" (99).[16] In addition, Fleishman's accounts of Eliot's known reading do not include Marx, Engels, or Nietzsche.[17] Nietzsche, for his part, having read at least some of Eliot's novels in German translation, dismissed the idea of German philosophical influence and disdained what he deemed to be her philosophical grounding in Christian morality and Jean-Jacques Rousseau.[18] Christopher Herbert points to instances of Eliot's contemporary critical reception that discard religious skepticism as the dominant reading of *Adam Bede*. He notes that some readers suspected the pseudonymous author was a clergyman, and critics found in *Adam Bede* "a pronounced religious strain" and an "appeal to religious sentiment" (158–159). [19]

A few critics present Eliot as devising her own views. Vanderbilt theologian Peter C. Hodgson distances Eliot from all ideological viewpoints, and Valerie A. Dodd also affirms Eliot's independence of thought. Dodd notes that Eliot "entertained [. . .] reservations which marred her experience of translating [Strauss]" and that her translation of Feuerbach spoke to "some of Marian Evans's main preoccupations" and "echoed [her] recoil from the over-theoretical cast of Positivism, and from Spencer's ignoring [. . .] the concrete complexity of life" (181). The important shift in Eliot's thinking about her inherited religion preceded her reading of Strauss, and Gaston contends: "Eliot's loss of Orthodox faith was precipitated in 1841 by her reading of Unitarian Charles Hennell's *Inquiry Concerning the Origin of Christianity*" (319).[20] Gaston finds Eliot resorting, nonetheless, to "Anglican frameworks" as contexts for representing characters of other religions—such as Methodism—and "represent[ing] religion as a difficult and ever-shifting relation between enthusiasm, egoism and ethics" (318). Reviewing the work of Strauss and Feuerbach as influences on Eliot's fiction, Gaston asserts that Eliot's "*later* reading of Strauss, Spinoza, Feuerbach, Spencer, Comte, Lewes, Darwin and others merely confirmed her own clear-sighted resolutions at the age of twenty-two" (319, emphasis added). Marilyn Orr, exploring the influences of religious debates on Eliot's early fiction, demonstrates "the importance to [Eliot] of the individual as a spiritual being" (7), independent of Strauss's and Feuerbach's views.[21]

Beyond Strauss's and Feuerbach's supposed influence on spiritual and religious elements in Eliot's fiction, their "scientific" perspectives are credited with shaping her approach to realism. Glenda Sacks, for example, asserts that in *Adam Bede*, Eliot's view of realism as encompassing a "moral enterprise of truth-telling" inspired her to compose "an anthropologically realistic account of rustic life in the form of a Feuerbachian allegory."[22] But Gail McGrew Eifrig's suggestion that

Eliot's approach to realism and history in fiction owed—much more broadly—to her translating and reviewing "immense amounts of history, philosophy, and literature" during the years before she took up the work of *Adam Bede*[23] likewise resonates with the priority of the particular in Eliot's theory of realism, a point I return to below. In her 1855 review of Otto Gruppe's consideration of German philosophy, for instance, Eliot writes that "a system of logic [. . .] which assigns the first place to general ideas [. . .] inverts the true order of things."[24] Moreover, Eliot's knowledge of contemporary painting and artistic theory is also germane to her "realistic" approach as an author of fiction. In her review of John Ruskin's *Modern Painters III* in 1856, Eliot emphasized *"realism"* as "the truth of infinite value"—"the doctrine that all truth and beauty are to be obtained by a humble and faithful study of nature and not by substituting vague forms, bred by imagination on the mists of feeling, in place of definite, substantial reality."[25] Luc Hermann contends that Ruskin's influence on Eliot in this regard "cannot be overestimated" (20), and to that point, Darrel Mansell describes Eliot's review as "enthusiastic" and notes that James D. Rust and Richard Stang take it as confirmation that Eliot is a realist (203).

Deborah Epstein Nord, however, expands Eliot's scope and understanding of realism, affirming that Eliot's wide, well-informed interests and taste drew her to multiple approaches to realism. According to Nord, Eliot's "interest in painting [. . .] was inseparable from her desire to practice and promote Realist fiction" ("Ethics" 361). Nord calls Eliot "perhaps the keenest and best educated observer of painting among the major novelists," and contends that far from a sole focus on Dutch paintings "as analogs" to her fictional realism, Eliot was also drawn to the "naturalism" of the Pre-Raphaelites' "idiosyncratic" realism, with the school's "focus on human relationships, and their infusion of the contemporary with symbolic and spiritual meaning" (361). Perkin, too, affirms Eliot's adherence to the tenet of "clear images" in the Pre-Raphaelites' "realist aesthetic": to create a mimetic reality "infused" with Eliot's "earnest ethical idealism."[26] It is the particular—the details of realism in fiction and Dutch or Pre-Raphaelite painting—that leads ineluctably to the general.

## Reading *Adam Bede*
### The Community and the Individual

*Adam Bede* opens on a series of similarly realistic scenes, vividly painted in their several frames of reference, and kinetic, too, as they show the forces of social evolution arriving in the community of Hayslope in 1799. The significance of these scenes grows increasingly complicated by problems of mythologizing and truth-telling, tensions with which Eliot was intimately familiar, and against the background of bucolic scenery and village custom, *Adam Bede* presents the productive development of some characters and the disintegration of others, patterns of their lives formed in community with others: Adam, Hetty, and Arthur are associated with the village of Hayslope and the estate owned by Arthur's grandfather, the squire, while Dinah comes from Snowfield, a bleak, factory town in Stonyshire, distinct from Hayslope in geographical features and in the occupations and perspectives of its people. Dinah lodges with her aunt and uncle Poyser at Hall Farm and is quickly accepted into Hayslope life in spite of her religious and cultural differences. The fates and actions of Adam, Arthur, Hetty, and Dinah are entwined by unfolding events. Their definitive personal characteristics and values determine their responses and the extent to which they develop in harmony or in conflict with community conventions.

Signs of change coming to Hayslope create tension in *Adam Bede*'s early chapters: Adam resolves a dispute among friends in the workshop, and "Methodism" pulls at the theological threads of village life; Adam nurtures his love for Hetty, but Arthur notices Hetty, and she is taken with Arthur, while Mr. Irwine, the rector and Arthur's tutor, sensing trouble, warns Arthur in general but dire terms about love's pitfalls. Dinah arrives as an outsider whose visible and conscientious identification with Methodism threatens the tranquility of Hayslope's religious orthodoxy. The conflict between Adam's love for Hetty and Arthur's clandestine love affair with her implies the nature of the novel's crisis: romantic delusions and secrets set in motion patterns of disintegration that menace individuals and the community.[27]

The narrator opens the novel by establishing a specific time and place to lend the story realism and nostalgia: it is late afternoon, the eighteenth of June, 1799, within the Hayslope workshop of Jonathan Burge. Brothers Adam and Seth Bede are foregrounded in the shop milieu and are so closely described, in terms of their Saxon and Celtic traits, that the reader, visiting Hayslope, might readily recognize them (1–12). As Adam walks home from his day's work, "an elderly horseman, with his portmanteau strapped behind him" stops to "admir[e]" Adam, the "stalwart workman" (12). From the narrator's close study of Adam in the shop, the reader, a mere step ahead of this outsider, has already "admired" Adam and knows something of his world. In the second chapter, "The Preaching," the unnamed "elderly horseman"—"the stranger" or "the traveller"—stops at the inn to water his horse and learns from the innkeeper that people are gathering in the village because Dinah, a newcomer to Hayslope, is about to preach on the town green (13).

In describing the traveler's entry into Hayslope's environs, the narrator opens the door to an essentially closed community, a village that is part of the "rich undulating district of Loamshire" (16), to expose the reader to the nostalgia of this bygone place, as well as to the workings of its prejudices. Within a few chapters, the narrator tours the clean and prosperous Hall Farm, where the Poysers, tenant farmers on the Donnithorne estate, oversee their impeccable dairy operation, robust livestock, and successful crops (64–80), and further on, overviews the luxury and leisure of the Donnithorne way of life (112–117). The landscapes of Loamshire and Hayslope suggest bountiful harvests and a pastoral idyll, in contrast to "a grim outskirt of Stonyshire" lying nearby (*Ibid.*), with its village of Stoniton and the nearly-treeless, "dreary bleak" mill-town of Snowfield, where discomfort and toil characterize community life (80–81). As Eliot makes clear, however, Hayslope's suggested bounty and beauty, the peace and work ethic of the farm, and the prosperity and comfort of the estate are subjects of myth making, and their inhabitants' flawed perspectives will threaten individuals and the community.

## Methodism in Hayslope

Hayslope's responses to Methodism and the stranger's impressions reveal not only the uncertainty of the community's traditional existence, but also Eliot's commitment to uncovering causes and describing their effects to the reader. Joshua Rann, village shoemaker and parish clerk, reveals his "simmering indignation" at the prospect of Dinah's preaching Methodism on the green. In his "resounding bass undertone," Rann inexplicably recites, "Sehon, King of the Amorites: for His mercy endureth for ever; and Og the King of Basan: for His mercy endureth for ever" (18).[28] The narrator parses this apparent "anomaly" by delving into Rann's hidden thoughts: he has sought "inwardly [to maintain] the dignity of the Church in the face of this scandalous irruption of Methodism," and the "argument" that comes to him emerges from "his own sonorous utterance" of the Psalm responses. Rann fuses the urge to preserve Anglican "dignity" with the lines "he had read the last Sunday afternoon" in his performance. The narrator counsels the reader that "adequate knowledge will show a natural sequence," the principle of cause and effect that Eliot makes fundamental to her fiction.

The traveler looking on from the inn has a more complex intellectual response to Dinah and her sermon, but like Rann's, his initial reaction is based on an emotional preconception. He expresses the surprise of a worldly outsider that there should be many Methodists in rural Hayslope, and affirms deprecatingly that he knows "but two types of Methodists—the ecstatic and the bilious" (21).[29] The narrator tells us that the traveler had "made up his mind to see [Dinah] advance with a measured step, and a demure solemnity of countenance" and "felt sure that her face would be mantled with the smile of conscious saintship, or else charged with denunciatory bitterness" (20–21). The traveler's expectations—perhaps shared by the novel's worldly readers—are challenged when Dinah walks toward her podium "as simply as if she were going to market" and appears to be as unselfconscious "as a little boy" (21). The stranger is spellbound by her voice and delivery—undermining his stereotypical and gendered preconceptions—and he is "chained to the spot against his will by the charm of Dinah's mellow treble tones, which had a variety of modulation like that of a fine instrument touched with the unconscious skill of musical instinct" (25).[30] Music and honesty, elements already associated with Adam's character and his work song, arise again in the stranger's impression of Dinah's sermon: "The simple things she said seemed like novelties, as a melody thrills us with a new feeling when we hear it sung by the pure voice of a boyish chorister; the quiet depth of conviction with which she spoke seemed in itself an evidence for the truth of her message" (25). This is the traveler's second metaphor comparing Dinah to a male child, evidently his standard for simplicity and innocence. His response to Dinah's sermon is emotional rather than intellectual because he cannot entirely escape his prejudices, having been swept up by Dinah's voice, appearance, and manner, rather than by what she says.

Eliot's first association of powerful feeling with music in the novel is significant because it counters the narrator's pattern of scientific demystification, and, in spite of some movement to backtrack, as I will show, the effect is to destabilize the unique power of science to convey truth—though critics have been virtually unanimous in affirming Strauss's and Feuerbach's work as essential to Eliot's use of demystification as a plot device. The scene at the close of Dinah's sermon demonstrates this destabilization: when Dinah's sermon concludes, the narrator describes the traveler's response first in intellectual terms, as an interest in "the development of a drama," but then highlights the traveler's emotional response, a "fascination in all sincere unpremeditated eloquence" that allows spectators to glimpse "the inward drama of the speaker's [Dinah's] emotions" (30). The traveler—and presumably the reader—is being pulled into an understanding of Dinah as a particular character, no longer simply a stereotyped "Methodist."

## Patterns of Disintegration

These opening narratives of emotional vulnerability, anxiety over the future, the appeal and denigration of female finery, and the interested male gaze serve partly as harbingers of the self-serving illusions and mutual attraction that soon overpower Hetty and Arthur. Arthur fantasizes about his future as the beloved master of the Donnithorne family estates, yet he soon longs to see Hetty again, heedless of her social station. Hetty wants to marry Arthur to have his attentions and enjoy the comfort and style implied in his wealth. During the weeks after Arthur has begun to notice her, Hetty develops a distorted view of their relationship described as "vague" and "atmospheric, shaping itself into no self-confessed hopes or prospects" (91). Hetty's new sensation "produces a pleasant narcotic effect, making her tread the ground and go about her work in a sort of dream, [...] showing her all things through a soft, liquid veil."

While this "beatified world" marks Hetty's alienation from her family and the larger community, the narrator affirms that Hetty's dream is based, in part, on a class illusion shared with the community. Arthur's superior social rank casts a spell over Hetty, "a simple farmer's girl, to whom a gentleman with a white hand was dazzling as an Olympian god" (92).[31] While chapter nine ("Hetty's World") works to demystify Hetty's delusions and to reveal Arthur's self-aggrandizing desire to be a beloved, exemplary squire, the reasons of each of them for desiring the other prove to be egoistic—the worst sort of mystification in the novel's value system, where sympathy with others is highly valued if not paramount.[32] Following their first meeting in the Grove, the two approach their second "chance" meeting with great anticipation: Hetty finds tears filling her eyes when she thinks Arthur is not coming, and Arthur is "full of one thought [...] of which she only is the object" (123–124). After their meeting, Arthur decides that "[h]e was getting in love with Hetty" and vows not to see her again (121), a resolution that he cannot keep. Through several more chapters, the narrator continues to reveal the self-gratifying, undiscerning nature of Hetty's and Arthur's yearnings.

When Arthur embraces Hetty for the first time, the narrator compares them to new-fallen fruit, "young unfurrowed souls" that "roll to meet each other like two velvet peaches that touch softly and are at rest"; moreover, their coming together is achieved "as easily as [that of] two brooklets that ask nothing but to entwine themselves" (120), suggesting that a natural inevitability governs their embrace. Time alters for them when Arthur's arms reach around Hetty and their eyes meet—"What a space of time those three moments were" (120)—and time disappears, along with geography and history, at their first kiss, when "for a long moment time has vanished" and encompassed the ages: Arthur "may be a shepherd in Arcadia [. . .], the first youth kissing the first maiden [. . . or] Eros himself, sipping the lips of Psyche" (124). Contrasted with Hetty and Arthur's illusion of timelessness as they make love, the calendar and clock in the world of the novel are demanding elements of shared, precise knowledge, and ignoring them has consequences. On several occasions, Hetty runs afoul of Mrs. Poyser's Hall Farm clock because it is set ahead of the Donnithorne's clock, putting Hetty in peril of discovery. Suggesting the consequences of Hetty and Arthur's carelessness, the narrator recalls the metaphor of new-fallen peaches to muse, "People who love downy peaches are apt not to think of the stone, and sometimes jar their teeth terribly against it" (139).

Arthur's desire for Hetty prevents him from considering the "stone" at the center of his "downy" attraction to her, and Arthur's need for community approval spins another illusion without his recognizing the danger his heedless infatuation poses to his aspirations as a well-loved landowner, but that romantic idea, too, is fraught with Arthur's lack of discernment. Arthur sees himself making improvements to equipment and modernizing farming methods on the estate, and his vision is to transform "what was a wild country, all of the same dark hue" to orderly holdings, "bright and variegated with corn and cattle" (154). He envisions his grateful laborers "touching their hats to him" as he passes. Contrasted with Arthur's painterly view of his future as a benevolent overlord, his future tenants hope for practical, useful improvements when Arthur takes the reins: "a millennial abundance of new gates, allowances of lime, and returns of ten per cent" (78). Though Arthur's place in the community is virtually assured by his birth and landholdings, Arthur "live[s] a good deal in other people's opinions and feelings concerning himself" (155) and holds the conviction that he can right every wrong with a compensating gift or gesture, as he does when Adam discovers his and Hetty's affair.

When Arthur visits Mr. Irwine to confess his conduct with Hetty, Arthur's desire to retain Mr. Irwine's good opinion defeats his intention to confess, but Arthur diverts his tutor onto the subjects of love and the weakness of one who "may be very firm in other matters, and yet be under a sort of witchery from a woman" (155). Suspecting that Arthur is in trouble, Mr. Irwine attempts, in general terms, to demystify the situation and the object of Arthur's fascination, suggesting that a man ("firm in other matters" but "under a sort of witchery") should keep reminding himself of the "unpleasant consequences" of falling in love (156). Mr. Irwine analogizes the bewitched man's necessity for truth to the use of a curious optical instrument "through which you may look at the resplendent fair one and discern her true outline"[33]; however, Mr. Irwine confides, the instrument "is apt to be missing just at the moment it is most wanted" (157). As Mr. Irwine fears, Hetty and Arthur's desire and delusions overcome Mr. Irwine's urging that Arthur foresee the truth of "unpleasant [future] consequences." Mr. Irwine affirms Eliot's view of the "irreparable collision between the individual and general" in response to one of Arthur's pretexts: "Consequences are unpitying. Our deeds carry their terrible consequences [. . .] that are hardly ever confined to ourselves" (156).

## The Accidents of Love

Hetty's and Arthur's perspectives on their affair are distinct—dependent on social status, education, and the nature of each one's urgency and degree of worldliness—but Arthur is, nevertheless, in love with Hetty, as he will vow to the end. The narrator describes Hetty's perspective as unseeing, of being in a dream-like state, and metaphors of "spinning" and "webs" in relation to Hetty's illusions are those Feuerbach uses to describe the nature of religious beliefs.[34] Eliot creates a similar metaphor in a domestic context to suggest that Hetty's lack of industry around the farm owes to Hetty's "spinning in young ignorance a light web of folly and vain hopes" (227). Hetty's plan to "be a lady in silks and satins," the narrator tells us, is a vision "all spun by her own childish fancy," but Arthur admits that it "was spun half out of his own actions" (282). Though Arthur acknowledges being implicated in Hetty's "web," he vows having spoken "no word with the purpose of deceiving her" (282). Yet their sexual intimacy, his purchase of valuables for her, and their exchange of love tokens are signs of his deception of Hetty and of his self-delusion: Hetty's locket and her gold pearl and garnet earrings are her "private treasures" (226), and Arthur retains a "small pink silk handkerchief" as a love token, taking pains to conceal it from Adam (275).

Arthur's delusions about his interactions with Hetty and his feelings for her begin to be unmasked in the sobering breakfast conversation with Mr. Irwine to which I referred above. The process continues in a darker mode when Adam catches sight of them in the Grove, well before Gyp's bark startles them apart (267), and Adam sees they are poised for a kiss.[35] Adam's earlier points of confusion about Hetty—"the locket and everything else that had been doubtful to him"—are resolved in a moment that shatters his illusions as "a terrible scorching light showed him the hidden letters that changed the meaning of the past" (268). When Arthur comes toward Adam, "saunter[ing]" past him "in evening dress of fine cloth and fine linen, his white jeweled hands half thrust into his waistcoat pockets," Adam stands unmoving and demands that Arthur stay (268). When Arthur tries to diminish his interaction with Hetty as an incidental, innocent flirtation, Adam counters that he is not "deceive[d]," calling Arthur a "light-minded scoundrel" (269). Arthur's aloof demeanor conceals his anxiety over the potential for public knowledge when he tells himself that Adam is "the best person who could have happened to see him and Hetty together," because Adam "would not babble about it to other people" (268). Arthur continues to present an unconcerned exterior when he tries a further rationalization on Adam: it is an old custom for the high-born man and the simple country girl to come together for an enjoyable flirtation (269).

Though Adam dismisses Arthur's effort to excuse and veil his actions, Arthur soon realizes, with "sudden relief," that "Adam can still be deceived" (270). When Adam parses Arthur's conduct under the principle of village morality, Arthur attempts to deceive Adam about his and Hetty's sexual intimacy (270), leading Adam to disclose his love for Hetty. Adam's revelation gives Arthur a reason for regret: "All screening self-excuse, which rarely falls quite away while others respect us, forsook [Arthur] for an instant, and he stood face to face with the first great irrevocable evil he had ever committed" (271). Despite that moment of truth, Arthur maintains his denials, and Adam reproaches him as a "double-faced man" (272). The physical blows that follow show the reader Adam's fierce sense of Arthur's wrongs toward Hetty, but Arthur won't admit the truth. The scene closes on Adam's fear that he may have killed Arthur with a heavy blow, but Arthur revives with time and brandy and continues the deception.

Adam, wary of Arthur's hold on Hetty, won't shake hands until Arthur has written a letter of definitive farewell to Hetty. Adam continues to reject Arthur's rationalizations, reminding him that "things don't lie level between you" and that the social distinction and Hetty's age—"[s]he's all but a child"—should make "any man with a conscience in him [. . .] feel bound to take care on" (278). Where Adam before had once viewed Arthur in "round, gentlemanly epithets," Adam has become Arthur's "Nemesis," taking the form of "some rude person"—a plain-spoken, clear-sighted working man— who "gives rough names to [Arthur's] actions" (281). Adam's pitiless characterizations of Arthur's "actions" reveal their true nature and make Adam an interpreter of the affair, as well as a sharer in the secret.

The next day Arthur continues to deflect his culpability and to misrepresent the extent of the affair to Adam. Arthur hides Hetty's pink silk neckerchief from Adam and is torn between impulses to get away on the one hand and to "carry Hetty away" on the other (283). Arthur is stricken briefly with "a sudden dread" when he considers the possibility that Hetty will attempt to kill herself over his departure and then entertains "another dread, which deepened the shadow" (284), a reference, surely, to the possibility that Hetty is pregnant from their "trifling and flirting" (278), as Arthur mischaracterizes their relationship to Adam. The narrator observes that had anyone practiced such a great deception upon Arthur, he would have "resented it as a deep wrong" (285), but Arthur, who envisions himself admired and beloved by his grandfather's tenants, is immune to an authentic I-thou consideration of working-class feelings in a world where sympathy is central to community. Nonetheless, before Arthur leaves with his regiment, he pens the farewell letter to Hetty that Adam has demanded and leaves it with Adam to give to Hetty— or to withhold from her—as Adam judges (286). While Arthur treats the letter lightly and continues to lie to Adam, the letter will unveil Arthur's faithlessness to Hetty.

The following Sunday, when it becomes clear to Adam that Hetty persists in nurturing her hope that Arthur "does care" for her (290), Adam gives her the letter (291), and a good many pages further on, the narrator describes the violence it practices on Hetty with phrases emphasizing destruction: the "*shattering* of all her little dream-world," a "*crushing blow* on her new-born passion," and "*overpowering* pain that *annihilated* all impulse to resistance" (301, emphasis added). Arthur's words crush Hetty's hopes, and her suffering is genuine: she "sobb[ed] until the candle went out, and then wearied, aching, stupefied with crying, threw herself on the bed without undressing" to fall into a troubled sleep (301). The next day, her misery deepens when she finds that Arthur's "little trinkets" offer no hope of "her future paradise of finery" (301). Hetty's emotions evolve through a process of demystification, and she confirms her judgment of the previous night that the letter is "cruel." Where her "anger" toward Arthur had been "suspended" by her grief the night before, she now "hate[s]" him (302–303) and views him and their relationship in an unforgiving light.

Though Adam fails to grasp the truth of the affair, Hetty, perhaps already fearing pregnancy, alters her attitude toward Adam and agrees to marry him. In part, at least, Hetty consents because a dull vision of a future with Adam provides at least a glimpse of her passion and pleasure with Arthur: "She wanted to be caressed—she wanted to feel as if Arthur were with her again" (323). In this sense, Hetty's "love" for Adam is "mediated," in René Girard's term, by her desire to re-experience with Adam sensations she enjoyed with Arthur, and Hetty's mediation fulfills her pattern of devising self-serving delusions.[36] Hetty's discovery of her pregnancy, however, crushes the fragile equilibrium won by the betrothal and initiates the crisis that uproots her from the community to flee to Windsor in search of Arthur, exposing their transgression to communities beyond Hayslope.

## "Out of all human reach"

Though Hetty fears leaving the farm and Hayslope for the unknown, she is also afraid to face "discovery and scorn among the relatives and neighbours who once more made all her world, now her airy dream had vanished" (329). For a month before she runs away from home, Hetty considers drowning herself in a "dark shrouded pool" in the Scantlands, but when she comes to such a pool, she "has not the courage to jump into that cold watery bed," and she rationalizes that if she had gone in, her family would be shamed when she was found (328). Hetty's rejection of the pool's dark, cold water leads her to imagine that Arthur will not cast her out into the parallel cold and dark of the world, but that he will "receive her tenderly," and these thoughts wrap Hetty in a sense of "lulling warmth" (329).

As she makes her way to Windsor, Hetty meets the coldness of a world where she knows no one and is, at best, a curiosity. She discards her fantasy that Arthur will take her in and longs to return to Hayslope, to the "people on whom she had an acknowledged claim"

(333). Her feelings of estrangement accentuate the humanizing value of her lost community. Compounding her disillusionment is Hetty's discovery that Arthur is no longer at Windsor but in Ireland, and she sets out, retracing the way she had come, yet without intending to return home (344). Hetty's desire to rejoin the Hayslope community is impossible to fulfill, and again she thinks of a dark pool like the one she visited earlier and wonders whether drowning is painful, associating her exile with the experience of death. Traveling toward Stratford-on-Avon, Hetty expects to find "just the sort of pool she had in mind," taking cues from the lay of the land and clumps of trees, until at last she discovers one (344–345). Hetty often sidesteps her resolve, but the narrator describes her alienation from community as a virtual death: "The horror of this cold, and darkness, and solitude—out of all human reach—became greater every long minute: it was almost as if she were dead already" (346). Alive still, but suffering from the cold, Hetty seeks shelter in a hovel of furze set among the sheep for lambing season (347). Looking to Feuerbach, one may interpret Hetty's isolation and resort to the hovel near the sheepfold as her definitive separation from community into an animal-like, instinctive mode of survival. Her plight demonstrates Feuerbach's view that alienation from the community is virtual madness or death and recalls his precept that only in community does one claim humanity.[37] Hetty's separation from the human world is the culmination of the pattern of disintegration that began when reading Arthur's letter shattered her "little dream-world."

Hetty is awakened the next morning by an elderly herder (348) whose quick, rude honesty recalls Adam's assessment of Arthur. The man scolds Hetty for wandering away from the road and says she looks like a "wild woman" and will be robbed if she "go[es] trapsesin' about the fields like a mad woman" (348–349), forthright observations that Hetty sets aside for future consideration. Her dread urges her toward Stonyshire, "within reach of Dinah" at Snowfield (349), because she dreams Dinah will comfort her—perhaps a foreshadowing of Dinah's offering Hetty spiritual consolation in prison—but Hetty's dread also counsels her that she can no more resort to Dinah than throw herself into a pool, because her shame would then become known, not merely to Dinah, but to the community (349).

## Revelations

With Hetty's dark musings, the narrator ceases relating her travels—their outcome uncertain—and turns the reader's attention to Hayslope and the effects of Hetty's long, unexplained absence on Adam and the community. As Adam grows impatient with Hetty's absence, events unfold in Stonyshire, at Stoniton, where the magistrate finds two names in Hetty's pocketbook, her own, with "Hayslope" written alongside, and "Dinah Morris, Snowfield" (367), but Hetty refuses to tell the magistrate who she is and where she comes from. Her silence functions internally to drive the plot through cause and effect: in refusing to own the name and place that would attach her to family and community, Hetty effaces her place in the world and silently asserts, as she thought earlier, that she is "dead already" (346). Because the magistrate must discover whom he has arrested, he inadvertently writes to the very man—Mr. Irwine at Hayslope—who will take pains to inform Adam of Hetty's fate.

After a fortnight of Hetty's absence, Adam fears that she has run away and decides to see Mr. Irwine to reveal what he believes will be the painful news that Arthur has seduced Hetty (365). But Mr. Irwine, with his own sad revelation to share, shows Adam the magistrate's letter describing Hetty's crime of infanticide and her arrest (366–367). When Mr. Irwine confirms Hetty's identity to the authorities in Stoniton, English justice goes forward, with each witness unveiling a heretofore hidden word or deed of Hetty's to implicate her in her crime, until the most reluctant to believe it must admit the truth of the jury's hard verdict.[38] Hetty's shame blackens the Poyser's name, too, and is cause for mourning, "a misfortune felt to be worse than death," because the family's honor, staked on generations of good repute in the community, has received "too keen [a hurt,] even in the kind-hearted Martin Poyser the younger, to leave room for any compassion towards Hetty" (371).[39] Adam, however, attends the court sessions and perceives "a deep horror, like a great gulf" looming between him and Hetty (392). Bridging the "gulf" between the self-effaced Hetty and her former community, Dinah secures permission from the magistrate to remain with Hetty as she awaits execution (399–400), and Dinah persuades Hetty to tell her story (404–408).[40] In Dinah's effort to redeem Hetty, she persuades Adam to visit Hetty in prison (408–409), but Adam sees Hetty there "as if she had come back to him from the dead to tell him of her misery" (412).

Ignorant of Hetty's pregnancy, her crime, and the discovery of their affair, Arthur returns to Hayslope for his grandfather's funeral. His delusions about Hetty are maintained by a weeks-old correspondence with Mr. Irwine telling of Hetty and Adam's betrothal. Arthur feels "at ease about Hetty" and expects to be greeted with joy by the community's familiar faces (393), but the screw turns at the close of a chapter dedicated to painting Arthur's nostalgia for his imagined community of admirers when Arthur opens a letter from Mr. Irwine that narrates recent events (398). Arthur's eleventh-hour arrival on horseback at the Stoniton scaffold (414) where Hetty was to have been executed announces that her penalty has been commuted to "transportation for life," but "life" in the British colonies severs forever her connections to her former community, and, as if to enforce the immutable nature of that separation, Hetty dies on the homeward voyage when she is pardoned after years of enforced deportation (480).

While Arthur remains untouched by the law, his delusion that one may err without incurring lasting consequences collapses under the weight of the suffering he witnesses, and he imposes self-exile with his regiment and lives out a remorseful, self-castigating existence. He is bereft of his native community, stripped of his hopes for being loved by cheerful, grateful tenants and workers, and he relinquishes the right to continue his family line. At Arthur's leave-taking, the watch and chain he gives Adam for Dinah is more than a sign of Arthur's respect for Dinah or a sacrifice of gentlemanly finery. In concert with this reading of the novel, the gift signals Arthur's acknowledgement of the reality that time has irretrievably unveiled his actions and will continue to unfold their "unpitying" consequences (156), and the gold links of the chain suggest the sequence of events that led predictably to that reckoning. The last the reader hears of Arthur, he has confirmed, through the years of his exile, what Adam had long ago told him (418), "There's a sort o' damage, sir, that can't be made up for" (480–482). As the narrator observes, perhaps echoing the sentiment of Eliot's Victorian readers, "God preserve you and me from being the beginners of such misery!" (350).

## Patterns of Love

*Adam Bede* opens with an incipient pattern of disintegration based on delusional, romanticized love and closes with a pattern of love and marriage embedded in community—but also romanticized. The delusions, subterfuges, and devastating consequences of Arthur and Hetty's affair contrast with the story of Adam and Dinah's falling in love and marrying, though their stories share some common threads. Like Arthur and Hetty, Adam, Seth, and Dinah end up in positions they do not anticipate for much of the novel. Seth hopes to marry the pious Dinah, who shares his Methodist beliefs; Dinah believes she will never marry because she has a spiritual calling; Seth believes Adam loves Hetty, and Adam knows that Seth wants to marry Dinah; everyone knows Adam loves Hetty and is working to deserve her.[41] Adam, Seth, and Dinah are open about their plans and have future expectations that are consonant with their personal histories and gifts. Their self-deceptions in matters of love are due to denial of personal feelings or resistance to circumstances that counter their beliefs. On the other hand, Hetty builds a delusionary world with unfounded visions of social and material advancement revolving around Arthur's wealth and position, and Arthur, deciding he is "getting in love" with Hetty, constructs an illusory future where he distributes beneficence and offers generous compensation to erase his missteps. Adam and Dinah harbor certain illusions about Hetty, crediting her with the capacity to respond with love and unselfishness toward others.

Like Arthur and Hetty's love, Adam's love for Hetty is a web woven of repeated misinterpretations. At Thias Bede's funeral, Hetty is saddened by Arthur's absence, and Adam, in his romantic delusion about Hetty's character, reads her mood amiss, interpreting it as a "sign that she had some sympathy with his family trouble" (188). The narrator likens Adam's erring conclusion to a universal desire to interpret the actions of others as best serves the interpreter: "Poor fellow! that touch of melancholy came from quite another source; but how was he to know? We look at the one little woman's face we love, as we look at the face of our mother earth, and see all sorts of answers to our own yearnings" (188). Adam later tells himself that Hetty's blushes and other indications of her desire to be with Arthur are, rather, evidence of her love for him (199–202). At the dance celebrating Arthur's birthday, the sleeping Totty is roused when she is passed between Hetty and Adam, and her peevish movements catch Hetty's simple beads, jerking Hetty's locket out of its hiding place in her bodice. Hetty first goes pale, an alteration that Adam notices, and she blushes "red" as Adam picks up the locket (259–260).[42] He retrieves the scattered beads and open locket from the floor and the locket—a gift that encases a lock of Hetty's dark hair with a tawny lock of Arthur's—gives Adam a "puzzled alarm," and he wonders whether Hetty has a lover (260–261). By the time he returns home, Adam has convinced himself that Hetty bought the locket for herself, and with that unlikely scenario reassuring him, Adam goes to bed "comforted, having woven for himself an ingenious web of probabilities," which the narrator ironically notes is "the surest screen a wise man can place between himself and the truth" (261).

Adam's "web of probabilities" consoles him that Hetty is kind and that she loves him, and afterward, when Adam sees Arthur and Hetty kissing in the woods, the narrator casts the demystification as an apocalyptic text revealing a formerly hidden truth.[43] Adam's calling Arthur to face a raw interpretation of his actions and their consequences, however, is only a temporary blow to Arthur rather than a crisis of conscience. Arthur consoles himself by entertaining prospects for a safe outcome and imagining compensating gestures toward Adam and Hetty. With the letter Adam has demanded from him, Arthur appends a note to Adam that it "may pain [Hetty] more" to read Arthur's rejection than to have only silence. By this means, Arthur "procures some relief to himself by throwing the decision on Adam with a warning," and gives Adam—"who was not given to hesitation"—reason to hesitate (286). Yet neither the irony nor the self-interest of his warning penetrate Arthur's conscience. When Adam studies Hetty for "signs" after Arthur's departure and decides that she has not loved Arthur very much and that she can still love him, the narrator demystifies his illusion for the reader by revealing Hetty's inward thoughts: "It was nothing to [Hetty]—putting her arm through Adam's; but she knew he cared a great deal about having her arm through his, and she wished him to care. Her heart beat no faster, and she looked at the half-bare hedgerows and the ploughed fields with the same sense of oppressive dullness as before" (322).

Hetty will not love Adam, and her mirroring the "half-bare" scene in her jaded view of Adam's affection is an index, not only of her feelings for Adam, but also for the nature of her feelings more generally. Adam wants to be married to Hetty, to think she loves him, and Hetty is now resigned to be married to Adam, "the one person" whom "her mind had rested on in its dull weariness" (323). Events soon push Adam to examine his delusions, and he discards his misinterpretation by recalling and reinterpreting signs from his and Hetty's times together under new light. This intellectual exercise foreshadows Adam's later openness to reexamining his relationship with Dinah, an essential step toward the restoration of family and community that concludes the novel

## Love, Religion, and Community

The link between love and religious feeling is central to Adam and Dinah's relationship, and the experience of each is presented as a kind of "mystery" in the estimation of characters whose views the reader is led to trust.[44] In spite of critical assessments that align one or more of Eliot's works with the thought of Strauss or Feuerbach, Eliot's approach to and interpretation of love and religious feeling in *Adam Bede* reflect a more traditional or sentimental conviction: they are mysteries insusceptible to scientific analysis.[45] Adam tells Arthur as they fight in the woods, for example, that his love for Hetty is "such as I believe nobody can know much about but them as feel it, and God as has given it to 'em" (278). Seth, in considering Adam's attraction to Hetty, tells Dinah, "It's a deep mystery—the way the heart of a man turns to one woman [. . .] and makes it easier for him to work seven year for *her*, like Jacob did for Rachel" (31, Eliot's emphasis). Seth appears to echo Adam, who "often check[s]" Seth's "argumentative spiritualism" with the phrase, "Eh, it's a big mystery; thee knows't but little about it" (46). Concerning Seth's love for Dinah, the narrator confides, "Love of this sort is hardly distinguishable from religious feeling" and affirms, "[O]ur love at its highest flood rushes beyond its object, and loses itself in the sense of divine mystery" (34). Adam, faced for the first time with Seth's depth of love for Dinah, concludes, "It's a mystery we can give no account of" (112). The narrator clarifies Adam's sense of what "mystery" is when Adam can only describe his love for Hetty as "frankly a mystery" because he is unable to "disguise mystery [. . .] with the appearance of knowledge" using an illusion painted by "fine words" (319). Here Eliot reverses Feuerbach's and Strauss's metaphors of demystification: instead of unveiling a hidden truth, "knowledge" may create an illusion from "fine words," obscuring the hidden truth—and denying the mystery—of love.

Rather than be distressed because he has no "fine words" to elaborate on his love for Hetty, Adam credits God as its giver (277–278), and following Arthur's departure, he sees her as accepting and affectionate, affirming to himself that God has given Hetty the spirit to overcome her disappointment and to love him (318). A Feuerbachian observer might observe that Adam here projects onto God his human feelings for Hetty, but Eliot does not take this demystifying step. The origins and condition of love as an ineffable mystery converge in an important sense with the origins and conditions of religious faith. At this convergence, one finds Dinah Morris's impulses toward Adam involuntary and visceral: she blushes, and her gazes follow him without her apparent awareness. To a keen observer like Lisbeth Bede, Dinah's responses reveal her attraction to Adam, and Lisbeth perceives by Adam's attentions to Dinah that Adam, unawares, is falling in love with Dinah. Dinah initially discounts the possibility that divine love and her call to the ministry could be challenged by love for a man, and Adam suppresses his feelings for Dinah even after Lisbeth Bede confirms them because he believes Seth hopes to marry Dinah.

The narrator describes Adam's love for Dinah in terms of "webs" and "music," metaphors earlier associated with Adam's love for Hetty. Before he becomes fully aware of his feelings for Dinah, Adam listens for her voice on his visits to the Hall Farm "as for a recurrent music" (437), equating her voice with the tones of a familiar refrain, and again relating the mystery of falling in love to the experience of listening to music. W. J. Harvey sees the novelist's "contriving hand" taking a shortcut in character development with Adam's unacknowledged love for Dinah (231–232), and views Dinah's eventual consent to marry Adam as a product of "psychological discontinuity" (181). But both developments, rather than supposed shortcuts of one kind or another, are consistent with the "mystery" that Eliot assigns to love's origins. The narrator compares Dinah and Adam, in a scene where they are under the power of their first attraction with "slight words" and "tremulous touches," to "two little quivering rainstreams" about to "mingle into one" (441), juxtaposing the inevitable, "indescribable" attractions of love with the likewise compelling yet gentle forces of nature that make one of two. This image may be read as comporting with Feuerbach's notion of a love that erases otherness between two people, and I would concur. But Feuerbach, goes further, as I observe above in the context of Adam's thinking Hetty loves him after Arthur departs. While Feuerbach questions the process that leads people to attribute their love to a divine source, Eliot adds no such demystifying doubt to Adam's reinterpretation of the signs of love between himself and Dinah.

Lisbeth, who is anxious that Dinah remain in Hayslope, tells Seth that Dinah is in love with Adam: "She'd ne'er go away, I know, if Adam 'ud be fond on her an' marry her [. . .]" (443). Though Seth has been thinking vaguely along similar lines, he presses his mother for specifics and sets the tone, in a sense, for Adam's later response: what Lisbeth knows by observation must be discovered by Adam—and by Seth—as a process of rethinking and reinterpretation. Seth urges Lisbeth to keep silent on the subject in Adam's presence (443), but shortly after, Lisbeth finds her opportunity with Adam, and though "frightened at her own courage" (446), she insists that her view of Dinah's feelings for him is accurate. Adam makes a series of disbelieving arguments against Lisbeth's certainty (447–448), but

Lisbeth's observations ultimately push Adam to grapple with his interpretation of the past.

As I noted above, Adam's reexamination of his beliefs about Dinah's attitude toward him builds on his previous reconsiderations of signs related to Hetty. As before, Adam hesitates at the threshold of examining his conclusions and essays rationalizations, but the truth is inescapable: "[N]ow the suggestion had been made to him, he remembered so many things, very slight things, like the stirring of the water by an imperceptible breeze, which seemed to him some confirmation of his mother's words" (448). In Adam's fresh reading of remembered signs, the experience of water stirred by a slight breeze joins "music" and "light" as an analogue for falling in love.

When Seth has given Adam his blessing to approach Dinah, Adam confides to Seth his final excuse for evading the truth of Lisbeth's assertion: "I'm afraid she speaks without book" (451). Adam's biblical reference resonates with subsequent events, because Adam and Dinah will feel compelled to affirm that their love is divinely inspired—mediated through God. When Adam declares his love to Dinah, his vow, "I love you next to God who made me" (453), emerges logically, but Dinah, fearing her love for Adam draws her away from God, decides to return to Snowfield to await divine guidance while she pursues her ministry (456–457), and matters hang fire from harvest until mid-October.

Adam's character, then, maintains integrity, prior to his proposal to Dinah, and when he makes his second journey to find an absent loved one—Dinah, this time—he is, as before, in an anxious state of mind, awaiting news that he may be loath to hear but hoping for the best.[46] The landscape he passes reminds him of his journey in search of Hetty, and although the memory is painful, Adam's purpose and his hope for Dinah's assent have altered his view of the countryside. The narrator explains the mechanism of his retrospective gaze and the groundwork it lays: "No story is the same to us after a lapse of time; or rather, we who read it are no longer the same interpreters: and Adam this morning brought with him new thoughts [. . .] which gave an altered significance to its story of the past" (472). As he rides along, however, Adam's confidence in Dinah's giving him a positive answer wanes with his fear that her "old life [will] have too strong a grasp upon her" for her love for Adam to hold sway (472). When he reaches Snowfield, he waits impatiently for her to appear (472). The narrator spends a full page explaining Adam's honest character, his past sorrows, and his deepening understanding. Without forgetting his first passion, Adam's thoughts now evolve toward his "more precious" love for Dinah (472–473), an integrated and motivated evolution in his feelings and desires.

The late afternoon shadows are lengthening when Dinah appears, and they "walk on in silence" for some time before she speaks, telling Adam that she now believes their marriage "is the Divine Will" and expressing her love for him in further religious terms: "My soul is so knit to yours that it is but a divided life I live without you" (475). Dinah's expression of their souls being "knit" together suggests, in Eliot's terms, a fabric of love created from their desire for oneness that has none of the superficial attraction that drew Adam and Arthur toward Hetty and drew Hetty toward each of them. Adam and Dinah's love is distinctive because it is based, not only on a shared worldview and mutual regard, but also because it is founded on their conviction of its being divinely ordained. Hayslope's community requires that love be made public, sanctioned in a religious ceremony under the eyes of witnesses, and so theirs is.

Some critics have found Dinah and Adam's union unsatisfactory. Harvey finds Dinah's and Adam's changes of heart arbitrary and claims that Dinah's "essentially static" character makes the reader uncomfortable about their marriage (*Art* 180). Eliot defends the realism of their mutual changes of heart by appealing to the reader's memory of being in love:

> [I]t is almost certain that you, too, have been in love [. . .] . If so, you will no more think the slight words, the timid looks, the tremulous touches, by which two human souls approach each other gradually, like two little quivering rain-streams, before they mingle into one— you will no more think these things trivial than you will think the first-detected signs of coming spring trivial, though they be but a faint, indescribable something in the air [. . .]. Those slight words and looks and touches are part of the soul's language; [. . .] words, such as "light," "sound," "stars," "music,"—words really not worth looking at, or hearing, in themselves, any more than "chips" or "sawdust": it is only that they happen to be the signs of something unspeakably great and beautiful. I am of opinion that love is a great and beautiful thing, too; and if you agree with me, the smallest signs of it will not be chips and sawdust to you: they will rather be like those little words, "light" and "music," stirring the long-winding fibres of your memory, and enriching your present with your most precious past. (441)

The narrator describes Adam's love for Dinah by musing on the insubstantial and compelling experience of being in love and returns to effects that can only be evoked in language that resonates mutually. The signs that prompted Adam's two experiences of love are "slight" in comparison to his "unspeakable" experience of love. If the narrator's claims as a realist and historian rest on a Straussian scientific detachment that systematically reveals the hidden meaning behind visible signs or the hidden causes of visible effects, or on Feuerbach's "sole sovereignty of reason," then those claims ultimately falter where love and religion are represented in *Adam Bede*.[47] But the sentimental realism of *Adam Bede*'s conclusion—the resolution of conflict and the reintegration of the Hayslope community—depends not on an application of rigorously scientific demystification, but on the reader's shared ineffable and inexplicable experience of falling in love. Neither the characters nor the narrator in *Adam Bede* enact Strauss's or Feuerbach's demystification of love and religion, and Eliot invites the reader's attention, instead, in an opposite direction, toward sympathetic identification based on shared feeling and mutually understood metaphors.

The reader's sympathetic identification with Adam's and Dinah's emotions is consistent with Eliot's idea of "tragedy." *Adam Bede*'s characters construct community through ordinary actions and discourse, extending a sympathetic heart toward those whose "collisions" with the "general" have threatened to dismember the community. In the aftermath of revelations about Hetty's and Arthur's errors, members of the community act to heal and sustain it in one way or another. Nevertheless, the "collision" is certainly "irreparable" in certain ways: Arthur can neither compensate his errors nor assume his future of beneficent affability as "squire," and his health is broken by remorse and his years abroad as a soldier (480). Hetty, cast out for her crime, will never be restored to her former community.

Adam and Dinah's love contributes continuity and stability to the community, particularly to the Poyser and Bede families, and Seth Bede, who first sought Dinah as a wife, finds his happiness in Dinah and Adam's household (479–481). Even Arthur Donnithorne seems to be destined to have redemption through the ministrations of Dinah and Adam (481–482). The community's viability and continuity are based on ties of love and family, and on the community's determination to overcome forces that would pull it apart. In the closing pages of *Adam Bede*, Eliot's images confirm the viability and human sympathy of the community: Adam and Dinah's affectionate household discourse touches on Mr. Irvine, Hetty, and Arthur; Adam is now Hayslope's master carpenter and lumberman; Dinah is a gentle wife and mother whose children bear nostalgic names; and the Poysers come in at the cottage door to visit the newly formed Bede family.

A skeptical reader, mindful of the influence of Strauss and Feuerbach on Eliot's thought, might interpret these pages as constructing an idyllic myth to conceal a psychological break that affects all *Adam Bede*'s principal characters. The close of *Adam Bede*, then, would be read as the author's uneasy compromise between her structural "invariability of sequence" and a sympathetic, but realistic approach to provincial life. Critics have argued that *Adam Bede*'s ending undermines Eliot's claims of realism, that her narrator stops short of concrete cause-effect exposition and demystification of Adam's religious and romantic feelings. Some have found authorial ambivalence toward narrative omniscience or, else, inconsistency in Eliot's claims to be a "judicious historian" of "realistic" provincial life and Adam's biographer. In fact, Eliot's realism does not falter in its analysis of the "webs" of delusion in Hetty's and Arthur's patterns of disintegration. But the patterns of reintegration that culminate in the marriage of Adam and Dinah and found a new equilibrium in the community of Hayslope rely on acceptance of the "mystery" of love and religion as foundational, both to their individual identities and to the identity of the community.

## After *Adam Bede*

An attentive reading of Eliot's later fiction is likely to make us different "interpreters" of her early fiction, because Eliot continues to develop her art and to experiment with realism. From the reader's perspective, the restored provincial community of *Adam Bede* remains well in the past, consistent with the narrator's claim to represent "homely" English village life at the close of the eighteenth century. After *Adam Bede*, in the spring of 1859, Eliot published "The Lifted Veil," a Gothic novella whose title suggests a conscious grounding in the principles of Feuerbach and, especially, in Strauss's frequent analogy between truth-telling and "lifting a veil."[48] In "The Lifted Veil," Eliot experiments with a constrained first-person narration, in contrast to the colorful, intimate, omniscient voice in *Adam Bede*, and the story's Gothic darkness in setting and character contrast *Adam Bede*'s pastoral scenery and its resolutely resilient and optimistic protagonists.[49]

In several of her subsequent novels—particularly *Romola* (1862–1863), *Middlemarch* (1871–1872), and *Daniel Deronda* (1876)—Eliot's fictional communities are experiments beyond the "homely" English village life represented in *Adam Bede* and *Silas Marner* (1861). The later novels' "collisions" with community and their amorous entanglements are more complex than *Adam Bede*'s straight-forward encounters, and their relationships have less to do with desire triangulated or mediated by religious faith. *Romola*, *Middlemarch*, and *Daniel Deronda* are set in more cosmopolitan surroundings with more worldly characters than those of *Adam Bede*, and no single form of community seems able to satisfy characters such as Dorothea Brooke or Daniel Deronda who have visions—quixotic or egoistic—in conflict with the values of their respective communities. Eliot's later narrators more frankly confront *Adam Bede*'s unanswered questions of interpretation and identity. In those novels, the influences of Strauss and Feuerbach remain, along with those of other thinkers of her time, but Eliot's explorations of myth, language, and the forms of community extend more fully the radical implications of Feuerbach's epistemology: forms of community, like forms of fiction, exist in the medium of language and necessarily become a community of (mis)interpretation.

**Notes**

1. "George Eliot" is, of course, a pen name. Naming Eliot in contexts of critical work and biography has had various resolutions: J. Hillis Miller calls Eliot "Mary Anne Evans," noting that "even her real given name is variable" (3–4). To that point, Marilyn Orr stipulates "Mary Anne Evans (as she was christened)" (12), and Tim Dolin prefers "Mary Ann Evans," but observes that Eliot began using "Marian Evans" in 1851 (17). Following her connection with Lewes and shortly after adopting George Eliot as her pen name, Eliot privately used "Marian Lewes" (Bodenheimer 129). I use her pen name in this chapter.
2. These observations appear in "Notes on *The Spanish Gypsy*." See *George Eliot's Life as Related in Her Letters and Journals* (Ch. 15 "April 29, 1868." 3.31–37), hereinafter, *Letters*. Eliot's second husband, John W. Cross edited its three volumes. Also see Nord's article on Eliot's notebook on *The Spanish Gypsy*.
3. The idea is Hegel's. Jonathan N. Badger explains that Hegel "points to a *tragic collision*" with "established ethical convention" lying "at the heart of a tragic drama" (36, Badger's italics). See Hegel's *Aesthetik* (I) for his theory of tragedy's "collision" (esp. 204–216). Knoepflmacher, for example, marks Eliot's "acceptance of Hegel's 'view of tragedy'" (*Early* 192 *ff*).
4. "Science" and "scientific" in this chapter refer to Strauss and Feuerbach's use of *Wissenschaft* as rational, systematic inquiry and organization of knowledge in various disciplines, including philosophy and theology. (Ed.)
5. Strauss and Feuerbach published their treatises in German in 1835 and 1841, respectively. Chapman issued Strauss's *Life* (3 vols. in 8vo) in

1846 without the translator's name and in 1854, published Feuerbach's *Essence* crediting "Marian Evans" as its translator and as the "Translator of 'Strauss's Life of Jesus.'"

6 Gooch notes that Feuerbach's affinity for Hegel did not extend to regarding "Christianity as the consummate religion" ("Feuerbach"), as Feuerbach wrote in his 1928 letter to Hegel (Hegel. *Letters* 546–550). Also see Feuerbach's "Towards a Critique of Hegel's Philosophy" in *Fiery Brook* (94) and n. 47, below.

7 See Paris's 1962 essay, for example. I do not seek to diminish the influence of Feuerbach's "model of Christianity" on intellectual life in England and Germany, which Gooch writes may be taken to mark a symbolic close to "the period of classical German philosophy" that began in 1781 with publication of Immanuel Kant's *Critique of Pure Reason* ("Feuerbach"). Feuerbach's *Essence* initiated a new wave of German thought forwarded by Karl Marx, who wrote to Feuerbach to acknowledge his giving "socialism a philosophical foundation," and Friedrich Engels recalled *Essence* having had a "profoundly 'liberating effect' on him and Marx by 'breaking the spell' of the Hegelian system" (*Ibid.*).

8 Editor David Carroll describes Simpson's "ease" with his materials (21–22) in referring to Eliot's basis in Strauss, Feuerbach, Comte, and Goethe.

9 See Paris ("Higher" 59; "Religion" 418, 420). Paris credits Eliot's view of Christianity's "subjective reality" to Feuerbach (*Ibid.* 428–429). Paris revisited his earlier views of Eliot in 2003.

10 A good number of critics cite Eliot's work on Spinoza as an influence, and Perkin calls it a "critical commonplace" that Eliot is a "Wordsworthian novelist" (132).

11 Knoepflmacher writes that the higher criticism not only "helped to undermine George Eliot's [Calvinistic] belief," but also "provided her with substitute values and ideals she incorporated into her novels" (31). He cites critics Barbara Hardy, George Levine ("Determinism"), and Neil D. Isaacs as divorcing Eliot's art from her philosophy (25 nn. 1–3).

12 See Kimberly VanEsveld Adams (42–46; 53 n. 18).

13 Quoting from Marian Evans's letter to Sarah Hennell, Loesberg (130 n. 16; 132), like Paris ("Religion"), omits Eliot's compelling, provisional final clause: "but of course I should, of myself, alter the phraseology." The letter is found in Haight's edition (2.153).

14 Mazaheri (73 n. 6) quotes from *Essence*.

15 Fleishman refers to Spinoza's *Tractatus Theologico-Politicus* and his *Ethica*. Eliot translated the *Ethica* from Latin in 1856, but because of a dispute over payment, the translation was left unpublished for decades. See Deegan's essay on these translations. Clare Carlisle edited the translation as *Spinoza's* Ethics.

16 Miller's "echo" may refer to Eliot's letter (December 26, 1860) to her intimate friend Barbara Leigh Smith Bodichon where "opium" is

associated with suppressing pain: "The highest 'calling and election' is to *do without opium* and live through all our pain with conscious, clear-eyed endurance" (*Letters* 3.366, Eliot's italics). Marx's "das Opium des Volkes" [the opium/opiate of the people/masses] appears in the Introduction ("Contribution" 1844) to his critique of Hegel's philosophy.

17 See Fleishman's chronologically arranged bibliography in "George Eliot's Reading" and his *Intellectual Life* for related insights.

18 Rignall cites Nietzsche's assessment of Eliot as a "little moralistic femal[e]" (*The Twilight of the Idols* 157), and Carol Diethe cites a letter from Nietzsche (November 24, 1887) "excoriat[ing] all those who admired Rousseau and emulated him," Eliot among them (66–67).

19 See David Carroll's Introduction for details of the contemporary reception. See also Pam Hirsch (esp. 79–81).

20 Eliot was introduced into the liberal Coventry circle of the Brays and Hennells in November 1841, soon after the second edition of Hennell's *Inquiry* was published (Haight 38–39). Hennell's ideas may have resonated with Eliot early on because she was thinking along similar lines.

21 See the treatments of Eliot's intellectual life by Dodd and Fleishman. Orr prefaces her material by assessing Feuerbach's and Strauss's philosophies. Note also Susan E. Hill's linking Eliot's assessment of Feuerbach and her activity as a translator to the construction of *Middlemarch*'s moral foundations.

22 Sacks (75, 76) recalls Levine's often-quoted phrase, "some moral enterprise of truth-telling" (*Realistic* 8).

23 Eifrig's reading makes Eliot's view of history and its associations with places and objects essential to *Adam Bede*'s milieu (esp. 409–415).

24 See Eliot's "The Future of German Philosophy" (151). See Fleishman's comments on Eliot's review (*Intellectual* 67–68).

25 See the American edition (343, italics original).

26 See Perkin (129; 132–133).

27 Feuerbach forwards the idea that men and women should respond positively to the "sexual instinct" rather than deny it as Christianity demands (*Essence* 167), but in Arthur and Hetty's response to their desire, Eliot sustains the idea that transgressing social boundaries has severe consequences to the individual and the community. Sacks marks the obvious disconnect between Eliot's private life and the moral views of her "conservative middle-class readers" (90).

28 Where direct speech, like Rann's, is quoted from *Adam Bede*, only double quotation marks are used.

29 Eliot's notebook contains the underscored sentence: "The class Wesley liked least were the farmers," as the "least susceptible of Methodism" because of its required meetings. See Martin's notes to the text of *Adam Bede* (500) and Joseph Wisenfarth (127–128).

30 Dinah refers to having witnessed Wesley's open-air preaching, but the narrator stipulates that Dinah "was not preaching as she heard others preach" (26).
31 The "shared illusion" is confirmed by the deference of the community toward the squire and Arthur at the coming-of-age celebration, and more generally by Martin Poyser and Adam in exchanges with the squire and Arthur, respectively. For Adam, as the narrator relates in chapter 16, "The word 'gentleman' had a spell" (245).
32 See Perkin on Eliot's portrayals of "human sympathy," especially in his chapter five, where he examines *Adam Bede* and *Silas Marner*. Anger (*Victorian*) proposes an "ethics of sympathy" grounded in Eliot's contemporary context as the most productive hermeneutic for reading Eliot's later fiction; see Anger's catalog of critical treatments of "sympathy" in Eliot's work (113–116). Also see Tom Sperlinger on Eliot as "sensitive," and Wendy Williams on Eliot as a "poetess."
33 Hetty's imaginary "toilette," too, is "resplendent" (140).
34 In addition to the image of the "web of delusions" for Feuerbach's descriptions of religious beliefs, Feuerbach uses "dreams" as an analogy for religious faith (xxxvi, xxxix). Eliot associates such "webs" with first love in *Adam Bede* and *Middlemarch* and, in *Middlemarch*, with Bulstrode's life of concealment. See Ian Adam's study of *Middlemarch*, *This Particular Web*.
35 Gyp, Adam's faithful dog, serves for illustrations of loyalty and human love: Adam tells his mother that Gyp wants Adam to look at him because Gyp "can't abide to think I love thee best" (446). Lisbeth tells Adam that Dinah has no more response to Seth coming near her than if he were Gyp, but she's "all of a tremble" when Adam sits beside her at breakfast (449) and argues for Adam's attraction to Dinah with an opposite comparison: "Thy eyes follow her about, welly as Gyp's follow thee" (448). See Sacks on the importance of Gyp and other animals in *Adam Bede* (82–85).
36 Girard is concerned with reader response and with causes and effects that are somehow veiled through a "romantic" interpretation; he presents "triangular" or "mediated" desire using examples from literary novels (1–52).
37 Feuerbach's assertion that "only community constitutes humanity" is realized starkly in the distinctions between Hetty's life in Hayslope and her anonymous, solitary wanderings, her isolation as a prisoner, and her subsequent exile.
38 See the testimony of Sarah Stone, who acts as midwife to Hetty (387–389). Her testimony is followed by that of John Olding, who observes Hetty's movements after she leaves Mrs. Stone's cottage, and who discovers the dead child (389–390). The jury finds Hetty "guilty" without recommendation for mercy (391).
39 Martin Poyser, the younger, shows his kindheartedness toward Hetty when he greets her late arrival amiably and excuses it (130, 158,

respectively); moreover, when Hetty vanishes in her "quest" for Arthur, Martin assures Adam that he won't "turn [his] back on her" (361).
40 Paris describes Dinah's interaction with Hetty in Feuerbachian terms as an "I-thou relation," in which Dinah is able to imagine herself in Hetty's place, and that sympathy restores Hetty's humanity ("Religion" 430; *Experiments* 104–105). In "Religion," Paris quotes from Feuerbach (2): "Man is himself at once I and thou; he can put himself in the place of another, for this reason, that to him his species, his essential nature, and not merely his individuality, is an object of thought."
41 Adam nurtures his illusions about Hetty for the greater part of the text, through the end of chapter 38. In chapter 39, Mr. Irwine informs Adam of the death of Hetty's child and Hetty's arrest.
42 Though the narrator records it in the moment (260), Eliot postpones revealing Adam's notice of Hetty's "changing color" to his later rethinking the incident (261).
43 The reader will probably recall the scene treated in a previous section where "[A] terrible scorching light showed [Adam] the hidden letters that changed the meaning of the past" (268).
44 Hetty and Arthur, the novel's least trustworthy characters where truth and community values are concerned, give neither religion nor any link between religion and love a thought.
45 Hill's conclusion that *Middlemarch*'s union of Dorothea and Will implies their having "learn[ed] to negotiate and balance duty and desire" and answers to the "Feuerbachian ideal of marriage" (652) is also suggested in the union of Adam and Dinah.
46 W. J. Harvey sees the novelist's "contriving hand" short-circuiting character development with Adam's unacknowledged love for Dinah (231–232) and views Dinah's eventual consent to marry Adam as a product of "psychological discontinuity"(181). These developments, nonetheless, are consistent with the "mystery" Eliot assigns to the origins of love and with the progression of events that incrementally influence Adam's and Dinah's emotional lives.
47 Gooch ("Feuerbach") cites Feuerbach's letter to Hegel identifying the historical task remaining in the wake of Hegel's philosophical achievement to be the "establishment of the 'sole sovereignty of reason' in a 'kingdom of the Idea' that would inaugurate a new spiritual dispensation." Gooch ("Atheism") describes Strauss's "sang-froid" in "applying the tools of historical criticism to the canonical gospels" (831).
48 In discussing Hetty's infatuation with Arthur, above, I refer to the metaphor in *Adam Bede*. Hetty sees Arthur's intentions "through a soft, liquid veil" (91).
49 See Royce Mahawatte's treatment of the narrative as a Gothic novel (esp. 75–96). "The Lifted Veil" first appeared in *Blackwood's Magazine* in July 1859 and was edited by Helen Small in 2009. Michael Carlson asserts that the story's protagonist-narrator, Lattimer, is unreliable (64). Eliot's views on facile plot elements and inept narration in examples of

women's fiction appear in her essay "Silly Novels by Lady Novelists" and are germane to these questions.

**Works Cited**

Adams, Kimberly VanEsveld. "Feminine Godhead, Feminist Symbol: The Madonna in George Eliot, Ludwig Feuerbach, Anna Jameson, and Margaret Fuller." *Journal of Feminist Studies in Religion* 12.1 (1996): 41–70.

Anger, Suzy. "George Eliot and Philosophy." Ed. George Levine. *The Cambridge Companion to George Eliot.* 76–97.

—. *Victorian Interpretation.* Ithaca, NY: Cornell UP, 2005.

Badger, Jonathan N. *Sophocles and the Politics of Tragedy: Cities and Transcendence.* Innovations in Political Theory. New York: Routledge, 2013.

Bodenheimer, Rosemarie. *The Real Life of Mary Ann Evans: George Eliot, Her Letters and Fiction.* Ithaca, NY: Cornell UP, 2018.

Carlson, Michael. "'Famished Tigress': Sympathy and the Other in George Eliot's Fiction." *George Eliot – George Henry Lewes Studies* 58/59 (2010): 61–76.

Carroll, David. Introduction. *George Eliot: The Critical Heritage.* Ed. David Carroll. New York: Routledge, 2000. 1–48.

Cross, John W. *See* Eliot. *George Eliot's Life (Letters).*

Deegan, Thomas. "George Eliot, George Henry Lewes and Spinoza's *Tractatus Theologico-Politicus.*" *George Eliot – George Henry Lewes Studies* 22–23 (1993): 1–16.

Diethe, Carol. *Nietzsche's Women: Beyond the Whip.* Monographien und Texte zur Nietzsche-Forschung 31. Berlin: Walter de Gruyter, 2013.

Dodd, Valerie A. *George Eliot: An Intellectual Life.* London: Macmillan, 1990.

Dolin, Tim. *George Eliot.* Oxford World's Classics. Authors in Context. Oxford: OUP, 2005.

Eagleton, Terry. *How to Read Literature.* New Haven, CT: Yale UP, 2013.

Eifrig, Gail McGrew. "History and Memory in *Adam Bede.*" *Soundings: An Interdisciplinary Journal*: Papers from The Drew Symposium 76.2/3 (1993): 407–420.

Eliot, George. *Adam Bede.* 3 vols. London: Blackwood, 1859.

—. *Adam Bede.* Ed. Carol A. Martin. Oxford World's Classics. Oxford: OUP, 2001.

—. *Daniel Deronda.* Ed. Graham Handley and K. M. Newton. 2nd ed. Oxford, UK: Clarendon P, 2014.

—. "The Future of German Philosophy." *Essays.* Ed. Thomas Pinney. London: Routledge & Kegan Paul, 1963. New York: Columbia UP, 1963. 148–153.

—. *The George Eliot Letters.* Ed. Gordon Haight. 9 vols. New Haven, CT: Yale UP. 1954–1956, 1978.

—. *George Eliot's Life as Related in Her Letters and Journals* [*Letters*]. Ed. John W. Cross. The Works of Eliot, Cabinet Edition. Edinburgh: Blackwood, 1878–1881. 3 vols. New York: Harper & Row, 1885.

—. "The Lifted Veil." *Blackwood's Edinburgh Magazine* 86.525 (July, 1859): 24–48.

—. *The Lifted Veil: Brother Jacob*. Ed. Helen Small. Oxford, UK: Clarendon P, 2009.

—. *Middlemarch: A Study of Provincial Life*. Ed. David Carroll. Oxford, UK: Clarendon P, 1986. Intro. Felicia Bonaparte (2008). Reissue, 2008. Ed. David Carroll and David Russell. 3rd ed. 2019.

—. *Romola*. Ed. Andrew Brown. Oxford: OUP, 1994.

—. *Silas Marner: The Weaver of Raveloe*. Ed. Juliette Atkinson. 2nd ed. Oxford, UK: Clarendon P, 2017.

—. "Silly Novels by Lady Novelists." *The Selected Essays, Poems, and Other Writings of George Eliot*. Ed. A. S. Byatt and Nicholas Warren. London: Penguin, 1990. 140–163.

—. *A Writer's Notebook, 1854–1879, and Uncollected Writings*. Ed. Joseph Wiesenfarth. Charlottesville: UP of Virginia, 1981.

Eliot, George. *See also* Evans; Spinoza.

Evans, Marian. "Contemporary Literature: Art and Belles Lettres" [Rev. of John Ruskin's *Modern Painters* III. London: Elder]. *Westminster Review* 65 British Ed. (April 1856): 625–633. American Ed. (January–April 1856): 343–347.

—. *See also* Eliot; Feuerbach (*Essence*); Strauss.

Feuerbach, Ludwig Andreas. *The Essence of Christianity*. Trans. Marian Evans. London: Chapman, 1854. The 1854 ed. is available electronically at the GeorgeEliotArchive.org. Ed. Beverley Park Rilett.

—. *The Fiery Brook: Selected Writings of Ludwig Feuerbach*. Trans. and Introduction, Zawar Hanfi. Garden City, NY: Doubleday, 1972.

—. *Das Wesen des Christentums*. Leipzig: Otto Wigand, 1841.

Fleishman, Avrom. *George Eliot's Intellectual Life*. Cambridge, UK: Cambridge UP, 2010.

—. "George Eliot's Reading: A Chronological List." *George Eliot – George Henry Lewes Studies* 54/55 (2008): 1–76.

Gaston, Sean. "George Eliot and the Anglican Reader." *Literature and Theology* 31.3 (2017): 318–337.

George Eliot Archive. Ed. Beverley Park Rilett. GeorgeEliotArchive.org, 2022.

Girard, René. *Deceit, Desire, and the Novel*. Trans. Yvonne Freccero. Baltimore, MD: Johns Hopkins UP, 1976.

Gooch, Todd. "Atheism." Ed. Michael N. Forster and Kristin Gjesdal. *The Oxford Handbook of German Philosophy in the Nineteenth Century*. Oxford: OUP, 2015. 829–851.

—. "Ludwig Andreas Feuerbach." Ed. Edward N. Zaita. *SEP*. Stanford, CA: The Metaphysics Research Lab, Department of Philosophy, Stanford U, 2016.

Haight, Gordon. *Eliot: A Biography*. Oxford, UK: Clarendon P, 1968.

—. *See also* Eliot. *The George Eliot Letters*.

Hardy, Barbara. *The Novels of George Eliot: A Study in Form*. London: U of London, Athlone P, 1959.

Harvey, W. J. *The Art of George Eliot*. London: Chatto & Windus, 1961.

Hegel, Georg Wilhelm Friedrich. *Hegel's Aesthetics: Lectures on Fine Art*. Vol. 1. Trans. T. M. Knox. Oxford, UK: Clarendon P, 1975. Rpt. 2010.

—. *Hegel: The Letters*. Trans. Clark Butler and Christiane Seiler. Bloomington: Indiana UP, 1984. 546–550.
Hennell, Charles. *An Inquiry Concerning the Origin of Christianity*. London: Smallfield, 1838. 2nd ed., 1841.
Herbert, Christopher. *Evangelical Gothic: The English Novel and the Religious War on Virtue from Wesley to Dracula*. Charlottesville: U of Virginia P, 2019.
Hermann, Luc. *Concepts of Realism*. Suffolk, UK: Camden House, 1996.
Hill, Susan E. "Translating Feuerbach, Constructing Morality: The Theological and Literary Significance of Translation for George Eliot." *Journal of the American Academy of Religion* 65.3 (1997): 635–653.
Hirsch, Pam. "Three Georges, Perie-zadeh and Spitting Critics, or 'Will the Real Mr Eliot Please Stand Up?'" *Critical Survey*: Literature, Fame and Notoriety in the Nineteenth Century 13.2 (2001): 78–97.
Hodgson, Peter C. *Theology in the Fiction of George Eliot: The Mystery Beneath the Real*. London: SCM Press, 2001. Also entitled *The Mystery Beneath the Real: Theology in the Fiction of George Eliot*. 2000.
Isaacs, Neil D. "*Middlemarch*: Crescendo of Obligatory Drama." *Nineteenth Century Fiction* 18 (1963): 21–34.
Knoepflmacher, Ulrich C. *George Eliot's Early Novels: The Limits of Realism*. Berkeley: U of California P, 1968.
—. *Religious Humanism and the Victorian Novel: George Eliot, Walter Pater, and Samuel Butler*. Princeton, NJ: Princeton UP, 1965.
Levine, George, ed. *The Cambridge Companion to George Eliot*. Cambridge, UK: Cambridge UP, 2001.
—. "Determinism and Responsibility in the Works of George Eliot." *PMLA* 77.3 (1962): 268–279.
—. *The Realistic Imagination: English Fiction from Frankenstein to Lady Chatterley*. Chicago: U of Chicago P, 1981.
Loesberg, Jonathan. "Aesthetics, Ethics, and Unreadable Acts in George Eliot." Ed. George Levine. *The Cambridge Companion to George Eliot*. 121–147.
Mahawatte, Royce. *George Eliot and the Gothic Novel: Genres, Gender, Feeling*. Cardiff: U of Wales P, 2013.
Mansell, Darrel, Jr. "Ruskin and George Eliot." *Criticism* 7.3 (1965): 203–216.
Martin, Carol. "Explanatory Notes." George Eliot. *Adam Bede*. Ed. Carol Martin. 497–541.
Marx, Karl. "Introduction: A Contribution to the Critique of Hegel's *Philosophy of Right* [Zur Kritik der Hegelschen *Rechtsphilosophie*: Einleitung]." *Deutsch-Französische Jahrbücher* 1 (Paris, February 1844): 7, 10. English translation at marxists.org.
Mazaheri, John. "Religion and Work in *Adam Bede*." *George Eliot – George Henry Lewes Studies*: In Memory of Kenneth J. Fielding (1924-2005) 48/49 (2005): 64–74.
Miller, J. Hillis. *Reading for Our Time*: *Adam Bede* and *Middlemarch Revisited*. Edinburgh: Edinburgh UP, 2012.
Nord, Deborah Epstein. "George Eliot and John Everett Millais: The Ethics and Aesthetics of Realism." *Victorian Studies* 60.3 (2018): 361–389.

—. "George Eliot's Notes for *The Spanish Gypsy*." *The Princeton University Library Chronicle* 72.2 (2011): 471–476.
Orr, Marilyn. *George Eliot's Religious Imagination: A Theopoetical Evolution*. Evanston, IL: Northwestern UP, 2018.
Paris, Bernard J. *Experiments in Life: George Eliot's Quest for Values*. Detroit: Wayne State UP, 1965.
—. "George Eliot and the Higher Criticism." *Anglia* 84 (1966): 59–73.
—. "George Eliot's Religion of Humanity." *ELH* 29.4 (1962): 418–443.
—. *Re-reading George Eliot: Changing Responses to Her Experiments in Life*. Albany, NY: SUNY P, 2003.
Perkin, James J. Russell. *Theology and the Victorian Novel*. Montreal: McGill-Queen's UP, 2009.
Rée, Jonathan. *Witcraft: The Invention of Philosophy in English*. New Haven, CT: Yale UP, 2019.
Rignall, John. *George Eliot, European Novelist*. Nineteenth Century Series. Surrey: Ashgate, 2011.
Sacks, Glenda. "The Shock of the New: Allegory and Realism in *Adam Bede*." *George Eliot – George Henry Lewes Studies*: In Memory of Kenneth J. Fielding (1924-2005) 48/49 (2005): 75–102.
Simpson, Richard. "George Eliot's Novels." *Home and Foreign Review* 3 (October 1863). Rpt. "Richard Simpson on George Eliot." Ed. David Carroll. 2000. 221–250.
Singleton, Jon. "Malignant Faith and Cognitive Restructuring: Realism in *Adam Bede*." *Victorian Literature and Culture* 39.1 (2011): 239–260.
Sperlinger, Tom. "'The Sensitive Author': George Eliot." *The Cambridge Quarterly* 36.3 (2007): 250–272.
Spinoza, Baruch [Bernard]. *Spinoza's Ethics [Ethica]*. Trans. George Eliot. Ed. Clare Carlisle. Princeton, NJ: Princeton UP, 2020.
—. *Tractatus Theologico-Politicus*. Trans. Samuel Shirley. Leiden: Brill, 1989.
Strauss, David Friedrich. *Das Leben Jesu, kritisch bearbeitet*. 2. verb. Aufl. 2 Bd. [2nd emended ed. 2 vols.]. Tübingen: C. F. Osiander, 1835.
—. *The Life of Jesus, Critically Examined*. 3 vols. [Trans. Marian Evans.] London: Chapman Brothers, 1846. Vols. 1–2 are available electronically at the GeorgeEliotArchive.org. Ed. Beverley Park Rilett.
Williams, Wendy S. *George Eliot, Poetess*. New York: Routledge, 2016.
Wisenfarth, Joseph. "George Eliot's Notes for *Adam Bede*." *Nineteenth-Century Fiction* 32.2 (1977): 127–165.

# ⋙ 8 ⋘
# The Hero's Journey to Redemption
## Re-envisioning the Dramatic Structure of *King Lear*

### Claudia M. Champagne

Gustav Freytag's "pyramid," presented in his 1863 *Technik des Dramas*, shows the two sides of a triangle labeled at the line-ends and at their midpoints with an alphabetical sequence representing dramatic junctures in classical and Shakespearean five-act tragedy. Freytag's simple graphic, with its open base, is a favorite visual aid in teaching. Its influence is further reflected in its online presence, in the many reprints and editions of Freytag's German text, and in Elias J. MacEwan's 1896 English translation where MacEwan gives Freytag's scheme:

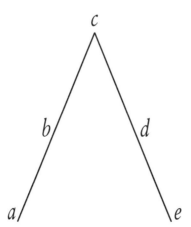

Fig. 1: *Freytag's Pyramid (MacEwan, 1896. 115)*

According to Freytag's basic model (Fig. 1), "These parts of the drama, (*a*) introduction, (*b*) rise, (*c*) climax, (*d*) return or fall, (e) catastrophe, have each what is peculiar [to it] in purpose and in construction" (115).[1] These terms for the plot structure of classical and Shakespearean tragedy figure importantly in this chapter and are defined as follows. The "introduction" is exposition, giving background information on the plot and characters and staging the inciting moment of the play (act one). The "rise" is the upward trajectory of the play's action, during which complications develop, heightening dramatic tension, while the hero remains in control of the action (act two). The dramatic "climax" marks the definitive turning point of the hero's fortunes, often due to a distinct error in judgment or action (act three). The "return or fall" is the downward turn of the hero's fortunes, as he or she loses control of the action (act four). The "catastrophe" occurs when the hero reaches the tragic end of the story and includes a moment of last suspense (act five).

In discussing Shakespearean tragedies, Freytag shows how parts *a* and *b* lead to *c* in *Romeo and Juliet*, with the climax achieved in the death of Tybalt (126–127). He argues that the climax of *Othello* occurs in act three "in the great scene in which Iago arouses Othello's jealousy" (130). Freytag gives his most detailed structural analysis to *Hamlet*, where he marks the "Introduction" and "Exciting Force" in the appearance of the Ghost (act one) and sets the "Ascending Action" in act two and the beginning of act three, ensuing in four stages: Claudius and Polonius conspire against Hamlet; Hamlet decides to test Claudius with his play; Hamlet delivers his most famous soliloquies ("O, what a rogue and peasant slave am I" in 2.2, and "To be, or not to be" in 3.1); and Claudius reveals his guilt by leaving the play in distress.[2] The "Climax," according to Freytag, is Hamlet's hesitation in killing Claudius at prayer later in act three, and the "Tragic Force or Incident" follows with the killing of Polonius. Freytag views the "Return" as occurring in act four and the first scene of act five and evolving in three stages that concern Ophelia's growing madness, the return of Laertes to conspire with Claudius, and Hamlet's reappearance during Ophelia's funeral. The "Catastrophe" of act 5, according to Freytag, focuses on "the killing" of Hamlet, Claudius, and Gertrude as its "chief scene" (190–192). Freytag gives much less attention to *Macbeth*, arguing that the climax occurs not with Macbeth's murder of King Duncan in act two, but with his murder-for-hire of Banquo in act three (186–187).

Making only passing references to *King Lear*, Freytag tracks a "rising action [. . .] of terrible magnificence" ascending to a climax in act three's "hovel scene," with its "play of the three deranged persons, and the judgment scene with the stool" (129). Freytag argues that the play's falling action opens with *Lear*'s "second mad scene," also in act three, but subsequently states that the "second mad scene" is "no intensifying of the first" (188), making it merely a continuation of the falling action. Freytag locates *Lear*'s moment of "last suspense" in act five at Edmund's dying attempt to rescind his order for the execution of Lear and Cordelia (136). While Freytag notes Lear's movement inexorably downward toward from the "second mad scene" to the catastrophe, his pyramid neglects the spiritual and regenerative aspects of Lear's journey that I address below.

The pyramid, according to Freytag, accurately represents the dramatic structure of Shakespeare's five major tragedies—*Romeo and Juliet*, *Hamlet*, *Othello*, *Macbeth*, and *King Lear*—as well as others Freytag mentions more briefly—*Antony and Cleopatra*, *Coriolanus*, *Julius Caesar*, and *Timon of Athens*—and several of the history plays. Because Freytag's pyramid aptly represents the structure of some of these dramas, I regularly use it in teaching Shakespeare's tragedies, making elaborations and modifications at appropriate points on his basic diagram, as shown in Fig. 2.

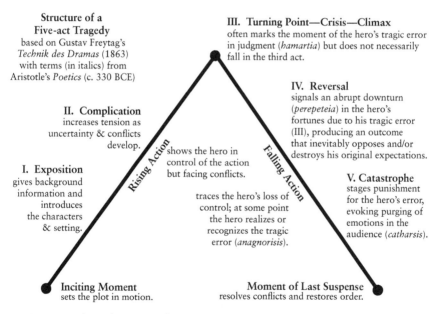

*Fig. 2: Aristotle's Elements of Tragedy* (Poetics) *Plotted on Freytag's Pyramid.*

Among my additions to Freytag's work in the context of Shakespearean tragedy, I incorporate the four elements of complex tragedy identified by Aristotle in his *Poetics*: *hamartia*, the hero's tragic error in judgment (distinguished from tragic flaw); *peripeteia*, the reversal of events; *anagnorisis*, the discovery of identity or recognition of truth; and *catharsis*, the purging or cleansing of the audience's emotions of pity and fear (Aristotle 15–18). In Shakespearean tragedy, the tragic error usually occurs at the climax in act three, the falling action of act four enacts the reversal of the hero's fortunes and his growing recognition of responsibility for his impending downfall, and the catastrophe in act five effects the audience's vicarious purging of emotions (Fig. 2). Freytag gives only limited consideration to the *Poetics*. Thus, locating Aristotle's elements of tragedy on the pyramidal structure of tragedy is my innovation. I return to it below as confirming the most remarkable features of *King Lear*'s structure.[3]

Shakespeare's plotting of *Lear* materially challenges Freytag's pyramid with its alphabetically ordered points because, as I will argue, Lear's path makes the play a distinctly redemptive tragedy whose effects transcend the final catastrophe and produce an uncommon audience response to a Shakespearean tragedy. Therefore, the most coherent and pedagogically useful visual representation of *Lear*'s dramatic structure is an *inverted* pyramid with its right side extended higher than its beginning point on the left side, as shown in Fig. 3.

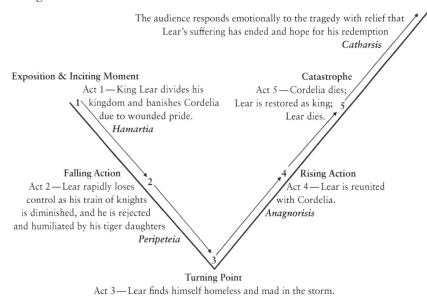

*Fig. 3: The Inverted Pyramid of* King Lear.

This inverted pyramid reverses the left and right sides of Freytag's upright pyramid to represent the reversed dramatic movement of the play.[4] The falling action comes first along the downward slope of the left side, precipitated by the grievous errors made by the hero in the first scene, and the right side represents the rising action of the second half of the play. The "climax" of act three occurs, therefore, at the nadir or low point of the inverted pyramid, exactly the opposite of Freytag's high point. From 3.4 onward, Lear's increasing awareness of his mistakes and his consequently growing spiritual regeneration move him upward along the right side of the inverted pyramid during the rest of the third act, all of act four, and well into act five. The play's catastrophe opens with Cordelia's execution and begins near the end of Lear's earthly suffering, at the penultimate point (5) on the pyramid's upper right side. The catastrophe closes with Lear's death, arguably occurring in response to Cordelia's hanging, and signals the beginning of the audience's response to the final scenes as *catharsis*, indicated by the extended right side of the inverted pyramid. The play's atypical tragic structure is accurately represented by my inverted pyramid.

To accommodate the inverted pyramid as representing the structure of *King Lear*, I have reconfigured the placement of Aristotle's elements, described generally above. Lear reveals his *hamartia* in the first scene of the play, rather than at the climax in act three. The *peripeteia* of Regan and Goneril's rejection of their father and the reversal of his fortunes occurs in act two, not in act four where it would otherwise be expected. Lear's *anagnorisis* constitutes the rising action that begins in the storm and hovel scenes of act three and continues through the last two acts. The catastrophes of the final scene—Cordelia's and Lear's deaths—result in *catharsis*, but rather than the pity and fear theorized for the audience of classical tragedy, the audience of *King Lear* likely responds with awe and satisfaction, sensing that Lear has achieved self-awareness—though he pays a heavy price for it. Audience members may even hope that Lear and Cordelia will be reunited after death. Aristotle's elements, then, sit coherently along my inverted pyramid, suggesting the most comprehensive, integrated, and useful visual image so far proposed of the play's unusual dramatic structure, which has perplexed critical analysis of the play for more than a hundred-and-fifty years.

## Critical Approaches to the Dramatic Structure of *King Lear*

During the twentieth century, three important critical studies of *King Lear*—those of A. C. Bradley in 1904, Karl P. Wentersdorf in 1965, and Fredson Bowers in 1980—acknowledged that the dramatic structure of this singular tragedy does not follow the typical pattern of the five-act Renaissance tragedy. A. C. Bradley found the structure of the play to be highly problematic, even going so far as to question whether Lear should be considered the protagonist of the tragedy, based on its dramatic structure:

> [...] it is impossible, I think, from the point of view of construction, to regard the hero as the leading figure. If we attempt to do so, we must either find the crisis in the First Act (for after it Lear's course is downward), and this is absurd; or else we must say that the usual movement is present but its direction is reversed, the hero's cause first sinking to the lowest point (in the storm-scenes) and then rising again. But this will not do; for though his fortunes may be said to rise again for a time, they rise only to fall once more to a catastrophe. (63)

Bradley hints at my reading of the dramatic structure as a reversal of the falling action and the rising action, but he rejects my view of the catastrophe as the culmination of the rising action. Bradley resolves the difficulty that these contradictions in the play's movements present by emphasizing the action initiated in act one by Goneril, Regan, and Edmund (the Earl of Gloucester's bitter, illegitimate son): Bradley notes that their fortunes rise to a height in act three (when the sisters cast Lear out into the storm, Regan and her husband, Cornwall, blind Gloucester, and Edmund is named the new Earl of Gloucester), and they fall to the catastrophes of their deaths, with Lear and Cordelia as collateral damage in the tragedy of the villains (63). Bradley concludes, "Thus we may still find in *King Lear* the usual scheme of an ascending and a descending movement of one side in the conflict" (63). However, Bradley's perspective not only fails to account for the placement of Lear's fatal error, as I will define it below, in act one, but also denies Lear's status as titular hero, since Bradley makes the story that of the villains or antiheroes. I argue that it is critically sound to visualize the plot in exactly the way Bradley rejected as "absurd" (63)—by reversing the falling and rising actions.

Fredson Bowers returned to the difficulties inherent in the plot movement of *King Lear* seventy-five years later in his essay "The Structure of *King Lear*." Taking the Aristotelian concept of *hamartia*, the hero's "crucial error that leads to a tragic instead of a comic ending" (7), as his point of departure, Bowers locates the "crucial error" in Shakespeare's plays as corresponding to the dramatic climax, a reflection of Freytag's basic structure of rising action followed by falling action that is precipitated by the tragic error in judgment. As Bowers asserts, "Tragic decision constitutes the climax," supporting my integration of Aristotle's terms with Freytag's pyramid (Fig. 2). Bowers illustrates his conclusion by offering Hamlet's terrible mistake in killing Polonius as an example of how the plot turns downward toward its unavoidable catastrophe (8). I would add that Romeo's decision to put honor over love by killing Tybalt and Othello's to trust Iago over Desdemona are similarly catastrophic. All three fatal errors occur in act three of the five-act plays. Bowers then considers where the climax of *King Lear* occurs and finds the storm scene in act three to be a turning point for Lear, as Freytag's model predicts, because, Bowers asserts, this scene depicts Lear's "new consciousness of his participation in the common humanity from which in his pride he had thought himself exempt" (11). The problem with this reading, as Bowers acknowledges, is that this act three turning point for Lear is not the moment of his *hamartia*, as it is for Romeo, Hamlet, and Othello. Lear's self-realization is not the crucial error required to fulfill Freytag's model. Indeed, Bowers concedes, Lear makes no tragic error in the storm scene of act three that turns the play into a tragedy (7). Lear's actions during the storm (3.2) and hovel scenes (3.4) constitute *anagnorisis* rather than *hamartia*, because Lear admits his failures as king and father, first, by recognizing that he has not considered the needs of his subjects before his own and, second, by bidding the Fool to take shelter from the storm ahead of him. As Bowers observes, "Lear's 'decision' to release his humanity and suppress his pride-based choler is in fact regenerative and morally sound, not a violation of the ethical fabric" (12).

Bowers concludes that act three presents no climax at all because *King Lear* is an "anomaly": Shakespeare's other tragedies (*Hamlet, Antony and Cleopatra, Coriolanus, Romeo and Juliet, Othello,* and *Macbeth*) "are conventional five-act, pyramidally-structured Renaissance tragedies" (13), with mid-point tragic decisions leading directly to catastrophes. Instead, Bowers calls *King Lear* "a modified classical tragedy" (13). In Sophocles' *Oedipus Rex*, Bowers explains, the hero's tragic error in judgment has taken place long before the play begins when Oedipus killed his father on the road, and the plot unfolds with his discovery of that mistake and its consequences (14). In *King Lear*, according to Bowers, Shakespeare modified the Renaissance tragic structure by placing the hero's terrible error in the first act, when Lear divides his kingdom and banishes Cordelia: "Shakespeare allows himself almost the full length of the play to work out the far-reaching and complex results of Lear's tragic decision" (14). Act one is, Bowers concludes, the climax of the play, and the storm scene in act three (Bradley's climax) is an "anticlimax," which does not avoid the final catastrophe but does bring about "the moral effect of the restoration of his reason over his passion [. . . and] in the tragic close [of the fifth act] a reconciliation of protagonist and audience" (17). Bowers recognizes that Freytag's pyramid does not work for *King Lear* and suggests, rather, the figure of a single sloping line [ ↘ ] whereby Lear starts at the top and falls inexorably downward to the nadir at the end of the play. This image does not, however, account for the positive change in Lear's character that begins in act three.

Like Bowers, Karl P. Wentersdorf responded to Bradley with a visual representation of *King Lear*, but Wentersdorf's figure embodies the play's unusual and complex movement more thoroughly than Bowers' single sloping line. Wentersdorf theorizes two opposing directions over the course of the drama and, agreeing that Freytag's pyramid does not work to illustrate them, contends that two diagonal, intersecting lines—"a Saint Andrew's cross," *i.e.*, ✗—are a more accurate image. He explains,

> [T]here are two contrasted lines of action: the external fortunes of the protagonist, which decline—with minor, suspense-raising advances—from the beginning to the end [ ↘ ] and the old king's spiritual fortunes, which slowly but surely progress until at last he emerges from the struggle, cleansed of his weaknesses by the purgatorial fire of earthly suffering [ ↗ ]. (648)

To this description, I have added directional arrows within brackets to indicate the trajectories of the two conflicting lines of plot movement. Though Wentersdorf does not designate the point in the play where the "contrasted lines" intersect, they most likely cross at act three, the midpoint of the play, when Lear is homeless in the storm (the lowest point of his "external fortunes") and begins to understand his tragic errors in the midst of his madness (his rising "spiritual fortunes").

However, none of these graphics quite succeeds in representing the play's dramatic structure. While I agree with Bowers' reading of Lear's tragic error as occurring in the first act, the sloping line figure fails to consider Lear's essential movements during the five acts. On the other hand, my inverted pyramid illustrates fully and accurately Lear's trajectory. While Wentersdorf's cross [X] embodies the falling and rising actions of the play in a more satisfying way than does Bowers' slope or Freytag's pyramid, it fails to account for the fact that Lear's external fortunes ultimately rise because, despite the defeat of Lear's defenders and the execution of Cordelia, Edgar defeats Edmund, and Albany cedes the throne back to Lear just before Lear's death. Those events, too, are elements of Lear's character path. As the discussion below shows, the inverted pyramid coherently represents Lear's regaining the political authority he held as king, as well as his spiritual redemption as man and father.

## The Inverted Pyramid as Model for *King Lear*

Unlike Othello and Macbeth, Shakespeare's other mature tragic heroes, Lear is entirely responsible for his own catastrophe: no one has misled him (as the witches' prophecies do Macbeth) or deceived him (as Iago does Othello). Lear is also distinguished from classical tragic heroes who are subjects, even victims, of fate. Unlike Oedipus, the quintessential Greek tragic hero fated by the oracle to kill his father and marry his mother, Lear has absolute agency over his poor choices. Indeed, the play begins with a series of errors. Presumably knowing his elder daughters' avaricious natures, Lear offers Goneril and Regan the opportunity and the motive to treat him cruelly by giving them his kingdom. Naming Goneril (his eldest daughter) and the Duke of Albany (her husband) his successors, following the order of primogeniture, would have likely kept the kingdom intact and avoided civil war.[5] The audience may also conclude that Lear's admitted favoritism of Cordelia may in some measure inspire Goneril and Regan to direct their jealousy and wrath against their father and younger sister. Lear's discourse and actions are the prime movers in the tragedy, and he will bear the consequences in the end, symbolized when he carries Cordelia's body onto the stage in the final scene (5.3.257).[6] The trajectory of Lear's journey is singular among those of Shakespeare's tragic protagonists, and tracing it demands a different geometrical figure, the inverted pyramid I have described.

The play opens at the upper extreme of the inverted pyramid's left side with Lear at the height of his power and majesty as the aged king of Britain (1.1), but his fall is imminent, represented by the downward arrows placed between acts one, two, and three (Fig. 3). Lear's multiple errors in judgment occur early in the first scene of act one and immediately set him on a path toward ruin. Having already "divided" his kingdom into three unequal portions (1.1.37–38), weakening it and making civil war inevitable, Lear then abdicates his throne, seeking rest and luxury in retirement, so that he may "[u]nburthen'd crawl toward death" (1.1.41). Finally, Lear determines the portions of his divided kingdom based on a test of his daughters' affection. He is pleased by Goneril's and Regan's hyperbolically insincere professions of love but banishes his youngest daughter, Cordelia, when she says that she loves him "[a]ccording to my bond, no more nor less" (1.1.92–93). Enraged, Lear disclaims

Cordelia as his daughter, reneges on his promise of her dowry, and banishes the Earl of Kent, his most loyal retainer, when he intercedes on Cordelia's behalf.

Lear's words and actions in the first scene reveal his fundamental inability to grasp the bond of natural love between parent and child. When he questions his daughters, "Which of you shall we say doth love us most / That we our largest bounty may extend / Where nature doth with merit challenge?" (1.1.51–53), Lear defines love as transactional: he gives to his daughters only when he receives from them the flattery he craves. When he asks Cordelia, "[W]hat can you say to draw / A third more opulent than your sisters'? Speak," her answer is "Nothing, my lord" (1.1. 85–87). Lear warns her, "Nothing will come of nothing, speak again" (1.1.89). Cordelia refuses to play Lear's game as her sisters do. She hears his praise of her sisters' oaths and reproves them for effectually denying their love for their husbands: "Sure I shall never marry like my sisters, / To love my father all" (1.1.103). But for Lear, Cordelia's just protest is inadequate: he wants all her love and swears a formal oath declaring that Cordelia is no longer his daughter (1.1.108–120). Pitying himself, Lear laments, "I lov'd her most, and thought to set my rest / On her kind nursery" (1.1.123–124). Having given Cordelia his favor, Lear expected to receive her care in his old age. Of Cordelia's two suitors, the Duke of Burgundy shares Lear's idea of love as transactional and refuses to marry Cordelia when Lear withdraws her dowry. The second suitor, the King of France, however, declares he loves her more than before, since "She is herself a dowry" (1.1.240) and assures Cordelia that she is "most rich being poor" (1.1.250). Just before Lear exits the stage in act one, he asserts to the King of France, "[W]e / Have no such daughter, nor shall ever see / That face of hers again" and banishes her from the kingdom, "Without our grace, our love, our benison" (1.1.262–265). Alone with Cordelia and France, Goneril and Regan heap further insults on Cordelia, and she charges them with cunning and concealment (1.1.268–281).[7]

Clearly, the first scene offers nothing to incite the rising action traced on Freytag's pyramid (Fig.1) but instead produces precipitous falling action depicted by the left side of my inverted pyramid. Lear falls short in stewardship and protection of Britain as a king and in love as a father, sending him, his dynasty, and the kingdom hurtling down the slope that traces his rapid descent. A brief exchange between Goneril and Regan at the end of the first scene gives us their view of their father. When Goneril notes his "poor judgment" in rejecting Cordelia (1.1.291), Regan answers, "'Tis the infirmity of his age, yet he has ever but slenderly known himself" (1.1.293–294), and Goneril agrees that his choleric nature is a "long-ingraff'd condition" (1.1.297). By the close of scene 1, Lear's impetuosity and failures of character and duty as both king and father have set in motion his destruction and the play's tragic consequences.

Lear continues along that downward path with the presumption that he can resign his kingship yet retain his title, power, and privilege, "all th' addition to a King" (1.1.136), symbolized by a train of one-hundred knights. Goneril, with whom he spends the first month of his retirement, soon complains that the knights are riotous and reduces their number by half, whereupon Lear lays on Goneril the worst possible curse for royalty: "Into her womb convey sterility" (1.4.278). He then rages offstage, shouting, "I have another daughter" (1.4.305), but as act one ends, the Fool promises Lear that Regan, his middle daughter, will act as Goneril has. In the next scene (1.5), Lear's cryptic "I did her wrong" (1.5.24) certainly refers to Cordelia, indicating that he has begun to realize that he has made a terrible mistake. Nonetheless, this fleeting expression of self-consciousness does not indicate that Lear is turning toward self-awareness since he does not act upon it by making some attempt to recall Cordelia. Instead, Lear prays, "O, let me not be mad, not mad, sweet heaven! / Keep me in temper, I would not be mad!" (1.5.46–47). Perhaps he senses that the consequences of privileging Goneril and Regan will be so dire that he will need to escape into madness to avoid facing his own culpability, as the falling action charted along the left side of the inverted pyramid continues in act two.

The second act presents Lear's rapid decline in fortune, represented by the downward-pointing arrows on the left side of the inverted pyramid (Fig. 2). In 2.4, Goneril and Regan join forces against Lear to reduce the number of his knights further and further. Regan declares, "I entreat you / To bring but five and twenty; to no more / Will I give place or notice," and Lear answers petulantly, "I gave you all—" (2.4.247–249). Goneril continues, "What need you five and twenty? ten? or five?" (2.4.261). Finally, Regan inflicts the *coup de grace* to her father's desire to preserve the pomp of kingship represented by his knights by asking rhetorically, "What need one?" (2.4.263). Understanding that physical need is not the point, Lear cries out poignantly, "O, reason not the need! our basest beggars / Are in the poorest thing superfluous" (2.4.264–265). He is, of course, not actually a solitary beggar, since he still has Kent and the Fool to assist him. Lear's point is that even beggars have something they need to survive emotionally if not physically, something that preserves their sense of dignity—like a cardboard box or a shopping cart, to evoke modern associations with the homeless. Lear does not *need* even one knight, but he *wants* his followers to retain his sense of identity as king. However, the king who was once at the peak of power and privilege, represented by the initial highpoint on the left side of the inverted pyramid, has fallen precipitously down the falling action of acts one and two. Yet Lear vows revenge in 2.4 as if he were still a powerful king: "I will do such things— / What they are yet I know not, but they shall be / The terrors of the earth!" (2.4.280–282). This eloquent but empty threat comes not from a king with armies to unleash on his enemies, but from an old man who has foolishly given away his power. The stage directions indicate that "*Storm and tempest*" (2.4.284) are heard outside as Lear leaves the stage, and in a moment of insight, he admits his vulnerability as the horror of being rejected by both of his remaining daughters begins to drive him out of his mind: "O Fool, I shall go mad!" (2.4.286). As night falls and the winds increase (2.4.300–301), Regan tells the Earl of Gloucester, whose castle she and Cornwall have occupied, "Shut up your doors" (2.4.304), abandoning Lear to the storm. With this series of reversals culminating at the end of act two, Lear is about to sink to the lowest point of the inverted pyramid in his journey as tragic hero.

Act three begins with a report that Lear has been raging madly as he runs about in the storm (3.1.3–15). Lear enacts that description in 3.2 with his apostrophe to the elements—"Blow, winds, and crack your checks! rage, blow!" (3.2.1)—establishing the storm's function as an external mirror of his rage and mental chaos. Lear then blasts the "rain, wind, thunder, fire" as "servile ministers" in league against him with his "two pernicious daughters" (3.2.15, 21, 22), calling himself "a man / More sinn'd against than sinning" (3.2.59–60). Consumed with hatred for those who have "sinn'd against" him, Lear reaches the nadir of his external and spiritual fortunes and observes, "My wits begin to turn" (3.2.67), expressing his fear of encroaching madness. But apparently because of his altered mind, Lear sees suffering in another for the first time in the play, asking the Fool, "How dost, my boy? Art cold?" (3.2.68). In 3.4, he again addresses the Fool with fatherly care, bidding him to enter the hovel that Kent has found: "In, boy, go first" (3.4.26). Lear, homeless in "this pitiless storm" (3.4.29), at last empathizes with all the "[p]oor naked wretches" (3.4.28) in his kingdom, as he urges himself, "Expose thyself to feel what wretches feel" (3.4.34). He acknowledges here that being king gives him responsibility for his people's welfare and that, while he has been focused on which daughter will house him and his knights each month, his poorest subjects are homeless and suffering in this storm. Lear laments, "O, I have ta'en / Too little care of this!" (3.4.32–33). This moment of understanding marks a change in Lear's character, and the direction of the inverted pyramid reverses. Only when he becomes a homeless former king because of his failings, does Lear begin to understand what is required of him as a king and a father, a dawning self-awareness that begins the *anagnorisis*.

With this new consciousness working on his mind in 3.4, Lear soon meets one of those "poor naked wretches" he has just been thinking about—Poor Tom, the mad beggar, who is actually Edgar, the legitimate son of old Gloucester, in disguise. Lear declares, "Thou are the thing itself: unaccommodated man is no more but such a poor, bare, fork'd animal as thou art" (3.4.106–108). Lear then tears off his clothes, identifying with the naked beggar and enacting his realization that adversity and loss equalize king and beggar. Nakedness also symbolizes Lear's movement toward spiritual purgation and rebirth in the apocalyptic storm, and his path begins to rise along the right side of the inverted pyramid, indicated by the upward directional arrows (Fig. 3).

In spite of these signs of Lear's spiritual awakening, the remainder of act three shows that Lear's anger with Regan and Goneril still consumes him and delays his upward movement. As the storm rages outside, Lear, in his madness, arraigns Regan and Goneril for a mock trial and assigns the Fool, Poor Tom (Edgar), and Kent to serve as justices. Lear remains mystified by his daughters' cruelty, wondering, "Is there any cause in nature that make these hard hearts?" (3.6.77–78). Later, in 4.6, Lear will return to this theme of his unnatural and ungrateful elder daughters when he encounters the blinded Gloucester, another father betrayed by his child (Edmund). Here, Lear acknowledges that Goneril and Regan were lying when they professed their love for him: "[T]hey flatter'd me like a dog [. . . .] they told me I was everything. 'Tis a lie" (4.6.96–105). Following this hint of a confession, Lear continues his tirade and ends by describing Goneril and Regan to Gloucester as monsters in disguise: "Down from the waist they are Centaurs, / Though women all above; / ... Beneath is all the fiends" (4.6.124–127), implying that they appear to be women, but underneath they are unnatural and evil monsters. This echoes the Duke of Albany's earlier claim that his wife Goneril and her sister Regan are "Tigers, not daughters" (4.2.40) when they put their father out in the storm. Albany tells Goneril, "See thyself, devil! / Proper deformity shows not in the fiend / So horrid as in woman" (4.2.59-61).[8]

Lear's fortunes turn again in 4.6 with the arrival of a Gentleman, one of Lear's knights, whom Cordelia, now returned from France, has sent to find Lear. The Gentleman reminds Lear, "Thou hast one daughter / Who redeems nature from the general curse / Which twain have brought her to" (4.6.205–207). Cordelia, as the Gentleman affirms, remains faithful to Lear and will mend the bond of nature he broke with her, making Regan and Goneril's deception and cruelty irrelevant. Though Lear remains erratic in these scenes, his growing understanding is indicated by the upward arrows on the right side of the pyramid that track his movement toward self-knowledge and his preparation for the spiritual redemption he finds in his reunion with Cordelia.

The upward directional arrows on the right side of the inverted pyramid (Fig. 3) also represent Lear's political movement toward the horizontal plane where he began. Earlier in act four, we learn from Kent that "from France there comes a power / Into this scattered kingdom" (4.3.30–31) led by Cordelia and the King of France. In 4.4, Cordelia avows that she is not motivated by "blown ambition," but by "love, dear love, and our ag'd father's right" (4.4.27–28); in other words, she is fighting to restore Lear to the throne not to advance herself. (She is, after all, already Queen of France.) Kent has told Lear that Cordelia has returned but reports to Lear's Gentleman (knight) that Lear has refused to see her:

> A sovereign shame so elbows him: his own unkindness,
> That stripped her from his benediction, turn'd her
> To foreign casualties, gave her dear rights
> To his dog-hearted daughters—these things sting
> His mind so venomously, that burning shame
> Detains him from Cordelia. (4.3.41–46)

Lear's "burning shame" reflects the growing consciousness of guilt that will lead him to ask for Cordelia's forgiveness, as well as his upward spiritual movement, indicated on the right side of the inverted pyramid. However, the news that the King of France must return to his own country due to "Something he left imperfect in the state" (4.3.3) does not bode well for Lear's political fortunes.

In 4.4, Cordelia anxiously shares with the Doctor reports that have come to her of Lear, raving and dressed in foliage, "As mad as the vex'd sea, singing aloud" (4.4.2). She dispatches a French officer to find Lear and bring him to her to be cared for. Cordelia asks the Doctor what will be needed to aid "in the restoring of his [her father's] bereaved sense" and offers "all my outward worth" for the cure (4.4.8–10). The Doctor assures Cordelia that "repose," induced with the help of "simples" (medicinal herbs) will "close the eye of anguish" (4.4.12–15). Cordelia's actions in this scene and her offer to "give all" for a cure demonstrate a love for Lear that abides despite his offenses against her. The upward directional arrows on the right side of the inverted pyramid (Fig. 3) represent his spiritual ascent under Cordelia's care, as well as his later political movement toward the horizontal plane where he began.

In his reunion with Cordelia in 4.7, Lear experiences a powerful moment of *anagnorisis* that marks his movement out of madness and toward full awareness of his losses and his culpability for them. Their meeting sits midway up the rising action of the right side of the inverted pyramid (Fig. 3). As Lear, still asleep, is carried in, Cordelia speaks to him, praying that "restoration hang / Thy medicine on my lips" and that her kiss will "[r]epair those violent harms that my two sisters / Have in thy reverence made" (4.7.25–28), in other words, that her love will be stronger than her sisters' hatred and "repair" the damage they have done, restoring him to himself. When Lear awakens to find himself with Cordelia, he sees her as a spirit in heaven, "a soul in bliss," and believes that he has died, his soul condemned to hell, "bound / Upon a wheel of fire" (4.7.45–46), recalling the "burning shame" of (4.3.46) that prevented him from seeing Cordelia sooner. Lear tries to kneel before her, but she stops him and asks him to "hold your hand in benediction o'er me" (4.7.57). Though he still does not recognize Cordelia, Lear describes himself with insight for the first time since he admitted during the storm in act three his failures as king: "I am a very foolish fond old man" (4.7.59), a profoundly honest statement, for this is exactly what Lear has been: an old fool.

Lear's progress toward self-knowledge continues its halting but forward movement as he professes that he is still "not in my perfect mind" (4.7.62) and cannot remember where he slept the night before. Then, in a moment of clarity in which he recognizes Cordelia, he says, "I think this lady / To be my child Cordelia" (4.7.68–69). With this declaration, Lear's *anagnorisis* is complete. In calling Cordelia his child and naming her, Lear revokes his earlier folly of disowning her, and when she answers, "And so I am, I am" (4.7.70), the bond of nature between parent and child is restored. Lear cannot erase his mistakes, because the political action has moved irrevocably forward into civil war and his decisions have caused universal harm, but in this scene, we see him on an upward spiritual path of self-knowledge made possible by Cordelia's love. Confessing and asking forgiveness of Cordelia are necessary to Lear's spiritual development and repentance, just as her military intervention is necessary if he is to be restored to the throne.

The movement up the pyramid's right side continues in 4.7 when Lear admits that, unlike her sisters, Cordelia has "some cause" not to love him, but she assures him, "No cause, no cause" (4.7.74–75). While acknowledging that Cordelia has "some cause" to hold against him may not seem like a full confession of his sins against her, even this admission is a significant act of humility for the once proud and egotistical king. The doctor confirms Lear's recovery to Cordelia, assuring her, "[T]he great rage / You see, is kill'd in him" (4.7.77–78). Once Cordelia has replaced her sisters' hatred with care, love, and forgiveness, he is rational, fulfilling Cordelia's hopes. For the second time, Lear begs for Cordelia's forbearance: "You must bear with me. / Pray you now forget, and forgive; I am old and foolish" (4.7.83–84). This is a chastened and humbled Lear, who has made significant strides on the upward path of the inverted pyramid toward redemption and spiritual regeneration.

Act five unfolds the catastrophic defeat of Cordelia's forces by those of Edmund and her sisters in 5.1 and the arrests of Lear and Cordelia in 5.2. However, despite these political reversals, Lear's spiritual course along the right side of the inverted pyramid continues to move upward. Even in the play's final scene (5.3), when Lear and Cordelia are being taken to prison, Lear professes to be happy, and as Cordelia weeps, he tells her to dry her tears:

> Come let's away to prison;
> We two alone will sing like birds i' th' cage;
> When thou dost ask me blessing, I'll kneel down
> And ask of thee forgiveness. So we'll live,
> And pray, and sing, and tell old tales, and laugh. (5.3.8–12)

If Shakespeare had ended the play here, with Lear sentenced to live out the remainder of his days in prison with Cordelia, *King Lear* would have been a comedy or tragicomedy, but Shakespeare's tragic design requires further catastrophic suffering.[9] Though Cordelia has forgiven Lear, his redemption does not end with confession and remorse but with severe penance: he must pay a heavier price than imprisonment for abandoning his divided kingdom to Regan and Goneril.

Lear's penance reaches its apex in 5.3, when Edmund's dying rescission of his warrant for the deaths of Lear and Cordelia (5.3.244–251) arrives too late to save Cordelia, and Lear enters, bearing her body. His "Howl, howl, howl!" (5.3.258) here echoes his furious opening address in 3.2 when he commands the storm, "Blow, winds and crack your cheeks" (3.2.1). Now, Lear roars in pain and heartbreak, recognizing the irrevocability of his loss: "She's gone for ever! / I know when one is dead, and when one lives; / She's dead as earth" (5.3.260–262). This is indeed the tragic catastrophe but also the pinnacle of Lear's development as a tragic hero. We have seen his path rise along the inverted pyramid from his spiritual and political nadir in act three. At that point, his spiritual regeneration begins, continuing along an upward path in act four with his reunion with Cordelia. In 5.3, Lear's tragic journey closes with the realization of his greatest loss.

The compelling distinction that makes *King Lear* structurally anomalous as a tragedy is that its action in following Lear's spiritual journey is not delineated by rising action followed by falling action but the reverse. Lear's tragedy is not that of the rise of the hero, followed by his error in judgment and his fall, the pattern of Freytag's pyramid. Instead, Lear falls immediately, sinks to a point of absolute loss, and then rises spiritually. At the end of the play, Lear is briefly king again when Albany cedes the throne back to him. However, he is a different king and man than he once was—broken now but also self-aware, humbled, and caring.

My inverted pyramid accommodates both Lear's transformation and the audience response that it prompts. Its right side projects upward, beyond the final catastrophe, to indicate the audience's reception of the play's conclusion, a reception that depends on how events affect the tragic hero and on the hero's response to them. Cordelia's execution breaks Lear's heart, all the more poignantly because he barely misses saving her from the hangman and assures the lifeless Cordelia, "I kill'd the slave that was a-hanging thee" (5.3.275). Gazing on Cordelia's body, Lear pitifully, repeatedly vacillates between hope that she lives and awareness that she is dead: "Lend me a looking-glass, / If that her breath will mist or stain the stone, / Why then she lives" (5.3.262–264). A few lines later, his hope is again awakened: "This feather stirs, she lives! If it be so, / It is a chance to redeem all sorrows / That ever I have felt" (5.3.266–268). But he soon despairs of his hope to "redeem all sorrows" and laments, "I might have sav'd her, now she's gone for ever!" (5.3.271). Immediately, he addresses Cordelia again, as though she is still alive: "Cordelia, Cordelia, stay a little. Ha! / What is't thou say'st?" and in a quick aside to Edgar, Kent, and Albany, he praises Cordelia's femininity: "Her voice was ever soft, / Gentle, and low, an excellent thing in a woman" (5.3.272–274), asserting that she, unlike her sisters, fully conforms to a woman's nature.

In Lear's final speech, he ignores his restoration to sovereignty and focuses on Cordelia. He again voices his despair that she is dead, followed by a final, desperate hope that she is, somehow, alive:

> And my poor fool is hang'd! No, no, no life!
> Why should a dog, a horse, a rat, have life,
> And thou no breath at all? Thou'lt come no more,
> Never, never, never, never, never.
> Pray you undo this button. Thank you, sir!
> Do you see this? Look on her! Look her lips,
> Look there, look there! (5.3.306–312)

Is Lear deluding himself that Cordelia is breathing, or does he see her as the "soul in bliss" he described (4.7.45) when he awakened and found her before him? Shakespeare does not make either reading clear. I suggest Lear's last two lines indicate a vision of reunion with Cordelia in the afterlife, where he will receive divine forgiveness and experience spiritual rebirth. In her 2004 online essay for the British Library, Christie Carson notes that Lear's last two lines were not present in the 1608 Quarto edition but were added to the 1623 Folio, and she argues, "The reintroduction of hope in Lear's last lines can be performed either as redemption and absolution or delusion. As is true of so much of Shakespeare's work, these lines are ambiguous." The stage direction that follows is simply "*He dies*" (5.3.312). When Edgar tries to revive Lear, Kent gently rebukes him: "Vex not his ghost. O, let him pass, he hates him / That would upon the rack of this rough world / Stretch him out longer" (5.3.314–316). Kent's metaphor of torture by the rack recalls Lear's own metaphor of the "wheel of fire" (4.7.46) upon which he is bound. Kent then asserts Lear's readiness for death, since "He but usurp'd his life" (5.3.318).

With Lear's death, Albany confers joint rule on Edgar and Kent, but Kent declines, resolved that he will soon accompany Lear in death: "I have a journey, sir, shortly to go: / My master calls me, I must not say no" (5.3.322–323). Edgar now finds himself by default king of Britain and delivers the final speech, reflecting on the lessons of the tragedy:

> The weight of this sad time we must obey,
> Speak what we feel, not what we ought to say:
> The oldest has borne most; we that are young
> Shall never see so much, nor live so long. (5.3.324–327)

Edgar emphasizes the "weight"—the moral or lesson—to be derived from the terrible suffering staged in the tragedy when he concludes, "we" should speak sincerely and truthfully, as Cordelia does in the first scene. His "we" includes his companions on stage, as well as the audience. Validating Lear's restored prestige, Edgar also acknowledges the debt of "we that are young" to their predecessors: "The oldest has borne most," he says, honoring not only Lear, who has lost and regained more than anyone, but also his father, the old Earl of Gloucester, who dies blinded but vindicated of treason and reunited with his loyal son Edgar. Carson observes that Edgar's speaking these lines in the First Folio corrects the Quarto version by shifting them to Edgar from Albany.[10] She further argues,

> [T]here is strong evidence the changes between the Quarto and the Folio were made as a result of the audience response to the play during Shakespeare's lifetime. The ending, in particular, is altered to change it from a scene of absolute despair to a scene of possible redemption and rebirth. Hope is reintroduced into the Folio ending of the play, something that makes this tragedy more poignant but also more bearable.

The extended line on the right side of my inverted pyramid represents the audience's cathartic response to the final note of hope for Lear's redemption as the play ends.

Shakespeare structured *King Lear* as a dramatic anomaly. The inverted pyramid, as I have described it in terms of dramatic movement and character development, offers an accurate visual representation of Shakespeare's dramatic vision in this remarkable play, with his singular hero's journey to redemption, whereas Freytag's pyramid and other graphic representations, including Bowers' sloping line and Wentersdorf's St. Andrew's cross, do not quite succeed. Aristotle's elements of complex tragedy assist in plotting the play's trajectory and support the inverted pyramid as fully depicting the structure of the tragedy. Indeed, my inverted pyramid visually represents the unexpected reversal of the tragic plot and the audience's unusually hopeful response to the play's tragic catastrophe. Ultimately, Shakespeare denies the audience's expectations of an orderly tragedy and flips the usual tragic structure on its head. In so doing, he creates an unmatched dramatic experience and, I would argue, his greatest tragic hero.

## Notes

1 Citations of Freytag's *Die Technik des Dramas* refer to MacEwan's English translation.
2 Quotations from plays are cited as act, scene, and line number(s), period separated. Read 3.2, for example, as "act 3, scene 2."
3 The placement of the tragic error in judgment as well as the climax in act three is characteristic of Renaissance drama rather than classical tragedy. Bowers reminds us that the *hamartia* has already occurred before the action begins in classical drama, as it does in *Oedipus Rex* (14).
4 The phrase "inverted pyramid" usually describes the presentation of data in descending order of importance in journalistic style and has not, as far as I am aware, been used in regard to dramatic structure.
5 According to the laws of primogeniture, Goneril, the eldest, would succeed, presumably because Lear has no living son and no deceased son whose legitimate sons survive. See Marguerite A. Tassi's view of Cordelia's gendered, political role.
6 Citations of *King Lear* refer to Frank Kermode's edited text (*The Riverside Shakespeare*).
7 No direct evidence in the play explains the difference in nature between Cordelia and her older sisters. As Goneril says, "He always loved our sister most" (1.1.290), and their father's open favoritism has probably inspired their jealousy. But no one hints at the reason why he loves Cordelia "most." We may speculate, based on the age difference between Cordelia and her sisters and Lear's age (over 80), that they did not have the same mother. Cordelia's mother was perhaps Lear's second wife in a marriage of love, whereas his first marriage to Goneril and Regan's mother was arranged, political, dynastic, and likely loveless. Therefore, he naturally favors the child born of love in his old age, though the play never actually refers to the sisters' mothers. Cordelia has somehow learned to love unconditionally, perhaps from her mother. One completely speculative possibility is that Cordelia's mother was Lear's mistress, whom he married after his first wife's death, provoking his elder daughters' bitterness and resentment on their mother's behalf.
8 A beautiful woman concealing fiendish features beneath her gown and Satan disguised as a woman to tempt man are medieval commonplaces.
9 James E. Hirsh notes the problematic dramatic structure of the play and the possibility of an untragic ending: "[T]he play has a confusing exposition, a falling action when it should have a rising action, a misleading climax, a rising action when it should have a falling action, and seems headed for a tragicomic resolution rather than a tragic catastrophe" (86). Hirsh argues, "Shakespeare botches the ending," making Cordelia's death not the result of "tragic fate" but of Edmund's "forgetfulness" (88). Hirsh concludes, however, that the disorderly nature of the play is not really the result of the playwright's incompetence but rather his deliberate construction of a play that fails as tragicomedy but succeeds as tragedy: "This structure [. . .] intensifies the painfulness of the play" (90). Hirsh

suggests here that Cordelia's death serves no purpose in the plot; rather, it deals a deathblow of pain to Lear. Critical studies after Hirsh's in 1986 focus on Cordelia's role as a Christ-figure and other Christian elements of the play, but none relates the redemption theme to the play's dramatic structure. See, for example, Kent R. Lehnhof's 2018 summary treatment of the question. As Lehnhof concludes, Lear and Cordelia's reconciliation is like other reunions in Shakespeare's late plays; consider Pericles and Marina's in *Pericles* and Leontes and Hermione's in *The Winter's Tale*, as Cotton describes it in his chapter of this volume. Lehnhof writes, "[I]f these climactic moments verge on the holy, they do so in a very humanistic way. What brings Lear and Pericles and Leontes to the threshold of the sacred is not the intervention of a divine being but the (renewed) experience of an interpersonal relation" (118).

10 The First Folio text given in *The Riverside Shakespeare* makes Edgar the speaker of the final lines. Two earlier Quarto texts assign the speech to Albany; however, the speaker refers to "we that are young" (5.3.326), a "we" only Edgar can participate in. Moreover, many of Shakespeare's tragedies end with a speech by the character charged with restoring order (*e.g.*, Prince Escalus in *Romeo and Juliet*, Fortinbras in *Hamlet*, and Malcolm in *Macbeth*), and that figure in *King Lear* is the new King Edgar. Carson explains the significance: "Edgar is presented in the Folio as the leader of the new generation and the representative of a gentler form of leadership."

**Works Cited**

Aristotle. *Poetics*. Ed. and Trans. Michelle Zerba and David Gorman. New York: Norton, 2018.

Bowers, Fredson. "The Structure of *King Lear*." *Shakespeare Quarterly* 31.1 (1980): 7–20.

Bradley, A. C. *Shakespearean Tragedy: Lectures on* Hamlet, Othello, King Lear, Macbeth. London: Macmillan, 1904. Rpt. Penguin Classics. London: Penguin, 1991.

Carson, Christie. "The Quarto of *King Lear*—Representing the Early Stage History of the Play?" *Treasures in Full: Shakespeare in Quarto*. Expert Views. London: BL, 2004. Online.

Freytag, Gustav. *Die Technik des Dramas*. Leipzig: S. Hirzel, 1863. New ed. Berlin: Autorenhaus Verlag, 2003.

—. *Freytag's Technique of the Drama: An Exposition of Dramatic Composition and Art*. Trans. Elias J. MacEwan. 2nd ed. Chicago: S. C. Griggs, 1896.

Hirsh, James E. "An Approach through Dramatic Structure." *Approaches to Teaching Shakespeare's* King Lear. Ed. Robert H. Ray. New York: MLA, 1986. 86–90.

Lehnhof, Kent R. "Theology, Phenomenology, and the Divine in *King Lear*." Ed. Moshe Gold and Sandor Goodhart with Kent Lehnhof. *Of Levinas and Shakespeare: "To See Another Thus."* West Lafayette, IN: Perdue UP, 2018. 107–122.

MacEwan, Elias J. *See* Freytag, Gustav. *Freytag's Technique*.

Shakespeare, William. *King Lear*. Ed. Frank Kermode. *The Riverside Shakespeare*. General Ed. G. Blakemore Evans and J. J. M. Tobin. 2nd ed. Boston: Houghton Mifflin, 1997. 1303–1354.

Sophocles. *Oedipus Tyrannus* [*Oedipus Rex*]. Trans. Hugh Lloyd Jones. *Ajax. Electra. Oedipus Tyrannus*. Cambridge, MA: Harvard UP, 1994. 323–483.

Tassi, Marguerite A. "The Avenging Daughter in *King Lear*." Ed. Lesel Dawson and Fiona McHardy. *Revenge and Gender in Classical, Medieval, and Renaissance Literature*. Edinburgh: Edinburgh UP, 2018. 111–121.

Wentersdorf, Karl P. "Structure and Characterization in *Othello* and *King Lear*." *College English* 26.8 (1965): 645–648.

## 9

# Overcoming the World
## Strategies of the Poet and the Sculptor

HELEN F. MAXSON

The evocative powers of art and subjectivity and the nature of the medium affect reception of the iconic theme of "Mary at the foot of the cross" interpreted in two generically distinct fifteenth-century creative works, the anonymous Middle English lyric "Lament of the Virgin," dated about 1450, and Michelangelo di Lodovico Buonarroti Simoni's Vatican *Pietà*, executed 1498–1499/1500.[1] Distilling Christianity's core principle of overcoming the limitations of the world by means of Christ's love and sacrifice, these works present the grieving mother holding the body of Christ, whose death is the first and most challenging crisis of the newly initiated Christian world. The task before each artist was to shape earth-bound elements into transcendent works of poetry and sculpture, and we may imagine the artist and the poet united by their representational object and shared faith and separated by language, geography, and materials laboring to express the psychic suffering and spiritual significance of the scene. The artists' creative labors, like their creations, suggest the transcendence of which Jesus speaks in describing himself as "of the world" and knowing its "tribulations" as a man and "overcoming" it as the Christ.[2] Among the stories Jesus told are those in which men and women are focused on some earthly circumstance and rise above it to respond to the higher call of the spirit. Some of Jesus' actions, too, call attention in a literal way to the principle of "overcoming the world" that he would enact in his death and resurrection. Jesus speaks to his disciples of it in John 15–16 and in familiar parables: the prodigal son (Luke 15), the pearl of great price (Matt. 13), the lost sheep (Matt. 18), and the good Samaritan (Luke 10) all suggest the value of superseding the world's trials and expectations by means of the spirit.[3] Accounts of Jesus' walking on water, calming a storm at sea, turning water into wine, and increasing a few loaves and fish into a sufficient quantity to feed a multitude illustrate his overcoming the constraints of the physical world by means of the spirit.

Like the narratives and artistic recreations of Jesus as the Christ, the life and figure of his mother, particularly honored in Catholic culture as the Virgin Mary, have offered artists in various media a compelling subject for inspiration since late antiquity; nevertheless, representations that foreground her humanity and emotional accessibility are a development generally—but not absolutely—attached to the high and later Middle Ages.[4] Mary's biblical biography sketches her as a pious young Jewish woman chosen as "the handmaid of the Lord" (Luke 1:38) and visited by the archangel Gabriel, who tells her that she is "blessed among women" and that having found favor with God, she will conceive and bear a son whom she will name Jesus. The prophecy and promise are fulfilled, and keeping vigil through his passion and death, she participates in his church following his death and eventually becomes Christianity's celestial symbol of maternal love, tenderness, and self-sacrifice, and a mediator between man and God.[5] By the twelfth century, Mary represented maternal suffering, compassion, and protection, and in 1215, the Fourth Lateran Council made the *Ave Maria* compulsory learning for laypeople, institutionalizing her role as the supreme mediator—Mary *Mediatrix* of all Graces—between man and God. As the *Mater Dolorosa*, "the sorrowful mother," Mary became the subject of lyric poetry generically known as "Marian laments," the *Planctus Mariae*, and "Mary at the foot of the Cross."[6] In painting, carving, and sculpture, the mourning mother of Christ is the *Pietà*. Both may be viewed as implying Mary's transformation into an eternal, spiritual presence linking heaven and earth.

A thirteenth-century Franciscan hymn of the *Planctus Mariae* genre, "Stabat Mater Dolorosa" [the grieving mother remained (there)], is attributed to an Italian poet-priest, whose verses emphasize the Virgin's affliction at the crucifixion, and Geoffrey Ashe marks the tendency in fourteenth-century Franciscan productions, too, to stress Mary's humanity.[7] Ashe notes Mary's evolution as an object of worship whose "[f]lesh and blood and natural feeling seemed to give her a positive advantage over the abstract Deity" (222) and affirms that her human and maternal qualities answered the era's embrace of emotion as a source of spiritual truth.[8] Editor R. T. Davies notes that in twelfth-century lament poetry "meditation on [Mary's] part in the drama of redemption" was "aimed at stirring the believer's heart" and offered its audience "appropriate sentiments" to that end (40). Davies gives the fifteenth-century "Lament" discussed here as number 112 in his edition, and he describes it as "fully and poignantly explor[ing] the heart-breaking potentialities" of a scene "chosen for its sentimental power" (38). Such representations of Mary gain persuasive force through emotional appeals to the audience rather than from a magisterial imperative. The scene of Christ's body laid across his mother's lap at the foot of the cross is charged with such pain, tenderness, and indelible grief that the "Lament" and the *Pietà* render those appeals in an especially powerful way.

One aspect of the affective argument shared by the "Lament" and the *Pietà* is the idea of Mary's dual identity at Christ's death. Each artist presents her as an earthly mother mourning in the flesh, "crucified in spirit," as she bears the weight of her son's body upon her maternal body for the second time. The events of Christ's crucifixion and death render her simultaneously a newly created figure of spiritual and religious significance.[9] In representing Mary's inexpressible agony over Jesus' body, the sculpture and the lyric respond to believers' emotional connections to the Virgin's trials as mother and holy figure, and each draws in its audience as witnesses to the scene. By rendering her features and form as youthful, as Michelangelo does, the artist gestures to Mary as the young woman she was when the archangel Gabriel set her on the path to the foot of the cross. In the "Lament," this message lies subtly in the discursive images of joyful mothers and their living sons.

In spite of the diverse results that one might expect in a comparative study of two obviously distinct creative products, the *Pietà* and the "Lament" offer a productive comparative approach because of their common subject with its fierce appeals to sympathy and Christian belief. The artists evidently shared a similar sense of the scene's representation of the redemptive value of Christ's death and his mother's suffering and of the layered narratives of temporal experience and memory in a context of sacrifice to imply transformative spiritual power over earthbound matters. The juxtaposition of these effects works as a persuasive argument, eliciting—as I have indicated—an emotional response for audiences sufficiently involved with each work. This artistic rhetoric answers despair and pain with Christ's hopeful injunction to "overcome the world" and with the Virgin's mediation between the earth's dark times and the hope of heaven.

## A Lyrical *Pietà*: Mary at the Foot of the Cross

Like the Virgin of Michelangelo's *Pietà*, Mary, in the eleven-stanza monologue of the "Lament," draws the viewer's attention to the scene at the foot of the cross, where the Gospel of John places her (John 19:25–27). She begins to speak almost immediately after her son's body has been laid across her lap, "taken from [the] tree [*i.e.*, the cross]" (l. 4), and she calls upon women who have witnessed the crucifixion, as recorded in the four Gospel accounts, to attend her.[10] With a collective address to "Woman," she appeals through eleven eight-line stanzas to the mothers of living sons in words that reflect her moving gaze. The poem is composed in a frequent medieval rhyme scheme (a b a b b c b c) with a constant thematic refrain—*my dere son, dere*—that hearkens to the bond of mother and child and the cost of Jesus' sacrifice. The refrain, of course, tends to linger in the memory with its predictable repetition. For most of seven stanzas, Mary directs attention to her disbelief and maternal anguish in response to the savagery of Christ's wounds, his tortured death, and her terrible loss. She paints a series of familiar scenes between mothers and children to mark the contrast between her listeners' continuing joy in their living sons and her profound dismay, and she urges them to witness her newly bereft state. Only in a single line of stanza 7 and in the second half of stanza 8, does she turn her thoughts to the meaning, purpose, and nature of Christ's sacrifice and her role in it. In my reading of the "Lament," Mary is the first witness to the great burden of Christianity, simultaneously embodying and describing it, while the attentive reader, gazing in the mind's eye on the grieving mother holding the tortured body of Christ, follows her gaze and responds to her poignant urgings, beginning with her opening appeal.

Mary opens by beckoning all women who share with her their love for a child to "stay and see" her dead son, "lying before me, upon my knee" (ll. 2–4), and her appeals to those women introduce nine of the stanzas. In the first, she describes the joyful reality of mothers whose "children you dance upon your knee / With laughing, kissing, and merry cheer" (ll. 5–6), imagining a series of homely scenes between them and their sons that evoke wrenching contrasts with her state. Holding her son's body—still warm and supple from life—Mary's distressed disbelief continues to build a discourse of pathos through the opening stanzas, appealing emotionally to the audience by addressing experience and feelings they know. In stanza 2, she recounts a mother's daily attentions to her child, no doubt recalling scenes of arranging her son's hair and cap and gazing upon his bright face (l. 11). She contrasts those images with her present occupation of picking thorns from Jesus' head (l. 15) and fruitlessly ministering to his wounds as she had done to heal minor scrapes when he was small. Mary continues to meditate on Jesus' wounds in images of contrast in stanza 3, envisioning the mother of a living child setting a green "garland" (*chaplet*) on her little one's head as an adornment (l. 17), but the mother's act, performed with "great pleasure" (l.19), and the fresh garland on her son's brow contrast with Mary's sorrowfully extracting the "thorns, sore pricking" (l. 21) from the "crown" forced derisively into Christ's scalp and brow. As any mother might, she kisses her son (l. 22) but is "full of woe" as she sits "weeping" while other mothers still "sing" (ll. 22–23).

In these stanzas, Mary voices explicit references to the Gospel tradition of the crucifixion and refers to the wounds on Christ's body, treating them systematically. In stanza 4, calling on her listener to "look to me again" (l. 25), Mary juxtaposes her interlocutor, a contented mother who kisses a living child, with herself, in anguish as she gazes at the *gret gap* in her son's breast and "innumerable wounds" on his body (ll. 26–29). Unlike the kisses of mothers who hold living sons, her kisses no longer work to diminish the hurt, yet she follows the custom and suggests the lesions remain wet with blood when she remarks that her lips are bloody with kissing his injured flesh (ll. 29–30). She argues that her fate (*me happys*) is a very harsh one indeed (l. 31). In stanza 5, rather than take Jesus by the hand, as other mothers do their sons, she now fears to see his "terribly bleeding" hands (ll. 33–35), and for the first time in the poem, at approximately its mid-point, Mary reminds listeners—and herself—that Christ willingly and purposefully went to his death, permitting his hands "to be bored with nail and spear" for "your sake" (ll. 37–38). She quickly returns, though, to focus on her loss and the existential divide between the joy (*myrth*) of her listeners and her own *gret sorow* (l. 39). In the following stanza (6) she gazes on his wounded feet and presents the gritty reality that she may put "the largest finger of either hand" through the openings bored through her son's feet, and that her fingers, when she withdraws them, are covered in his blood (ll. 45–47).

With that gruesome image calling attention to the enormity of Christ's suffering and to her pain as a mother envisioning it, Mary's argument in stanza 7 opens with a summary call to action, admonishing listeners, "therefore" (l. 49) to "think on my son" (l. 52) and to understand how her heart was "made all cold" seeing her son so abused (ll. 53–56). Mary emphasizes her audience's duty to acknowledge her loss as a mother when she again points to the contrast between the sons of her listeners and her own in stanza 8, summarizing the difference in terse images: "Thou has thy son full whole and sound, / And mine is dead upon my knee: / Thy child is loose and mine is bound, / Thy child is in life and mine dead is he" (ll. 57–60). These contrasts make forceful emotional appeals to the poet's audience, but Mary's discourse soon turns its tone and focus toward the audience's understanding of the spiritual significance of Jesus' sacrifice.

In summarizing the final contrast, "[yours] alive" and "[mine] dead," with terse and simple finality midway through stanza 8, Mary's gaze surely turns to fall again upon Jesus' body, but with the next line, she lifts her gaze toward her audience of women, challenging them with a rhetorical question to justify Christ's death: "Why was this done except for you?" (l. 61). Should they have any doubt as to whether an innocent man has endured an ordeal and died as an intentional sacrifice, Mary stipulates that no wrongdoing could justify his punishment and death: "For my child never did wrong here" (l. 62).[11] With that claim of Christ's righteousness, she demands that her listeners pay their debt: they are "obligated" to weep with her over Christ's death (l. 63), and she justifies the mandate by returning to the original refrain, "For now lies dead my dear son, dear" (l. 64).

In the two stanzas that follow, Mary enlarges her audience to include "both man and wife" (l. 65) and expands her affective argument by asserting that her son is now their son, too, and loves them greatly (l. 66). She then appeals to them to think how a son's death would affect them, imagining that they "would weep at every meal" (l. 68) and chiding them for failing to weep for her son, who, moreover, "has no peer" (l. 70) and "sends *your* sons both hope and healing" (l. 71, emphasis added). She closes by rephrasing the opening to the refrain to underscore her audience's indebtedness: "And *for you died* my dear son, dear" (l. 72, emphasis added). In the penultimate stanza, Mary calls on "all women of good sense" (l. 73), directing their collective gaze to her "child, on my knees dead" to counsel them to "weep not" for their own children, but to mourn his death, and she assures them that by so doing, they will gain an "absolute reward" (ll. 74–76), namely, the soul's redemption. Mary then emphasizes the immeasurable importance of Christ's sacrifice in a conditional scenario: "He would again for *your* love bleed / Rather than see *you* damned" (ll. 77–78, emphasis added) and closes the stanza with a "prayer" to her listeners to "heed" his sacrifice (ll. 79–80).

In the final stanza, Mary's discursive gestures are generous. She vows to speak no further of her son's torment, because doing so may precipitate her death (ll. 81–82); moreover, she gives her listeners permission to "laugh when [they] will" even though she mourns (l.

83). Mary's meditations on her son's wounds in the middle stanzas and the significance of his death in the final stanzas temper her initial, subjective focus on witnessing his agony and facing his death in a worldly sense, but the opening stanzas compel the audience's sympathy and interest, and the shift in her perspective works as a spiritual model. Mary has come to accept the reality of her "weep[ing]" while other mothers "laugh at will" (l. 83), and the bitter contrasts and reproofs of the opening stanzas give way in the final stanzas to love that suggests Mary's position as *mediatrix*: "That you may see if you look to me again / To love my son, if you be willing, / I will love yours with a full heart" (ll. 84–86). In these lines, Mary assumes an overarching maternal role toward the living sons of all other women, assuring her interlocutors, along with the reader, that if they have the will to look to her and to love her son, he will bring them and their children to the place of bliss where he resides: "And he shall bring your children and you, certain, / To heaven. where is my dear son, dear" (ll. 87–88). Mary explicitly avows the soul-saving power of love through Christ and her participation in his divine mission.

The poet's arrangement of Mary's song explores the Virgin's process of "overcoming the world," reflecting her theological insight as it narrows its focus to the purpose of Christ's sacrifice. No longer bound by subjective experience, Mary's understanding of that purpose emerges through a discursive evolution that begins with her deeply felt torment as she focuses on her son's lifeless body and her own existential pain. I noted above that we hear the first note of Mary's movement toward an expansive, universal view in stanza five and a second reflection of her shifting perspective in stanza seven. Expressing these fleeting insights in contexts of heart-wrenching comparisons, Mary moves in stanza 8 toward an absolute justification and call to action. The final three stanzas refer to the everlasting debt that Christ's sacrifice and her loss impose on her audience, requiring that rational, sympathetic witnesses share her feelings and accompany her spiritual growth in understanding and embracing Christ's sacrifice. In the final stanza, with no further will to share her woe, Mary gives her listeners leave to enjoy life as they may while she weeps (ll. 87–89). She then falls silent, and her performance ends, followed by a standard Latin formula: *Explicit fabula*.

Mary's "story" (*fabula*) has repeatedly demanded her internal audience's emotional involvement in witnessing the damage done to Christ's body, wound by wound. Her anguished maternal discourse over the bloodied corpse works rhetorically to fill her audience with pity and awe, deepening their emotional bond with her. Mary's initial expressions of mourning and her sad, envious references to mothers with living sons spring from her immediate meditation on Christ's wounds and her loss, while the shift in stanza 8 that reflects her spiritual and intellectual journey bespeaks Mary's movement toward an encompassing love—the Greek Bible's *agape*—and she validates Jesus' death and unjust punishment as the means by which believers have hope of redemption, affirming her part in his sacrifice as model and *mediatrix*.[12]

## Michelangelo's *Pietà*, St. Peter's Basilica, Rome

Michelangelo's *Pietà* presents a stricken Mary holding Christ's remains across her knees at the foot of the cross, where her gaze is fixed on his body, and her suffering frames the work (Pl. 1). Like the "Lament," the *Pietà* conveys the Virgin's fragility, as well as her underlying strength, and locates the process of transcending the world in the luminescent Virgin and the dead Christ. The grace and beauty of the *Pietà* counter Leonardo da Vinci's assessment of sculpting as "arte meccanicissima" [extremely mechanical] rather than scientific, a view based on the rationale that the true sciences originate in "abstract intellectual speculation" (Clark 136–137). The sculptor's labor with his material, as Leonardo describes it in his *Trattato della Pintura* [*Treatise on Painting*], serves to help us imagine Michelangelo's intimate and earthy connection with the huge block of raw marble he shaped into the Vatican's *Pietà*:

> The [. . .] sculptor when making his work uses the strength of his arm in hammering, to remove the superfluous marble or other stone [. . . . by] an extremely mechanical operation, generally accompanied by great sweat which mingles with dust and becomes converted into mud [. . .]. His face becomes plastered and powdered all over with marble dust, which makes him look like a baker, and he becomes covered in minute chips of marble, which makes him look as if he is covered in snow. His house is in a mess and covered in chips and dust from the stone.[13]

Clark observes that Leonardo's derisive description of the strenuous and filthy work of the sculptor were unmistakably aimed at Michelangelo, Leonardo's rival, who "records [them] with a kind of sardonic pride in [his] letters and sonnets" (136). Michelangelo's intellectual and imaginative grasp of his work is indicated in the care with which he pursued the commission. The *Pietà* began and was finished according to his imagination—his "abstract intellectual speculation"—working from the historical foundations and the mysteries of his faith, as he might represent them in the right block of marble. These matters of the sculptor's intellect and imagination applied to his faith and base material are formative to my viewing of the *Pietà*.

Michelangelo's biographers William E. Wallace and Miles J. Unger signal Michelangelo's personal attention to his marble for the *Pietà*. Wallace emphasizes the sculptor's diligence in procuring the best section of stone from a chosen site and his understanding of its commerce (*Artist* 21–22), and Unger notes that Michelangelo began his search for "a suitable piece of marble" only when he had finally determined "the statue's overall composition and proportions" (58). In November 1497, Michelangelo, on horseback, "set out for the quarries of Carrara to obtain the flawless block" (*Ibid*). Wallace describes that early winter as an unpropitious time for inspecting or cutting marble in Carrara, a place of "staggering peaks and distant heights," where nobody "had ever quarried a block the size Michelangelo desired, but with the promise of money and employment, [villagers] rose to the challenge" (*Artist* 20–21). Even with local cooperation, Wallace writes, Michelangelo "took nearly a month to find the marble," and his December decision was merely "the beginning of a long and dangerous operation of lowering the valuable block down the mountain slope, transporting it by oxcart to the sea, and shipping it to Rome" where it arrived six months later (21–23). Though his approach would have been costly for most sculptors in terms of studio time and compensation, as Wallace asserts, it convincingly reflects Michelangelo's practical and artistic consciousness of the attributes of his medium and his desire for the fullest control over it. These circumstances are comparable to a poet's desire for precision in poetic expression.

Michelangelo's focus on the qualities of his marble figures significantly into recent critical approaches to the *Pietà*. Suggesting a concrete and pragmatic rationale for the distinct nature of the *Pietà*'s marble, art historian Aileen June Wang explains that the sculptor brought a high polish only to those surfaces of the *Pietà* that viewers would see, leaving the rear of the piece roughly finished (453). Nevertheless, rough marble elements remain visible to viewers (Pls. 2, 3). Wallace, too, praises the highly polished areas of the sculpture as "a miracle of marble carving" (*Artist* 23) and, in a 2011 essay on Michelangelo's "craftsmanship," he focuses on the delicacy of the Virgin's extended arm and left hand and fingers (Pl. 4), marveling at Michelangelo's transformation of abrasive stone into "pliant flesh and supple folds of drapery" as displays of his artistry and originality (Pl. 5).[14] The responses of nineteenth-century art theorist Walter Pater and twentieth-century art historian H. W. Janson, however, suggest that Michelangelo's handling of the *Pietà*'s substance reveals the kind of mature spiritual understanding and emotional awareness that we might compare with that found in the "Lament." Pater and Janson trace at least one aspect of this quality to the marble itself.

Pater, in his 1873 study, explored the notion that the finished figures remain partially bound in the rough marble (Pl. 1) and remarked that this "puzzling" and "studied" state of "incompleteness" found in "nearly all" Michelangelo's sculpture, lends his work an unfinished quality by "combin[ing . . .] passion and intensity with the sense of a yielding and flexible life" (53). Noting a similar spirit in Michelangelo's painting, Pater writes that the body of Adam, coming from dust into human form on the Sistine Chapel ceiling, has in it "something rude [. . .], something akin to the rugged hillside on which it lies" (59). Participating in this vein of *Pietà* criticism almost ninety years after Pater's study was published, Janson, in his global history of art published in 1969, notes that Michelangelo himself speaks of "'liberating the figure from the marble that imprisons it'" (10). Biographer Unger, too, stipulates that "for Michelangelo, the true art of sculpture was subtractive, a process of removing excess material and exposing forms latent in the mass" (61); moreover, Unger suggests that the block of marble represents "the earthly body while the form that emerges slowly [from] beneath the chisel represents the soul struggling to free itself from its material prison" (61).

Michelangelo's practical and artistic intimacy with his medium has contributed significantly to the *Pietà*'s reception by its viewers and critics. For Unger, its message is about the power of the spirit over the physical world. Pursuing the idea that for Michelangelo, the "soul" of the marble is freed under the work of the chisel, Unger cites several lines from a poem of Michelangelo's:

> Just as by removing, lady, one forms
> from hard mountain stone
> a living figure,
> which grows more as stone grows less;
> so the little good that I possess
> trembles 'neath the body's fleshy form,
> imprisoned in its hard carapace. (61)[15]

Michelangelo's poetic analogy of forms "imprisoned" shows his participation in a system of thought that "has deep roots in Greek philosophy, as well as in Christian theology," according to Unger (61–62), and suggests Michelangelo's deliberate philosophical path in creating the *Pietà*. What Unger characterizes as Michelangelo's "metaphor of the body as the prison of the soul" (61) validates the *Pietà*'s spiritual dimension, one that speaks physically as well as philosophically to overcoming the world with the spirit. Unger's perspective supports earlier critical views of the *Pietà* that focus on its transformation from rough marble to polished figures shown emerging from the stone. These perspectives invite us to locate in Michelangelo's artistic worldview his love of earthy materials and of working with them, his deep spirituality, and his theoretically grounded process.

Michelangelo's involvement with his raw material suggests that the physical form he gives Mary in the *Pietà*, like his figure of Adam on the ceiling of the Sistine Chapel, speaks to his idea of freeing form and spirit with art, of transcending the material world by transforming matter into a statement about the spirit. Michelangelo's avowed Christian belief accords with the idea of the transcendent power of art, as Clark's critical biography of Leonardo da Vinci argues in the following contrast Clark poses between Leonardo and his rival, Michelangelo:

> In no accepted sense can Leonardo be called a Christian. He was not even a religious-minded man. [. . . .] Michelangelo, on the other hand, was a profoundly religious man, to whom the reform of the Roman Church came to be a matter of passionate concern. His mind was dominated by ideas—good and evil, suffering, purification, unity with God, peace of mind—which [. . .] to Michelangelo were ultimate truths. (137)

Indeed, Clark's assessment of Michelangelo as a deeply religious man who considered substantial theological and philosophical questions comports with the viewing I suggest of the *Pietà*, and Michelangelo's most abiding concerns, as Clark summarizes them, are precisely what one sees in the Vatican *Pietà*.[16]

## Common Threads and Distinctions

In the "Lament," Mary's implied physical position supporting Christ's body on her lap at the foot of the cross and her discourse suggest, respectively, the gaze of the *Pietà*'s Virgin intent on Christ's wounds and her unspoken thoughts. The *Pietà* shares with the medieval "Lament" not only the image of a grieving Mary meditating on her dead son, but also the suggestion of a young mother who once held a living child on her lap. It is remarkable that the poet and the sculptor suggest layered, familiar images of Mary to their medieval and early modern audiences in their scenes at the foot of the Cross and that they do so according to the potential and limitations of their media. Lyric and sculpture present the amazed, grief-stricken mature woman mourning the murdered son, but the pious girl receiving the news of the archangel, the new mother gazing at her newborn in the manger, the young mother at play with her child, guessing nothing of what the future might hold for him: these figures may be discerned there, too, along with the transcendent, eternal Mary, who "overcomes the world" with a spiritual epiphany. Unger notes the layered representations in the *Pietà* when he remarks that "Christ's body retains its perfection even in death, so Mary's face remains unmarked by time" (66). In concert with Unger, I suggest that Michelangelo's *Pietà* responds to his aim at a "higher truth" (69).

Unger further maintains that Michelangelo evokes "Mary's dignity at this most trying moment" to present "the theological message of Jesus' sacrifice, the paradoxical mystery at the heart of Christianity" (69). Unger's statement may describe the *Pietà*'s reception by viewers who contemplate the layered qualities of its figures, wondering that their features and the finish given their flesh appear to be inconsistent with their ages and with the ravages of the event that precedes the scene at the foot of the cross. Finding coherence within that tension, however, speaks to the core of Christian belief, and the response I propose suggests an epiphany—or something akin to that experience—for the viewer. Although Michael Hirst and other critics may insist that Michelangelo's sculpture does not offer a narrative (52), those who find a story in the *Pietà*'s implied layers imaginatively transcend the boundaries of chronology and over-determination of subject. Perhaps this response is even more accessible to the *Pietà*'s viewers than to readers of the lyric, where Mary's narrative is marked by specified grammatical categories. Michelangelo's rendering of Mary cradling Jesus' body evokes a fluid succession of moments for receptive viewers. The Virgin's youthful appearance contests the maturity of the adult son in her lap, suggesting simultaneous evocations of the Annunciation, the Nativity, the present event, and its future promise as recorded in Hebrew and Christian narratives, and the grip of Michelangelo's rough marble on those polished figures implies both the unredeemed nature of man in the Old Testament and, in the figures' emergence from that marble, the promise of redemption that lies ahead for followers of Christ. A meditative viewer of the *Pietà* may perceive there, too, a parallel to the tension that exists between the pressures and griefs of the physical world, on one hand, and man's desire to transcend the world in mind and spirit, reaching for an intimation of Divinity, on the other.

Art historian Wang suggests that the artist's separating the morphemes of his name as *Michael Angelus* on the Virgin's strap (Pl. 6) is done deliberately to suggest a kinship between Divine artistry and Michelangelo's perception of his art.[17] Wang explains that Michelangelo's arrangement of the letters and morphemes of his name "transform[s]" its meaning into "Michael the Angel" to call attention to his baptismal saint, the warrior archangel St. Michael (Pls. 7, 8). Wang theorizes that by emphasizing *Angelus* and placing the strap across the Virgin's breast, the sculptor represents himself "as a vehicle for conveying God's thought" (466), a concept from Marsilio Ficino's 1475 commentary on Plato's *Symposium,* with which Michelangelo is supposed to have been familiar (466–467). For viewers open to Michelangelo's archangelic allusion, his work as a sculptor and a David-like warrior contending with the stone speaks authentically to the *Pietà*'s message.[18] Furthermore, Michelangelo's inscription, with himself as the subject of the incompletely visible imperfect verb *faciebat* [was making] humbly implies the im-perfection of his earthly artistry compared to the perfection God—the absolute poet and creator—achieved.[19]

Michelangelo's awareness of the interaction between the Divine and human creativity also resonates with the contemporary view of Mary as "the embodiment of the union of God and humankind" (Saupe 7), and the intimacy between mother and son in the *Pietà* emblematizes that relationship. In a similar sense, Mary's evolution in "The Virgin's Lament" might be read by the faithful as God's plan of redemption working through Mary's movement from subjective despair toward a mystical, all-encompassing understanding. Both the poem and the sculpture express tensions between connection and disjunction at one level and between media and meaning at the intersections of flesh and spirit at another. These tensions invite the audiences of the poem and the *Pietà* to grapple authentically with their experiences of sorrow, despair, and anguish in contexts of love and sacrifice, answering the sculptor's and the poet's implied grappling with physical limitations and materials to express spiritual and artistic visions.

**1** *Michelangelo's Vatican* Pietà *(December 2013, St. Peter's Basilica). Note rougher surfaces of the marble. This image and details shown in the other color plates here are used courtesy of Jebulon (Xavier Espinasse). Wikimedia Commons, CC0, public domain.*

2 *Detail of the Virgin's face and upper body. Courtesy, Jebulon (Xavier Espinasse).*

3 *Detail of rough and polished marble elements. Courtesy, Jebulon (Xavier Espinasse).*

4 *Detail of the Virgin's extended left arm and her fingers. Courtesy, Jebulon (Xavier Espinasse).*

5 *Detail of "pliant flesh" and "subtle folds." Courtesy, Jebulon (Xavier Espinasse).*

OVERCOMING THE WORLD | 243

**6** *Detail of the Virgin's strap. Courtesy of Jebulon (Xavier Espinasse).*

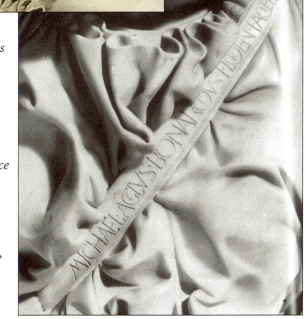

**7** *Detail of the Virgin's strap. Images for plates 7 and 8 are provided and permissions granted for their use by Professor Marilyn A. Lavin. Both appeared in Irving Lavin's "Divine Grace and the Remedy of the Imperfect. Michelangelo's Signature on the St Peter's Pietà" (Artibus et Historiae, 2013). We further acknowledge the support of Joanna Wolańska for IRSA.*

MICHAEL·AG̃LVS·BONAR⊕VS·FL®ENT·FACĩEBA
MICHAEL·ANGELUS·BONAROTUS·FLORENTINUS·FACIEBA(T)

**8** *Irving Lavin's transcription of Michelangelo's wording on the Virgin's strap, image courtesy of Professor Marilyn A. Lavin.*

Notes

1 Wording and dates for Michelangelo's creating the *Pietà* come from Irving Lavin's 2013 article (277). I designate my subject in this chapter as "the Vatican *Pietà*" because Michelangelo sculpted two later examples of the subject: his Rondanini *Pietà* (Castello Sforzesco), known as his final work, in which Mary stands behind and supports the form of Jesus, and his "collaborative" four-figure Florentine *Pietà* (Museo dell' Opera del Duomo, Florence), about which, see Wallace's 2000 article. A fourth *Pietà*, the Palestrina *Pietà* (Galleria dell'Accademia, Florence) is a three-figure group, "long-doubted" as Michelangelo's work and "convincingly removed from the Michelangelo canon" by John Pope-Hennessy in 1968 (Schulz 367 n. 5); nevertheless, it is yet "sometimes attributed" to Michelangelo, as Wallace observes (*Ibid*. 95 n. 13). The Vatican *Pietà* is also called the St. Peter's or Rome *Pietà*.

2 See John 16:33. In the Greek Bible, the words signaled in the main text here are νενίκηκα, transliterated *nenikēka* [I have conquered / prevailed over / subdued / overcome (the world)] and θλιψιν, transliterated *thlipsin* [pressure / affliction / tribulation] (Englishman's, Strong's). The Vulgate translates: *haec locutus sum vobis ut in me pacem habeatis in mundo pressuram habetis sed confidite ego vici mundum*, with *pressuram* [a pressing, pressure] and *vici* [I conquered, overcame] translating, respectively, the key words.

3 In this context, see the Pearl Poet's *Pearl* (discussed here by William T. Cotton), where Pearl is the embodiment of the pearl of great price. Pearl instructs her father in the meanings of several of these parables.

4 See Karen Saupe's Introduction to *Middle English Marian Lyrics* for a historical perspective of Marian devotion through the Middle Ages and also R. T. Davies's comments on Marian lyrics in his Introduction to his *Medieval English Lyrics* (esp. 38–40).

5 For biblical citations of these characterizations and those that immediately follow, see Luke 1:26–42 and 2:19, 51; John 19:25; and Acts 1:14, which speaks of women in the early Church.

6 Davies entitles his version of the "Lament," "Mary Complains to Other Mothers" (210–211). See also Sandro Sticca's study of the genre as medieval drama examined in literary, historical, and theological contexts.

7 *Stabat* is the imperfect form of *stare*, a verb that may convey the idea of standing or being firm toward adversity or holding ground against odds in battle; the imperfect has durative aspect, denoting a continuous state or action in the past: she was standing, continued, or remained (there). In 1900, John Thein supposed that the hymn's composer was probably Jacopone da Todi, a thirteenth-century Franciscan friar (645), and a few years later, Daniel Joseph Donahoe credited Jacopone as the composer of "many spiritual songs and hymns," assigning him the "Stabat Mater Dolorosa" (195–199), which James J. Wilhelm characterizes in 1990 as "the most famous Marian hymn" (23).

8 See essays edited by Dale M. Coulter and Amos Yong in *The Spirit, the Affections, and the Christian Tradition* (2016). Simo Knuuttila (2018) provides a critical summary with primary and secondary bibliographies in "Medieval Theories of the Emotions" (*SEP*).
9 The Department of Medieval Art and the Cloisters at the Metropolitan Museum ("The Cult of the Virgin Mary in the Middle Ages") explains this frequent phrase as follows: "Theologians established a parallel between Christ's Passion and the Virgin's compassion: while he suffered physically on the cross, she was crucified in spirit."
10 The "Lament" is cited parenthetically by line number(s). Modern English translations from it, set within quotations, are the editor's. Middle English is given in italics.

The text, based on Saupe's No. 42 (94–96), is given here on pp. 294–297. See also Saupe's edition for bibliographical notes, glosses, and variants (224–225) and her historical study of Marian lyrics in England (Introduction). Davies's earlier edition gives selected variants and omits the last four stanzas given by Saupe.

John places Mary at the cross, recording Christ's words, spoken from the cross to his mother and John (19:16). The four gospels mention the presence of women around Jesus before, at, or following the crucifixion: see Matthew 27:55–56 and (at the tomb) 27:61; Mark 15:40–41; Luke 23:27–28 and 55; and John 19, especially 25–27. Jesus addresses his women followers essentially as "mothers" in Luke 23:27–28 as he carries his cross: "Daughters of Jerusalem, do not weep for me, but for yourselves and your children." The Gospels offer no direct biblical testimony of Mary's emotional response at the crucifixion, as Davies observed (40).
11 Luke's and John's accounts suggest the clearest justifications for Mary's claim ("my son never trespassed here"). See Luke 23: 4–22, 40–41, and 47; John 19: 6–22; and Matthew 27:24.
12 Strong's gives ἀγάπη [agape] as "love, benevolence, goodwill." John, for example, sets *agape* into Christ's spoken injunctions on several occasions (5:42; 13:35; 15:9–10; 15:13; 17:22–25) to describe Christ's followers' love for one another, Christ's love for them, and the love of God. See Sarah Rolfe Prodan's comments on her viewing of the *Pietà*'s exemplification of *caritas* and "reciprocal agapic love," which the Virgin both receives and returns (151).

While "the flesh" has long evoked ideas of weakness, vulnerability, and uncleanness in contrast to the value and purity of the spirit, and while believers of some faith traditions hope to pass beyond what they view as its base state into spiritual purity, "flesh" in the Judeo-Christian tradition likewise recalls the Hebrew story of God's transforming the dust of the world into mankind, his highest creation. For Christians, Christ is the word made flesh, and Christians participate in the Mass with "the blood and the body" of Christ.

13 The quotation comes from Leonardo's *Trattato della Pintura* (Codex Urbinas Latinus 1270). Wallace adopts the translation (*The Artist* 144) from Martin Kemp's *Leonardo on Painting* (38–39). Clark provides it in *Leonardo* (136).
14 See Wallace's essay (85–87).
15 "Sì come per levar, donna" appears in full, along with an English translation, in James M. Saslow's edited volume *The Poetry of Michelangelo* (152):

> Sì come per levar, donna, si pone / in pietra alpestra e dura / una viva figura, / che là più cresce u' più la pietra scema; / tal alcun'opre buone, / per l'alma che pur trema, / cela il superchio della propria carne / co' l'inculta sua cruda e dura scorza. / Tu pur dalle mie streme / parti puo' sol levarne, / ch'in me non è di me voler né forza.

16 Michelangelo's letters, edited by Irving and Jean Stone, often express Michelangelo's faith in God and in Christ's purpose on earth.
17 Wang writes that Michelangelo "signed" letters with the Tuscan "Michelagniolo," but letters archived with that spelling appear to be those from Michelangelo's correspondents rather than those he signed. Deborah Parker cites Giovan Francesco Fattucci's salutation, "Michelagniolo charissimo," and Giorgio Vasari's "Moltomagnifico messer Michelagniolo signior mio" and "Michelagniolo charissimo" (96).
18 Michelangelo's marginal comparison, "David with his sling and
I with my bow [*arco*]," has been quoted in many contexts. Charles Seymour (7 *ff.*), whose chain of ideas on this subject Saul Levine explores in the contemporary context (97–98), suggested that Michelangelo's *arco* refers to his hand drill, operated by a "bow." Leonard Barkan, citing Seymour and Marcel Brion's 1939 work, notes that the tool was "more normally *archetto*" (115).
19 Irving Lavin's view of the strap's detail and his diplomatic transcription of Michelangelo's inscription accompany this article through the courtesy of Professor Marilyn A. Lavin. In addition to Wang's 2004 article on the Virgin's strap, see earlier work by David Cast (esp. 676–677, nn. 8–9) and Lisa Pon (esp. 18–19) and more recent perspectives from Lavin† (esp. 279–282) and Nicole Hegener.

**Works Cited**

Anonymous. "112: Mary at the Foot of the Cross: 42." Ed. Karen Saupe. Kalamazoo, MI: Western Michigan U and Medieval Institute Publications, 1998. 94–96.

—. "Mary complains to other mothers." *Medieval English Lyrics: A Critical Anthology*. Ed. R. T. Davies. Chicago, IL: Northwestern UP, 1964, 1991. 210–211.

Ashe, Geoffrey. *The Virgin*. London: Routledge and Kegan Paul, 1976.

Barkan, Leonard. *Michelangelo: A Life on Paper*. Princeton, NJ: Princeton UP, 2011.

Brion, Marcel. *Michel-ange*. Paris: Albin Michel, 1939.
—. *Michelangelo*. Trans. James Whitall. New York: Greystone, 1940.
Buonarroti, Michelangelo. *I, Michelangelo, Sculptor: An Autobiography Through Letters*. Eds. Irving and Jean Stone. New York: Doubleday, 1962.
—. *The Poetry of Michelangelo: An Annotated Translation*. Ed. James M. Saslow. New Haven, CT: Yale UP, 1991.
Cast, David. "Finishing the Sistine." *The Art Bulletin* 73.4 (1991): 669–684.
Clark, Kenneth. *Leonardo da Vinci*. Intro. Martin Kemp. London: Penguin, 1988. This edition substantially maintains the revised edition text (1967) and integrates notes from the 1939 edition (subtitled *An Account of His Development as an Artist*) earlier excluded from the "pocket version" (35).
Coulter, Dale M., and Amos Yong. *The Spirit, the Affections, and the Christian Tradition*. Princeton, NJ: Princeton UP, 2016.
Davies, R. T. Introduction. *Medieval English Lyrics: A Critical Anthology*. 13–49. *See also* Anonymous, "Mary complains."
Department of Medieval Art and the Cloisters. "The Cult of the Virgin Mary in the Middle Ages." *Heilbrunn Timeline of Art History: Essays*. New York: The Metropolitan Museum of Art, metmuseum.org, October 2001.
Donahoe, Daniel Joseph. *Early Christian Hymns: Translations of the Verses of the Most Notable Latin Writers of the Early and Middle Ages*. New York: Grafton, 1908.
Hegener, Nicole. "*Faciebat, non finito* und andere Imperfekte Künstlersignaturen neben Michelangelo." Ed. N. Hegener and F. Horsthemke. *Künstlersignaturen von der Antike bis zur Gegenwart* [Artists' signatures from antiquity to the present]. Petersberg, DE: Michael Imhof, 2013. 14–43.
Hirst, Michael. "The Artist in Rome 1496–1501." Ed. Michael Hirst and Jill Dunkerton. *The Young Michelangelo*. London: National Gallery Publications, 1994. 13–82.
Janson, H. W. *History of Art*. Englewood Cliffs, NJ: Prentice-Hall, 1969.
Knuuttila, Simo. "Medieval Theories of the Emotions." *SEP*, 2018.
Lavin, Irving. "Divine Grace and the Remedy of the Imperfect. Michelangelo's Signature on the St Peter's *Pieta*." *Artibus et Historiae*: Papers dedicated to Peter Humfrey, Pt. II. 34.68 (2013): 277–328.
Levine, Saul. "Michelangelo's Marble *David* and the Lost Bronze *David*: The Drawings." *Artibus et Historiae* 5.9 (1984): 91–120.
Michelangelo. *See* Buonarroti, Michelangelo.
Parker, Deborah. "The Role of Letters in Biographies of Michelangelo." *Renaissance Quarterly* 58.1 (2005): 91–126.
Pater, Walter. *The Renaissance: Studies in Art and Poetry*. Berkeley, CA: U of California P, 1980.
The Pearl Poet. *Pearl: A New Translation*. Trans. Marie Borroff. New York: Norton, 1977.
Pon, Lisa. "Michelangelo's First Signature." *Notes in the History of Art* 15.4 (1996): 16–21.

Prodan, Sarah Rolfe. *Michelangelo's Christian Mysticism: Spirituality, Poetry, and Art in Sixteenth-Century Italy.* New York: Cambridge UP, 2014.
Saslow, James M. *See* Buonarroti. *The Poetry.*
Saupe, Karen. Introduction. *Middle English Marian Lyrics.* 1–41. *See also* Anonymous. "Mary at the Foot of the Cross: 42."
Schulz, Juergen. "Michelangelo's Unfinished Works." *The Art Bulletin* 57.3 (1975): 366–373.
Seymour, Charles, Jr. *Michelangelo's David: A Search for Identity.* Pittsburgh, PA: U of Pittsburgh P, 1967.
Sticca, Sandro. *The* Planctus Mariae *in the Dramatic Tradition of the Middle Ages.* Trans. Joseph R. Berrigan. Athens, GA: U of Georgia P, 1988.
Stone, Irving, and Jean Stone. *See* Buonarroti. *I, Michelangelo.*
Thein, John. *Ecclesiastical Dictionary: Containing, in Concise Form, Information Upon Ecclesiastical, Archaeological, and Historical Subjects.* New York: Benziger, 1900.
Unger, Miles J. *Michelangelo: A Life in Six Masterpieces.* New York: Simon and Schuster, 2014.
Wallace, William E. "*La bella mano*: Michelangelo the Craftsman." *Artibus et Historiae* 32.63 (2011): 85–99.
—. *Michelangelo: The Artist, the Man, and His Times.* New York: Cambridge UP, 2010.
—. "Michelangelo, Tiberio Calcagni, and the Florentine *Pietà*." *Artibus et Historiae* 21.42 (2000): 81–99.
Wang, Aileen June. "Michelangelo's Signature." *Sixteenth Century Journal* 35.2 (2004): 447–474.
Wilhelm, James J., ed. "Anonymous Franciscan Hymn to Mary: 'Stabat mater dolorosa.'" *Lyrics of the Middle Ages.* Garland Reference Library of the Humanities 1268. New York: Garland, 1990. 23–34.

# ❦10❧
# Religious or Irreligious
## The Reader's Response to *Pearl*, Shakespeare's *The Winter's Tale*, and Flannery O'Connor's "Revelation"

### William T. Cotton

The category of the "irreligious" reader is—perhaps—mildly confrontational, so a clarification may be useful. By "irreligious" I mean not merely the declared atheist or agnostic, but a person lacking any defined spiritual instinct. Nonetheless one who adheres to no religious system may feel very strongly the beauty of various forms of religious art and be deeply moved by passages from the Bible and other holy texts, as one may be equally affected by devotional literary works created by and for believers, though one is not a part of that group. The experience involved is neither ersatz nor some surrogate for what the faithful enjoy, but somehow an emotional, perhaps a spiritual response in a different register. In this chapter, having chosen readings from three accessible, diverse, and well-known literary touchstones, I explore whether such a reader response is likely and suggest why.

The alliterative dream vision *Pearl*, dated 1375–1400, the final scene of William Shakespeare's 1610 romance *The Winter's Tale*, and Flannery O'Connor's "Revelation," first published in 1964, are a diverse group of literary texts in essential ways, but they have in common their eliciting a strong emotional response from the reader or audience, and each may be read as having deeply affecting religious and spiritual significance.[1] While one might readily expect such a reading of the Middle English *Pearl*, an overtly confessional dramatic poem composed for a devout fourteenth-century audience, less readily the other two, which are not usually said to nurture religious feeling.[2] Distributed over five-hundred years of English-language literature, the three possess diverse religious roots: *Pearl* emerges from the Western Roman Catholic tradition, *The Winter's Tale* from Shakespeare's English Protestant milieu, and "Revelation" from the post-war American South and a profoundly Catholic woman writer.[3] As literary texts, they represent distinct genres: *Pearl* is an elegy in the form of a medieval dream vision, *The Winter's Tale* is a stage play categorized as a comedy in the mode of romance, and "Revelation" is a short story in a postmodern realistic vein.[4] These well-differentiated texts offer distinct generic, cultural, and historical contexts for examining the nature of a reader's spiritual or religious response to literature.

## Consolation in *Pearl*

Many of its readers will view *Pearl* as a lesser-known attachment to the more widely read *Sir Gawain and the Green Knight*, whose manuscript is bound in the same codex with *Pearl*, *Cleanness*, and *Patience*, but *Pearl*'s human drama may be as compelling for the reader as the strange chivalry of *Sir Gawain*. Where the reader of *Sir Gawain* may initially be amused or intrigued, the reader's first and overriding response to *Pearl* is likely to be pity and sympathy for the grieving father, who dreams of being led through a heavenly garden by his little deceased daughter. His emotional state is poignant, compellingly persuasive of the reader's sympathy. This intimate connection between the speaker and the object of his loss and the consolation he finds in his vision make the poem an elegy and give it profound claims on the reader's involvement with the text. It is also a dream vision whose beatific guide is that recently deceased two-year-old child, a much-beloved, unlettered innocent probably known only to her family, circumstances that give her an intimate reason to guide the dreamer. The most affective feature of the poem is its presentation of the melancholy of mourning. The poem's pathos and any legitimate claim to involve the reader emotionally in the speaker's intense grief arise from the gradual and subtle revelation of who "Pearl" is and how the speaker's grief is therefore worthy of sympathy. Even in a scholarly reading that views the poem as a dream vision validated by Christian doctrine and an enactment of Christian consolation, Pearl's identity as the spirit of the speaker's dead child takes on the greatest weight and significance.[5] The speaker's little guide, then, we may coherently name "Pearl," and the speaker, who is a father, a dreamer, and a seeker of Christian truth and consolation, styles himself the "joyless jeweler," an ironic reference to the loss of his little "Pearl." I will refer to him as her father and as the "Jeweler."[6]

The poem opens with the word "Pearl," and in the second stanza, the Jeweler describes his "grief" as so deeply intense that his "breast would swell and burn" (l. 17), the kind of sorrow we would attach to the death of a cherished loved one.[7] In stanza 13, the Jeweler frankly states that what he has lost is beyond the value of a rare "gem": "Then a finer thing I found at hand / That stirred my spirit more and more" (ll. 155–156). He suggests here his growing realization, and "more and more" becomes a refrain, increasing the poem's emotional intensity thematically through five stanzas. In stanza 14, the Jeweler is suddenly enthralled by what he sees and exclaims that his "mind ran wild!" as he gazed "beyond the water" upon a fiery "crystal cliff" (ll. 158–159) at whose foot he sees "a child, / A maiden" in a "little robe all gleaming white" (ll. 161–163). He remembers her, saying, "And I knew her—knew I had seen her before" (l. 164), for she is "that beautiful child" and the "fairest of fair" (ll. 166–167), the one to whom he alludes with superlatives in the first stanza. He confirms in the concatenated refrain that the "longer" he looks, he knows "her more and more" (l. 168). In the following stanza (s. 15), the reader is swept "more and more" along in the Jeweler's unfolding emotions:

> Still more I searched her sweet, fine face
> And her figure when I found her there;
> Such gladness hammered and hit in my chest
> As seldom stirred my heart before.
> I longed to call out to the child at once,
> But my heart was hurt with the pain of wonder;
> I saw her here in so strange a place,
> No wonder if wonder numbed my heart!
> And then she lifted her face as fair
> And white as ivory, and more pure;
> It made heart sing, struck all astray,
> And ever the longer, more and more. (15.169–180)

The poet's alliterative phrasing in these lines follows the Jeweler's gaze as he searches the opposite shore: his heart stirs, he longs to call out and feels pained, then numbed with amazement, and finally, his "heart sing[s]" when Pearl lifts her face to confirm his hopes. The Jeweler's wonder, joy, longing, sorrow, and delight are responses with which the reader will be likely to empathize through imagination or experience as the poet's refrain of "ever the longer, more and more" intensifies the Jeweler's—and the reader's—emotional progress. The dark sixteenth stanza continues to play upon the reader's feelings by reversing the Jeweler's emotions from joy to fear with the repetition of "more" and the ominous alliterations of /d-/ (*dread, dead, dared, drawn, dark*) and /h-/ (*hawk, hall*), and a mirror of the Jeweler's apprehensive face:

> More than I liked my dread arose;
> I stood dead still and dared not call—
> My eyes wide open, mouth drawn close—
> I stood as still as the hawk in the hall; (16.181–184)

The poet contrasts this heavily shaded anxiety with an abrupt turn: the "gentle child" rises from her seat, eliciting a dazzling series of images in stanzas 17–19, where the poet's words emphasize the Jeweler's perception of light (*fair, brilliant, gleaming, white, brightest, dazzling, blazing, light*), purity (*pure, purest, innocence, clean, clear*) and the intrinsic worth (*royal price*) of the pearls adorning Pearl's gown (ll. 193–228).

Like the Jeweler's experience of the Earthly Paradise and the Heavenly Paradise in this poem, our dreams, too, may come with preternatural clarity or else, more commonly, as indistinct and troubled visions. We might imagine the Jeweler's perception of the form and, particularly, the face of his departed child as temporarily pixilated while he comes to terms with the remarkable event he witnesses, so that only gradually is he able to recognize and accept her for who she is. The course of the narrative, then, is a process of testing and growth for the Jeweler, another kind of human experience with which the reader can probably identify. Under Pearl's tutelage, the Jeweler learns to embrace the truth of her message. A way of reading this process calls upon Stoicism, a philosophical school with considerable appeal at the period at which *Pearl* was composed. Stoicism contextualizes this process and validates the Jeweler's experience in the essential principle of *exercitatio*, understood as discipline and training, which affirms that one becomes one's truest, fullest self only gradually, by trial-and-error and suffering. The Jeweler undergoes that process in *Pearl*, and it results, for the Jeweler and perhaps for the reader, too, in a literary *consolatio*, a philosophical discourse where someone who has suffered misfortune receives wise counsel for comfort and encouragement.[8] *Pearl*'s *consolatio* consists of Pearl's rhetorically re-aligning her father's value system away from the earth's materiality to prepare him for a life of patience before the will of God. *Pearl*'s alliterative verse and scripturally grounded rhetorical arguments place the reader in sympathy with the Jeweler's changing emotions and enlarged perspectives in the *consolatio*. Its textual elements ask for the reader's intellectual engagement, deepening the power of the poem's emotional argument in this section.

Those who are biblically literate and many who are less so will find material that resonates in one way or another, as I show in the examples that follow.

To reconcile the Jeweler's objections to the apparently unequal heavenly rewards accorded to believers, Pearl presents a series of arguments having scriptural and doctrinal bases. She attempts to show her resistant father how the inhabitants of Heaven, the "members" of Christ, may enjoy different degrees of beatitude without the more lowly placed envying those set above them, whom the lowly consider no more worthy—or even less worthy—than themselves. Beginning in stanza 39, Pearl applies a colorful analogy known as "the members and the body" (ll. 457–468).[9] According to this parable, it would be ridiculous to imagine the foot envious of the belly as the recipient of all the food, or the hand begrudging the head its position as seat of the intelligence because all are members of one living body, incorporate, as the blessèd in Heaven are "members" of Christ. Pearl then turns in stanzas 42–49 (ll. 493–588) to Christ's vineyard parable and repeats what he has said there about how the workers will be blessed equally, no matter how long they have toiled.

Pearl's extended application of Christ's parable of the laborers in the vineyard (Matt. 20:1–16) answers the Jeweler's charge (s. 41) that she has been unjustly received into a very high position in Heaven, despite, he says, her never having learned her Pater Noster or her Creed, nor how to please God, while those who led long, arduous lives of probity and service would receive the same reward. Like the Jeweler, the reader is perhaps wondering at how all those people receive the same "penny" in heaven for their labors on earth. For contemporary readers, Pearl's retelling of Christ's parable (ss. 42–49) should work as a crushing rejoinder to the Jeweler's complaint of unjust rewards: Pearl explains that a lord has enlisted a crew of laborers to harvest his grapes, and as the day wears on, he engages more workers at the same pay. When the workers are paid, those who worked the entire day complain that the lord is unjust in paying the half-day workers with the same coin he has paid them. The lord responds that all received what they had bargained for.[10] Yet the Jeweler remains unconvinced, telling Pearl he sees no "reason" in her explanation. The reader, too, may remain unconvinced in the face of the father's earthly logic and, like him, be unwilling to accept Pearl's scriptural rationale.

Pearl pursues her argument in stanza 48 by quoting Christ, "The last shall be first and the first shall be last, for many are called but few are chosen" (ll. 569–572; Matt. 20:1–66), but the Jeweler is so disgruntled that even the Savior as an authority fails to convince him. He cavils at her quoting scripture (s. 50), and his quibble elicits Pearl's "gentle" response in the final line of stanza 51, her strongest rebuke: "For the grace of God is great enough." This aphorism is the poem's most memorable message, repeated through stanzas 51–55. Pearl next tries to teach her obdurate father that, as in her case, "But he who never once walked wrong, / The innocent, is saved by right" (56.671–672), and she extends the principle into stanza 61, where she enunciates Christ's parable of the pearl of great price (Matt. 21:45–46). According to this parable, a merchant was counseled to sell his goods, no matter how valuable, in order to purchase one perfect pearl, the parable's symbol of heavenly reward. Pearl closes the parable in stanza 62, addressing her father directly, "I beg you, sell off all earth's madness; / Buy that flawless pearl of price" (ll. 743–744). The parable takes on the greatest poignancy in the reader's consciousness as Pearl, compassionate toward her father's desperation, yet grieved by his obduracy, pleads with him from the other side of Jordan to dedicate his life to Christ's principles. Because of her position of knowledge and the perfect pearl she wears on her dress as the emblem of her heavenly reward, Pearl is, for her father, the embodied vision of that reward.[11]

Like the Jeweler's fourteenth-century readers, biblically versed twenty-first-century readers hear familiar texts and doctrine in Pearl's arguments.[12] For any reader, though, the Jeweler's resistance to consolation for the loss of his child, along with his great need to find peace, is likely to have an emotional appeal. Pearl's repeated, gentle insistence on "grace enough" and the vision the Jeweler is allowed of heaven displace the poem, at least in this reading, from being primarily a doctrinal exposition or even a catechetical work because of the human drama it enacts between the sorrowing, earth-bound man and the blissful, heavenly child. Today's reader—believer or not—finds in *Pearl* not merely the promulgation of a fourteenth-century doctrine of the blessedness of innocents, but also its embodiment in the figure of Pearl; she is a revelation of what Christians were (and are) called to believe about life, death, God, and heaven. Her father, from this perspective, is a sorrowing man given God's grace by her presence and discourse. Whether or not the reader adopts this doctrine, *Pearl* may yet gain emotional appeal within that context, and the stronger that appeal, the greater will be the poem's elegiacally cathartic effect, its ability to offer consolation in grief. What greater consolation than to see and know that the little child who has died is in a better place than the one we presently inhabit? Resonant chords in the father's expressions of his changing emotions will help readers hear Pearl's consolation as both touching and challenging.

## *The Winter's Tale*

Like *Pearl*, *The Winter's Tale* treats the loss of loved ones and the desire to be reunited with them; yet, further, *The Winter's Tale* gives its audience the impression of having been present at an earthly resurrection—a raising of the dead in body and spirit. Regardless of its climactic "miracle," the play stages an apparently non-religious drama whose action unfolds in a Classical never-time where inhabitants frequently invoke gods—but not the Christian God because on the Elizabethan-Jacobean stage, God could not be named, nor could overtly Christian subject matter be staged.[13] Shakespeare divides the play's imaginative geography between "Sicilia" and "Bohemia," whose famous "bear-ridden seacoast" is essential to the plot.

King Leontes' jealousy through the first three acts is an unmotivated malignity that in short order becomes pathological. In act one, Leontes is convinced that his old friend Polixenes, King of Bohemia, who has been visiting Leontes' court, is having an affair with Leontes' queen, Hermione, and that their young son, Mamillius, and their unborn child were both fathered by Polixenes. Leontes attempts to poison Polixenes by suborning the worthy counselor Camillo, but Camillo, conscience stricken, instead flees Sicily with Polixenes, leaving Queen Hermione and Mamillius unprotected, and the audience, now alert to the dangerous king's extremes, sympathizes all the more with his potential victims. In the second act, Hermione is arrested on charges of adultery and treason, and the little prince falls ill in response to Leontes' dishonorable treatment of Hermione. The queen gives birth in prison to a daughter, Perdita, whom Leontes declares a bastard. Hermione's friend Paulina tries unsuccessfully to reason with Leontes, but he orders his chief minister, Antigonus, Paulina's husband, to take the newborn and expose it to the elements and animals in a desolate place. Leontes, despite his desperate order, dispatches men to obtain a reading from Apollo's oracle at Delphos to confirm his suppositions about Hermione and Polixenes and the two children (2.1.180–187). In act three, Leontes compels Hermione, now weakened by childbirth and other woes and supported physically by Paulina and her ladies, to stand trial.

Hermione's debilitated appearance, bereft state, and desperate speech at her trial in the second scene of act three are staged to be particularly affecting to the audience. When the sealed report from the oracle at Delphos is read in Hermione's presence (3.2.132–136), it vindicates all except Leontes, warning him of losing everything if he persists.[14] The audience's relief is short lived when Leontes recklessly declares the oracle "mere falsehood" (3.2.140–141) and continues with the trial, only to learn immediately that Mamillius has died (3.2.144–146). Leontes, in private prayer, repents, but Hermione faints at the news of her son's death, and Leontes orders her carried out. Paulina returns to court to denounce Leontes with a colorful litany of his errors (3.2.175–202) before she delivers her final blow: Queen Hermione has died (3.2.200–202).[15] In the further upheavals of the third and final scene of act three, the audience shares in the continuing rise of tension as the party charged with leaving newborn Perdita to die of exposure arrives on the seashore of Bohemia, where the faithful Antigonus is dismembered and partially eaten by a bear. The ship bearing the others then sinks with all hands, and local shepherds arrive to save Perdita and bury Antigonus' remains. This series of deadly events marks a low point in the world of the play: the queen and her two offspring are now presumed dead. Shakespeare has the chorus, Time, move his "patien[t]" audience sixteen years into the future and to the hinterlands of Bohemia (4.1.5–15) for the pastoral interlude of the fourth act, shifting tonality from winter to spring, with singing, dancing, love, and delightful flower passages that are soon darkened with the problem of star-crossed lovers. In scene two, Camillo and King Polixenes exit the court in disguise, bound for the countryside, to prevent the union of Polixenes' son, Prince Florizell, and the beautiful shepherdess Perdita. Polixenes now behaves as harshly as Leontes had done before his repentance, and when Florizell and Perdita, pursued by Polixenes, escape Bohemia to the supposed sanctuary of Sicilia, this further shift in setting prepares for the play's resolution, namely, the rehabilitation of Leontes and the reunion of his surviving family under the sponsorship of Paulina, who has subjected Leontes to a course of contrition over the years, even exacting from him a promise that he will marry again only at her bidding.

The stage is now set for the *coup de théâtre* of Paulina's play within the play (5.3).[16] What, then, in this concluding scene will constitute for the audience the sense of participating in a resurrection? The following series of excerpts from the so-called "statue scene," comprising all of scene three (5.3.1–155), shows how that sense of participation arises. Leontes views—with great wonder—a remarkably lifelike statue of Hermione, his deceased queen. Paulina cautions him:

> Either forbear,
> Quit presently the chapel, or resolve you
> For more amazement. If you can behold it,
> I'll make the statue move indeed, descend
> And take you by the hand; but then you'll think—
> Which I protest against—I am assisted
> By wicked powers. (5.3.85–91)

In these lines, Paulina demands that Leontes promise to witness the statue come to life, and she stipulates that she is not assisted by "wicked powers" when she revives Hermione before our eyes, giving assurance that no demonstration of the black arts threatens the audience.[17] Leontes further builds the audience's anticipation when he dismisses Paulina's "I know what you'll think" and asks for more than she has promised:

> What you can make her do,
> I am content to look on; what to speak,
> I am content to hear; for 'tis as easy
> To make her speak as move. (5.3.91–94)

Their exchange elevates the dramatic tension line by line as Leontes vows to remain in place as a witness and urges Paulina to cause the statue to "speak" as well as "move." Paulina prolongs the suspense, requiring additional elements of cooperation from Leontes:

> It is required
> You do awake your faith. Then all stand still.
> [Or] those that think it is unlawful business
> I am about, let them depart. (5.3.94–97)

Leontes immediately reassures Paulina of her audience with a royal command that binds all present: "Proceed, / No foot shall stir" (5.3.98). We, the audience, should we suspect the truth, must also suspend disbelief in order to participate fully in the drama from Leontes' and Perdita's unknowing perspectives. Paulina directs Leontes through the scene, and her next speech—"Music! awake her! Strike!" (5.3.98)—is followed by stirring musical effects that not only "awake[n]" the statue of Hermione, but must also stir some members of the audience as the music heightens their emotional involvement in Hermione's unfolding resurrection, an uncanny theatrical event.[18] Having commanded Hermione to awaken, Paulina coaches her star through the scene for which Hermione has been preparing for sixteen years. Paulina, of course, knows the reason for Hermione's reluctance to begin her charade, but she implies that Hermione's hesitancy owes to the coldness of death:

> [. . .] 'Tis time; descend; be stone no more; approach;
> Strike all that look upon with marvel. Come;
> I'll fill your grave up. Stir; nay, come away;
> Bequeath to death your numbness; for from him
> Dear life redeems you. You perceive she stirs. (5.3.99–103)

When Paulina assures Hermione, "I'll fill your grave up," the two of them understand that Paulina refers to the power of her play-within-the-play to close Hermione's death-in-life exile by restoring her to her throne and family. Paulina's commanding direction and Hermione's obedience confirm Paulina's control of the scene, and Paulina affirms to the awe-struck witnesses on stage and in the audience that they have—indeed—seen Hermione "stir." The stage direction stipulates, "*Hermione comes down*," signaling a movement that thrills through the theater.

The following exchange between Paulina, who knows all, and Leontes, who responds as one seeing the dead come to life, transfixes the audience, who occupy both positions at once. Paulina admonishes the startled Leontes, "Start not" and assures him that what he is witnessing "shall be holy as / You shall hear my spell is lawful" (5.3.104–105). She then teases Leontes, now struck motionless and dumb by what he sees, and reminds him, "When she was young, you woo'd her; now, in age, / Is she become the suitor?" (5.3.108–109). Leontes touches Hermione's extended hand in response, and marvels, "O, she's warm," and then appeals to heaven, "If this be magic, let it be an art / Lawful as eating" (5.3.109–111).

As the audience views this most affecting scene, a brief interjection by two onlookers, King Polixenes and Camillo, perhaps speaks for the audience as for the dazed witnesses on stage when Polixenes marvels, "She embraces him," and Camillo quickly makes the scene more explicit: "She hangs about his neck" (5.3.111–112). Camillo and Polixenes act as mediating forces between the audience and the scene, directing two requests to Paulina: that the "statue" speak and that Paulina explain what has happened. Paulina dodges Polixenes' question by pointing out that the court would "hoot at" the mere explanation "[t]hat she is living" (5.3.116–17) and smoothly puts in train the reunion of Perdita and Hermione. She instructs Perdita to kneel and ask her mother's blessing (5.3.119–120), and playing on Perdita's name (the Lost One), reassures Hermione, "Turn good lady. / Our Perdita is found" (5.3.120–121). Paulina's understated discourse intensifies the dramatic effect and recalls the oracle's prophecy to the minds of the audience.

Hermione, too, is reminded of the oracle. Her awe increases, and her questions flow as she gazes at Perdita and then exults:

> You gods look down
> And from your sacred vials pour graces
> Upon my daughter's head! Tell me, mine own,
> Where hast thou been preserved? where liv'd? how found
> Thy father's court? For thou shalt hear that I,
> Knowing by Paulina that the oracle
> Gave hope thou wast in being, have reserved
> Myself to see the issue. (5.3.121–128)

Hermione's rejoicing affirms for the audience that the oracle is fulfilled. The play is done, and Leontes' final, brief speech is directed to "Good Paulina," whom he has just given to Camillo in marriage: "Lead us from hence, where we may leisurely / Each one demand, and answer on his part / Performed in this wide gap of time since first / We were dissevered" (5.3.151–155). Leontes' speech serves as a sort of dénouement to Hermione's resurrection and fulfills a Shakespearean requirement that an authority figure discursively round off the action, sending the characters off the stage to ponder events, and take leave of the viewers, who depart to reflect upon what they have witnessed.

The audience's takeaway from *The Winter's Tale* is that its theatrical legerdemain arouses wonder and awe, but we, its audience, have no sense of being hoodwinked, for, like King Leontes, we enter the final scene believing that Hermione is dead—perhaps forgetting that Hermione's "death" is known only through Paulina's reports. Because no on-stage character voices skepticism, the audience is a collective victim of Paulina and Hermione's conspiracy and, with Leontes and the court, is apt for the surprise at the ending.[19] I suggest the possibility that witnessing Queen Hermione alive and the fulfillment of the prophecy that a lost child will be restored is somehow a simulacrum for what believers experience at the sacralizing of the Mass. For non-believers, the event may be something of a religious experience, too, perhaps a suggestion—in its theatrical analogy—for meditation. The resurrection-reunion scene of *The Winter's Tale*, furthermore, enacts a yearning like that Pearl's father expresses in his dream and that viewers may have experienced, that a dead loved one might—somehow—be returned to life.

## Epiphany in O'Connor's "Revelation"

Among the tortured Southern souls of Flannery O'Connor's novels and short stories, the saints are sinners, so profoundly flawed that regarding them as in any way capable of redemption requires a virtual contortion of our understanding.[20] Some readers of O'Connor's "Revelation" (1964) may feel, at an unsympathetic first reading, that its biblical title is blazingly ironic, but even at the first reading, we cannot escape understanding what an epiphany is because we accompany Mrs. Ruby Turpin in hers, perhaps asking ourselves, "Where in the procession of saints up to heavenly bliss viewed at the end of the story would *we* fit?"[21] For the reader to be somehow complicit with Mrs. Turpin is, indeed, a humbling experience.

O'Connor achieves this complicity in four scenes and two stirring narrative climaxes. The story opens in the waiting room of a doctor's office, where Claud has come to get treatment for a leg injury and where the Turpins meet other locals whom Mrs. Turpin mentally assesses. Its action climax occurs at the close of this scene when the deplorable Mary Grace hurls her college psychology textbook at Mrs. Turpin's head, creating a brawl that involves most of the characters in the doctor's office. It ends with Mary Grace's verbally insulting Mrs. Turpin and then losing consciousness. The second scene moves to the darkened bedroom of the Turpins' comfortable farmhouse, where they retreat to recuperate from their respective wounds, and where Claud sleeps while Mrs. Turpin lies awake pondering Mary Grace's insult. From the interior of the farmhouse, the action moves to its backyard later that day, after Claud has returned with the field hands, and Mrs. Turpin comes out to the truck to greet the women, telling them of the ordeal that produced her facial injury and offering them a bucket of ice water. The fourth and final scene takes Mrs. Turpin to the "pig parlour," the farm's swine enclosure, where she takes the water hose from Claud before sending him away to care for his leg, and where, alone with the pigs and her thoughts, she experiences her epiphany, the story's thematic climax. Its dénouement takes her from the pig enclosure back toward the house.

The attraction in the doctor's office scene between Mrs. Turpin and Mary Grace is central. Mrs. Turpin is, at first, fascinated by Mary Grace and even drawn to her, though she finds the girl repulsive. Mary Grace is singularly graceless in every respect, and soon Mrs. Turpin comes to perceive her as a nemesis. It turns out that Mary Grace is a graver threat, and her abrupt assault-by-textbook of Mrs. Turpin creates a fast-paced, chaotic, and bewildering climax seen entirely from Mrs. Turpin's point of view:

> Claud's face crumpled and fell out of sight. The nurse ran in, then out, then in again. The gangling figure of the doctor rushed out of the inner door. Magazines flew this way and that as the table turned over. The girl fell with a thud and Mrs. Turpin's vision suddenly reversed itself

and she saw everything large instead of small. The eyes of the white-trashy woman were staring hugely at the floor. There the girl, held down on one side by the nurse and on the other by her mother, was wrenching and turning in their grasp. The doctor was kneeling astride her, trying to hold her arm down. He managed after a second to sink a needle into it. (645)

Mary Grace, moving into unconsciousness, speaks quietly to Mrs. Turpin: her "gaze locked with Mrs. Turpin's" and she "whispers" a dreadful imprecation: "Go back to hell where you came from, you old wart hog" (646). The locking of their gazes and Mary Grace's judgment on Mrs. Turpin constitute the understated climax of the scene, and the reader stands in Mrs. Turpin's shoes.

Being called out in this dreadful fashion is appalling to Mrs. Turpin. As she lies awake weeping in the second scene, she engages in a colloquy with Jesus, protesting, "'I am not,' she said tearfully, 'a wart hog. From hell.' But the denial had no force. [. . . .] She had been singled out for the message [. . .]" (647). Finally, she comes to perceive Mary Grace as God's evangel—a messenger of good news—and Mrs. Turpin's very own "grace." In the third scene, when the field hands arrive, Mrs. Turpin repeats Mary Grace's imprecation to the women workers in response to their questions. In doing so, she makes a public confession of the insult, the ultimate stage in her preparation to be the object of an epiphany, to receive the titular "revelation."

What I refer to as the "complicity" into which O'Connor casts us as readers is one of the great strengths of the story. In the first scene, the reader is led into judging disapprovingly of Ruby Turpin, mirroring Mrs. Turpin's running assessments and categorizations of her companions in the waiting room, where she is particularly harsh toward those whom she despises. If Mrs. Turpin is a bigot, then, we, too, come out looking like bigots for our hasty and uncharitable judgment of Mrs. Turpin. An author's involving and implicating the reader in the moral dilemmas of a text is foregrounded by Stanley Fish in *Surprised by Sin*, his study of John Milton's *Paradise Lost*. Fish demonstrates how the narrative voice in *Paradise Lost* (1667) is continually maneuvering the reader into the position of acceding to the moral errors of Eve and Adam, placing the reader in no position, then, to stand aloof and judge them; like it or not, the reader participates in their sin. When Ruby Turpin focuses her attention upon her own kind as they progress up to heaven, she realizes they will have to pass through Purgatory, observing "even their virtues were being burned away," and "her eyes small"—perhaps like pigs' eyes—remain "fixed unblinkingly on what lay ahead" (654). This observation is precisely the story's "revelation," that Mrs. Turpin's final judgment is to be humiliated—she's among "the last" (654)—and her fate is purgatorial. Even what she perceives as her "virtues" are "burned away," though in the end she will be blessed. Mrs. Turpin's "revelation" is the grace of self-knowledge.

At the first reading, whether readers are steeped in Christianity or ignorant of its principles, they may find the story's "revelation" abrupt and puzzling if not jolting. A closer reading, however, will show how O'Connor prepares us for its abruptness, its contradictory aspects, and its jolts. Two sections of the narrative in particular provide the reader with discernable foreshadowing, drawing us into Mrs. Turpin's thoughts. Her bedtime categorization of people into classes, no matter that it bogs her down into complexity that she cannot fathom, confirms her ingrained bigotry, and the two fugue states she enters as a reaction to being assaulted in the doctor's office indicate that she is in a fragile psychic condition, perhaps open to unusual spiritual experience:

> Sometimes Mrs. Turpin occupied herself at night naming the classes of people. On the bottom of the heap were most colored people, not the kind she would have been if she had been one of them, but most of them: next to them—not above, just away from—were the white trash; then above them were the homeowners, and above them the home-and-landowners, to which she and Claud belonged. Above she [sic] and Claud were people with a lot of money and much bigger houses and much more land. But the complexity of it would begin to bear in on her, for some people with a lot of money were common and ought to be below she and Claud and some people who had good blood had lost their money and had to rent and then there were colored who owned their own homes and land as well. [. . . .] Usually by the time she had fallen asleep all the classes of people were moiling and roiling around in her head [. . .]. (636)

By its end, this scene has assumed the nature of a dream whose phantasmagoria foreshadow the categories of souls rumbling up into heaven in Mrs. Turpin's vision in the hog enclosure.

O'Connor's lighting effects in the epiphany at the end of "Revelation" (653–654) tend toward the crepuscular rather than the blinding, but they are flamboyant nevertheless:

> Until the sun slipped finally behind the tree line, Mrs. Turpin remained there with her gaze bent to [the hogs] as if she were absorbing some abysmal life-giving knowledge. At last she lifted her head. There was only a purple streak in the sky, cutting through a field of crimson and

leading, like an extension of the highway, into the descending dusk. She raised her hands from the side of the pen in a gesture hieratic and profound. A visionary light settled in her eyes. She saw the streak as a vast swinging bridge extending upward from the earth through a field of living fire. (653–654)

With her eyes filled with the external light of her vision, Mrs. Turpin's experience, unlike that of Pearl's father, is open-eyed, but the effects of Mrs. Turpin's looking into the distance, across a physical barrier—like the river across which Pearl's father sees her—to what becomes a bright and surprising heavenly vision are similar. Mrs. Turpin interprets it in the language and with the associations of her lower-middle-class, mid-century culture:

> Upon it a vast horde of souls were rumbling toward heaven. There were whole companies of white trash, clean for the first time in their lives, and bands of black niggers in white robes, and battalions of freaks and lunatics shouting and clapping and leaping like frogs. And bringing up the end of the procession was a tribe of people whom she recognized at once as those who, like herself and Claud, had always had a little of everything and the God-given wit to use it right. She leaned forward to observe them closer. They were marching behind the others with great dignity, accountable as they had always been for good order and common sense and respectable behavior. They alone were on key. (654)

Her vision recalls her earlier colloquy with Jesus, in which Mrs. Turpin complains that the biblical paradox "the first shall be last and the last shall be first" is essentially specious because no matter what, there always *will* be first and last (653). In her vision, even as she congratulates herself on being among the only group singing on key, she is amazed to find not only that her group has been placed last, but also to realize "by their shocked and altered faces" that their virtues are being burned away with their sins (654). There in the hog pen, her eyes fixed on her vision, Mrs. Turpin enters a fugue state: "She lowered her hands and gripped the rail of the hog pen, her eyes small but fixed unblinkingly on what lay ahead. In a moment the vision faded, but she remained where she was, immobile" (654). Mrs. Turpin's silence and immobility contrast her usual volubility and movement, and the vision and its sound effects persist, even as she moves slowly toward home: "In the woods around her the invisible cricket choruses had struck up, but what she heard were the voices of the souls climbing upward into the starry field and shouting hallelujah" (654).

Surely this is a moving scene, with its effects of light and motion and jubilant song stimulating Mrs. Turpin's confused response to the inescapable memory of her vision—and yet many details undercut its joyous tone. On the whole, the tone is of elevated, almost religious observance: "abysmal life-giving knowledge" is compelling; to speak of a "gesture hieratic and profound" virtually makes Mrs. Turpin a celebrant priest; and she receives a "visionary light" (653). Most readers will sense the lack of dignity in Mrs. Turpin's seeing the procession of saints as a "horde" who "rumbl[e]" along toward heaven, and the descriptors of the representatives of society who make up this procession, along with their conduct—"shouting" and "leaping" and singing off key—contest usual ideas of what a heavenly vision ought to be (654). Not only are the two largest cadres referred to in the crude terms we have come to expect from Mrs. Turpin, but these figures are also accompanied by "battalions of freaks and lunatics shouting and clapping and leaping like frogs." Hieronymus Bosch in Georgia! No wonder the complacent countrywoman is taken aback to see her own people cast in a subsidiary role. Mrs. Turpin's vision cannot help but be a revelation to her—but what sort of revelation is it?

The epiphany that is Mrs. Turpin's "revelation" has two key features. First, its elements are vivid and true to what one expects of an epiphany, based on the tradition going back to the conversion of St. Paul on the road to Damascus.[22] Second, despite Mrs. Turpin's vision concluding gloriously with "the voices of the souls climbing upward into the starry field and shouting hallelujah" (654), the tone of narrative voice undercuts the effect, setting it into the register of the Southern grotesque. As we readers experience it, we have to ask, does this woman at all *deserve* such a revelation? And, we might ask—as readers who have judged Mrs. Turpin—who are we to judge that? We, too, have had a revelation, because we readers have arrived at the height of complicity in our participation in O'Connor's story. We have been enthralled by Mrs. Turpin's wrenching epiphany—and have received condign warning not to be self-righteous in our acceptance of it.[23]

A possible takeaway from our complicity as readers of this short story—a story written by a near contemporary of some of us—is that the religious life is not dead in our time and place, but that it persists, even now, in various guises. O'Connor insisted that *all* her fiction had religious themes—though, necessarily, those took bizarre and even perverse forms in order to catch the attention of her early-1960s American audience.[24] If O'Connor's critical work is strongly polemical, it is that she perceived herself as a writer embattled, as one resisting superficiality and commonplaces and revealing challenging and compelling truths to resistant readers. As we read "Revelation" and O'Connor's other stories, we realize that we *can* participate in specifically religious experiences through fiction.

O'Connor's death in August 1964, following complications from surgery the previous February, and her having written "Revelation" in 1963 means that it holds some of her final words.[25] Her sparse but determined manifestos make clear the intentions she had for her readers, whether they were from Georgia or Connecticut: to shock them into recognition of spiritual malaise and also to offer them a perverse sort of grace. With what consummate skill she draws us in! And for that skill, ironically, O'Connor became the darling of readers whom we might suppose to be the most naturally resistant to her evangel. As such, "Revelation" is this chapter's fitting final example of literature that offers a spiritual experience to the religious and the irreligious—here, through the ordinary, desperate characters in O'Connor's Christ-haunted fiction.[26]

## Notes

1 *Pearl*'s composition is dated by the British Library in the late fourteenth century, and its manuscript, bound in a decorated, illustrated compilation known as BL MS Cotton Nero A X, dates to the early fifteenth century, making it approximately contemporary with Chaucer's *Canterbury Tales*. *The Winter's Tale*'s composition is conjectural, falling in a narrow range from 1609–1611 (Chambers 1.271); Shakespeare died in 1616. See n. 25, below, for publication details for "Revelation."

2 Cecilia A. Hatt, for example, finds a unifying theological vision in the *Pearl* codex's poems. In Works Cited, see The Pearl Poet for texts of *Pearl*.

3 Maurice Hunt, setting *The Winter's Tale* among the "pagan" plays, examines Christian elements suggested in J. A. Bryant's probe of its "Christian aspects" and Huston Diehl's theory of its "theatrical and theological wonder" (46–48). David N. Beauregard points to the play's discursive references to Christianity in several examples, including Leontes' referring to confession in "priest-like, thou / Hast cleans'd my bosom. I from thee departed / Thy penitent reform'd" (1.2.235–239), and Cleomines' telling Leontes, "you [. . .] have performe'd / A saintlike sorrow" and using "penitence" and "trespass" (5.1.1–4) to characterize Leontes' deeds (37–38).

4 Over the past 45 years, Howard Felperin, Harald W. Fawkner, and Grace Tiffany have characterized *The Winter's Tale* as a "miracle play." In O'Connor's work, Mark Bosco sees a naturalistic expression of the "experience of faith" in the aesthetics of the "Catholic baroque," where

"a visceral style aimed at the senses" challenges the viewer rather than offering comfort.

5  Scholars began to advance allegorical readings of *Pearl* soon after Richard Morris prepared his edition of *Pearl* in 1864, and some have denied the existence of a grieving father or a dead child. Nevertheless, the poem has more often been regarded as an elegy whose speaker is a father narrating a dream in which he sees and speaks with his deceased child. Although the narrative and debate are laced with clearly identifiable allegories, it is more profitable to think of its material as symbolism. Gardner affirms that view in his Introduction: "Properly speaking the poet's mode is symbolic, not allegorical" (46). A. C. Spearing (*Gawain-Poet*) directly addresses the distinction, the place of allegory, and the weight of symbolism in *Pearl* (esp. 128–137) and emphasizes its "Symbol and drama" (137 ff.). Also see Spearing's earlier article and Angela Carson's discussion of *Pearl*'s genre as elegy.

6  The British Library's catalogue description of the *Pearl* manuscript casts the speaker as the father and Pearl as his deceased child (The Pearl Poet), reflecting what Jean-Paul Freidl and Ian J. Kirby, in their 2002 discussion of the Pearl-Maiden's perfection, call the "generally accepted" critical consensus (395). Though the internal evidence for Pearl as the dead child is glancing and minimalist—scattered through 101 stanzas in 1212 lines—it is concentrated in a few places (ss. 14–17, for example), and the effect is cumulative and compelling. In the opening stanza, the speaker refers to Pearl with gendered pronouns—"her" four times (as objects and a possessive pronoun) and "she" once—and repeats "her" (a possessive pronoun) in stanza two. The line "She was nearer to me than aunt or niece" (l. 233) is the strongest single indication in the poem corroborating Pearl's identification, yet a degree of indirection remains, for we might suppose her to be the speaker's sister or mother, as well as considering her as his daughter, or even his wife, and Jane Beal argues that Pearl is the Jeweler's late beloved, while Charlotte Gross finds courtly romance in *Pearl*. Further examples of this creative line of thinking include W. H. Schofield (655–656), Walter K. Greene (817–818), G. G. Coulton (40), and Carson (19, 24). Because of explicit statements about Pearl's age and her "innocence" meriting a place in heaven, however, these blood and marital relationships are implausible.

7  Modern English quotations from *Pearl* are Gardner's. Gardner numbers stanzas only, while other translations include line numbers. Stanza and line numbers are period separated, and parenthetical citations of wording from the poem are given in italics. Osgood's 1906 edition is accessible electronically. Malcolm Andrew and Ronald Waldron give *Pearl* in modern English prose (2013), based on their earlier lyric version.

A useful perspective on reading *Pearl* as a consolation for the death of a loved one lies in Chaucer's *The Book of the Duchess* (1368), a dream-vision consolation on the death of Dame Blanche, the wife of John of Gaunt, Chaucer's patron. Chaucer displaces the elegiac voice

in the *Duchess* from the experience of the bereaved husband, whereas *Pearl*'s speaker directly expresses the trials of grief and longing, creating a more poignant and affecting reading. See the following note.
8 *Pearl* has long been noted as a *consolatio*. Especially relevant to *Pearl*, Cicero's lost *Consolatio* was written to console himself for the death of his daughter, Tullia. See Han Baltussen's and Marcus Wilson's essays on the *consolatio* tradition as contextualized, respectively, in Cicero and in Seneca, who exemplified Stoic *consolatio*. Michael H. Means's influential generic study (1972) of English medieval *consolatio* describes it as a didactic work of debate and dream-vision literature where instruction elicits a "psychological or spiritual change" (9), most often for the first-person narrator. Along with *Pearl*, Means cites Dante's *Commedia*, Boethius' *Consolation of Philosophy*, and William Langland's *Piers Plowman* among the genre's well-known examples.
9 The parable of the members and the body comes from biblical and patristic sources, namely, 1 Corinthians 6:15 and St. Augustine's *De civitate dei* [*The City of God*] 21:30, respectively.
10 Stanzas 36–60 argue the problem of unequal rewards in heaven.
11 The layered constellation of meaning for the pearl as a symbol will have the reader's attention as the "debate" goes forward. Gardner (46), considering the generic classification of the poem, identifies as many as eleven foci for pearl symbolism in the poem: 1) at first, the pearl is a literary figure, a metaphor for the father's greatest treasure, his child, whom he has lost; 2) the lost pearl, assumed to have fallen into the ground, is the "seed" of John 22, which must be lost and die before it can be resurrected; 3) because of the pearl's spherical shape, it suggests the Neo-platonic good. Variously, too, the pearl is identified with 4) immutability, 5) art, 6) virginity, 7) the soul in bliss, 8) Christ, 9) Heaven itself, 10) the figurative wages of the faithful Christian, and 11) the order of the cosmos.
12 The several scriptural allusions selected for mention here—fewer than ten percent of those in the poem—indicate the degree to which *Pearl* is imbued with details of scripture in support of Christian sentiment and doctrine. Borroff, in her 1977 verse translation, finds *Pearl* containing ninety-seven biblical passages (11 ff.), and I cite here eight of its parables. See also Jennifer Garrison's chapter treating *Pearl*.
13 All citations from Shakespeare come from 1977's second edition of *The Riverside Shakespeare* and follow the usual pattern of act, scene, and line(s), period separated. Shakespeare's comedies, so-called problem plays, and romances have notoriously fanciful settings, and those of *The Winter's Tale* come from Robert Greene's prose romance *Pandosto* (Bullough 8.156–199). Reversing Greene, Shakespeare makes Sicilia the kingdom of Leontes—Greene's King Pandosto—and the not-quite-neighboring "Bohemia," the kingdom of Polixenes.
14 See Christopher J. Cobb's notes on staging the scene and its discourse (257–258, nn. 15–19).

15 Beauregard finds the play structured by movement stemming from the Catholic sacrament of penance and culminating in a "miraculous" springtime resurrection (109–123).
16 Informed members of the audience may now anticipate three reunions: Leontes and Perdita's, Leontes and Hermione's, and Hermione and Perdita's. Shakespeare shrewdly does not stage the first of them—Leontes and Perdita's—but instead has it affectingly reported (5.2)—to better preserve the emotional impact of the second, even on the well informed.
17 Shakespeare's contemporary audience would have fully understood the weight of Paulina's avowals against necromancy and her warning to "depart" as addressing the Puritan canard against the theater. In sixteenth- and seventeenth-century England, Puritans objected to the theater as undermining the people's sense of reality. Regarding whatever was not "real" as untrue, Puritans saw the theater as a species of lie and, therefore, a threat to religious observance because theater and religious observances are both performances. Jonas Barish's survey of attitudes toward the theater devotes two chapters to the Puritans' attack on the stage in Shakespeare's time. Puritanical earnestness was made clear when Puritans progressed from a repressed minority to become England's rulers and closed London theaters in 1642. Clearly, Shakespeare and his character Paulina, his stage manager here for the play-within-a-play, are less worked up over Sicilian mores than over the laws of a contemporary Jacobean polity.
18 The "striking" chords evoke the period's high regard for music's curative powers. The *locus classicus* for scholarly study of Renaissance concepts of music is John Hollander's *The Untuning of the Sky*. See also Renata Pieragostini's 2021 study using late-fourteenth-century Bolognese documents.

On the "uncanny" effect of the "resurrection scene," see Cynthia Marshall's 1986 discussion citing "actors and audiences offer[ing] repeated testimony that something strange, something uncanny, is felt at the moment when Hermione's statue steps from its pedestal" (296). The idea of "the uncanny" in this critical context comes from Sigmund Freud's 1919 "Das Unheimliche" ["The Uncanny"].
19 Some of the audience may understand that Paulina is the most likely character to conspire with Hermione to save her life and convince the world of her death. Paulina is Shakespeare's chief alteration to Greene's *Pandosto*, mentioned above. See Bullough's count of Shakespeare's sixteen departures from Greene (8.123–124).
20 O'Connor addressed the "saints and sinners" dilemma in her 1960 essay, "Some Aspects of the Grotesque in Southern Fiction," which forthrightly demands that her fiction be accepted on its own terms. Her essays appear in 1970's *Mystery and Manners* (hereinafter MM), so named for two of three key terms—"mystery," "manners," and "grace"—in O'Connor's lexicon of self-commentary. Essays cited here come from MM. O'Connor's 1988 *Collected Works* includes only eight

of the fourteen pieces in *MM*. On O'Connor's view of her task as a Catholic writer, see n. 24, below.
21 A "revelation" or an epiphany is a "showing forth" of a god or some powerful aspect of the godhead. It is a shocking event, often accompanied by blinding light, and the person who experiences it is likely to be physically and emotionally prostrated. Also see the following note.
22 Saul of Tarsus experiences a blinding, epiphanic vision resulting in his conversion. In Acts 8, Saul persecutes Christians, making "havoc of the church, entering into every house," arresting men and women and jailing them (KJV). In Acts 9, Saul continues "breathing out threat[s] and slaughter" against Christians and sets out for Damascus with a group of men, but as they near the city, a light suddenly shines around Saul, and a heavenly voice upbraids him, leaving him "trembling and astonished"—and blind. Saul has remained sightless and unable to eat or drink for three days when Ananias, sent by God, comes to heal Saul and to tell him that he will be "fill[ed] with the Holy Spirit" (Acts 9:17 KJV), remaking Saul as the Apostle Paul.
23 The reading of "Revelation" offered here is largely in accord with critical opinion. See Michael Dunne's and Ralph C. Wood's chapters on "Revelation" in their respective book-length studies of O'Connor. The concept of the complicity of the reader in the bigotry of the central character, however, is my own theory, stemming from Fish's insights into reader response, acknowledged above.
24 See, for example, "Good Country People." The reader who wishes to understand O'Connor's religious aims will find her essays useful. "The Church and the Fiction Writer," "Novelist and Believer," "Catholic Novelists and Their Readers," "On Her Own Work," and "The Catholic Novelist in the Protestant South" confront the relationships between fiction and faith and between the writer's obligations to art and religion and show O'Connor at her most polemical and, indeed, defensive. She addresses them primarily—if not solely—to her most challenging audiences, Catholic laity and Church hierarchy.
25 With "Revelation," "Parker's Back" and "Judgement [*sic*] Day" were published in the short-story collection *Everything That Rises Must Converge* after O'Connor's death. "Revelation" appears in 1964 in *The Sewanee Review* (178–202), in 1965 in *Everything That Rises* (191–218), and in O'Connor's *Collected Works* (633–654).
26 O'Connor wrote, "I think it is safe to say that while the South is hardly Christ-centered, it is most certainly Christ-haunted" ("Some Aspects of the Grotesque in Southern Fiction" 44).

## Works Cited

Baltussen, Han. "Cicero's *Consolatio ad se*: Character, Purpose, and Impact of a Curious Treatise." *Greek and Roman Consolations: Eight Studies of a Tradition and Its Afterlife*. Ed. Han Baltussen. Swansea: Classical P of Wales, 2013. 67–91.

Barish, Jonas. *The Anti-theatrical Prejudice*. Berkeley: U of California P, 1981.
Beal, Jane. *The Signifying Power of* Pearl: *Medieval Literary and Cultural Contexts for the Transformation of Genre*. Studies in Medieval Literature and Culture. New York: Routledge, 2017.
Beauregard, David N. *Catholic Theology in Shakespeare's Plays*. Newark: U of Delaware P, 2008.
Bosco, Mark. "Flannery O'Connor as Baroque Artist: Theological and Literary Strategies." *Renascence* 62.1 (2009): 41–61.
British Library. *See* The Pearl Poet.
Bryant, J. A., Jr. *Hippolyta's View: Some Christian Aspects of Shakespeare's Plays*. Lexington, KY: U of Kentucky P, 1961.
Bullough, Geoffrey, ed. *Narrative and Dramatic Sources of Shakespeare. Volume VIII: Romances*: Cymbeline, The Winter's Tale, The Tempest. New York: Columbia UP, 1975. *See also* Greene, Robert.
Carson, Angela. "Aspects of Elegy in the Middle English *Pearl*." *Studies in Philology* 62.1 (1965): 17–27.
Chambers, E. K. *William Shakespeare: A Study of Facts and Problems*. Vol. 1. Oxford, UK: Clarendon P, [1930] 1966.
Chaucer, Geoffrey. *The Book of the Duchess*. Ed. Colin Wilcockson. *The Riverside Chaucer*. Ed. Larry D. Benson. 3rd ed. Boston: Houghton Mifflin, 1987. 329–346; 966–976.
—. *The Canterbury Tales*. Ed. Larry D. Benson. *The Riverside Chaucer*. 3rd ed. 3–328.
Cobb, Christopher J. *The Staging of Romance in Late Shakespeare: Text and Theatrical Technique*. Newark, NJ: U of Delaware P, 2007.
Coulton, G. G. "In Defence of *Pearl*." *MLR* 2.1 (1906): 39–43.
Diehl, Huston. "'Strike All That Look Upon With Marvel': Theatrical and Theological Wonder in *The Winter's Tale*." Ed. Bryan Reynolds and William N. West. *Rematerializing Shakespeare: Authority and Representation on the Early Modern Stage*. New York: Palgrave Macmillan, 2005. 19–34.
Dunne, Michael. "Flannery O'Connor: 'Funny Because It Is Terrible.'" Michael Dunne. *Calvinist Humor in American Literature*. Baton Rouge: Louisiana State UP, 2007.
Fawkner, Harald W. *Shakespeare's Miracle Plays:* Pericles, Cymbeline, *and* The Winter's Tale. Rutherford, NJ: Fairleigh Dickinson UP, 1992.
Felperin, Howard. "Shakespeare's Miracle Plays." *Shakespeare Quarterly* 18.4 (1967): 363–374.
Fish, Stanley E. *Surprised by Sin: The Reader in* Paradise Lost. Berkeley: U of California P, 1971.
Fitzgerald, Sally, and Robert Fitzgerald. *See* O'Connor, Flannery. *Mystery and Manners*.
Freidl, Jean-Paul, and Ian J. Kirby. "The Life, Death, and Life of the Pearl-Maiden." *Neuphilologische Mitteilungen* 103.4 (2002): 395–398.
Freud, Sigmund. "Das Unheimliche [The Uncanny]." *Imago: Zeitschrift für Anwendung der Psychoanalyse auf die Geisteswissenschaften* 5.5–6 (1919): 297–324.
Gardner, John. "Introduction and Commentary." *The Complete Works of the Gawain Poet*. 3–90. *See also* The Pearl Poet.

Garrison, Jennifer. *Challenging Communion: The Eucharist and Middle English Literature*. Columbus, OH: The Ohio State UP, 2017.
Greene, Robert. *Pandosto. The Triumph of Time*. (1588). Ed. G. Bullough. 8.156–199.
Greene, Walter Kirkland. "The *Pearl*: A New Interpretation." *PMLA* 40.4 (1925): 814–827.
Gross, Charlotte. "Courtly Language in *Pearl*." Ed. Robert J. Blanch, et al. *Text and Matter: New Critical Perspectives of the Pearl-Poet*. Troy, NY: Whitson, 1991.
Hatt, Cecilia A. *God and the Gawain-Poet: Theology and Genre in* Pearl, Cleanness, Patience, *and* Sir Gawain and the Green Knight. Rochester, NY: D. S. Brewer, 2015.
Hollander, John. *The Untuning of the Sky: Ideas of Music in English Poetry, 1500-1700*. New York: Norton, 1970.
Hunt, Maurice. "A New Taxonomy of Shakespeare's Pagan Plays." *Religion and Literature* 43.1 (2011): 29–53.
Marshall, Cynthia. "Dualism and the Hope of Reunion in *The Winter's Tale*." *Soundings: An Interdisciplinary Journal* 69.3 (1986): 294–309.
Means, Michael H. *The Consolatio Genre in Medieval English Literature*. Gainesville, FL: The U of Florida P, 1972.
O'Connor, Flannery. "The Catholic Novelist in the Protestant South." *MM*. 191–209.
—. "Catholic Novelists and Their Readers." *MM*. 169–190.
—. "The Church and the Fiction Writer." *MM*. 143–153.
—. *Collected Works*. Ed. Sally Fitzgerald. New York: Library of America, 1988.
—. "Good Country People." Ed. Sally Fitzgerald. *Collected Works*. 263–284.
—. *Everything That Rises Must Converge*. Intro. Robert Fitzgerald. New York: FSG, 1965.
—. "Judgement [sic] Day." *Everything That Rises Must Converge*. 245–269.
—. *Mystery and Manners: Occasional Prose* (MM). Ed. Sally Fitzgerald and Robert Fitzgerald. New York: FSG, 1970.
—. "Novelist and Believer." *MM*. 154–168.
—. "On Her Own Work." *MM*. 107–118.
—. "Parker's Back." *Everything That Rises Must Converge*. 219–244.
—. "Revelation." *Collected Works*. 633–654.
—. "Revelation." *Sewanee Review* 72.2 (1964): 178–202.
—. "Revelation." *Everything That Rises Must Converge*. 191–218.
—. "Some Aspects of the Grotesque in Southern Fiction." *MM*. 36–50.
—. "Writing Short Stories." *MM*. 87–106.
The Pearl Poet. *Pearl*. Collection Items [catalogue description]. BL Cotton Nero A X. London: British Library. bl.uk/collection-items/pearl. 2022.
—. *The Pearl*. Trans. Richard Morris. *Early English Alliterative Poems in the West-Midland Dialect of the Fourteenth Century*. EETS 1. London: Trübner, 1864. Rev. ed. 1869. 1–37.
—. *The Pearl: A Middle English Poem*. Trans. Charles G. Osgood, Jr. Belles Lettres Series. Boston: D. C. Heath, 1906. Also digitized at Archive.org.
—. *Pearl*. Trans. John Gardner. *The Complete Works of the Gawain-Poet*. Carbondale, IL: Southern Illinois UP, 1970.

—. *Pearl: A New Translation*. Trans. Marie Borroff. New York: Norton, 1977.

—. *The Poems of the* Pearl *Manuscript in Modern English Prose Translation: Pearl, Cleanness, Patience, Sir Gawain and the Green Knight*. Trans. Malcolm Andrew and Ronald Waldron. Liverpool, UK: Liverpool UP, 2013.

Pieragostini, Renata. "The Healing Power of Music: Documentary Evidence from Late-Fourteenth-Century Bologna." *Speculum* 96.1 (2021): 156–176.

Schofield, W. H. "Symbolism, Allegory, and Autobiography in *The Pearl*." *PMLA* 24.4 (1909): 585–675.

Shakespeare, William. *The Winter's Tale*. Ed. Hallett Smith. *The Riverside Shakespeare*. 2nd ed. Ed. G. Blakemore Evans and J. J. M. Tobin. Boston: Houghton Mifflin, 1997. 1527–1731.

Spearing, A. C. *The Gawain-Poet: A Critical Study*. Cambridge, UK: Cambridge UP, 1976.

—. "Symbolic and Dramatic Development in *Pearl*." Ed. Robert J. Blanch. Sir Gawain *and* Pearl: *Critical Essays*. Bloomington: Indiana UP, 1966. 98–119.

Tiffany, Grace. "Shakespeare's Miracle Plays." *English Studies* 93.1 (2012): 1–13.

Wilson, Marcus. "Seneca the Consoler? A New Reading of His Consolatory Writings." *Greek and Roman Consolations: Eight Studies of a Tradition and Its Afterlife*. Ed. Han Baltussen. Swansea: Classical P of Wales, 2013. 93–121.

Wood, Ralph C. "'Climbing into the Starry Field and Shouting Hallelujah': O'Connor's Vision of the World to Come." *Flannery O'Connor and the Christ-Haunted South*. Grand Rapids, MI: Eerdmans, 2004. 251–265.

# ❧11❧
# "Shape and Meaning and Point" in Katherine Anne Porter's "The Grave"

## Elizabeth Moore Willingham

Katherine Anne Porter's "The Grave," first published in *The Virginia Quarterly Review* in April 1935, is one of Porter's "Miranda stories," so called for their young protagonist. This tale of Miranda's childhood found a wider audience with publication in *The Best American Short Stories* in 1936 and *The Leaning Tower and Other Stories* in 1944.[1] "The Grave" recalls events on a farm in Central Texas on a summer's day in 1903 when Miranda, nine years old, and brother Paul, twelve, are ostensibly out for a hunt on family land, though their greater desire is to meet with some small adventure. They initially find distractions from the ordinary in an abandoned family cemetery, but when Paul shoots a pregnant doe rabbit and shows Miranda the developing fetuses, she soon reacts to the sight with profound unhappiness, and Paul hides the evidence and swears her to secrecy. After a few days, Miranda's memory of the rabbits fades, and when she involuntarily recalls the scene with horror nearly two decades later, a second vision gives her peace. The story's proverbial title echoes through these narrative movements, and ideas or images of literal or figurative death and burials lie at their respective centers. This curious story, with its shifting narrative time, digressions, thematic vagaries, and supposed "symbolism," has had years of thoughtful, earnest critical attention. The following brief summary of that work will suggest its general nature and theoretical scope.

## "The Grave" and the Critics

Readings of "The Grave" adopt various points of departure: Porter's biography, feminist perspectives, Freudian theory, patriarchal dominance, biblical echoes of character and situation, Greek mythology, and trauma studies. Daniel Curley, in 1963, reads Miranda's reaction to the final movement of the rabbit scene as the beginning of her "reject[ing] the whole bloody female mess" (378), but Curley's contextualizing his conclusions between biography and fiction finds that Porter's constant themes of "loss" and "terror" get unique treatment in "The Grave," where she represents "the Christian fable [. . .] in its entirety with the final phase of redemption cleverly disguised in the really obvious treasure in the grave" (384). Sister M. Joselyn's 1964 article emphasizes the poetic elements that make "The Grave" a "lyric" short story with a "syllogistic plot," thereby inviting the reader's participation in the story's quest for knowledge; she remarks its many religious associations and potent "interlocked symbols" (217–220). Constance Rooke and Bruce Wallis's 1975 reading presents the story as a heavily parallel narrative of the biblical Fall and Christianity's account of resurrection and redemption; for Rooke and Wallis, the Apostle Paul's conversion on the road to Damascus resonates with Paul's character in the story's final scene.[2] In her 1983 study of "Porter's women," Jane Krause DeMouy views the Miranda stories generally as being "about feminine conflicts" (113), and in "The Grave," she finds "a personal story" that "parallels Adam and Eve's archetypal fall" and creates "the story of one young girl's repulsion at sexual knowledge" in "primal images" (140). DeMouy finds Paul and Miranda's being on their own a reinforcement of the biblical creation myth with the male–female "pairing essential to the continuation of life" and the story's hunting motif linking its Edenic references with its sexual symbols (141), including the ring's implication of the "preciousness of [Miranda's] virginity," and Miranda's "evoking simultaneously the primacy of Eden and the phallus" when she "defers" to Paul, mentioning "snakes" in admitting her ineffectiveness as a hunter (142–143). Darlene Harbour Unrue (*Truth*) also relates Miranda to Eve, "her archetypal mother," and suggests Miranda's mention of "snakes" as symbolizing knowledge of "sexuality" (52). Patricia Yeager, in 1992, forwards a sexual-religious interpretation that recognizes the "Holy Ghost" in its reproductive capacity. Yeager writes, "This is, in short, a story about the construction and deformation of a modern reproductive unconscious" (270) and an "angry narrative about women and reproductive danger" (271). She credits Porter's "bizarre folding of reproductive anxiety back into the master tropes of Western theology"—"the impregnating fleshlessness of the holy ghost" and "the apostolic radiance of still another 'Paul'"—to be part of its success (271).

Cleanth Brooks in 1966, characterizes "The Grave" in superlatives: It is "so rich," "full of subtleties and sensitive insights," and "has so many meanings" but is yet "an almost unbelievably economical" coming-of-age story about Miranda's "discovery of the truth. [. . .] about birth and her own destiny as a woman," with "the secret of birth [. . .] revealed in the place of death and through a kind of bloody sacrifice" (112–114). Porter's chosen biographer Joan Givner sets "The Grave" among Porter's "many" stories that "have seemed to be quintessential renderings of women's experience" (513) and notes that critics "have continued to explore the suggestions of such objects as the coffin screw shaped like the dove of Venus (symbol of earthy love) and the womb-grave of the dead rabbit" (71). Givner resorts to a consideration of the story "against the events of [Porter's] life" to locate its "impact" and attributes its power to Porter's "compression of so much intensely felt experience" (71). In 1988, Mary Titus casts "The Fig Tree" and "The Grave" as Porter's "explorations of the sexual terror and guilt" connected with the author's memory of losing her mother, suggesting that the fragrance of "mingled sweetness and corruption" in the grandfather's grave reflect "the two sides of memory, the nurturing and destruction that surround the relation of mother and child" (119). In his 1990 study of Porter's fiction, James T. F. Tanner emphasizes knowledge of sexuality and "womb-tomb" imagery as thematic (84), and Mary Ann Wimsatt's article of 2000 emphasizes Paul and Miranda's unexpected confrontation with "pregnancy and death" in the story and views the experience as helping Miranda to "lear[n] what she had to know" (459). For Wimsatt, "The Grave" propounds the idea "that love of any kind ends in death," and she relates it thematically in that sense to "The Fig Tree" (461). In her 2013 study, Janis P. Stout, one of the most prolific critics of Porter's work and biography, points out that "sex and death" and "sex and violence" converge in "The Grave" as they do elsewhere in Porter's fiction, and she affirms the possibility of redemption in the story's concluding scene (73, 75). George Cheatham sets death as "the obsessive center" of all the Miranda stories ("Death" 610). All these critics pose questions of significant critical interest, and several find compelling parallels among the Miranda stories. It is noteworthy in the present context that Stout and Cheatham set death as a perennial concern of the stories, that Stout finds redemptive signs in the final scene, and that Curley calls attention to the "really obvious treasure in the grave."

## Reading Porter and Miranda

This chapter's reading of "The Grave" draws on the dreadful finality of the image named in its title and its relevance to the story's emphasis on "shape, meaning, and point," qualities vested in its material culture and natural objects. Porter recalled them as foundational properties of the stories she heard growing up in a family of "great letter writers, readers, great storytellers," and she claimed those principles as her writing legacy.[3] The idea of literature creating order from chaos and meaning from confusion, of writers whose work is to give the disordered world and the confusion of experience—particularly the experience of death—shape, meaning, and point illuminates "The Grave." Porter philosophizes in a similar vein in "St. Augustine and the Bullfight," where she asserts that she possessed an innate, "incurable tendency to try to wangle the sprawling mess of our existence in this bloody world into some kind of shape" and declares that a writer must "take hold firmly, and draw the exact line between what really happened, and what you have since imagined about it" (93). She cautioned against "giving [. . .] meanings" to events "that they do not possess" and stipulated to the writer's first task: "Only by remembering, comparing, waiting to know the consequences can we sometimes, in a flash of light, see what a certain event really meant, what it was trying to tell us" (94).

Porter's confessions about the importance she attached to "The Grave" and how she regarded childhood are also telling. In a letter dated January 12, 1942, Porter wrote to Glenway Wescott, segueing from her praise of a favorite story of his, as follows: "I love of my own stories, 'The Grave,' perhaps best of all," and she lamented that "no one mentions it or hardly ever" and "no one seems to remember it . . .".[4] Some of Porter's statements should certainly be weighed skeptically, but this somewhat abrupt, laconic expression of parental adoration and regret, recorded as a parenthetical reflection in a brief note asking a favor of a friend, conveys a genuine sense of value and regret. In 1974, with a similar tone of regret and revelation, Porter wrote frankly about her sense of childhood in a way that bears on "The Grave": "I do not believe that childhood is a happy time, it is a time of desperate cureless bitter griefs and pains, of shattering disillusionments, when everything good and evil alike is happening for the first time, and there is no answer to any question . . ." ("Autobiographical" 1016). The stories of Miranda's childhood, like Stephen's story in *The Downward Path to Wisdom*, are shaped by those elements, and amid their confusion and "griefs," the two child protagonists of the stories struggle for understanding and yearn for love and an escape from their torment.

For readers less familiar with Miranda, a few notes may be useful. Called "Baby" by her father, Miranda is a (barely) nine-year-old female in 1903. She is reared by mid–nineteenth-century middle-class "Christian" standards because her grandmother's old-fashioned values govern the household.[5] In Miranda's house, no one has a sex partner, no babies are born, and adults converge to shield her from sexual awareness. In Miranda's limited and immature understanding, her experience of events is apt to become imaginatively self-focused, as happens in "The Grave" and in other stories. In "The Fig Tree," for example, Miranda calculates the "signs" of death and obsessively buries small dead animals she encounters. When the chirping of frogs convinces Miranda that she has buried a live chick in the opening of the story, she suffers dramatically with her guilt until a scientific explanation from her Aunt Eliza absolves her (361). In "The Circus," the other children coax her to feel guilty for ruining Dicey's afternoon at the circus with what they view as Miranda's whimsical hysteria (345). "The Grave" and "The Fig Tree" concur in showing us that Miranda "hated dolls" and "never played with them" except to deprive them of their clothes and wigs to dress the kittens.[6] Indeed, what Miranda notices and adores are baby animals. In "The Circus," the other children taunt her by playing up exactly what she will regret having missed: "darling little monkeys" riding on "wonderful little ponies" and a "baby elephant" (346). In "The Fig Tree," her father distracts her from crying by promising "about forty fresh kittens" when they arrive at the farm, and we are told that "her usual interests" are "the kittens and other little animals on the place, pigs, chickens, rabbits, anything at all so it was a baby and would let her pet and feed it" (360).[7]

## Reading "The Grave"

"The Grave" opens "one burning day" in 1903 when Paul, age twelve, and Miranda, nine, are hunting on family land soon after their grandmother's death (*Collected* 362). By the terms of her will, a part of the family farm is to be sold, and because the sale "happened to include" a family cemetery of "about twenty graves," the narrator tells us, it "was necessary to take up the bodies and bury them again" (362) in the town's "big new" cemetery where the grandmother is buried. Among the remains to be moved are those of the grandfather.

The grandmother's death and the sale of the land have altered Paul and Miranda's social status.

Aware of their déclassé status, the children steal into the cemetery as trespassers to inspect the "graves lying open and empty," a series of "pits all shaped alike with such purposeful accuracy" (362). Graves discovered "lying open and empty" echoes biblically, but the image of Paul and Miranda confronting these signs in that familiar but newly alienated place, where each empty grave confirms an erasure of family ties, custom, and ownership, stifles the echo. The fact of death, the family's beliefs and rituals connected to dying and death, the grandmother's living actions in that regard, and the legal provisions she willed to be enacted after her death gave shape, meaning, and point to life—her life, the family's, and the children's. The destination sitting in the title suggests that kind of power. But neither of the children is touched by awe or grief or feels humbled in mind or spirit by the weight of "the grave" or by their connections to twenty or so dead family members. Aware that some "special, suitable emotion" should come to them under the circumstances, they can only summon "an agreeable thrill of wonder" as they gaze upon a site of prospective adventure (362). They share, nonetheless, "a small disappointment at the entire commonplaceness" of open graves and the new knowledge that an empty grave is "just a hole in the ground" (363), perceptions that suggest an impending comeuppance.

The likelihood of an approaching reversal strengthens when Miranda, beckoned by an "agreeable thrill of wonder," abruptly "leap[s] into the pit that had held her grandfather's bones" (363). The reality of "pits" and the idea of "bones" in the landscape fail to touch Miranda, and the "purposeful accuracy" and "alike[ness]" that shape the graves contrast the aimlessness and ignorance that drive her reckless seeking. At the bottom of the "pit," Miranda, like "any young animal," begins "scratch[ing] around aimlessly and pleasurably" (363) in the dirt. Her primitive archeology produces "a lump of earth," "scooped up" and "weighed" in her hand, its "pleasantly sweet, corrupt smell" is an earthy, woodsy perfume. The little clod falls apart on her palm to reveal a small metal object, "a silver dove" of "hazel-nut" size, with outspread wings, "a neat fan-shaped tail," and a "deep round hollow" in the breast. From within the "pit," Miranda turns the dove "up to the fierce sunlight" and sees that the hole tooled in the breast is "cut in little whorls." The dove's shape, color, and tooling, prescribed by religious and funereal culture and purpose, spark neither recognition nor curiosity in Miranda, and she tightens her fingers around it and "scramble[s] out" of her grandfather's grave for the next phase of the adventure—showing her treasure to her brother—and she calls to Paul whose "head appear[s] smiling over the rim of another grave."

Paul calls out that he has found something, too, and "wave[s] a closed hand" toward her before they "r[un] to compare treasures" (363). Following a game to guess the other's treasure that ends in a "showdown" of revelation on open palms, Paul reveals his find: a "thin wide gold ring carved with intricate flowers and leaves." Miranda is "smitten" immediately, and Paul is keen on the dove because, he, in contrast to Miranda, knows—or thinks he knows—its purpose. They engage in "some little bickering" and exchange artifacts. With his "treasure" (367) in his hand, Paul asks Miranda (rhetorically), "Don't you know what this is?" and answers, "[A] screw head for a *coffin!* . . . " (363, Porter's emphasis). He proudly speculates on its rarity: "I'll bet nobody else in the world has one like this!" Miranda, unimpressed, merely "glanc[es] at it without covetousness," absorbed in the sight of the gold ring on her thumb, where it "fit[s] perfectly."

In addition to narrating a property trespass and a bit of grave-goods robbing, the story's opening movement develops commonalities and distinctions between Paul and Miranda. The narration of their discoveries, with its digressions and recalled events (363–365), shows Miranda to be sensual, capricious, ignorant, impatient, and pleasure seeking. Paul, on the other hand, appears to value knowledge, order, skill, and fair play and is generally more thoughtful and deliberate than Miranda. The story's opening also emphasizes ideas of shape, meaning, and point in descriptions of the cemetery, graves, dove, and ring. The dove representing the Holy Spirit is implied as having been an element of coffin hardware selected by the grandfather's widow. The ring's description makes it a wedding band, and the circumstances of its discovery in a family grave suggest Miranda as one of its rightful legatees, but her visceral response—being "smitten at the sight" of it—expresses only her desire to possess its value and sparkle. Never in play is the ring's symbolism for Miranda as the circle of her future life, shaped by spousal and maternal duty and devotion and familial legacy; its "fitt[ing] perfectly on her thumb" (the wrong digit) tends to un-say those traditional ideas. Neither the "silver" dove nor the "gold" ring is apparently felt to require further parsing.

As they leave the cemetery, a digression opens to describe Paul and Miranda's past "hunting" relationship (363–364). Paul's scrupulous attitude toward hunting contrasts Miranda's habitually inappropriate conduct, her ignorance and pretense, and her habitual lack of fair play towards Paul. She has often "lost her head" in "excitement at seeing birds whizz up suddenly before her face, or a rabbit leap across her very toes," and "almost without sighting," she has "flung her rifle up and pulled the trigger," but she "hardly ever hit any sort of mark" (364). Her conduct often "spoil[s]" Paul's shots, and she adds to the chaos by claiming whatever animal falls as her own. Miranda asserts that she hunts because she likes to "walk around," pull the trigger, and hear the gunfire (364). Paul's knowledge, experience, and skill mark him as Miranda's mentor and contrast Miranda's aimlessness, self-absorption, and casual injustice. When Paul tries to correct her, she goads him with a claim to "the first snake" they see, but it's a trifling claim because she has already "lost interest in shooting." Miranda only has eyes for the ring "shin[ing] with the serene purity of fine gold," and a second digression is folded into her "idl[e]" thoughts (364).

Miranda's contemplation of the ring on her thumb recalls events in the recent past, leading her to long for imagined luxury and despise her boyish clothes and pastimes. She recalls her shame when "bad-tempered" old women have chastised her attire and wants to return to the "farmhouse" to have "a good cold bath, dust herself [in secret] with plenty of Maria's violet talcum powder," put on her "thinnest, most becoming dress" and "sit in a wicker chair under the trees . . ." (365). Miranda has "vague stirrings," too, for "a grand way of living" that she lacks the resources to imagine. Lost in her reverie, Miranda "lag[s] far behind Paul," and is about to say that she's turning back for the house when a rabbit "leap[s]," and Miranda, in another performance of omission, uncharacteristically "let[s] Paul have [his shot at the rabbit] without dispute." The terse assertion "He killed it with one shot" shifts the narrative lens toward the story's second scene.

## Paul's *post-mortem*

Miranda catches up to Paul as he examines the carcass, and declaring his shot to have caught the rabbit "[r]ight through the head," he immediately begins skinning it "very cleanly and quickly" under Miranda's calm, admiring gaze (366). The mention of skinning leads to a brief digression that connects the act to Miranda's childish vanity of "always ha[ving] fur coats for her dolls" by means of a hired man's skill in tanning rabbit hides, for although Miranda "never cared much for her dolls[,] she liked seeing them in fur coats." She and Paul kneel over "the dead animal" placed on the ground, and Miranda looks on "admiringly" as he strips away the skin destined for a doll's fur coat: "The flayed flesh emerged dark scarlet, sleek, firm," and "with thumb and finger," Miranda traces "the long fine muscles with the slivery flat strips binding them to the joints." When Paul notices the "oddly bloated belly" and realizes that his kill is a pregnant doe rabbit, he offers Miranda a field autopsy of the abdomen. The narration emphasizes Paul's knowledge and skill and evokes Miranda's curiosity and wonder as she continues to kneel over the corpse, across from Paul, watching him work:

> Very carefully he slit open the thin flesh from the center ribs to the flanks, and a scarlet bag appeared. He slit again and pulled the bag open, and there lay a bundle of tiny rabbits each wrapped in a thin scarlet veil. The brother pulled these off and there they were, dark gray, their sleek wet down lying in minute even ripples, like a baby's head just washed, and their unbelievable small delicate ears folded close, their little blind faces almost featureless. (366)

This perspective is Miranda's; nonetheless, she speaks "under her breath" voicing a child's typical desire for inclusion: "Oh, I want to *see*" (Porter's emphasis). She "look[s] and look[s]," feeling, the narrator stipulates in a sentence loaded with significance, "excited but not frightened, for she was accustomed to the sight of animals killed in hunting." In this *un*accustomed instance though, Miranda was "filled with pity and astonishment and a kind of shocked delight in the wonderful little creatures [. . . because] they were so pretty." Still anxious to "see" and avid to "know," Miranda reaches in and touches "one of them ever so carefully," unaware, it seems, that they are already dead, and with a preface of surprised dismay, she reports, "Ah, there's blood running over them" and begins to tremble "*without knowing why*" (emphasis added). Miranda's visceral alteration betrays a disruption in the nature of her perception based on her touch and the sight of "blood running over them" near her fingers. The quick calculus of touching and seeing and pronouncing her conclusion—death, euphemistically declared in "blood running"—alters Miranda's view of the fetuses, and it seems she regains her feet at that point, distancing herself from what has been converted from "wonderful" and "pretty" into a "bloody heap" (367) of uncomfortable implications. Following about nineteen lines of stream of consciousness narrative, magical claims to knowledge, character-developing asides, and telling recollections (366–367), we find Miranda on her feet, "quietly and terribly agitated," holding her rifle (again) "under her arm" (367). True to her age, nature, and rearing, Miranda has identified the closest link between herself and the dead rabbits: she connects her vanity in "lik[ing] to see" rabbit-fur coats on her dolls with the dead rabbit "babies," and it gives her the fantods, as did her false sense of guilt for the death of a chick in "The Fig Tree."

The narration referred to above, opening at Miranda's "beg[inning] to tremble," asserts that despite the setback, she "[y]et" desires "most deeply to see and to know" (366) and quickly feels that by seeing, she "ha[s] known all along" because "her former ignorance fade[s]," and she "ha[s] always known just this"—a "just this" that nobody "ha[s] ever told her anything outright" about. The silence around Miranda on "just this" flows awkwardly into her being habitually "rather unobservant of the animal life around her because she [is] so *accustomed* to [seeing] animals," both those "killed in hunting," mentioned just above, as well as living animals that she finds "*not very interesting*" but "simply disorderly and unaccountably rude in their habits" (366, emphasis added).[8] Miranda's alleged lack of observation and indifference where animals are concerned tends to undermine her anxious claims to want to "see" in order to "know." Miranda next recalls that Paul "spok[e]"—evidently, when he says, "It was going to have young ones"—"as if he had known about everything all along," and as if he "may have seen all this [presumably, fetuses inside a dead animal's body] before," though he "had never said a word to her."

The narrator next dials back Miranda's degree of enlightenment, saying she "[knows] now *a part at least* of what [Paul] knew" and shifting her means of knowledge to magic: "She understood *a little* of the secret formless intuitions in her own mind and body, which had been clearing up, taking form so gradually and steadily she had not realized that she was learning what she had to know" (366–367, emphasis added). Paul's voice, pitched low, interrupts the narration, and his speech is described from Miranda's perspective in contrary-to-fact-terms, "as if he were talking about something forbidden" (367). Paul begins to explain that the fetuses "were just about ready to be born," and when he falters over "born," Miranda supplies familiar parallels: "I know [. . .] like kittens. I know, like babies." While she claims rote bits of knowledge in clipped comparisons, the important thing Miranda "know[s]" now is that the fetuses are dead, never to be born, and she gazes "down at the bloody heap," its particular shapes effaced by her altered view, and she speaks, "quietly and terribly agitated": "I don't want the skin. I won't have it." In a childish echo of matriarchal repudiation, Miranda renounces her role in the economy of doll fur coats.

In the final movement of the rabbit (mis)adventure, Paul "burie[s]" the fetuses within the mother's body, wraps the skin around them, and hurriedly "hid[es] her away" beneath a clump of sage bushes (367). This is the story's third grave-of-sorts, but rather than casual buried treasure, guilt and fear are hidden away. Returning to Miranda "at once," Paul shares with her his only worry in connection with the adventure: that she will "tell Dad." From Paul's caution, we may suppose his experience with Miranda suggests that she will be voluble in her distress and get him into trouble. But whatever extreme conclusion Paul must be envisioning their Dad—fearful of female contamination—leaping to, Paul has not shown Miranda about "sex."

## Treasure in the Grave Goods

On another "very hot day," "nearly twenty years" later, Miranda is making her way through the sensory chaos of a "foreign" market in the environs of Mexico City (367).[9] A tray of colorful candies shaped like small animals—"birds, baby chicks, baby rabbits, lambs"—unexpectedly "held up before her" in the hand of a native vendor prompts "the episode of that far-off day" to "lea[p] from its burial place" (367). For Miranda, the unexpected visual assault of colorful diminutive shapes amid the market's olfactory melting pot of over-warm fresh meat, wilting vegetables and flowers, and "vanilla, maybe" filling the air bring her to a halt before the tray of colored shapes, "reasonlessly horrified" by a vision from an afternoon that "she had remembered always until now vaguely as the time she and her brother had found treasure in the opened graves" (367). The passage runs over with Proustian implications and the Japanese flower analogy from *Swann's Way*, but unlike Proust's "I," Porter's narrator is unspecific: "[W]ithout warning, plain and clear in its true colors as if she looked through a frame upon a scene that had not stirred nor changed since the moment it happened, the episode of that far-off day leaped from its burial place before her mind's eye" (367).[10] The vendor's gesture and the material furnishings suggest the paten of the Eucharist, its wafers metamorphosed into diminutive colored sugar animals—including a lamb—offered up to Miranda as communicant.

Miranda's horror is "reasonless"—irrational in the place and time where she finds herself—perhaps because in recalling, decades afterward, the sight of rabbits "killed in hunting," Miranda might have expected to be beyond "horror." Miranda had lost her soldier–lover,

Adam, to influenza in 1918, only barely escaping death herself, and awakening to the knowledge—and guilt—that Adam had become infected while caring for her.[11] But the "horror" that assaults Miranda's senses "among the puddles and crushed refuse of a market street in a [. . .] strange country" belongs to the nine-year-old child, who began to tremble and rose, "terribly agitated," moving away from a sight that weighed too heavily on her conscience. Miranda's alarm finds its remedy when a second vision—clear, detailed, and serene—"instantly" effaces the "dreadful" one (367–368), setting Paul's forgotten young face before her as he was on that day, "standing again in the blazing sunshine, again twelve years old, a pleased sober smile in his eyes" (368). Miranda's attention moves to the "silver dove" that Paul turns "over and over in his hands" as one might handle a rosary. Paul's demeanor and his connection to the silver dove erase Miranda's unreasoning horror, and with that intimation, the last of the Miranda stories ends.

Miranda's sense of her vision of Paul is yet another element of the story that Porter must have regarded as needing only a gesture. The dove in Paul's hands and the "pleased sober smile in his eyes" speak to Miranda's sudden terror, returning an ineffable message of peace, love, and reassurance. If Miranda sees and knows something now, it is because she feels the message as keenly as her nine-year-old self felt shock and guilt over the death of "baby rabbits." Her second vision arrives as a reminder, an ethereal sticky note conveying a once-familiar lesson that has been put aside and forgotten.

The Christianity of Paul and Miranda's fictional milieu is essentially the one that Porter recognized, claimed, doubted, yearned toward, or disdained through her long life. In life or fiction, the shape and color of the dove from the grave represent but one possibility: the grace and gifts of the Holy Spirit, the "comforter" that "will teach you all things and make you remember all that I have told you."[12] In the churches and grave yards of Mexico, Colorado, Louisiana, and Texas, the geographies of Miranda's life, and on the coffin of a Cumberland Presbyterian, a Kentucky Baptist, a Texas Methodist, or a Louisiana or Texas Catholic, the denominations that figure into the Miranda stories, the dove descending to earth with its head and beak outstretched in profile signifies the Holy Spirit. At the Annunciation to the Virgin, at Jesus' baptism, and in representations of the Trinity, its shape tells its meaning and point. The crisis of conscience Miranda suffers and buries following her intimate encounter with the cost of rabbit-fur doll coats to little lifeless rabbit fetuses finds resolution—grace, forgiveness, perhaps an understanding of some ineffable truth about life and death—in a bright vision of her brother handling the dove in an easy, secure, familiar way. Paul's face and demeanor offer Miranda spiritual peace, and she appears to be receptive to it. A hindsight reading of this vision from Miranda's nine-year-old thinking is that Paul is finally sharing what he "had known about everything all along" but had never told her (366).

Whether her view of Paul and the dove and its intimations of peace have lasting value for Miranda or will soon be buried, like her childhood memory—or whether she will remember and vacillate between the starkness of the horrifying vision and the comforting reassurance of grace—we get no word. That the text fails to provide an explicit certainty may make an unsatisfying ending for some readers. The answer we seek in our questions about the closing scene lies, so I think, in the convergence of shape, meaning, and point that, for Miranda, produces a moment of epiphany, Porter's "flash of light" in which we "see what a certain event really meant, what it was trying to tell us."[13]

**Notes**

1 Porter's fiction is cited here from *The Collected Stories of Katherine Anne Porter* (*Collected*) of 1965. The text of "The Grave" is also available online courtesy of the *Virginia Quarterly Review* (vqronline.org/fiction/grave). Porter's non-fiction is cited here from *The Collected Essays and Occasional Writings* (*Essays*), prepared by Porter, or from *Collected Stories and Other Writings* (Ed. Unrue) and is indicated accordingly in Works Cited.

2 *Cf.* Acts 9:3–19. George Cheatham rejects this particular parallel ("Literary" 114).

3 Barbara Thompson's interview with Porter elicited this response. The interview first appeared in *The Paris Review* in 1963 and is reprinted elsewhere. Myron Mandell (Mike) Liberman comments on Porter's assertion (43). See also Porter's June–July 1953 correspondence with University of Colorado Classics professor Donald Sutherland edited as "Ole Woman River" and Porter on "symbols" in James Ruoff's account (64–65).

4 The letter is a holding of the University of Maryland's Libraries' Special Collections and University Archives that include Katherine Anne Porter papers (Letter from Porter to Glenway Wescott, January 12, 1942. Box 39, Folder 1, Item 18 [Mixed Materials]). Miss Porter is given to continuous strings of adjectives, phrases, and clauses unrestrained by punctuation, and she uses ellipses on occasion. Rather than insert an intrusive [*sic*] at each instance, the reader may consider the text as presented to reflect the original unless I have erred in the transcribing; only bracketed punctuation and morphemes are meant as editorial additions.

5   For instances of the father's "babying" Miranda, see "The Circus" (347) and "The Fig Tree" (356–357).
6   See "The Fig Tree" (357–358) and "The Grave" (366).
7   Porter addresses other childhood sentiments concerned with animals in "St. Augustine and the Bullfight" (97–98).
8   The author apparently felt this reference to animals' "habits" to need no enlargement; it's not obscure but simply enough a euphemistic reference to what animals do around the yard and in their pens through the day: defecate and urinate whenever and wherever, and sometimes sniff at or eat the result. Some critics go in another direction: Corinne Andersen, for example, describes animals mating as "fornicat[ion]" (7–8) and credits Miranda with having "seen animals fornicate" to support a Freudian reading. DeMouy writes, "Miranda's dim awareness of sexuality and fertility among the farm animals expands to include an understanding of the reproduction of human life" (140).
9   Porter was in Mexico City for the Feast of the Virgin on December 12, 1920 and published an English-language article on her visit to the Basilica for *El Heraldo Mexicano*'s edition the following day. See *Essays* for "The Fiesta of Guadalupe," assigned a 1923 date without notice of its 1920 appearance, along with Thomas Walsh's related article.
10  See Proust (65–69). In any edition or translation, the final half-dozen or so pages of the opening chapter presents the passage cited. Miranda is evidently meant to envision, in a fast-forward flash, the entire "episode" of shooting, skinning, and eviscerating the rabbit, and discovering the kits are dead.
11  See *Pale Horse, Pale Rider* (313–317).
12  In the Synoptic Gospels, as well as in the Book of John, the Holy Spirit descending to Jesus at his baptism arrives in the form of a dove (Matthew 3:16; Mark 1:8–10; Luke 3:22; and John 1:32). For Jesus' description of the Holy Spirit, see John 14:26. The KJV is the Bible likely to have been used by Texas and Kentucky Presbyterians, Methodists, and Baptists in Porter's time. For a Catholic Bible, see Douay-Rheims (1899, U.S. edition), which retains the Greek ὁ Παράκλητος : the Paraclete [helper, comforter, counselor], who "will teach you all things, and cause you to recall all the things whatsoever I have said to you." The Holy Spirit in depictions of the Trinity, at Jesus' baptism, and descending to the Virgin at the Annunciation is generally shown as a dove with the outspread wings and fan-shaped tail described in "The Grave."
13  See "St. Augustine and the Bullfight" (94).

**Works Cited**

Andersen, Corinne. "'Instantly upon this thought the dreadful vision faded': The False Epiphany of Katherine Anne Porter's 'The Grave.'" *South Central Review* 33.3 (2016): 1–17.

Brooks, Cleanth. "On 'The Grave.'" *Yale Review* 55 (1966): 275–279. Rpt. Robert Penn Warren, ed. *Katherine Anne Porter: A Collection of Critical*

*Essays*. Twentieth Century Views (series). Englewood Cliffs, NJ: Prentice Hall, 1979. 112–116.
Cheatham, George. "Death and Repetition in Porter's Miranda Stories." *American Literature* 61.4 (1989): 610–624.
—. "Literary Criticism, Katherine Anne Porter's Consciousness, and the Silver Dove." *Studies in Short Fiction* 25.2 (1988): 109–115.
Curley, Daniel. "Treasure in 'The Grave.'" *Modern Fiction Studies* 9.4 (Winter 1963–1964): 377–384.
DeMouy, Jane Krause. *Katherine Anne Porter's Women: The Eye of Her Fiction*. Austin: U of Texas P, 1983.
Givner, Joan. "A Fine Day of Homage to Porter [*The Dallas Morning News*. May 23, 1976]." *Conversations*. Ed. Givner. 189–191.
—, ed. *Katherine Anne Porter: Conversations* (*Conversations*). Jackson: U of Mississippi P, 1987.
—. *Katherine Anne Porter: A Life*. Rev. ed. Athens: U of Georgia P, 1991. (1st ed. New York: Simon & Schuster, 1982.)
Liberman, M. M. *Katherine Anne Porter's Fiction*. Detroit: Wayne UP, 1971.
Sister M. Joselyn, O.S.B. [Eileen Baldeshwiler]. "'The Grave' as Lyrical Short Story." *Studies in Short Fiction* 1.3 (1964): 216–221.
Porter, Katherine Anne. "Autobiographical: The Land That Is Nowhere." Ed. Darlene Harbour Unrue. *Collected Stories and Other Writings*. New York: Library of America, 2008. 1010–1016.
—. "The Circus." *Collected*. 343–348.
—. *The Collected Essays and Occasional Writings of Katherine Anne Porter* (*Essays*). Boston: Houghton Mifflin, 1970.
—. *The Collected Stories of Katherine Anne Porter* (*Collected*). New York: Harcourt, 1965. 362–368.
—. *Collected Stories and Other Writings*. Ed. Darlene Harbour Unrue. New York: Library of America, 2008.
—. *The Downward Path to Wisdom*. *Collected*. 369–386.
—. "The Fiesta of Guadalupe." *Essays*. Boston: Houghton Mifflin, 1970. 394–308.
—. "The Fig Tree." *Collected*. 352–362.
—. "The Grave." *The Best American Short Stories 1936: and the Yearbook of the American Short Story*. Ed. Edward Joseph O'Brien. Boston: Houghton Mifflin, 1936. 245–250.
—. "The Grave." *Collected*. 362–368.
—. "The Grave." *The Leaning Tower and Other Stories*. New York: Library of America, 1944. 69–78.
—. "The Grave." *The Virginia Quarterly Review* 11 (January–April 1935): 177–183.
—. *Katherine Anne Porter: Conversations*. See Givner, Joan, ed.
—. "Ole Woman River: A Correspondence with Katherine Anne Porter." *Essays*. 271–283.
—. *Pale Horse, Pale Rider*. *Collected*. 269–317.
—. "St. Augustine and the Bullfight." *Essays*. 91–101.
—. *See also* Ruoff, James; Thompson, Barbara.
Proust, Marcel. *À la recherche du temps perdu I: Du côte de chez Swann*. Paris: Gallimard, 1919.

Rooke, Constance, and Bruce Wallis. "Myth and Epiphany in Porter's 'The Grave.'" *Studies in Short Fiction* 15.3 (1975): 269–275.

Ruoff, James. "Katherine Anne Porter Comes to Kansas [1961]." Ed. Joan Givner. *Conversations*. 61–68.

Stout, Janis P. *South by Southwest: Katherine Anne Porter and the Burden of Texas History*. Tuscaloosa, AL: U of Alabama P, 2013.

Tanner, James T. F. *The Texas Legacy of Katherine Anne Porter*. Texas Writers Series 3. Denton, TX: U of North Texas P, 1990.

Thompson, Barbara (Barbara Thompson Mueenuddin Davis), interviewer. "Katherine Anne Porter: The Art of Fiction 29." *The Paris Review* 29 (1963): 87–114. Rpt. "Katherine Anne Porter." *Writers at Work:* The Paris Review *Interviews*, Second Series. Intro. Van Wyck Brooks. 137–163. Rpt. *Conversations*. Ed. Givner. 78–98.

Titus, Mary. "'Mingled Sweetness and Corruption': Katherine Anne Porter's 'The Fig Tree' and 'The Grave.'" *South Atlantic Review* 53.2 (1988): 111–125.

Unrue, Darlene Harbour. *Truth and Vision in Katherine Anne Porter's Fiction*. Athens: U of Georgia P, 1985.

—. *See also* Porter, *Collected Stories and Other Writings*.

Walsh, Thomas. "That deadly female accuracy of vision: Katherine Anne Porter and *El Heraldo de Mexico*." *Journal of Modern Literature* 16.4 (1990): 635–643.

Wimsatt, Mary Ann. "Katherine Anne Porter (1890–1980)." Ed. Blanche H. Gelfant and Lawrence Graver. *The Columbia Companion to the Twentieth-Century American Short Story*. New York: Columbia UP, 2000. 456–462.

Yeager, Patricia. "The Poetics of Birth." Ed. Domna C. Stanton. *Discourses of Sexuality from Aristotle to AIDS*. Ann Arbor: U of Michigan P, 1992. 262–296.

# 12
# New Orleans' St. Louis Cemetery No. 1

## Judith H. Bonner

Visitors to New Orleans soon notice its cemeteries of aboveground burial vaults that Mark Twain called "Cities of the Dead." Early French colonists learned quickly that the swampy soil in the New Orleans region made underground burial impractical because coffins and bodies would resurface during periods of high water, and they subsequently adopted aboveground tombs. Aboveground tombs in the European tradition were introduced into the city principally by Spanish colonizers whose tombs were constructed of brick, covered with stucco, and lime-washed in white or various colors in keeping with the Spanish custom.

The oldest existing and most mysterious cemetery in the city is St. Louis Cemetery No. 1, the site of the cover photograph. It was established by Spanish royal decree on August 14, 1789. Built at the edge of the French Quarter to replace the overcrowded St. Peter Street Cemetery that no longer exists, St. Louis Cemetery No. 1 is located at 425 Basin Street between Conti and St. Louis and is bordered by Tremé St. to the north, parallel to Basin. The cemetery is entirely enclosed, with its boundaries partly composed of wall vaults constructed in the Spanish style. Along the Basin St. side, for example, are "oven vaults," so-called because their arched brick faces recall ovens. In New Orleans' subtropical climate, the oven vault indeed works like an oven, decomposing bodies rapidly, usually within a year, after which families place the remains of the deceased into a muslin bag set at the rear of the tomb to allow for the next interment. Family tombs house successive generations, and should a death occur within a year of a previous burial, local cemeteries offer the family a temporary vault to house the remains of the more recently deceased until space is available in the desired tomb.

Historically, New Orleans has been dominantly Catholic, and today the city remains culturally Catholic. French colonists introduced *La Toussaint*, All Saints Day, celebrated on November 1st, to the city. The day has long been recognized as a state holiday, with offices and public businesses closed. On this annual day of remembrance, families honor those gone before them with prayer and dedication. Traditionally, they spent the day in the cemetery picnicking and tending to the family tomb, trimming its overgrowth and repairing crumbling plaster and resealing it with whitewash—a mixture of lime and water. As children helped tend the family tomb, they learned of their heritage and genealogy through the carved inscriptions commemorating those buried there. In the nineteenth century, handmade funerary art called *immortelles* were placed on the tomb. *Immortelles* were elaborate constructions that originated in France, sometimes made in the shape of wreaths with such durable materials as glass beads and wire. Often, immortelles bore sentimental messages dedicated to the deceased family member. To this day,

*Wording on the reverse of this postcard photograph describes the scene as a group of women "[d]ecorating graves in St. Louis Cemetery on All Saints' Day 1900," but the site of the photo may be St. Roch's Cemetery rather than St Louis No. 1, and name of the photographer and exact date are unknown. Dover Publications features the card, along with this text, as one of a booklet entitled* Thirty-two Picture Postcards of Old New Orleans *(1979) and notes that it appears there "Courtesy Koch and Wilson, Architects." Though the photo is regarded by all as being in the public domain, the image is used with the blessing of Koch and Wilson, Architects, of New Orleans, and of Dover Publications.*

families honor their dead by placing wreaths, bouquets, and candles on the tomb.[1]

St. Louis Cemetery No. 1 has 700 tombs, and more than 100,000 people are buried within its boundaries. Areas were once designated for white and free African American Catholics and Protestants and for people of color.[2] Legendary and historical figures—aristocrats, diplomats, politicians, pirates, soldiers, authors—and citizens at large are its permanent residents. New Orleans' first mayor, Étienne de Boré, a pioneer in the sugar industry, is entombed here. Homer Plessy, the plaintiff who challenged the separate-but-equal doctrine in the U.S. Supreme Court case Plessy vs. Ferguson in 1896, was buried here in 1925. The most storied person buried in St. Louis Cemetery No. 1 is the "notorious 'Voodoo Queen,'" Marie Laveau,[3] and although the cemetery offers admittance only with a licensed tour guide, there are those who, to this day, manage to slip in and mark Laveau's tomb with three consecutive Xs—for good luck, certain spells, or personal requests. The cemetery allows a small number of new burials and continues to fascinate citizens and visitors alike.

# Tomb No. 577

## Elizabeth Moore Willingham

The tomb designated as No. 577 in St. Louis No. 1 is the large three-vault structure that dominates the front-cover photograph.[4] This view, taken several years before the tomb's restoration, reveals components of its underlying structure and serves as an example of St. Louis No. 1's "tangible record of a continuously developing cultural history."[5] No. 577 also functions, in company with its neighbors, as witness to the effects of climate and neglect on monuments and the landscape. While the aboveground burial structures and their ornaments may suffer acute blows from major weather events, a consistent lack of human intervention, along with the area's subtropical climate, means ongoing losses to inscriptions, carvings, artistic embellishments, tablets, and structural features. In extreme cases, tombs have had to be razed.

No. 577 is made of the stucco-covered red brick described above by Judith Bonner. Several runs of brick form the base that supports the tomb's walls and its high, ornamental pediment, raising No. 577's profile above those of most other structures in the frame. Its generous triple-vault accommodation also sets the tomb apart in physical dimensions.

Yet in the style and spirit of many of its neighbors, No. 577 is a modestly ornamented "house tomb." Like the house tombs of ancient Roman burials, those of nineteenth-century U.S. cemeteries suggest that loved ones reside in "houses" where they are reunited in death. Like some Roman examples, No. 577 and similar tombs in New Orleans may house the remains and honor the memories of multiple generations related by blood or marriage, along with their close associates, a practice that Judith Bonner points to above. The tomb's three original tablets, inscribed in English and French, memorialize New Orleanians surnamed Folger, Hunter, Malard, and Moore.[6] The flowing inscriptions also confirm that prominent French-speaking inhabitants of the city might follow the Spanish custom of aboveground entombment.

No. 577's rectangular shape, symmetrical architecture, straight-line geometry, and pragmatic details give it a classical sensibility and speak to its architect's attention to elements that would protect the tomb from adverse weather effects. The designer's foresight has served that purpose remarkably well during the tomb's nearly 200 years of exposure.[7] Perhaps half-a-dozen years after this photograph was made, a process of restoration and preservation was undertaken, and by June 6, 2011, the badly damaged center tablet seen in the photo had been replaced with a plain white-marble tablet lacking inscriptions.[8] The muddy, puddle-prone path had been graded and laid with crushed stone, and missing brickwork and other materials were replaced. One of the tomb's graceful touches, a large ornament using a central Greek cross encircled by a wreath of olive leaves, was restored to its place, its ribbon-ends unfurling across the ornamental gable. The modified pediment and entablature, the tomb's many moldings, and its roof were again intact following these efforts, and exposed bricks were plastered over with a natural red-clay-pigmented stucco. These efforts speak to the ingrained New Orleans spirit of contending with things of the earth to restore the art and crafts of the old city.

At the time of Mardi Gras 2016 (January 23–February 9), the plain marble tablet covering the center opening remained secure, as did the surrounding crushed-stone pathway. The tomb's post-restoration surfaces had acquired stains of patina, suggesting that the tomb had resumed its visible process of graceful aging.

## Notes

1 This quotation and other information on New Orleans' funeral and death customs appear at Louisiana State Museum Online Exhibits.
2 Peter Dedek writes that in 1822 the city demolished part of St. Louis No. 1's Protestant section to lay a road. Christ's Church (Episcopalian) then established Girod Street Cemetery for Protestant burials (34–35). A small "Protestant Section," noticeable for its ground level tombs, exists today along Tremé and Conti in St. Louis No. 1. See also the New Orleans Catholic Cemeteries' online presence for its historical account of St. Louis No. 1.
3 The plaque attached to Marie Laveau's "reputed burial place" in St. Louis Cemetery No. 1 records this phrase.
4 Judith Bonner accorded me access and direction to THNOC's databases, an essential source of material on this tomb. Tombs in THNOC's 1981 survey of structures in St. Louis No. 1 are identified numerically.
5 The apt characterization of the cemetery's cultural legacy comes from the Dead Space Collaborative Studio's report (28).
6 The tomb is called "the Malard tomb" in some references. See Leonard Huber's essay, for example.
7 "Nearly two hundred years" is speculative but conservative. The earliest death whose dates remained legible as memorialized on the tomb at THNOC's 1981 survey is recorded as August 13, 1819, and the next is September 29, 1836. Other years of death that were legible in 1981 are recorded at mid-century or later. It may be that the tomb as we see it or some portion of it dates to one of those early burials, but it is possible that it was erected or completed sometime after one or both deaths, and the remains of those family members were relocated to lie there.
8 I am grateful to Diona Dickerson for sharing her 2011 photo.

## Works Cited

Dead Space Collaborative Studio. *Dead Space: Defining the New Orleans Creole Cemetery: A Site Conservation and Management Plan for St. Louis I Cemetery*. Philadelphia: U of Pennsylvania, Department of Historic Preservation and Landscape Architecture, Graduate School of Fine Arts, 2001.
Dedek, Peter. *The Cemeteries of New Orleans: A Cultural History*. Baton Rouge: Louisiana State UP, 2017.
Huber, Leonard V. "New Orleans Cemeteries: A Brief History." Ed. Mary Louise Christovich. *New Orleans Architecture. Volume III: The Cemeteries*. Gretna, LA: Pelican, 1974. 3–62.
Louisiana State Museum Online Exhibits. "Antebellum Louisiana I: Disease, Death, and Mourning." *The Cabildo: Two Centuries of Louisiana History*. Baton Rouge: Louisiana Department of Culture, Recreation and Tourism, 2018.
New Orleans Catholic Cemeteries [nolacatholiccemeteries.org]. New Orleans: The Archdiocese of New Orleans, 2022.

# Appendix
## Mary at the Foot of the Cross

This text of "Mary at the Foot of the Cross" is No. 42 in Karen Saupe's *Middle English Marian Lyrics* (1998) and one of eighteen versions she edits on this theme. Dr. Saupe's text appears here with her permission and that of Medieval Institute Publications at Western Michigan University in Kalamazoo.

Read aloud, the lyric may be fairly well understood by English speakers. Brief glosses are given in order of appearance by stanza as footnotes. Glosses arise from Dr. Saupe's text (94–96) and from entries at Michigan's MEC, the CMED, and MED. Errors and omissions are the editor's.

1.
Of alle women that ever were borne
That berys childur, abyde and se
How my son liggus me beforne
Upon my kne, takyn fro tre.                                4
Your childur ye dawnse upon your kne
With laghyng, kyssyng, and mery chere:
Behold my childe, beholde now me,
For now liggus ded my dere son, dere.[1]                   8

2.
O woman, woman, wel is thee,
Thy childis cap thu dose upon;
Thu pykys his here, beholdys his ble;
Thu wost not wele when thu hast done.                      12
But ever alas I make my mone
To se my sonnys hed as hit is here:
I pyke owt thornys be on and on[,]
For now liggus ded my dere son, dere.[2]                   16

---

1  *berys*–bear. *childur*–children. *abyde*–stay. *se*–see. *now*–at the present time. *liggus*–lies. *beforne*–(adv. loc.) before, in front (of me), on/over (my knees). *kne*–knee(s). *fro*–from. *tre*–(the) tree (*i.e.,* the cross). *ye*–you. *dawnse*–dance, dandle. *laghyng*–laughing. *kyssyng*–kissing. *mery*–merry. *chere*–joy. *dere*–precious, costly.

2  *wel*–fine. *thee*–you. *childis*–child's. *thu*–thou, you; used in various genres to address a reader. *does upon*–does put on. *pickys*–comb. *here*–hair. *beholdys*–gaze upon. *ble*–fairness, brightness of skin, complexion, face. *wost*– knowest. *not*–nothing/nought. *wele*–well/much. *alas*–an intense exclamation of woe.

3.
O woman, a chaplet choysyn thu has
Thy childe to were, hit dose thee gret likyng[.]
Thu pynnes hit on with gret solas;
And I sitte with my son sore wepyng.                    20
His chaplet is thornys sore prickyng;
His mouth I kys with a carfull chere.
I sitte wepyng, and thu syngyng,
For now liggus ded my dere son, dere.[3]                24

4.
O woman, loke to me agayne[,]
That playes and kisses your childur pappys[.]
To se my son I have gret payne,
In his brest so gret gap is,                            28
And on his body so mony swappys.
With blody lippys I kis hym here;
Alas, full hard me thynk me happys,
For now liggus ded my dere son, dere.[4]                32

5.
O woman, thu takis thi childe be the hand
And seis, "My son, gif me a stroke!"
My sonnys handis ar sore bledand,
To loke on hym me list not layke.                       36
His handis he suffyrd for thi sake
Thus to be boryd with nayle and speyre;
When thu makes myrth, gret sorow I make,
For now liggus ded my dere son, dere.[5]                40

---

*make my mone*–I lament, grieve. *se*–see. *sonnys*–son's. *hed*–head. *hit*–it. *pyke*–pick. *owt*–out. *thornys*–thorns. *be*–by. *on and on*–one by one.

3  *chaplet*–wreath worn on the head, garland. *chapelet of thornes*–the crown/wreath of thorns. *choysyn*–chosen, selected. *were*–wear. *hit*–it, the *chaplet*. *dose*–does, brings, makes. *gret*–great, much. *likyng*–pleasure. *pynnes (on)*: secure, attach to, pin on. *solas*–pleasure, joy. *sitte*–sit. *sore* (adv. of intensity, associated with suffering) painfully, agonizingly. *wepying*–weeping. *thornys*–(of) thornes. *sore prickyng*–painfully piercing, stabbing. *kys*–kiss. *carfull*–full of woe, sorrow. *chere*–face. *thu*–thou, you. *syngng*–singing.

4  *loke*–look, attend. *childur*–children's. *pappys*–breast. *se*–see. *payne*–pain. *gap*–wound, opening. *so mony*–innumerable. *swappys*–slashes, blows, strokes. *lippys*–lips. *me*–I (the first person nominative pronoun). *kis*–kiss. *hym*–him. *ful*–very. *me thynk*–I think, judge. *me happys*–my fate.

5  *thu*–thou, you. *takis*–take(s). *thi*–thy, your. *be*–by. *seis*–you say. *gif*–give. *stroke*–caress (Saupe notes here a pun on the punishing blows given Jesus). *loke*–look, gaze. *me list not layke*– lit. my desire not likes; i.e., I have no pleasure (in —).

6.
Beholde, women, when that ye play
And hase your childur on knees daunsand:
Ye fele ther fete, so fete are thay,
And to your sight ful wel likand.  44
But the most fyngur of any hande
Thorow my sonnys fete I may put here
And pulle hit out sore bledand,
For now liggus ded my dere son, dere.⁶  48

7.
Therfor, women, be town and strete,
Your childur handis when ye beholde,
Theyr brest, theire body[,] and theire fete
Then gode hit were on my son thynk ye wolde,  52
How care has made my hert full colde,
To se my son, with nayle and speyre,
With scourge and thornys manyfolde
Woundit and ded, my dere son, dere.⁷  56

8.
Thu hase thi son full holl and sounde,
And myn is ded upon my kne;
Thy childe is lawse, and myn is bonde,
Thy childe is an life and myn ded is he;  60
Whi was this oght but for thee?
For my childe trespast never here.
Me thynk ye be holdyne to wepe with me
For now liggus ded my dere son, dere.⁸  64

---

    *handis*–hands. *suffryd*–allowed, permitted. *thi*–thy, your. *boryd*–bored, pierced. *nayle*–nail. *speyre*–spear. *thu*–thou, you. *makes myrth*–amuse (yourselves), are joyful.

6  *beholde*–gaze at. *hase*–have. *daunsand*–dancing, bouncing. *fele*–touch, feel. *fete*–feet. *so*–(adv. of degree) + *fete*–very comely, skilful (as *fet, fait*). *thay*–they (the child's feet). *ful wel*–completely (superlative). *likand*–beautiful. *most*–largest. *fyngur*–finger. *thorow*–through. *hit*–it (my finger). *sore bledand*–covered in blood, terribly bloodied.

7  *be*–(adv. loc) near, within (the town). *strete*–in public, on the road (from one town to another). *handis*–hands. *beholdys*–see, gaze upon. *ye*–you (all). *gode*–good. *hert*–heart. *scourge*–whip, lash. *manyfolde*–many times, in many places, greviously, terribly. *woundit*–wounded. A comma is suppressed from Saupe's text following *manyfolde*, read here as an adverb describing *woundit*.

8  *holl*–entire, healed. *sounde*–safe, secure. *myn*–mine. *lawse*–loose, free. *bonde*–bound, not free. *an life*–in life, living. *whi*–why. *oght*–anything. *trespast*–injured/wronged anyone, committed a wrong, broke the law. *holdyne*–charged,

9.
Wepe with me, both man and wyfe:
My childe is youres and lovys yow wele.
If your childe had lost his life,
Ye wolde wepe at every mele, 68
But for my sone wepe ye never a del.
If ye luf youres, myne has no pere;
He sendis youris both hup and hele,
And for yow dyed my dere son, dere.[9] 72

10.
Now alle wymmen that has your wytte
And sees my childe on my knees ded,
Wepe not for yours, but wepe for hit,
And ye shall have ful mycull mede. 76
He wolde ageyne for your luf blede
Rather or that ye damned were.
I pray yow alle, to hym take hede,
For now liggus ded my dere son, dere.[10] 80

11.
Fare wel, woman, I may no more
For drede of deth reherse his payne.
Ye may lagh when ye list, and I wepe sore,
That may ye se and ye loke to me agayne. 84
To luf my son and ye be fayne,
I wille luff yours with hert entere,
And he shall brynge your childur and yow sertayne
To blisse[,] wher is my dere son, dere.[11] 88
    *Explicit fabula.*

---

    obligated. *wepe*–weep, visibly or audibly mourn.

9  *wife*–wife. *lovys*–loves. *yow*–you. *mele*–meal, parts of the day. *del*–small degree, portion. *never a del*–not at all. *if*–(conditional) as much as. *luf*–love. *myn*–mine. *pere*–peer, equal. *sendis*–sends. *youris*–yours (your sons). *hup*–hope. *hele*–soundness, wellbeing. *dyed*–died.

10  *wytte*–good sense, wisdom. *hit*–it (the sight/fact of my dead son). *ful mycull*–perfect, fullest. *mede*–reward, gift. *ageyne*–again. *luf*–love. *or*–than. *alle*–all. *take hede*–listen, attend.

11  *may no more*–can (say, stand) no more. *drede*–dread. *rehearse*–continue to talk, describe. *list*–to will, to desire. *and*–though. *sore*–(adv. of intensity) bitterly, agonizingly. *that*–which (my weeping). *se*–see. *and*–if, should (you). *loke to*–seek me. *agayne*–again. *luf*–love. *and*–if, should (you). *fayne*–willing. *luff*–love. *hert entere*–all my heart, a full heart. *brynge*–bring. *sertayne*–certainly, without fail. *blisse*–heaven. *Explicit fabula*–the narrative (is [thus]) unfolded, laid open.

# Notes on Contributors

**Thomas Bonner, Jr.,** is Professor *Emeritus* at Xavier University of Louisiana, where he was W. K. Kellogg Professor and Chair of English for twenty years. He served as editor of *Xavier Review*, and executive editor for Xavier Review Press and has twice been Distinguished Visiting Professor at the United States Air Force Academy. In addition to *The Kate Chopin Companion with Chopin's Translations from French Fiction*, Bonner's books and monographs are concerned with William Faulkner, Edgar Allan Poe, and Southern fiction and poetry. Bonner's work on Kate Chopin began in 1969, and he is considered a pioneer in Chopin studies. In 2018, he published new essays on Chopin, along with a short story called "Léonce," inspired by Chopin's fiction, in *Parterre: New and Collected Poetry and Prose* (2018). His most recent book, edited with Judith Bonner, is their edition of William Spratling and William Faulkner's 1926 *Sherwood Anderson and Other Famous Creoles* (Gretna, Louisiana: Pelican Publishing, 2018). An early version of the essay published here was presented during a symposium at the Mabel Dodge Luhan House in Taos, New Mexico.

**Judith Bonner** is Senior Curator and Curator of Art for The Historic New Orleans Collection (THNOC) and publishes widely on Southern art and art criticism. Bonner has taught at Xavier University of Louisiana and the United States Air Force Academy and has curated exhibitions at Newcomb College, Tulane University, THNOC, and the New Orleans Museum of Art. For twenty years, Bonner compiled the annual bibliography on *Art and Architecture of the South* (*The Southern Quarterly*, University of Mississippi), and she co-edited the *Art and Architecture* volume of *The New Encyclopedia of Southern Culture* (University of North Carolina Press and the Center for the Study of Southern Culture, University of Mississippi, 2013). For a new edition of William Spratling and William Faulkner's *Sherwood Anderson and Other Famous Creoles*, Bonner and Thomas Bonner, Jr., authored critical biographies of the French Quarter personalities caricatured in the original, privately printed book.

**Claudia M. Champagne** holds the doctorate in English from Tulane University with concentrations in British literature of the Renaissance and nineteenth century. She is Professor of English and Chair of the Department of Humanities at the University of Holy Cross (New Orleans), where she has taught British literature, tragedy, and the works of William Shakespeare for thirty years. Champagne has published on Renaissance drama and on the poetry of Edmund Spenser and John Milton in the *Milton Quarterly*, *Christianity and Literature*, and *The Encyclopedia of Christian Literature*, and serves as a consulting editor for the *Variorum Commentary on the Poems of John Milton* (Duquesne University Press). She has presented on Shakespeare, Milton, and Lacan at meetings of the Modern Language Association, the Renaissance Society of America, the World Shakespeare Congress in Stratford-upon-Avon, the Conference on Christianity and Literature's "The Hospitable Text: New Approaches to Religion and Literature" (London, Notre Dame Center), and the South Central Conference on Christianity and Literature, for which she was executive director for 5 years.

**José Juan Colín** is a native of Mexico City and holds the Ph.D. from The University of New Mexico. Colín is *Emeritus* Associate Professor of Spanish at the University of Oklahoma, where he taught courses in Hispanic literature, culture, and cinema and served as executive director of the South Central Modern Language Association for five years (2016–2021). His research focuses on Latin American literature and culture of this and the last century, primarily on the social-struggle literature that flourished throughout Latin America after the mid-twentieth century. He has presented and published articles and essays on contemporary Central American, Mexican, and Caribbean writers, including Parménides García Saldaña, Sergio Ramírez, Rafael Menjívar Ochoa, Gloria Guardia, Tatiana Lobo, Mayra Montero, Leonardo Padura Fuentes, Horacio Castellanos Moya, and Laura Esquivel. Colín is the author of two books of criticism, *Los cuentos de Sergio Ramírez* (2004) and *Sergio Ramírez: acercamiento crítico a sus novelas* (2013). He is preparing studies of the novels of Salvadoran writer Horacio Castellanos Moya and the *literatura de la onda* [new wave literature] produced during the 1960s and 1970s by Mexican writers born 1938–1951.

**William T. Cotton** holds the B.A. in English from Cornell University and the M.A. and Ph.D. from the University of New Mexico. He taught English Renaissance literature, particularly Spenser and Milton, and utopian and epic literature at Loyola University in New Orleans for forty-six years, where he served as department chair, directed the University Honors Program, and was named *Dux Academicus*. His published work reflects similar interests, and includes essays and review articles on chivalric romance, poetry, and utopian and dystopian narrative. Cotton is co-founder of the New

Orleans Fencing Academy and continues fencing and teaches literature in New Orleans' lively literary venues. He was a volunteer in the Pfizer COVID-19 vaccine trial and later learned that he had received the vaccine.

**Martha Greene Eads** studied literature and theology at Wake Forest University, the University of North Carolina at Chapel Hill, and the University of Durham (UK) and is Professor of English at Eastern Mennonite University in Harrisonburg, Virginia. She has taught at the North Carolina Correctional Center for Women and at Valparaiso University in Indiana, where she held a Lilly Fellowship in Humanities and the Arts from 2001–2003. Eads's research and teaching interests include twentieth- and twenty-first-century drama, English modernism, and contemporary Southern fiction. Her articles on those topics have appeared in *Appalachian Journal*, *The Carolina Quarterly*, *Christianity and Literature*, *The Cresset*, *Modern Drama*, *The Southern Quarterly*, and *Theology*.

**Barbara E. Hamilton** earned the Ph.D. in comparative literature from Rutgers University. She is Professor of English and World Literature at Mercer County Community College and Adjunct Professor of English and Liberal Studies at William Paterson University. She recently received Mercer's 2022 Distinguished Teaching Award. Hamilton is chair of the General Education Committee, past chair of Liberal Arts, and an active participant in assessment and Diversity, Equity, and Inclusion initiatives at Mercer. She serves on the New Jersey General Education Coordinating Committee and as co-convener of the Women's Section for the American Folklore Society. Hamilton frequently presents on literature and pedagogy, contributing to academic journals such as *Interdisciplinary Humanities* and *Breaking Ground*.

**Michael P. Kuczynski** holds the M.A. and Ph.D. degrees in English and American literature from the University of North Carolina, Chapel Hill, and is Professor of English and Chair *Emeritus* of the Department of English at Tulane University, where he teaches courses on medieval literature and book history, often focusing on the relationships between medieval poetry, religion, and art. Kuczynski has published widely in the fields of text study and medieval English religious literature. A second, e-book edition of his *Prophetic Song: The Psalms as Moral Discourse in Late Medieval England* (University of Pennsylvania Press, 1995) has been reissued as part of the press's Anniversary Collection. His essay "Vox ecclesiae, vox Christi: the Psalms and Medieval English Ecclesiology" appears in *The Psalms* and *Medieval English Literature from the Conversion to the Reformation* (Ed. Francis Leneghan and Tamara Atkin. Boydell & Brewer, 2017). His two-volume edition, *A Glossed Wycliffite Psalter: Oxford, Bodleian Library MS Bodley 554*, includes his study of a Middle English commentary on the Psalms (EETS, OS 352 and 353. Oxford University Press, 2019). Kuczynski frequently presents his research at English medieval studies conferences and gave the plenary address at the Early Book Society meeting at Trinity College, Dublin, in 2019. He is currently completing *The True Portrait of Christ: A Medieval Forgery and Its Afterlife*, a monograph on an influential piece of New Testament apocrypha, and presented portions of his work at the Medieval English Research Seminar at Oxford University (February 2022).

**Lowry Martin** holds the J.D. from the Texas Tech University Law School and the Ph.D. from the University of California at Berkeley. He is Associate Professor of French Language and Linguistics at the University of Texas at El Paso where he is chair of the Department of Languages and Linguistics and teaches French. Martin's work has appeared in *French Forum* and in *Lingua Romana*. His chapter on francophone writers in the Americas, "The Making of the Other Americas," appears in *Teaching Diversity and Inclusion* (Taylor & Francis, 2021). Martin has been a Fellow of the NEH and was awarded a 2022 grant from Brandeis University's Schusterman Center's Summer Institute for Israel Studies. He has been a member of the South Central Modern Language Association's executive committee for several years and serves as its president for 2023–2024.

**Helen Maxson** holds the Ph.D. from Cornell University, where she focused on lyric and narrative modes in twentieth-century U.S. poetry and is Professor *Emerita* at Southwestern Oklahoma State University. Maxson taught high school English for seventeen years prior to earning the Ph.D. Maxson is a long-time presenter at the South Central Modern Language Association, where she served as secretary and chair of twentieth-century literature sessions for many years, and at annual seminars of the South Central Conference on Christianity and Literature. Her presentations and published work have concerned the fiction of Southern writer Wendell Berry and the poetry of Wallace Stevens, Walt McDonald, and Dan Schwarz. Maxson and Daniel Morris edited *Reading Texts, Reading Lives: Essays in the Tradition of Humanistic Cultural Criticism in Honor of Daniel R. Schwarz* (University of Delaware Press, 2012). Her articles have appeared most recently in *Western American Literature* and *The CEA Critic*.

**David O. Thompson** holds the B.A. in English from Northwestern University and the Ph.D. from Yale University, specializing in English literature, particularly in Victorian literature and the fiction of George Eliot. Following several years of teaching at Baylor University and Phillips Exeter Academy, he entered Harvard Law School, receiving his J.D. in 1986. Thompson practiced law in Seattle, Washington, from 1986–2020 and is a retired attorney and independent scholar.

**Elizabeth Moore Willingham** holds the Ph.D. from the University of Texas at Austin. Her critical essays and reviews have appeared in *Arthuriana, La corónica, Hispania, Revista de Estudios de Género y Sexualidades (Letras femeninas), Revista Monográfica, Sixteenth Century Journal, Speculum,* and *Harvard Celtic Studies*. She is a contributor to *A Student's Companion to Shakespeare* (Ed. Joseph Rosenblum. Westport, CT: Greenwood, 2005) and to reference works in medieval and Latin American topics published by ABC-CLIO, Oxford University Press, Routledge, and Scribner's. She is the author of *The Mythical Indies and Columbus's Apocalyptic Letter* (Sussex, 2016), which was awarded the St. Louis Mercantile Library and Bibliographical Society of America prize for American Bibliography. Her work has had the support of the National Endowment for the Humanities several times for medieval text studies, and she serves as series editor for three text editions and an essay collection for the Old French *Lancelot* of Yale 229 series for Brepols. She is editor of *Laura Esquivel's Mexican Fictions* (Sussex 2010), which was awarded the Harvey L. Johnson Book Prize of the Southwest Council of Latin American Studies. She has taught under-graduate and/or graduate courses at The University of Texas at Austin in the College of Liberal Arts (the Department of Spanish and Portuguese and the Department of English) and in the School of Education (Foreign Language Education), at The College of William and Mary, Texas A&M University, and Baylor University.

# Index

Making the volume's many primary materials and its critical complexities accessible and navigable is the aim of our index. Its designations, differentiations, and structures accommodate those ends.

Cross references headed by "*See*" and "*See also*" use opening word(s) or a personal name. Within complex main entries, the directions "(below)" and "(above)" signal companion entries (subheads) within a section. The scribal *&* (italicized unless it precedes an italicized term) holds internal cross references together, separating them from those signaling main entries, which are period separated. Because the Introduction follows the usual format of contributor volumes by treating each chapter in the prescribed order, it gets few notices here.

Abimelech 150
Abraham, previously Abram (Hebrew patriarch) 148, 149–150, 155, 165nn4,6*&*8, 167n29
  in Muslim prayer life 164–165n1
Acts (Acts of the Apostles, Christian Bible) 244n5, 269n22, 285n2
Adam, in *The Creation of Adam* (Michelangelo) 236, 237
*Adam Bede*. *See* Eliot, George
Adam and Eve (the Fall, creation myth). *See* Eden. Genesis
Adams, Kimberly VanEsveld 172, 173
Afghanistan, women of 97, 104
Africa, culture of 101, 104, 114. economy of 10. life of women in 106. reporting on 102
  *See also* African Americans. conflict minerals. Nottage, *Ruined*
African Americans, burials of, in New Orleans 291. as descendants of enslaved people 114. in fiction 58. — men 110. — women 100. *See also* racism
*agape* (Greek) 227, 234, 245n12
agnostic, as a theological position 30, 249. *See also* Huxley
Aguilar, Delia D. 95, 104
Ajax (prayer to Zeus) 20n14
alliterative verse 249, 251–252
All Saints' Day (*La Toussaint*) 289–290. Illus. 290
*The American Jewess* (Chopin's "Cavanelle") 30
Ames-Lewis, Francis 91n40
Andersen, Corinne 286n8
Anderson, Porter 166n18
Andrew, Malcolm, and Ronald Waldron 266n7

Anger, Suzy 173, 199n32
Anglicanism 174. *See also* Psalms
Annunciation. *See* Virgin Mary
anti-democratic forces 90
Ardennes, Battle of. *See* Reutlinger
Aristotle, *Poetics* 20n15. elements of tragedy in 207–208, 209, 210–211, 223. Illus. 207, 208
Arms, George 43
Arnold, Matthew, on "high seriousness" 4, 20n15. on Chaucer 4–5
Arons, Wendy, and Theresa J. May 105, 116n14, 117n19
Ashe, Geoffrey 228
Aston, Elaine 115n3
atheism, in criticism and theology 19n7, 172–173, 249, 200n47. *See also* Feuerbach. Strauss
Attridge, Michael 45n13
Auden, W. H. ("Musée des Beaux Arts") 64, 88n20
audience (critic/reader/viewer) reception/response xxii, 199n36, 249, 250, 265, 269n23. *See also* authorship. Ensler, *TVM*. Fish, Stanley. "Lament." Michelangelo, Vatican *Pietà*. Nottage. O'Connor. *Pearl*. Ramírez, political response. Shakespeare, *King Lear* & *The Winter's Tale*
Auerbach, Erich 3, 19–20n9
Austen, Gillian 21n41
author(ship), anonymity of 8. effect on reception 9
*The Awakening*. *See* Chopin

Badger, Jonathan N. 196n3
Báez, Silvio José (Bishop) 148, 165n3
Baltussen, Han 267n8

303

Baptist (a Christian denomination) 284, 286n12
Barber, Benjamin 73, 90n30
Barge, Elaine Zook 109, 113, 114, 115
Bargone, Frédéric-Charles 139
Barish, Jonas 268n17
Barkan, Leonard 246n18
Barrie, J. M. 50
Barrus, Ben 45n23, 46n26
Basu, Srimati 104
Bataille, Georges 139
Beal, Jane 266n6
Beauregard, David N. 265n3, 268n15
Bede, the Venerable. *See* St. Bede
Beer, Janet, and Elizabeth Nolan 43n2
Beethoven, Ludwig van (Symphony No. 9) 2
Bel Geddes, Norman (Futurama Pavilion) 84–85, 90n39
La Belle Époque 122, 123
Belle-Île (France, off the Brittany coast) 122–123, 125
Bembo, Pietro 85, 91n40
Benjamin, Katie 166n19
Benson, Larry D. 20n17
Bermúdez, Manuel 166n13
*Best American Short Stories 1936* 273
the Bible, Protestant vs. Catholic 44n10. in Tevis 66. Search books by name. *See also* Catholicism. Judaism. Protestantism
*bignonia* trumpet vine 143n30
Boccaccio, Giovanni 21n35
Bodley MS 554 (Wycliffite Psalter) 11, 301
Boethius (*Consolation of Philosophy*) 267n8
Bonner, Thomas, Jr. 32, 44n4, 45nn14&15, 45n22
*Book of the Duchess* (Chaucer) 266–267n7
Borges, Jorge Luis 165–166n10
Borroff, Marie 267n12
Bosco, Mark 265–266n4
Bourgogne (Burgundy) 122
Bowers, Fredson 209, 210–212, 223. *hamartia* 224n3
Boyd, Lois A., and R. Douglas Brackenridge 46n25
Bradley, A. C. 209–210, 211, 212
Bray, Charles (1811–1884) 172, 198n20
Brecht, Bertolt (*Mother Courage and Her Children*) 97. influence on Nottage's *Ruined* 97, 101, 102–103, 105, 116n14. on realistic theater 100. *See also* Ensler. Nottage
Breughel, Pieter, l'Ancien (*Landscape with the Fall of Icarus*) 64–65, 88n19
Brion, Marcel 246n19
Britain, pre-Christian, in Shakespeare's *Lear* 213, 214, 222
British Library 9, 222, 225n10, 265n1, 266n6. *See also* Carson, Christie
Brooks, Cleanth 275
Brown, Carleton 20n28
Bryant, J. A. 265n3
*Bulletin mensuel* (Bibliothèque Nationale) 124
Bullough, Geoffrey (*Pandosto*) 267n13, 268n19
Buonarroti, Michelangelo. *See* Michelangelo
Burgaud, Françoise 126
Bury St. Edmund's 11–12

Calhoun, David 45n24
Canada, literary award of 166n17
Canning, Charlotte 102–103
Čapek, Milič 54, 86n8
*Captain Blood* 61
*Carátula* (Central American cultural magazine) 165nn3&9
Cardenal, Ernesto (*Salmos*, "Psalm 5") 153–154
Caribbean 97, 106. literature of 51, 153–154. *See also* Ramírez
Carlson, Michael 200n49
Carlyle, Thomas 172
Carroll, David 197n8, 198n19
Carson, Angela 266n5&6
Carson, Christie 222, 223, 225n10
Caruth, Cathy 143n33
Cast, David 246n19
Catel, Mylène, and Rosemary Lloyd 143nn22–23
Catholicism/the Roman Catholic Church 25–26, 27, 28–31, 32, 34, 37, 41, 45n13, 139, 144n29, 228, 249–250, 284
baroque aesthetic of 265–266n4
the Church as a mystical body (Christ and members) 253, 267n9
Douay-Rheims (Bible) xi, 20n23, 41, 167n32, 286n12
as incentive for civil war 46n29

in literature 43n1. *See also* Chopin, regional and religious. Geoffrey of Vinsauf. Hopkins. Jammes. McCullers. Rice, Anne. Rossetti. O'Connor. *Pearl*
in popular/local culture 289–290. *See* also New Orleans. St. Louis (Missouri). St. Louis No. 1
purgatory/Purgatory, doctrine of 11, 261
sacraments and liturgy of 41, 253, 259, 245n12, 268n15
universities affiliated with 95
Vulgate 6, 11, 20n23, 45, 244n2. *See also* Stuttgart in Abbreviations
*See also* Church Fathers. Damasus. Feltin. Garesché, Kitty. Leo XIII. liberation theology. Lourdes. Michelangelo, faith of & Vatican Pietà, figures. Pius IX. Vatican II. Virgin Mary. Zola
Central America 152, 153. *See also Carátula*. Costa Rica. Nicaragua
Certeau, Michel de (*Mystic Fable*) 69, 70, 83
Cervantes Prize 165n9 (documentary film), 166n17
Chalmette (Louisiana), site of the Battle of New Orleans 41
Chambers, E. K. 265n1
Champagne, Claudia. *See* inverted pyramid
Chandler, Brian T. 166n21
Chaucer, Geoffrey 2, 5, 9–10, 11, 20n17, 20–21n31, 66, 265n1
   allusions to, in Tevis 87n12, 87–88n13, 89n22
   *The Book of the Duchess* 266–267n7
   *The Canterbury Tales*,
    elements of, "Franklin's" 9. "Knight's" 10. "Miller's" 10. "Nun's Priest's" 20n17. "Parson's" 9–10. prayer 9–10, 20–21n3. "Prioress's" 4–5, 20n17. Prologue 66, 67, 87n12, 89n22. "Wife of Bath's" 10
   the sublime, contexts of in 9–10
   *See also* Arnold. Geoffrey of Vinsauf
Cheatham, George 275, 285n2
Chekhov, Anton 71–72
Chile, literary award of 166n17
Choi, Won 82
Chopin, Kate
   childhood (as Katie O'Flaherty) 25, 29–31, 45nn14&16
   reading, writing, and *juvenilia* 30, 35, 37, 45n16
   De Maupassant, influence of 25. Chopin's translations of 44n4
   feminist perspectives of 31, 43n1, 44nn3&5
   marriage and motherhood of 32, 41, 42. as an "other" 33, 46n30
   novels of
    *At Fault* (1890) 31–32
    *The Awakening* (1899) 25–29, 35–43
    character development and conflicts in
     as bound/repressed vs. free (divided life, veiled rebellion) 36–37, 40, 44n11
     in cultural and social clashes 43n1, 44n11, 46n29. as maternal vs. non-maternal values 35–36, 40–41, 47n34. as the other 34–35, 38–39, 43n2, 44n11, 47nn34&37. *See also* "mixed marriage" (below)
     as inward vs. outward life 29, 32, 35, 37–38, 39, 40–41, 42, 43
     as negative space xviii, 27–28, 29, 41
     in sleeping vs. waking trope 39
    marriage in 32, 46n32. as a sacrament 28–29, 40
    "mixed marriage" in 28–29, 33–37, 38, 40, 45n13. as a source of external tension 28–29, 38–39, 40–41. as a source of marital discord 28–29, 38–39, 42, 47n37
    patriarchal culture in 28, 34, 38, 40, 42–43, 43n2, 44n9
    regional and religious cultures in Catholic Creole 25, 26, 27–28, 33, 35–36, 40, 41, 42, 43n2, 45n13
    as Catholic images/types 27–29, 35–36. "the lady in black" 25, 35, 36.

Marian figure 41. Old Mrs. Pontellier 35, 36
Presbyterian (Cumberland, Calvinistic) 5, 27–28, 33–34, 40, 42
as sources of difference/tension 25, 26, 27–28, 33–34, 35–37, 38–39, 40, 41, 42, 43nn1&2, 44nn10&11, 45n12, 46n29. *See also* settings (below)
settings and locales with cultural/religious relevance
Chênière Caminada 39, 45n21
France, Louisiana's culture as "French Catholic" 25–26, 27
Grand Isle 26, 27, 36–37, 38–39, 42, 46n33
Gulf of Mexico 26, 35, 47n37 *See also* Chênière Caminada & Grand Isle (above)
Iberville (home of Old Mrs. Pontellier) 35–36
Kentucky 25, 26, 27, 28, 33, 34, 36, 37, 40, 44n8
Mexico 27
Mississippi 25, 27, 36, 44n8
New Orleans 26, 28, 30, 35
Our Lady of Lourdes (church) 32 *See also* Chênière Caminada (above)
sexual attraction in 37–38, 43nn1&2, 44n3
*See also* music. short stories (below)
reception of as a novelist 25–26, 43nn1&2, 44nn3,5&6, 45n12
regional and religious culture in other fiction of xviii, 25, 27, 31–32, 35–37, 43n2, 45n12, 46nn26,27&29. See also *The Awakening* (above). short stories (below)
religious formation and views of 25–26, 29–31, 32–33, 37, 41, 43n1, 46nn26–27&31
review of Zola's *Lourdes* 47n36
sexuality in fiction of 43n2, 44n3
short stories of, with regional-culture interest, "At the 'Cadian Ball" 32. "At Chênière Caminada" 32. "Loka" 33. "The Maid of Saint Phillippe" 32. "The Night Came Slowly" 33, 34, 46n27. "Odalie Misses Mass" 32. "The Return of Alcibiade" 32. "A Sentimental Soul" 32. See also *The American Jewess*
Christ-figure 64. Adam Bede as 172. Cordelia as 225n9
Christianity
as an aesthetic xxii, 7, 9, 19–20n9, 20–21n31, 265nn2–3. See also *The Cloud of Unknowing*. Hopkins. "The Lament." Lydgate. *Pearl*. Melville. Michelangelo, Vatican *Pietà*. Nottage, *Ruined*. *Pearl*. "Revelation." Shakespeare, *King Lear & The Winter's Tale*. the sublime, Middle Ages. Thomas, R. S.
in education 94–95, 114
in fine arts and literature 10, 43n1, 45n22, 46, 71, 227, 228ff., 244n7, 245n9, 253–254, 261–265, 265n3, 267nn11&12, 274, 277, 284
derived from Jewish narrative 236, 237
presented as fundamentalist 56, 88n16
prohibition against 255
*See also* as an aesthetic (above). David, King of Israel. Eden. Milton
philosophical views of, Psalm 129, as a statement of Christian existentialism 12
*See also* Eliot, George. Feuerbach. Hegel. Hennell, Charles. higher criticism. Nietzsche. Spinoza. Strauss
theology and doctrine in 5–7, 11–12, 171–172, 197n15, 198n27, 227, 229, 230, 236–237, 238, 244nn2, 245nn9&12, 250, 254, 263. duty to others in 106, 114–115, 115n1. as existentialist 12. principles of, as authoritative 35, 174
*See also* Anglicanism. Baptist. Catholicism. Jesus. Judaism. liberation theology. Methodism. Presbyterianism. Protestantism. St. Paul. Virgin Mary
Christian, Mervyn 115n2

Church Fathers 5, 41. *See also* Catholicism/the Roman Catholic Church. St. Augustine. St. Jerome
Cicero 267n8
Civil War, English, U.S. parallels to 46n29
Clark, Kenneth 234, 237, 246n13
Claudel, Paul 139
the Cloisters (Metropolitan Museum, Heilbrunn Timeline of Art History) 245n9
*The Cloud of Unknowing* (anonymous) 8
Cobb, Christopher J. 267n14
Coleridge, Samuel Taylor 19n7
Colette, Sidonie-Gabrielle "Gabri"
Colette, Illus. 140
  death of 139, 144n39
  early life, family, friends, and marriages 122, 123, 141nn3,4&5, 142nn10,13&15 *See also* de Jouvenel. de Morny. Gauthier de Villars. Moreno. Jammes
  genres/interests/subjects of, in fiction and sketches
    animals 121, 123–124, 126, 126–129, 130–140, 141n2, 143n31, 144nn33&38
    domestic life 125–129 *See also* (below) works of, *Dialogues*
    landscapes/nature passages 121, 123–124, 125, 128–129, 133, 138–139
    "love" novels 121, 123, 124, 141n6. *See also* works, "love" novels (below)
    trauma narratives xx, 137, 143n33. *See also* "La Chienne" & "La Chienne qui en revient" (below)
    war sketches and stories 129–137 *See also* animals & trauma (above)
  professional life of xx, 128–132, 139, 140
    as journalist and war correspondent 129–132, 143n23
    as novelist 121, 123, 124–125, 142n14. *See also* genres (above) and works of (below)
    as performer 129
    reception of 128, 129–130, 139, 144n39. Jammes' defense of 126
  spiritual life of 121, 124, 139–140
  works of
    *Celle qui en revient* 138–139
      *See also* "La Chienne qui en revient"
    *La Chambre éclairée* 138–139
    *La Chatte* 138
    "La Chienne" 132–134, 143n31
    "La Chienne qui en revient" (*Celle qui en revient: suivi...*) 134–137, 143n32
    "Chiens sanitaires" (two sketches by this name exist) 130–131, 143n28
    the Claudines. *See* "love novels" (below)
    "Conte pour les petits enfants des poilus" 144n36
    "Les Couleuvres" 139
    *De la patte à l'aile* 138
    *Dialogues de bêtes, Sept, & Douze* 121, 124, 125–129, 142nn15–18, 143n32. *See also* "Toby-Chien parle" (below)
    *En Pays connu* 137
    *Gigi* xx
    *Les Heures longues 1914–1917* (*HL*) 130–134, 138–139
    *Histoires pour Bel-Gazou* 138
    *L'Ingénue libertine* 141n6
    "love novels," early
      the "Claudines" 121, 123. *Claudine à l'école* 123–124, 141nn6&8. nature writing in 123–124. *Claudine en ménage* 141n6. *Claudine à Paris* 124, 141n6. *Claudine s'en va* 141n6. *La Retrait sentimentale* 125, 141n6. the Minnes 141n6. *Égarements de Minne* 124–125. *L'entrave* 121, 124–125
    *La maison de Claudine* 141n3
    *Mes apprentissages* 125, 140n1, 143nn12–13
    the Minnes. *See* "love novels" (above)
    *Mitsou* 142–143n21
    *La Paix chez les bêtes* 137, 138–139, 142n16, 143n34, 144nn36–37
    *Paradis terrestre* 138
    *Pour un herbier* 141n4

*Prrou, Poucette et quelques autres* 138
"Renouveau" (*HL*) 143n26
"La salivation psychique" (*La Paix*) 137
*Sido, ou les points cardinaux* 138, 139, 141n3
"Toby-Chien parle" 129, 142n18, 142–143n21
*La Vagabonde* 142–143n21
*Les Vrilles de la vigne* 141n3
See also de Jouvenel. de Morny. Gauthier de Villars. Jammes. Moreno.
Colín, José Juan 165n2, 166n17
colonialism (European) 104, 106, 114–115, 152. British, in Eliot 187, 199n37. See also post-colonialism. St. Louis No. 1, colonial
coltan. See conflict minerals
Comfort, Cathy 141n2
Coming to the Table 114
*Commonweal* 144n39
Comte, Auguste 173, 174, 197n8
conflict minerals/metals 97, 104–105, 106, 114, 117n20. in theater 106
See also DRC. Nottage
Congo. See DRC
*consolatio*. See "Lament of the Virgin." Michelangelo, Vatican *Pietà*. *Pearl*. Stoicism
Cooper, Christine 98
Cooper, Merian C. 59, 88n13
1 Corinthians (Christian Bible) 34, 267n9. See also Jesus, parables
2 Corinthians (Christian Bible) 7
Costa Rica 151. in literature 152
Cottom, Daniel 173
Cotton, William T. xxii, 46n28, 225n9, 244n3
Coulter, Dale M., and Amos Yong 245n8
Coulton, G. G. 266n6
creation, biblical. See Eden
Cross, John W. 196n2
Crowley, John 84–85, 90n39
Cuadra, Pablo Antonio (*Libro de horas*) 153
Curley, Daniel 274, 275
Curtis, William (Lydgate's abbot) 12
Curtiz, Michael 61
cyborg 50, 87n11. See also posthuman. Shteyngart. Tevis, Spofforth
Cycles of Violence/cycles of violence 112, 113

"Daedalus and Icarus" (Ovid's *Metamorphoses*) 64–65. See also Tevis
Damasus, Pope 5
Dante (*Commedia*) 267n8
Darío, Rubén ("Margarita, está linda la mar") 152
Darwin, Charles 173, 174
David, King of Israel xviii, 239, 246n18. in Michelangelo's philosophy 246n18. Psalms of, as autobiographical 10–11. See also Boccaccio. Psalms
Davies, R. T. 244nn4&6, 245n10. on aims of lament poetry 228–229
Davis-Weyer, Caecilia 20n22
Dawson, Gary Fisher 116n11
the deadly sins 9–10
Dead Space Collaborative Studio 293n5
Debayle, Margarita 152
de Boré, Étienne (Louisiana French Creole planter) 291
de Certeau. See Certeau
Dedek, Peter 293n2
Deegan, Thomas 173, 197n15
de Jouvenel, Henri ("Sidi") 129, 130
de Maupassant, Guy 25, 44n4
DeMille, Cecil B. 61
de Morny, Missy (Mathilde) 129, 142n20
DeMouy, Jane Krause 274, 286n8
*De Profundis*. See Psalm 129
Deroze, Phyllisa Smith 95, 107, 109, 110, 114, 116n11
Derrida, Jacques (*The Animal That Therefore I Am*) 144n38
devil(s). See Satan
diegetic theory (sound perceived within the dramatic milieu) 116n11
Diehl, Huston 265n3
Diethe, Carol 198n18
Dionigi da Borgo 20n24
*les Dix* 139. See Goncourt, Académie
Dodd, Valerie 174, 198n21
Dolan, Jill 105
Dolin, Tim 173, 196n1
Donahoe, Daniel Joseph 244n7
Doyle, Molly (*A Memory*) 99. See also Ensler, works, *A Memory*
DRC xix, 95, 97, 102, 105, 107, 110, 111, 114, 115n2. See also Africa. conflict minerals. Goma. Nottage, *Ruined*. Uganda
dream vision in literature. See *Book of the Duchess*. *Pearl*, genres

Duarte Somoza, Missael 165n9
Dumas, Alexandre (*The Three Musketeers*) 45n14
Dunne, Michael 269n23

Eagleton, Terry 173
early modern era. *See* Renaissance
Eble, Kenneth 26, 40, 44n6
ecological criticism/dramaturgy 105, 141n2
Eden as biblical creation 68, 274. *See also* Eden, narrative. Genesis
Eden narrative and types in art and literature
  Adam 57. Michelangelo's 236–237. Milton's 63, 68–69. "pseudo-Adam" 61
  Eden, allusions to, as "crumbling" 52. as Earthly Paradise 252. in ironic naming (*el barrio El Edén*) 150–151. as "lost" (Wordsworth) 54. as pseudo-Eden 89. as a sexual myth 274. as a "silicon" Eden (Morozov) 89n28
  Eve 57, 274
  God in 63
  Satan (serpent, snake) 88, 274
  sin and fall of Adam and Eve 57, 63, 261, 274. their banishment 68–69
  *See also* Eden, as biblical. Milton, *Paradise Lost*. Satan
Eifrig, Gail McGrew 174–175, 198n23
Eliot, Charlotte Stearns 30, 45n17
Eliot, George (née Marian or Mary Ann Evans)
  essays and reviews by
    "Contemporary Literature: Art and Belles Lettres" 175. "The Future of German Philosophy" 198n24. "Notes on The Spanish Gypsy" 196n2. "Silly Novels by Lady Novelists" 200–201n49
  fiction of
    *Adam Bede* 196–197
      community, alienation from, in 179, 184–186, 198n27, 199nn31&37, 200nn40&44.
      community in 170, 172, 176, 177, 179, 180, 183, 184–185, 186–187, 189, 194, 195. as sympathy 194, 199n32

community standards in ("the general") 170, 176, 177–178, 187, 198n27
critical reception of 170–175, 190, 195, 197nn8–11. author of as clergyman 174. *See also* Nietzsche
ending of 191–193, 194, 195, 200n46.
history, theory of, in 198n23. as an element of community 170, 175. Loss of history 180 *See also* realism (below)
I-thou relationship in 183, 186, 194, 199n32, 199–200n39, 200n40
language 193–194, 196
love in 187–188, 189–194, 199nn34&35. Gyp, as an analogue for 199n35
marriage 187, 193, 195, 200n45
  as "a mystery" 190, 191, 200n46&48
realism and love 192–194
religion and love 192, 193, 200n44
sexual relations 181, 182, 183, 186, 198n27
metaphors in 171, 178, 180, 181, 190, 191, 192 (analogue), 194, 200n48
music in 178, 191, 192, 193. as a "dance" 188
myth in 176, 177, 196. *See also* ending (above). veiling, etc., (below)
religious culture in 187–188, 189–191, 193, 194, 195, 197n9, 199n34, 200n44
  Anglicanism 174, 177–178. implicit in Mr. Irwine, esp. 176, 181, 186, 187
  Methodism 174, 176, 177–179, 187–188, 198n29, 199n30
tragedy in 170, 181, 194, 195–196. as "damage" 187 *See also* on tragedy (below)
veiling/unveiling or misinterpretation/demystifying 176, 179, 180, 181, 182, 183–185, 186–187, 188, 189, 190, 191–192, 195,

199nn31,34&38, 200nn41–43&48. *See also* Girard. love (above)
*See also* colonialism, British, in Eliot
*Daniel Deronda* (a "later novel") 173, 195–196. Gwendolen Harleth in 170
"The Lifted Veil" (*The Lifted Veil*) 195, 200n49
*Middlemarch* (a "later novel") 195–196, 198n21, 199n34, 200n45
*Romola* 195, 196
*Silas Marner* 170, 195, 199n32. Godfrey Cass in 170
"The Spanish Gypsy" 196n2
reading and thought of 172–175, 196, 197nn11&13, 197–198n16, 198nn17,20–24&29
realist aesthetic of 170–171, 174–175, 176, 193–194, 195. demythologizing 178, 195
on tragedy 170, 194, 196nn2–3
translations by. *See* Evans, Marian
Eliot, Thomas Stearns (T. S.) 45n17, 66. "A Song for Simeon" 66, 68, 89n21
Eliot, William Greenleaf 45n17
Emerson, Ralph Waldo 39
The Empire State Building, in fiction 59, 66, 67, 84. in film 88n13. as a metaphor 84
EMU ix, 112, 117n20
ending, as happy/romantic/conventional 51, 68, 71, 89n24, 105, 106, 116–117n16, 193–195
Engels, Friedrich 173–174. — and Marx on Feuerbach 173, 197n7
England, literary figures of. *See* Eliot. "Lament." *Pearl*. Protestantism. Romanticism. Shakespeare. the sublime, as an aesthetic. Victorian
Ensler, Eve (now known as "V")
as author of *The Vagina Monologues* (*TVM*) 94, 96, 99
creative process of 96–97, 98, 115–116n6. "Vagina Queens," role in, of 96–97, 98
expectations for *TVM* 103, 104
as playwright 96, 100
works of
*A Memory, a Monologue, a Rant, and a Prayer*, with Molly Doyle 99

*The Vagina Monologues* (*TVM*)
accomplishments and aims 94, 95, 97, 98, 99, 100, 104, 113, 115–116n6. *See also* (below) audience & critical & fundraising
audience and performer responses 96, 97, 98, 99, 100, 102. traumatic responses of 99
Brechtian (realist) perspective on material 100
compared with/contrasted to *Ruined* 94, 95, 101, 102, 103, 104–105
critical reception/views 94–95, 96, 97, 98–100, 102, 104, 107–108, 113, 115–116n6
in education/on college campuses 94–95, 97, 98–99, 117n20
feminist perspectives of/on 98, 99, 110, 115–116n6
fundraising, marketing, merchandising campaigns of 96, 97–98, 100, 103, 104
gender considerations in 98, 99–100, 115–116n6
genre(s) of 98, 99, 100, 102
global reach of/implications for 97–98, 104
humor in 98
LGBTQI characters in 98–99, 115–116n6, 117n17
male–female relationships in 95, 117n17
men in, attitudes toward/implications for 95–96, 104
monologues/performances 97
"Because He Liked To Look At It" 95
"If Your Vagina Got Dressed, What Would It Wear?" 98, 104
"I Was There in the Room" 95
"The Little Coochi Snorcher That Could" 98, 102, 117n17
"My Vagina Was My Village" 98
"The Vagina Workshop" 117n17
"The Vulva Club" 95, 98
"They Beat the Girl Out of My Boy" 115–116n6

problems in content and
staging 99. See also *V-Day Organizer's* (below)
pruriant interest of 99
sexual violence in 94, 95, 97, 98, 99. as childhood memory 102, 115–116n6, 117n17. as erotic 102. See also purient (above)
violence, attitude toward 95
*V-Day Organizer's Handbook* 99, 116n7
See also "Letters and Stories." "One Billion." pornography of violence. sexual abuse. V-Day
Eos (goddess) 87n13
Ephesians (Christian Bible) 31
Epiphany 3, 238, 269nn21&22. theophany 3. See also O'Connor, "Revelation"
Espinasse, Javier (photographer) 240–243
Evans, Marian 173, 196n1, 196–197nn5&13
  her translations, of Feuerbach 171, 174, 196–197n5. Spinoza 197n15. Strauss 171, 196–197n5
Eve. See Eden
*Excelsior* 143n23
*exercitatio.* See "Lament." *Pearl.* Stoicism
Exodus (Torah, Pentateuch) 88n13

Fairbanks, Douglas 61
*Fambul Tok* (documentary film) 114
Farfan, Penny, and Leslie Ferris 115n3
Fattucci, Giovan Francesco 246n17
Fawkner, Harald W. 265n4
Felipe IV of Spain 166n17
Felperin, Howard 265n4
Feltin, Maurice Cardinal (d. 1975) 144n39
Feuerbach, Ludwig Andreas 170–173, 174, 178, 194, 195, 196, 196–197n5, 197n7, 198n21
  on Christianity 171–173, 190, l97n6, 200n47
  on community and humanity 172, 185, 199n37, 200n40
  on faith 181, 199n34. See also on Christianity (above)
  on Hegel 171, 197n6. Feuerbach's letter to Hegel 200n47

"I-thou" relation 200n40
  on love/marriage 190, 191, 200n45
    See also on sex (below)
  moral philosophy of 198n21
  on sex 198n27
  on unveiling myth/illusion 190. metaphors for 171–172, 190.
    See also *Wissenschaft* (below)
  *Wissenschaft* (based on Kant and Hegel) xxi, 178, 196n4
Ficino, Marsilio (on Plato) 239
Filewood, Alan 116n11
Fish, Stanley (*Surprised by Sin*) 261, 269n23
fistula 101, 103–104, 107, 108, 116n8. Fistula Foundation 116n8. See also Nottage
*Le Flambeau* 143n23
Flanagin, Jake 117n20
Fleishman, Avrom 173–174, 197n15, 198nn17,21&24
Florence (Italy), the Galleria dell'Accademia (Palestrina Pietà) 244n1. Museo dell' Opera del Duomo (*Pietà*) 244n1
Foreman, Mozelle 166n13
Fox-Genovese, Elizabeth 39
France xx, 25, 122–123, 128, 129, 139, 290
  awards of, literary and national 139, 166n17
  "countryside," landscapes, and animal life of 128, 141n9, 143n30. See also Colette, genres
  literary figures. See Claudel. Colette. Jammes. Mallarmé. Proust. Zola
  in literature (*King Lear*) 214, 218
    See also Colette
  magazines and journals of. See *Bulletin mensuel. Excelsior. Le Flambeau. Le Matin. Paris Review. La Vie parisienne*
  philosophers and theorists. See Comte. Certeau. Derrida. Lacan
  places mentioned. See Belle-Île. Lourdes. Mont Blanc. Les Monts-Bouccons. Paris. La Rochelle. Saint-Sauveur-en-Puisaye. Versailles. Les Vosges
  See also La Belle Époque. Chopin. Douay-Rheims. Feltin. Moreno. New Orleans. St. Louis No. 1. World War I (Ardennes. Marne, Verdun)

Francis, Claude, and Fernande Gontier 141nn3–5, 142n20, 144n39
*Frankenstein* 90n36. protagonist of (Dr. Frankenstein) 80, 81, 88
Frechon, Marie (photographer) 111, 115n2
Freidl, Jean-Paul, and Ian J. Kirby 266n6
Freud, Sigmund 273. theories of, Oedipal 81. *Todestreib* (death drive) 54. "Das Unheimliche" (the uncanny) 268n18. *Urvater* (forefather) 88n17. *See also* Lacan
Freytag, Gustav, on the structure of tragedy 205–207, 208, 212, 214, 223. Illus. 205
Friedman, Sharon 104–105
Friedrich, Caspar David, *Chalk Cliffs* 19n6. *The Wanderer* 2, 19n6.
Frost, Robert, in Tevis 63, 65–66

Gabriel (archangel) 228, 229, 238
Galbraith, Mary 116n11
*A Game of Thrones*. *See* Martin, George
García Márquez, Gabriel 165–166n10
Gardner, John 266n7
Garesché, Kitty (Katherine Milligan) 45n14
Garrison, Jennifer 267n12
Gascoigne, George 14–15, 21n41
Gaston, Sean 173, 174
Gauthier de Villars, Henry ("Willy") 122, 123, 124–125, 125–126, 129, 141n4, 142nn10&15. life with Colette 122–123, 141n5. separation from Colette 125, 129, 142n13. *See also* Les Monts-Bouccons
*Gawain*. *See Sir Gawain*
Gehl, Paul 21n33
gender, in criticism and literature 98–99, 104–105, 110, 125, 158, 273–274, 275. *See also* Deroze. LGBTQI
Genesis (Hebrew Bible, Torah/Pentateuch) 16, 20n14, 50, 63, 107, 149–150, 156, 157, 164–165n1, 165nn4–8, 167nn22,29–31&33, 245n12. *See also* Eden
Geoffrey of Vinsauf, caution to poets (*Poetria Nova*) 55. Church Fathers as influence on 5. influence on contemporaries of 5, 20n17
Gerah 150

German criticism and philosophy (19th century) xxi, 173–174, 175, 197n7, 198n24. *See also* Eliot, "The Future of German Philosophy." Engels. Evans, translations. Feuerbach. Freytag. Goethe. Kant. Marx. Nietzsche. Strauss
German expressionism 101. *See also* Brecht
Germany 197n7. *See also* German criticism. German expressionism. Romanticism, German.
Gerth Van Wijk, Hugo L. (Dutch botanical lexicographer) 143n30
Gettleman, Jeffrey, and Marcus Bleasdale 117n20
Gilbert, Sandra M. 40
Gilbert, Sandra M., and Susan Gubar 25–26, 44n5
*Gilgamesh, The Epic of* 50, 51
Girard, René 184, 199n36
Givner, Joan 275
Glare, P. G. W. 19n4
Glass, Philip 81, 90n37
global conflicts 134. and economic expansion 104–105, 106, 114–115, 117n20. *See also* Basu
God 7–10, 13, 33, 70, 86–87n9, 149–150. as the foundation of justice 6–7. *See also* Eden. Feuerbach. Lacan. Psalms. Ramírez, Sara. Strauss. the sublime, Middle Ages
Goethe, Johann Wolfgang von 173, 197n8
gold. *See* conflict minerals
Goma 111
Goncourt, Académie 144n39
Gooch, Todd 171, 197nn6–7, 200n47
Gospels. *See* John. Luke. Mark. Matthew
Gospels, Synoptic. *See* Luke. Mark. Matthew
Gothic, as church architecture 39. as a quality of narrative 195, 200n49
Grand Isle (Louisiana) 26, 27
"The Grave." *See* Porter
The Great Depression 84
The Great War. *See* World War I
Greene, Robert (*Pandosto*) 267n13, 268n19
Greene, Walter Kirkland 266n6
Gross, Charlotte 266–267n6
Gross, Terry 89n27
Grummt, Christina 19n6

Gruppe, Otto 175

Haddox, Thomas F. 43n1
Hagar (Abrahamic narrative, mother of Ishmael) 149, 165nn5&7
Haight, Gordon 197n13, 198n20
Haiti 97
Hallam, Arthur Henry 16
Hammers, Michele L. 98, 104
Haran (Abraham's brother) 167n29
Haraway, Donna (*Cyborg Manifesto*) 87n11
Hardy, Barbara 197n11
Harvey, W. J. 191, 193, 200n46
Hatt, Cecilia A. 265n2
Hawthorne, Nathaniel 15
Hebrews (Christian Bible) 164–165n1
Hegel, Georg (Hegelian philosophy) 59, 87–88n13, 171–172, 196n3, 197nn6–7, 197–198n16, 200n47 *See also* Feuerbach, *Wissenschaft*
Hegener, Nicole 246n19
Hemingway, Ernest, his "iceberg" theory 29
Hennell, Caroline (Hennell Bray) 198n20. *See also* Bray
Hennell, Charles 172, 173, 174, 198n20
Hennell, Sarah 197n13
*El Heraldo Mexicano* 286n9
Herbert, Christopher 174
Hermann, Luc 175
Hesiod 4–5
higher criticism xxi, 172, 197n11
Hill, Susan E. 198n21, 200n45
Hirsch, Pam 198n19
Hirsh, James E. 224–225n9
Hirst, Michael 238
Hodgson, Peter C. 174
Hollander, John 268n18
Holmes, Diana 142–143n21
Holy Spirit (*Paraclete* or comforter) 16, 18, 62, 269n22, 286n12. represented symbolically 274, 279, 284, 286n12
Homer "To Aphrodite" 87n13. as nodding 4, 20n13. prayer to Zeus (*The Illiad*) 4, 20n14
Hopkins, Gerard Manley 21n46. medievalism in poetry of 1, 19n1. "No Worst" 1, 17–18
Horace, on Homer 4
Houston, Whitney 81
Howell, Elmo 39
Huber, Leonard V. 293n6

Huete, Ulises 157–158
Huguenots 29, 45n14
Hunt, Maurice 265n3
Hussain, Amir 164n1
Huxley, Thomas H. 173. *See also* agnostic
hymns 9, 10, 87n13, 228, 244n7. *See also* Coleridge

Icarus 64–65, 67. *See also* Breughel. Ovid. Tevis, *The Man Who Fell*
*imago dei* (divine image) 8
the Immaculate Conception. *See* Virgin Mary
*immortelles* 290
imperialism. *See* colonialism. post-colonialism
injustice, structural roots of 96, 103–105, 116n14–15. *See also* liberation theology. race
inverted pyramid 224n4. as a graphic for *King Lear* 208–209. Illus. 208
Isaac 165nn1&6
Isaacs, Neil D. 197n11
Isaiah (Hebrew Bible) 6–7, 164n1
Ishmael (protagonist of *Moby Dick*) 15
Ishmael (son of Abraham and Hagar) 149, 165n7
Islam (Muslim faith) 107, 148, 164–165n1
Israel, Babylonian captivity of 11
Italy. *See* Florence. Milan. Rome. Vatican

Jacopone da Todi 244n7
Jaeger, Stephen C. 20n9
Jammes, Francis 124. *L'Église* 139, 144nn40. Préface (*Dialogues*) 126, 129, 142n17
Janson, H. W. 236
Janzen, Marike 116n14
Jean-Charles, Régine Michelle 106–107, 116–117n16
Jesus
 ministry of healing of, as a model for Christians 94–95, 114
 parables and teachings of 227, 244n3, 245n12, 253–254, 267nn9–12. See also *Pearl*
 represented in criticism, literature, music, or visual art 61, 62–63, 69, 71, 87–88n13, 172, 229*ff*., 261, 263. *See also* Christianity. "Jesus Loves Me." Judaism.

"Lament." Michelangelo, faith & sculpture. *Pearl*. Virgin Mary theological significance of 233, 234, 238–239, 244n2
"Jesus Loves Me" (children's hymn) 28, 44n10
John (Christian Bible) 227, 230, 244nn2&5, 245n10–12, 267n11, 286n12
John of Gaunt 266–267n7
Jones, Sam 165n18
Jouve, Nicole Ward 141n6, 142n19
Joyce, James 166n12. *See* Oreamuno
Juárez (Mexico) 97
Judaism 6–7, 30, 107, 245n12
  biblical 148–150, 155, 164–165n1, 228
  God, as foundation of justice in 6–7
  in Marian biography 228
  narratives and figures of, in art and literature 74, 80–81, 148, 153–154, 155ff.
  *See also* Abraham. *The American Jewess*. Cardenal. David, King of Israel. Eden. Exodus. Genesis. God. Hagar. Isaiah. Ishmael. Martínez Rivas. Psalms. St. Louis, Missouri. Sarah

Kant, Immanuel 172, 173, 197n7
Kaplan, Abraham 103, 116n12
Kaveny, Cathleen 95
Kelley, Hannah 112
Kemp, Martin 246n13
Kentucky 284, 286n12. *See also* Chopin, *The Awakening*, settings. Presbyterianism
Kermode, Frank 225n10
*The Killer Angels* 46n29
*King of Kings* 61
*King Kong* and King Kong 59, 88n13
*King Lear*. *See* Shakespeare
Kirwan, James 19n3
Knoepflmacher, Ulrich C. 171, 172, 173, 196n3, 197n11
Knuuttila, Simo 245n8
Kolbenheyer Dr. Friedrich 30–31, 45n18
Kuczynski, Michael 21n37. *See also* Bodley
Kurzweil, Ray 69, 80, 85n1, 86–87n9, 89n25, 90n36. *Transcendent Man* 90n36

Lacan, Jacques xix, 82, 76, 90n31

Lacanian psychoanalysis, applied to literary criticism
  desire 54, 59, 66, 69, 70–72, 77–78, 84–85, 86–87n9. *See also* (below) God & *infans* & *jouissance*
  God 69, 70, 86n6, 87n9. as *dieu obscure* (dark god) 87–88n13, 89n23. as *nom du père* 63, 79, 82. *See* the Symbolic (below)
  the Imaginary 55, 56, 57, 58, 60, 61, 67–68, 76, 78, 86n8
  *infans* 69, 79. Certeau on 83
  *jouissance* 54, 60, 67, 86n7. *plus du jouir* 67–68. *See also* the Symbolic, phallic (below)
  méconnaissance 50–52, 54, 55, 60, 65, 71, 76, 78, 79, 81, 84, 85, 90n39
  Mirror Stage 60–61, 79, 83
  m/Other 58, 60–61, 82
  Other/Otherness 59, 82, 87n11, 88n17. *See also* desire (above). Haraway. woman (below)
  the Real 54, 55–56, 57, 58, 70–71, 76, 82, 86nn6–7, 87n12, 88n17
  the Symbolic 55, 56, 58, 60, 61, 63–64, 65, 67, 71, 75, 76, 78, 79, 82, 88n17. as phallic 87n10
  *tessera*, language as 61–62, 65–66
  *Urvater* (Lacan's) 63, 88n17, 89n23
  woman, in *Le sinthome* (*pas-toute*) 57–58. in Sem. XX 87n10. *See also* (above) Mirror Stage. m/Other. Other. Real. Symbolic
  *See also* Certeau. Choi. Kurzweil. Morozov. Shteyngart. Tevis
*LALT* 166n17
"Lament of the Virgin" ("Lament")
  biblical text reflected in 227, 228, 229–230, 231, 244nn2&5, 245n12
  compared/contrasted with Michelangelo's Vatican *Pietà* 227, 229, 237–238, 239
  criticism on
    dating 227
    texts/editions of xxii, 228–229, 245n10. as appendix, glossed text (Saupe) 294–297
    views of 228–229
  discourses of
    flesh and spirit as "overcoming the world" 227–228, 229, 232, 233, 239, 244n2, 245n12

humility/submission 232–233
love, as *agape* 232, 233, 245n12
love, as maternal/parental 228, 230, 232, 233
pathos in existential contrasts
  in disbelief and mourning 229, 230–232, 233–234
  in meditation on/witness of suffering/injustice/sacrifice 230–231, 232–233, 234
  persuasion, in emotional appeals 227, 228–229, 230–231, 232, 233–234
  in ethical appeals 230, 231, 232, 233, 234
  redemption, promise of 229, 231, 232, 233–234, 239
Jesus (Christ), descriptors of, in 227, 233, 245nn9&11. See also theological (below)
reader reception 238, 239
structure of 229–230
  internal audience 228, 229, 230, 231–233
  narrative shifts 232–234
  refrains 230, 232
  speaker's physical perspective 227, 229–230
theological ideas in 227, 228, 229, 230, 231, 233, 239, 245n12
Virgin, roles of in 227–229, 230, 233, 234, 237–238, 239
Langland, William (*Piers Plowman*) 20–21n3, 267n8
Laughland, Oliver 115–116n6
Laveau, Marie (Voodoo Queen) 291, 293n3
Lavin, Irving 244n1, 246n19. Illus. 243
Lawrence, D. H. 44n3
Leader, Zachary, and Michael O'Neill 19n7
Légion d'honneur (France) 139
Lehnhof, Kent R. 224–225n9
Leo XIII (on the Virgin of Lourdes) 41
León (Nicaragua) 152, 166n15
Leonardo da Vinci, religious faith of, contrasted with Michelangelo's 237. as Michelangelo's rival 236. on sculpting 234. *Trattato* of 246n13
"Letters and Stories" 115n5
Levine, George 197n11, 198n22
Levine, Saul 246n18
Lewes, George Henry 173, 174, 196n1

LGBTQI xii, 107. literary representations of 98–99, 115–116n6, 117n17, 129. See also gender
liberation theology 150, 153, 154, 155, 164, 166n19. relation to feminism 155. See also Cardenal. Cuadra. injustice
Liberman, M. M. (Mike) 285n3
Lifetime (cable network) 100
Lispector, Clarice 165–166n10
Loesberg, Jonathan 172–173, 197n13
López Pérez, Rigoberto 152
Los Alamos (tantalum) 117n20
*Los Angeles Times* 116n10
*The Lost Chord* 61
Lot (Abrahamic narrative) 161, 167nn29–30
Lot's wife (Abrahamic narrative) as a pillar of salt 167n30. See also Martínez Rivas
Louisiana xviii, xxiii, 25, 26, 27, 28, 29, 31, 32, 33, 36, 38, 40, 41, 43n2, 284. See also Chopin. New Orleans. St. Louis No. 1. THNOC
Louisiana State Museum 293n1
Lourdes (France) 47n36. See also Leo XIII. Our Lady of Lourdes. Zola
Lucifer. See Milton. Satan
Luiselli, Valeria 156
Luke (Christian Bible) 87–88n13, 227, 228, 244n5, 245nn10–11, 286n12
Luso-Hispanic literature, biblical echoes in 153–155, 165–166n10
Lydgate, John ("On *De Profundis*") 11–12, 21n37

Macaulay, Thomas Babington 30, 31
McCullers, Carson 43
MacEwan, Elias J. 205
Machado de Assis 165–166n10
Mahawatte, Royce 200n49
Mallarmé, Stéphane 61–62, 88n14
Manhattan Theater Club 109
Mansell, Darrel, Jr. 175
Mardi Gras (2016) 292
Marian lyric. See "Lament"
Mariani, Paul 21n46
Mark (Christian Bible) 245n10, 286n12
Marklein, Mary Beth 117n20
Marne, Battle of the 131
Marshall, Cynthia 268n18
Martin, Carol 198n29

Martin, George R. R. (*Game of Thrones*, A Song of Ice and Fire series) 2
Martin, Lowry 141n2, 143n33
Martínez Rivas, Carlos (*Besos para la mujer de Lot*) 153
Marx, Karl 173–174, 197n7. "das Opium des Volkes" 198n16. *See also* Engels, on Feuerbach
Mary (mother of Jesus). *See* "Lament." Michelangelo. Virgin Mary
*Le Matin* 143n23
Matthew (Christian Bible) 227, 245nn10–11, 253, 254, 286n12
Mazaheri, John 173
Means, Michael H. 267n8
*méconnaissance*. *See* Lacan. Shteyngart. Tevis, *Mockingbird*
"Media vita, in morte sumus" (Gregorian antiphon) 85
Melville, Herman. *See Moby Dick*
Menton, Seymour 166n12
*Mercure de France* (literary magazine) 126
Mercure de France (publisher) 126
Merrill, Stuart (expatriate U.S. poet) 128–129, 143n22
Mervyn, Christian 115n2
Methodism 174, 198n29, 284, 286n12
*See also* Eliot, *Adam Bede*
#MeToo (social/cultural movement) 94, 95–96. *See also* Ensler, *TVM*, in education. sexual abuse
the Metropolitan Museum (New York City) 245n9. *See also* the Cloisters
Mexico 27, 97, 284, 286n9. literary awards of 166n17
Mexico City 283, 286n9
Michael (archangel) in Michelangelo's philosophy 239. in Milton 68. in Ramírez's *Sara* 159
Michelangelo 234, 246nn16–17
faith of 237, 238, 239, 246n16
intellectual life of
philosophy/theology of art 234–235, 236–237, 238, 239
poetry of 239, 246n15
sculpture of 236, 237
Florentine *Pietà* (Florence, Museo dell' Opera del Duomo) 244n1
Palestrina *Pietà* (Florence, no longer attributed to Michelangelo) 244n1
Rondanini *Pietà* (Milan, Castello Sforzesco) 244n1
Vatican *Pietà* (St. Peter's Basilica) xxi, 243n1. Illus. 240–243
creation of
the commission, management of 234
craftsmanship of 235–236, 237, 238. polished and rough surfaces 235, 236–237.
material of 227, 234–235
critical contexts for
art-historical reception of 235–237, 238–239. dating of 227. *See also* craftsmanship (above)
the artist's signature 239, 246nn17&19. Illus. 243
contemporary theology and worldview 227–228, 229, 234–235, 238, 239, 244n2, 245n12
as "narrative" 229, 238
tensions between the physical and spiritual 227, 229, 236–237, 238–239, 245n12
figures of 238, 239. Illus. 240–243
emotions implied in 229, 234, 237, 238
Jesus/Christ, body of 238
the Virgin Mary
dual identity of 229, 238
fragility–strength of 234, 238
as transcendent 238
viewer reception 227, 237, 238, 239
*See also* Eden, Adam. Leonardo
the Middle Ages, current interest in 2. in later literary movements 13–19
Middle English literature. *See* Chaucer. "Lament." Langland. *Pearl*. the sublime, Middle Ages
Milan (Italy), the Castello Sforzesco 244n1
Mill, John Stuart 173
Miller, J. Hillis 173, 196n1, 197–198n16
Milton, John 6, 50, 52, 66. *Paradise Lost* 6, 52, 68, 87–88n13, 88n18
*See also* Eden
Minsky, Marvin 50

Missouri 34. *See also* St. Louis (Missouri)
"mixed marriage" 45n13
*Moby Dick*, as a mystic pilgrimage 15–16
*Mockingbird*. *See* Tevis
modernism 128
Mont Blanc (along the French-Italian border, partly in Switzerland) 2, 7, 9, 18
"Mont Blanc." *See* Shelley, Percy
Les Monts-Bouccons (an estate in Besançon, France) 125, 142nn10&12
MONUC xii. *See also* Frechon
Moreno, Marguerite (French actress) 130
Morozov, Evgeny 72, 89n28
Morris, Richard (1864 ed. of *Pearl*) 266n5
*Mother Courage and Her Children*. *See* Brecht
Le Moulin Rouge (Paris) 129–130, 142–143n21. *See also* de Morny
Mount Helicon (seat of the Muses) 2
Mount Holyoke College 115–116n6
Mount Ventoux (as poetic inspiration) 7
Mukwege, Dr. Denis 103. *See also* fistula. Nobel
Murray, Penelope, and T. S. Dorsch 20n10
the Muses 2
music, in literature, theater, and criticism xviii, 38, 81, 101, 107, 108, 113, 114, 116n9, 178, 188 (dancing), 191, 192, 263, 264, 251. as heightening emotional response 257, 268n18. as a metaphor for contentment 220, 257. Romantic poetry compared to 2, 18

"negative space" xviii, 27, 29, 132. *See also* Hemingway
Neo-Platonism 266n11
Neruda, Pablo 165–166n10
New Orleans 42
cemeteries of 289. Christ's Church (Episcopalian) 293. New Orleans Catholic Cemeteries (online) 293n2. St. Peter Street 289. St. Roch 290. *See also* St. Louis No. 1

culture of 26, 289–292, 293n1, 298. Mardi Gras 292. *See also* All Saints' Day. Louisiana. THNOC
locales, historic (non-cemetery) 26. the French Quarter 26, 289, 298. St. Louis Cathedral 26. *See also* Chalmette. Our Lady of Prompt Succor
New York City 39, 90n39, 129, 245n9. *See also* Empire State Building. *King Kong*. Metropolitan Museum. Shteyngart. Tevis, *Mockingbird*
*The New Yorker* 144n39
Nicaragua 152. *See also* León (Nicaragua). Ramírez
literature of 165n10. biblical elements in 153–154
in literature 150–154. political resistance as thematic in 153–154, 165n10
politics of 152–153, 166n16
*See also* Cardenal. Cuadra. Darío. liberation theology. Martínez Rivas. Ortega regime. Ramírez. Somoza dictatorship
Nietzsche, Friedrich, on George Eliot 173–174, 198n18. the *Übermensch* 50
Nobel Prize, nomination for Literature 139, 144n39. Peace Prize Laureate (Mukwege) 103
Nord, Deborah Epstein 175, 196n2
Norell, Donna M. 144n39
North, Gary 46n26
Nottage, Lynn
creative process of 96, 97, 102, 103
expectations/goals for *Ruined* 102–104, 104–105
genre perspectives of 103
global theater of 101, 102
as playwright 94, 96, 101, 102
*See also* accomplishments & African & Brechtian (below)
*Ruined* xvii, 94, 106
accomplishments/ aims of 94, 95, 96, 100–101, 102–103, 105–106, 107, 108–109, 110, 113, 114
African culture and performance practices in 101–102. *See also* DRC (below). Basu. Ozieblo.
audience response to 107, 108
*See also* critical reception & educational (below)

boundedness vs. freedom in
116n15. *See also* female
characters (below)
Brechtian elements in 100, 101,
102, 103, 105, 106, 116n14
compared with/contrasted to *TVM*
94, 95, 96, 101, 102, 103,
104–105, 107–108, 110
critical reception/views of 95–96,
102–103, 105, 116n14. as
faith-centered 107–108,
114–115, 116n15. *See also*
Brechtian (above). ending of
& feminism & patriarchy
(below)
DRC culture/violence/war in 95,
97, 101, 102, 105, 107, 108,
110. *See also* Africa. conflict
minerals. DRC. Frechon.
Mukwege
educational/pedagogical uses of 96,
101–102. at church-related
universities 114–115. *See also*
DRC. Jean-Charles
ending of 105–107, 107–110,
116–117n16
female characters in 100–101,
105–106, 108, 109–110, 113,
116–117n16. *See also* identity
& patriarchy & sexual
violence (below)
feminism and feminist perspectives
in/on 105, 107, 110, 116–
117n16. *See also* ending of &
female characters (above) &
male characters (below)
fistula, as traumatic injury in
116n8. *See also* fistula
genre of 103, 116n11
German expressionism in 101
global implications/reach of 101,
102, 104, 106, 110, 114–115
*See also* African culture &
DRC (above)
identity altered in, due to trauma
100–101, 108–109, 116n8
injustice in 101, 104–105, 106,
116n14. *See also* sexual
violence & trauma (below)
male characters in 95, 101, 105,
108, 109–110, 117n18.
casting of 110. *See also* ending
& identity (above)
music in 101, 107, 108, 113, 114.
as diegetic 116n9

patriarchy, representation of, in
106
pregnancy in 109
as realistic 108–109. *See also*
Brechtian (above)
religious implications of, African
101. other 107, 109
sexual violence, representation of,
as economically driven 106,
110, 114–115. *See also* DRC
& female characters (above)
& trauma in (below). sexual
abuse. trauma
trauma in, responses to 96,
100–101, 102–103, 105–106,
108, 109, 110, 113, 114–115.
as despair 108–109. as
forgiveness 96, 109. as hope
107. as love/sacrifice 108,
114, 117n18. subjectivity in
105, 106–107. *See also* sexual
violence (above)
Noy, Wilfred. See *The Lost Chord*
Numbers (Torah, Pentateuch)
164–165n1
*NYT* 144n39

O'Connor, Flannery
as a Catholic writer 264–265. essays
on being a Catholic writer
268–269n20, 269nn24&26
death of 269n24
fiction of 259–260, 269nn24–25
"Revelation" 249, 250, 260
critical reception of 269n23
epiphany (revelation) in 260, 261,
262–264, 269n21
narrative structure of 260–261,
262
publication of 249, 269n25
reader complicity elicited in 260,
261, 264. compared to that in
*Paradise Lost* 261, 269n23.
as inward projection of events
and details 260, 261–262,
263–264. in mirroring
attraction and revulsion
260–261, 262, 263, 264.
religious and biblical ideas in 260,
261–264, 269nn21–22
*Oedipus Rex* (Sophocles) 213. Bowers
on 211, 224n3
Olopade, Dayo 103
Olsen, Christopher 101, 117n18

"One Billion Rising" 97, 115n4. *See also* St. Valentine's Day
Oreamuno, Yolanda 151, 166n12
Orr, Marilyn 174, 196n1, 198n21
Ortega regime (Nicaragua) 151, 152
Osgood, Charles G. (*Pearl* edition. 1906) 266n7
Ostman, Heather 43n1
Our Lady of Lourdes 41, 45nn20–21 *See also* Virgin Mary. Zola
Our Lady of Lourdes Church (Chênière Caminada) 26, 32, 39, 45n21
Our Lady of Prompt Succor (Ursuline Academy, New Orleans) 41. *See also* Chalmette. Virgin Mary
Ovid 50. *See also* Icarus
Ozieblo, Barbara 101, 102–103, 116nn10–11

Pacheco, Patrick 102
*El País* 166n17
pantheism 172
the Pantheon (Rome) in fiction 84. as metaphor 84, 85. as site of Raphael's tomb 85
parables. *See* Jesus
Paraguay 166n16
Paris 39, 122, 123, 125, 126, 129–130, 132. *See also* Moulin Rouge. *Paris Review*. *La Vie parisienne*
Paris, Bernard J. 172, 173, 197nn7,9&13, 200n40
*Paris Review* 285n3
Parker, Deborah 246n17
Pater, Walter 236
patriarchal culture in literature and criticism xx, 273. as related to violence 95, 106. as theologically based 32, 34, 40, 42–43, 95, 150, 151, 153, 154, 155, 160, 162, 162–163, 164
Paul. *See* St. Paul
Pavlov, Ivan 137
*Pearl* 250–255
audience of, contemporary 249
critical reception
attribution of authorship. *See* Pearl/Gawain Poet
dating of 249, 265n1
editions of 266nn5&7
genres proposed for
allegorical vs. symbolic 266n5
*See also* Pearl, identity (below)

*consolatio* 250, 252, 266–267n7, 267n8
didactic debate 253–254, 266n5, 267n8
drama 266n5
dream-vision 250, 266n5, 266–267n7, 267n8
elegy 250, 266n5
father/Jeweler, identity of and epithets for 250, 266n6
Neo-Platonism in 266n11
Pearl, identity of 250, 266nn5–6. the pearl, as a symbol 267n11
reader response to in
affective appeals
*consolatio* 252
fantastic heavenly imagery 251, 252. *See also* features of language (below)
kinship with the father, as resonant experience 250, 251–252, 254–255
the melancholy of mourning (pathos) as a discourse 250, 251–252, 254
reading Pearl as the speaker's deceased child 250–251, 252, 254–255
ethical appeals
biblical texts, including parables 253–254, 265n3, 267nn9,10&12
*exercitatio* 252
Pearl's effort to teach her father 253–254
theological authority 250, 253–254
use of language, as alliterative verse and alliteration 251–252. in descriptive detail 252. in repetition 251
*See also* Stoicism
Pearl/Gawain Poet 266. theological perspectives conveyed in work of 265n2. works credited to 250. *See also Pearl*
*Peri Hypsous* (Pseudo-Longinus) 4–5, 6. quoting Hesiod 20n16
Perkin, J. (James) Russell 173, 175, 197n10, 199n32
1 Peter (First Epistle of Peter, Christian Bible) 164–165n1
Petrarch (Petrarca), Francis (Francesco) 7, 20n24, 21n35. on Psalms 11.

320 | INDEX

reading Augustine 11, 20n25. on sublimity 7
Pharoah (in Abrahamic narrative) 150
Pieragostini, Renata 268n18
*Piers Plowman. See* Langland
*Pietà. See* Michelangelo. Thomas, R. S.
Pitts, ZaSu 61
Pius IX, Pope 47n35
Plato (*Symposium*) 239. *See also* Neo-Platonism
Plessy, Homer (Plessy vs. Ferguson) 291
*poilu* 135, 136
Polaire (French actress) 123
Polit-Dueñas, Gabriela 166n14
Pon, Lisa 246n19
Pope, Alexander (*Essay on Man*) 115n1
Pope-Hennessy, John 244n1
pornography, in reporting on Africa 102
pornography of violence 101–103
Porter, Katherine Anne
  on childhood 276–277
  on childhood memory 276, 285
  essays of, "Autobiographical" 276. "Fiesta of Guadalupe" 286n9. "Ole Woman River" 285n3. "St. Augustine and the Bullfight" 276, 286n7&9
  in Mexico 286n9
  "Miranda stories" of 273, 274, 275, 276–277, 283–284, 286n5.
  novellas of, *The Downward Path to Wisdom* 276–277. *Pale Horse, Pale Rider* 283–284, 286n11
  on "shape and meaning and point" 276, 285n3
  short stories of
    "The Circus" 277, 286n5
    "The Fig Tree" 277, 282, 286nn5–6
    "The Grave" xxii–xxiii, 273
      critical views of 273–275.
      as *Bildungsroman* 275.
      Christian and biblical material of 274, 287n12.
      death, as focus of 275.
      Freudian reading of 273–274, 286n8. sexual/gendered content of 275–276, 285n8. symbols in 275
    milieu(s), cultural, of 273, 283, 284, 286n12
    publication of 273
    religious culture in 278–279, 283, 284–285, 286n12. *See also* critical views (above)
    shape, meaning, and point, or lack of, in 276, 278, 279–280, 284, 285
  on writing fiction 276
post-colonialism. *See* Aguilar. Bidaseca. colonialism. Rajan. Sontag. Spivak
posthumanism 50, 51, 85n1, 89n28, 90n36. fiction on 50–52. as "ultimate other" 87n11. *See also* Kurzweil. Shteyngart. Tevis
postmodernism 51, 250
post-Romantic, ideas of, in Lacanian contexts 76. *See also* Romanticism
Pre-Raphaelite art, "realistic aesthetic" of 175
Presbyterianism (U.S.) xviii, 33–34, 45nn22–23, 45–46n24, 46nn26, 284, 286n12. Arminian views in 46n26. ministers in 46nn26–27. *Westminster Confession* of 33, 45–46n24. women in 34, 46n25 *See also* Protestantism
Prodan, Sarah Rolfe 245n12
Protestantism
  in England 49. effect on theater 268n17. as rationale for Civil War (1642–1651) 46n29
  KJV (King James) xii, 28, 34, 41, 45n22, 116n15, 167n32, 269n22, 286n12. RSV 167n32
  in literature. *See* Chopin, *At Fault & The Awakening.* Eliot, *Adam Bede.* Porter, "The Grave"
  in the U.S. 29, 30, 35, 44n10, 45n22, 269n24, 284, 293n2. as divisive 35, 46n29. as Huguenot 29, 45n14. *See also* Anglicanism. Baptist. Methodism. Presbyterianism
Proust, Marcel 139. *Swann's Way* 283, 286n10
the Psalms of David, the Psalter xviii, 10–11
  Anglican liturgical responses to, in *Adam Bede* 177–178
  literary tradition based on 10–13, 13–19. *See also* Cardenal. Psalm 129 (below)
  in the Office of the Dead 11
  Penitential Psalms 10–11. *See also* Psalm 129 (below)

Psalm 41 (*Quaemadmodum desiderat*) 12, 13
Psalm 129 (*De Profundis*) 11–12, 13–15, 21n36
used in public and private space 11, 12
See also Bodley MS 554. David, King of Israel. St. Augustine
Pseudo-Apollodorus 50
Pseudo-Longinus 20nn10&16. See also *Peri Hypsous*
Ptolemy, Brian 90n36
PTSD (post-traumatic stress disorder) 137, 143n33. See also trauma
Puritanism 255, 268n17. See Protestantism. Reformation. St. Bernard, on church decoration

Qu'ran 164–165n1

rabies 136–137, 144n35
race/racism, as institutionalized 110, 291. as represented in literature 81. See also African American. Plessy
Ragland, Ellie 57, 87n10
Rajan, Rajeswari Sunder 116n8
Ramírez, Sergio
  anti-Ortega movement, involvement in 152–153
  awards of 152, 166nn16&17
  documentary on 165n9
  essays of 152, 166n14
  exile of xx, 152–153
  female protagonists of 150–151, 152, 155
  feminist perspectives of 150, 155, 163
  government persecution of 152–153
  military career of xx, 150
  patriarchal culture in work of 151
  perspective on fatherhood in work of 166n14
  philosophy/theory of literature 151, 152, 154
  political career of xx, 152, 165n9, 166n14
  political elements in work of 150–151, 152–153, 166n14
  political response to works of 152–153
  works of
    *Adiós muchachos* 166n14
    *Castigo divino* 152
    *El cielo llora por mí* 150, 151
    *La fugitiva* 151, 152
    *Margarita, está linda la mar* 152, 155, 166n21
    *Sara* 148–149, 153
      biblical text, as source of, in 149–150, 164–165nn1&4–8, 167nn22,25,29–31&33
      critical response to 150, 153, 155, 165n10, 166n20.
      marginality/marginalization in 148, 155–156, 159–160, 167n28
      narrator, function and nature of 148, 157–159, 160, 165n8, 167n28
      novel/novelistic approach to 148, 150, 153, 155, 156–157, 161, 165n8, 167n32
      patriarchal culture in xx, 150, 151, 153, 154, 155, 160, 161–163, 164
      (proto)feminist protagonist of 150–151
      (proto)feminist resistance in 148–149, 154, 156–157, 160–161, 163
      subaltern reading of 156, 164, 167n23
    *Tiempo de fulgor* 152, 166n15
    *Tongolele no sabía bailar* 152–153
    *Ya nadie llora por mí* 152
Rankin, Daniel S. 25, 29, 30–31, 45nn13&18
Raphael (archangel), in fiction 159, 160
Raphael (Italian architect and painter) 85, 91n40
reader/viewer response theory. See audience response
realism, as an aesthetic 25, 32, 170, 250. in Dutch painting 175. in the medieval sublime 3, 19–20n9. in Pre-Raphaelite painting as "idiosyncratic" 175. in the theater 100, 101, 102–103, 109. See also Brecht. regional writers
Rée, Jonathan 173
Reformation 46n29. post-Reformation 27. See also Huguenots. Protestant. Puritanism
regional writers 151. U.S. xviii, 26, 27, 32. See also Chopin. Eliot, George, *Adam Bede*. O'Connor. Porter
Reiser, Alyssa 99, 100
the Renaissance (early modern era)

English 1, 237–238, 268n18, 224n3
  metrical psalm tradition in 13–15
  *See also* Gascoigne. Wyatt
music, curative powers assigned to, during 268n18
Tudor theater. *See* Bowers. Bradley. Freytag. Greene, Robert. Shakespeare. Wentersdorf
Italian. *See* Ficino. Leonardo. Michelangelo. Petrarch. Raphael. Vasari
Reutlinger, Jean (Paris photographer) Illus. 140
revelation. *See* epiphany
"Revelation." *See* O'Connor
Rice, Anne 43
Richards, Sandra L. 102
Ricks, Christopher 21n43
Rignall, John 173, 198n18
Rolle, Richard 10, 21n32
Romans (Paul's Epistle to the Romans, Christian Bible) 164–165n1
Romanticism 1, 70, 71
  English 9, 19, 50, 54. *See also* Coleridge. Shelley, Mary. Shelley, Percy. Wordsworth
  German 2, 7, 173. *See also* Beethoven. Friedrich. Goethe. Schleiermacher
  U.S. 70–71 *See also* Emerson. Melville
  *See also* post-Romantic. sleeping-waking. the sublime, Romantic period
Rome (Italy) 235. Pantheon 85. Rome *Pietà* 244n1. *See also* St. Peter's Basilica
Ronson, Jon 115n1
Rooke, Constance, and Bruce Wallis 274
Rossetti, Christina 1, 16–17, 21n46
Rousseau, Jean-Jacques 174, 198n18
*Ruined*. *See* Nottage
Ruoff, James 285n3
Ruskin, John (*Modern Painters III*) 175

Sacks, Glenda 174, 198n22&27, 199n35
St. Anne 32
St. Augustine
  *Confessions of* 5. on "dark interiority" 13, 17. on Psalms/ the Psalter 10–11, 13, 17, 21n38. on rhetoric 5, 7, 20n19. on sublimity 7
  *De civitate dei* 267n9
  influence of, on Catholics 41

*See also* Church Fathers. Petrarch. Porter, essays
St. Bede (Venerable Bede) on rhetoric 6
St. Bernadette (Soubirous) 41. *See also* Our Lady of Lourdes
St. Bernard of Clairvaux, on church decoration 6
St. Gabriel. *See* Gabriel (archangel)
St. Jerome 5–6. influence of, 19th c. 41. Stuttgart xiii. Vulgate xiv
St. John the Baptist 32
St. Louis (Missouri) 29, 30, 33, 45n17. in fiction 32. revision of Douay-Rheims 41
St. Louis Cathedral (New Orleans) 26
St. Louis No. 1 (cemetery, New Orleans) xxiii, 289, 290, 291–292, 293n2
  burials, by section 291, 293n2. of well-known persons 291
  colonial cultures, influence of on xxiii. French 289–290, 292. Spanish 289, 292
  funerary culture of 289–291, 292, 293nn1–3&5, Illus. 290
  THNOC survey of 293n4
  Tomb No. 577 in 291–292, 293nn6–7. Illus. front cover
  *See also* All Saints' Day. de Boré. Laveau. Plessy
St. Michael 239. *See also* Michael (archangel)
St. Paul, the Apostle 7, 264, 269n22, 274, 285n2. *See also* 1&2 Corinthians
St. Peter Street Cemetery (New Orleans) 289
St. Peter's Basilica (Vatican City) xxii, 234, 244n1. Illus. 240
Saint Petersburg (Russia) 137
St. Raphael. *See* Raphael (archangel)
Saint-Sauveur-en-Puisaye (French township) 122, 123, 141n3
St. Valentine's Day 104, 115n4
2 Samuel (Hebrew Bible) 11
Sánchez-Palencia, Carolina, and Eva Gil 99–100, 101
*Sara*. *See* Ramírez
Sarah, previously *Sarai* (Hebrew matriarch) 148, 149–150, 155, 164–165n1, 165nn4,6&8, 167nn22–33
Saramago, José 165–166n10
Sarde, Michèle 141n3, 142n20, 144n39
Saslow, James M. 246n15

Satan, in Milton 6, 59, 63, 64, 67,
  87–88n13. poets and devils 5.
  in relation to women 217–218,
  224n8. *See also* Eden. Milton. St.
  Jerome
Saul of Tarsus. *See* St. Paul, the Apostle
Saupe, Karen 239, 244n4, 245n10,
  294, 295n5
Schiesari, Julianna 141n2, 142n12
Schleiermacher, Friedrich 173
Schulz, Juergen 244n1
Scott, Shelly 99–100
Seneca, *consolatio* of 267n8
*sermo humilis* 3, 27, 19–20n9
the seven deadly sins 9–10
*Sewanee Review* 268n25
sexual abuse and violence 94
  child victims of 111
  churches/church-related institutions,
    in relation to 94–95, 112
  efforts at healing 94, 96, 111–114
    forgiveness, role of, in 112
    story- and truth-telling in
      113–114
  (female) genital mutilation 97, 104
  in literature, representations of, as
    pornographic 102–103. *See also*
    Ensler. Nottage
  male victims of 97, 115n2
  perpetrators of 95–96, 114.
    compassion/forgiveness toward
    95, 96, 114. shaming of 115n1
  pregnancy due to 111
  in slavery 114
  trauma due to xix. experienced as
    reliving events 99, 111, 112,
    143n33. *See also* efforts (above)
  in war xix. effects of 97, 105, 106,
    111, 112, 115n2, 116n8. as
    tactical 97, 115n2
  *See also* Barge, Elaine Zook. trauma.
    war, trauma in
Seyersted, Per 25, 30, 44nn3–4&7
Seymour, Charles, Jr. 246n18
Shaara, Michael (*The Killer Angels*)
  46n29
Shakespeare, William, plays of
  *Antony and Cleopatra* 207, 211
  *Coriolanus* 207, 211
  *Hamlet* 206, 207, 211, 225n10
  *Julius Caesar* 207
  *King Lear*
    audience response
      to the closing scene of 207, 210,
        211–212, 213
      to the closing speeches of
        222–223, 225n10
      as unusual 208, 209, 221, 223,
        225n9. *See also* tragedy,
        elements (below)
    Lear, as tragic hero
      contradictions in 210, 213, 221
      development of xxi, 207, 208–
        209, 210, 211, 212–217,
        218–222, 223
      redemption of xxi, 212–213,
        221, 222, 223, 225n9. *See
        also* structure (below)
      trajectory of 211–213, 213–222.
        Illus. 208. *See also* structure
        & tragedy (below)
    structure of
      as anomalous xxi, 208–210,
        211–212, 219–220, 221,
        224–225n9. Illus. 208.
      falling action 206–207, 208–
        209, 210, 212, 214–216,
        221
      Lear at the nadir 209, 212, 216,
        221
      as a "redemptive" process 208,
        211–212, 220, 224–225n9
      reversals in 208–209, 211, 221,
        223
      rising action 206, 209, 210, 212,
        214, 217, 218–220, 221
      turning point 206, 211, 217
      *See also* tragedy (below)
    tragedy, Aristotle's elements of,
      Illus. 207, 208
      *anagnorisis* (discovery/
        recognition) 207, 208, 209,
        217, 218–219
      catastrophe 210, 220–221, 223
        *See also* Hirsh, James
      *catharsis* (purging) 207,
        208, 209, 221, 223. as
        "reconciliation" 211–212
      climax 205–206, 208, 209, 210,
        211, 224n3
      *hamartia* (tragic errors in
        judgment) 207, 208–209,
        212, 224n3, 224–225n9
      *hubris* (tragic flaw) 207. *See also*
        Tevis, *Mockingbird*
      *peripeteia* (reversal) 207, 209
  *Macbeth* 206, 207, 211, 213, 225n10
  *Othello* 206, 207, 211, 213
  *Pericles* 225n9

324 | INDEX

*Romeo and Juliet* 206, 207, 211, 225n10
*Timon of Athens* 207
*The Winter's Tale*
  closing scene 255–259. *See also* "the statue scene" (below)
  contemporary audience of 249, 268nn17–18
  criticism on 250, 265–266nn3–4, 267n14. dating of 249, 265n1. source of 267n13, 268n19
  dramatic categories of, as comedy/romance 250, 267n13. as miracle play 265–266n4, 268n15. as pagan play 265n3. as problem play 267n13
  Puritan law, effects of, on 255, 268n15
  "the statue scene," audience response to anticipating reunions/reconciliations 268n16
    founded on preceding events 255–256
    music in 257, 268n1
    "participating in a resurrection" 255, 256–257
    Paulina's "stage management" 268n19
    witnessing the "uncanny" 268n17
    *See also* Puritan (above)
Shelley, Mary Wollstonecraft (*Frankenstein*) 58, 66, 88n13, 90n36
Shelley, Percy Bysshe 2–3, 12–13, 17–18, 19n7, 66
  "Mont Blanc" 2–3, 7, 8, 9, 12–13, 18, 19n7
  *Prometheus Unbound* 21n46
Shteyngart, Gary 89n27
  *Super Sad True Love Story* (*Super Sad*)
    compared with/contrasted to *Mockingbird. See* Tevis, *Mockingbird*
    Lacanian theory in reading of 76, 78, 85
      desire in 50, 51, 71, 72, 77, 78, 79, 84
      for death, along with the fear of death 74, 80, 83, 85
      for the father-figure (*Urvater*) 72, 73–74, 82, 90n29
      for love (parental) 78–79, 80, 81, 82–83. *See also* 90n36
      for the maternal figure 80, 82–83
    *méconnaissance* in 50, 52, 75, 79, 81, 84, 85
    mirror stage in 79
    *nom du père* in 79, 82
    Oedipal conflict in 81
    registers (Real, Imaginary, Symbolic) in 75, 76, 78, 82
    *See also* Freud. Lacan, Jacques. Tevis, *Mockingbird*
  literary allusions in 71, 80
  messianic delusion in 80–81
  New York City in 71, 72, 73, 76, 82. people of 72. compared to *Mockingbird*'s 71
  posthuman project of 76–77
    ethnicity in 72, 74, 75, 76, 77, 81, 82
    language, literature, and literacy in 71–72, 75, 78, 80, 81
    sex in 74, 78, 90n32
    social Darwinism in 72–74, 77, 78–79
    technology in 72, 73, 75, 84
    *See also* posthuman(ism). utopia
Siep, Ludwig 88n13
Sierra Leone 114
Silicon Valley 89n28
Simeon (Jewish prophet in Luke 2:25–35) 68, 87–88n13. *See also* Eliot, T. S.
Simpson, John, and Jennifer Speake, on Homer 20n13
Simpson, Richard 172, 173, 197n8
Singleton, Jon 173
*Sir Gawain and the Green Knight* 250
Sister M. Joselyn 274
Sivakumaran, Sandesh 115n2
slavery, sexual 101, 111, 114
sleeping-waking motif, in Romantic literature 39
Socratic dialogue 163
Sodom (and Gomorrah) 165n1, 167n30
Somoza dictatorship (Nicaragua) 152. as a political dynasty 166n16
Sontag, Susan 106
Sophocles. *See Oedipus Rex*
South Atlantic MLA 98–99
The South (U.S.) as "Christ-haunted" 269n26. fiction of 268n20. *See*

also Chopin. O'Connor. Porter. Shaara
Spain xx, 152–153, 166n17. *See also* Felipe IV
Spangler, George M. 44n6
Spearing, A. C. 20n26, 266n5
Spencer, Herbert 173, 174
Spencer, Sharon 141n2
Sperlinger, Tom 199n32
spider, heather/crab 124, 141n9
Spinoza, Baruch (Portuguese-Dutch philosopher) 172, 173, 174, 197nn10&15
Spivak, C. Gayatri 156, 167n23
St. *See as* "Saint"
Sticca, Sandro 244n6
Stoicism, as *exercitatio* 252, 253. as literary *consolatio* xvii, 252, 267n8. *See also Pearl*
Stone, Irving, and Jean Stone 246n16
Storr, Will 115n2
Stout, Janis P. 275
Strauss, David Friedrich (*Life of Jesus*) 170–172, 173, 174, 178, 190, 195, 196, 196n4, 196–197n5, 198nn8&21, 200n47. on religion 171. on revealing truth, metaphors for 171, 190. *See also* Feuerbach, *Wissenschaft*
Striff, Erin 99–100
the sublime, as an aesthetic
  in the Middle Ages
    ahistorical idea of 3. *See also* Romantic Period, contrasted (below)
    in art, architecture, poetry, and scholarship 2, 3, 5, 6, 7, 8–9, 10
    authority for and exemplars of biblical (Vulgate) 6–7, 9. *See also* Psalms (below)
    Church Fathers 5–6, 7, 13. *See also* St. Augustine
    Geoffrey of Vinsauf 5–6
    God, as foundation of justice 6–7. as incarnate in Christ 7
    Psalms/Psalter 10–13, 21nn37–38. as *locus classicus* 10 *See also* Psalms
    St. Bernard of Clairvaux 6
    Venerable Bede 6
    *See also* Chaucer. Lydgate. Petrarch
  expressed interrelatedly as
    awareness of the ordinary 3

    coherence between height and depth 7, 9–10
    "dark interiority" of the soul and self-scrutiny 3, 13, 19
    God vs. man's "radical alterity" 6–7, 8, 9, 10
    reason and discipline in creative work 2, 5. the poet as "architect" 5
    *sermo humilis* 19–20n9
    *via negativa* 7–9, 10. *See also The Cloud of Unknowing*
  in Renaissance (early modern) and later literature 1, 13–19, 19n7
  in the Romantic period
    authority for xviii, 4, 5. *Peri Hypsous*, as the *locus classicus* 4–5, 10
    contrasted with the medieval sublime xvii–xviii, 1, 2–3, 5–6, 7, 8, 9, 12–13, 18
    in the fine arts and literature 1–3, 6, 7, 9, 18, 19nn6–7
    values of
      idealizing artist and art/valorizing "exteriority and ego" 1, 2–3, 4, 5
      subjectivity of the artist 2, 3, 4, 5, 7, 19n3
      "virtuosity" and loftiness of expression over technique 3, 4–5, 7
    *See also* Kirwan, James. Pseudo-Longinus
*Super Sad True Love Story* (*Super Sad*). *See* Shteyngart
surrealism 128
Sutherland, Donald 285n3
Swaim, Don 89n26
Swan, Susan Celia 98, 99

Tanner, James T. F. 275
tantalum. *See* conflict minerals
Tassi, Marguerite A. 224n5
Tennyson, Alfred, Lord, medieval sublimity and Psalm 129 in poetry of 16, 21n43
Tennyson, Hallam 16
Terah (father of Abraham) 165n8
Terry, Sara. *See Fambul Tok*
Tevis, Walter 52, 64–65, 68, 85–86n3, 88nn16&19, 89n26
novels of
  *The Hustler* 85–86n3

*The Man Who Fell to Earth*
52, 68, 85–86n3. *See also* Brueghel. Icarus
*Mockingbird* 85–86n3
  baptism in 62
  compared with/contrasted to *Super Sad* 50–52, 71–72, 76, 78, 82, 84, 89n28, 90n29
  critical response to 85–86n3
  cyborgs and robots in 52–53, 54, 58, 64, 88n15. as caretakers 53, 58. emotional lives of 59, 63. suicides of 58. as a Thought Bus 70. *See also* Spofforth (below)
  dystopia in 58, 84–85
  ending of 51, 66–71
  family, archetypal, in 67
  Lacanian theory in reading of 55–56, 57–58, 60, 65–66, 87n12
    desire in 52, 54, 55, 56, 62, 63, 66, 70–71, 84–85. as culturally driven 60. as "mere efficiency" 60. for the Real 56
    father-figures and patriarchy in 56, 57, 62, 72
    *méconnaisance* in 52, 54, 55, 60, 65, 71. defined 50
    *See also* Freud. Lacan, Jacques. Shteyngart. Spofforth (below). utopia.
  literary allusions/cultural references in 59–60, 68–69, 87–88n13, 88n14. *See also* Auden. Chaucer. Frost. Milton. Wordsworth
  music in 65, 67, 104
  New York City in 52, 56, 61, 66, 69, 84. compared with *Super Sad*'s 71
  posthuman project/posthumanism in 50, 55, 58–59, 85n1. technology 58, 70, 72, 84. *See also* cyborgs (above). Spofforth (below)
  reader involvement in 66
  Romantic elements in 70–71
  Spofforth as protagonist in death wish/suicide of 59, 60, 65, 67–68, 87n9, 89n22
    emotional life of 55, 58–60, 63, 87n12, 88n18.
    memory of 66
    roles of, as Chaucerian pilgrim 59–60, 89n22. "dark god" 67, 68. Icarus 64, 67. *nom du père* 63. the Other 59. Satan/Lucifer 59, 63, 64. Simeon 68. *Urvater* in 90n29. *See also* (above) Lacanian & *The Man Who Fell*
    as tortured cyborg 52–53, 56, 58, 59–60, 64, 67, 72, 87–88n13, 88n15
  utopia in 50
*The Queen's Gambit* 85–86
Texas 273, 284, 286n12
Thein, John 244n7
THNOC xiii, xxiii, 293nn4&7
Thomas, R. S. "This to Do" (*Pietà*) 18–19
Thompson Mueenuddin Davis, Barbara 285n3
Thurman, Judith 122, 125, 126, 141nn3–5
Tiffany, Grace 265n4
Tilburg, Patricia A., on a Colettian landscape 141n7
tin. *See* conflict minerals
Titus, Mary 275
Tomb No. 577. *See* St. Louis No. 1
Toth, Emily 25, 29, 30, 43n2, 45nn14–16&18, 46n27
tragedy, theorized (Hegel, Eliot) 170, 194, 196n3. *See also* Aristotle
*Trattato della Pintura* (Leonardo, 1270) 246n13, 234
trauma 89n26, 99, 106, 109, 110, 113–114, 137, 143n33. Illus. 111–112
  represented in art and literature xix, xx, 134, 136–137, 229, 233–234, 273–274
  represented in drama, as owing to sexual violence 94–96, 97, 98, 99–101, 108, 109
  *See also* Colette. "Lament," pathos. PTSD. sexual abuse. war, trauma in
Trinity (Holy) 9, 284, 286n12. literary comparison to 68
Tullia 267n8
tungsten. *See* conflict minerals
Twain, Mark (*Huckleberry Finn*) 70, 289

Uganda 97, 109
UN (United Nations) xii, xiii, 95. *See also* Frechon
University of Maryland 285n4
Unrue, Darlene Harbour 274, 285n1
Urbina, Nicasio 165n17, 166n14
Ur of the Chaldeans (Abrahamic narrative) 167n29
Ursulines (religious order in New Orleans) 41
the U.S. (the United States of America)
    cemeteries of 292
    economic effect of, on other nations 97, 114–115
    economic prosperity or lack of, in 104, 110, 114–115
    literary awards in 50, 96, 166n17
    religious groups 45n22, 46n25. *See also* Catholicism. Protestantism
    sexual attitudes in 94–96, 114–115
    states of. *See* Kentucky. Louisiana. Mississippi. Missouri. Tennessee. Texas
    Supreme Court of 191
    *See also* African Americans. Coming to the Table. conflict minerals. Ensler. New Orleans. New York City. St. Louis. Plessy. racism
utopia, in liberation theology 153.
    vision of, as a misreading 50–51, 69, 71, 72, 84–85. *See also* Lacan, desire & *méconnaissance*

*The Vagina Monologues* (*TVM*). *See* Ensler
Vasari, Giorgio (art historian/biographer, artist, and architect) 246n17
the Vatican *Pietà*. *See* Michelangelo
Vatican II 29, 31, 45n13
V-Day 100, 104. *See also* Ensler, *V-Day Organizer's*. "One Billion Rising"
Verdun 129, 130. Battle of 143n25
Versailles (France) 129
*via negativa* xviii, 7–8
the Victorian era (British) 170, 187, 199n32
    literary figures of 1, 16, 13. *See also* Arnold. Eliot, George. Hopkins. Rossetti. Tennyson
    philosophers of 173–174. *See also* Darwin. Hennell, Charles. Huxley. Lewes. Mill. Spencer
*La Vie parisienne* 129, 142n21, 143n23
Villarruel, Patricia 151

*Virginia Quarterly Review* 272, 285n1
the Virgin Mary 284, 286n12
    in art, literature, music xxi, 9, 32, 41, 47n34, 227–239, 244nn1&6–7, 244n7. Illus. 240–243
    attributes of 227, 228
    *Ave Maria* 228
    as crucified in spirit 245n9
    the Immaculate Conception of (*Ineffabilis Deus*) 41, 47n35
    Mother of God (Madonna) 9, 41
    sites associated with 32, 39, 41, 45nn20&21, 47n36, 286n9
    *See also* Our Lady of Lourdes. Our Lady of Prompt Succor. Virgin of Guadalupe
the Virgin of Guadalupe 286n9. *See also* Virgin Mary
Les Vosges 131

Wales. *See* Thomas, R. S.
Walker, Nancy 33, 40, 43n2, 45n12
Wallace, William 235–236, 244n1, 246n13
Walsh, Thomas 286n9
Wang, Aileen June 235, 239, 246nn17&19
war, trauma in xix, 111, 116–117n16
    *See also* Colette. DRC. *Fambul Tok*. Nottage. sexual abuse
Warner, H. B. (actor, *King of Kings*) 61
Wehner, David Z. 43n1
Weiner, Andrew 52, 88n16
Wentersdorf, Karl P. 209, 212, 223
Wescott, Glenway 276, 285n4
Wesley, John, as noted by Eliot 198n29
Westerink, Herman 88n13, 89n23
*Westminster Confession* 33, 45–46n24
White, Norman 21n46
Whoriskey, Kate 110, 117n19
Wilhelm, James J. 244n7
Williams, Wendy S. 199n32
Willingham, Elizabeth 44n10
Wilson, Edmund (*Patriotic Gore*) 44n3
Wilson, Marcus 267n8
Wimsatt, Mary Ann 275
Winsor, Morgan 117n20
*The Winter's Tale*. *See* Shakespeare
Wisenfarth, Joseph 198n29
*Wissenschaft*. *See* Feuerbach
Wood, Ralph C. 268n23
Wordsworth, William, influence on Eliot of 172, 197n10. pantheism of 172. poetry of, "Intimations of Immortality" 54, 86n6

World War I (the Great War) xx, 129*ff*. *See also* Ardennes. Colette. de Jouvenel. Marne. Verdun
Wyatt, Sir Thomas, erotic verses of 13. on *De Profundis* 13–14. "Penitential Psalms" 13–14. sublime in 14, 15

Yeager, Patricia 274

Yoder, Carolyn 112

Ziff, Larzer 40
Zimmerman, Michael E. 75, 76, 87n9
Ziolkowski, Jan M. 19–20n9
Zola, Emile, Chopin's review of 47n36
Zucconi, Mike, and Chris Yoder 117n20